THE AMERICA
—— THAT ——
REAGAN BUILT

THE AMERICA
—— THAT ——
REAGAN BUILT

J. David Woodard

PRAEGER

Westport, Connecticut
London

Library of Congress Cataloging-in-Publication Data

Woodard, J. David.
  The America that Reagan built / J. David Woodard.
    p. cm.
  Includes bibliographical references and index.
  ISBN 0-275-98609-8 (alk. paper)
  1. Conservatism—United States—History. 2. United States—Politics and government—1945-1989. 3. United States—Politics and government—1989- 4. Presidents—United States—History—20th century. 5. Political culture—United States—History—20th century. 6. Elections—United States—History—20th century. 7. United States—Social conditions—1980- I. Title.
E839.5.W665 2006
973.92—dc22   2006009797

British Library Cataloguing in Publication Data is available.

Copyright © 2006 by J. David Woodard

All rights reserved. No portion of this book may be reproduced, by any process or technique, without the express written consent of the publisher.

Library of Congress Catalog Card Number: 2006009797
ISBN: 0-275-98609-8

First published in 2006

Praeger Publishers, 88 Post Road West, Westport, CT 06881
An imprint of Greenwood Publishing Group, Inc.
www.praeger.com

Printed in the United States of America

The paper used in this book complies with the
Permanent Paper Standard issued by the National
Information Standards Organization (Z39.48-1984).

10 9 8 7 6 5 4 3 2 1

Do not say, "Why were the old days better than these?"
For it is not wise to ask such questions.

Ecclesiastes 7:10

Contents

Prologue		ix
1.	Malaise	1
2.	1980 Election	17
3.	I, Ronald Wilson Reagan	33
4.	A Rising Tide	63
5.	Morning in America: The Second Term	79
6.	A Thousand Points of Light	103
7.	From a Distance	123
8.	Don't Stop Thinking About Tomorrow	141
9.	The Postmodern Nineties	161
10.	Triangulation	183
11.	9/11	203
12.	Misunderestimated	225
Epilogue: Epochs		247

Notes	251
Select Bibliography	269
Index	277

Prologue

The America That Reagan Built is an analysis of the political history of the United States from the 1980s to the second administration of George W. Bush. In the course of these twenty-five dramatic years, between the collapse of the Carter presidency and the two thin election victories of President George W. Bush, a growing public suspicion has emerged that the nation is dramatically divided in its culture and politics. The purpose of this book is to understand these changes in the nation by examining the cultural and political history as reflected in voter discontent and election outcomes. It is also a chronicle of the country around us today.

The book is guided by three convictions about the nature of American politics in the early years of the twenty-first century. The first tenet is that the premises of American cultural life shifted from modern to postmodern beliefs in the period of this narrative. The ideals of modernity in the twentieth century came from a faith in the relentless development of objective knowledge, a confidence in reason, and optimism about the future. These principles were epitomized in the person and presidency of Ronald Reagan, whose unbridled optimism about America sprang from his confidence in the nation's founding principles and technological might. Postmodernity emerged in the late twentieth century as a social construction of the world with a lack of objective meaning, and emphasized the natural impulses and emotions of the moment as superior to any abstract conception. Bill Clinton's presidency was one of immediate pragmatism, which emphasized discontinuity and irony over consistency and conviction. "Bill Clinton has thrived as a public performer because he is a postmodern character attuned to a postmodern moment in American political history."[1] American politics was caught in a conflict between these two philosophical ideas during this period of history. As a result, politics became more strident, and by the beginning of the new millennium, debate was almost as partisan as at any other time in our national history.

The second conviction is, as Michael Barone said in his book *Our Country*, "politics more often divides Americans along cultural than along economic lines."[2] Only two presidential elections, in 1992 and perhaps 1980, of the seven examined here were decided primarily for economic reasons. For the others, the strain of politics was more regional, racial, ethnic, religious, and personal than it was economic. While the state of the economy is an important factor in any presidential election, political campaigns are often more about who we are as a nation, what we want to be, and what we want for our children. In the words of journalist Ben Wattenberg, "values matter most."[3]

At times, the voters express themselves clearly about what they like, but at other times they are confused and the country is divided. However, at all times voters have a visceral understanding of the things they hold dear, and they can tell when those beliefs are being threatened or encouraged. In the twenty-five years studied here, almost more than in any comparable period in American history, the populace was mainly concerned about its rights. Unlike any other nation in the world, America is identified not by geography, cuisine, religion, or war—but by a preoccupation of what it is that we are about.

Consequently, national politics is a struggle over these values. Should the United States confront the Soviet Union, or act as a bargaining partner? Should the rogue states of the Middle East be attacked, or should they be subjected to diplomatic pressure? Does a woman have a right to choose an abortion, or does an unborn child have rights in the womb? Are government programs for health and welfare destructive of individual rights and liberties, or are they helpful to those who need them? Is the death penalty cruel and unusual punishment, or is it necessary for social order? Should same-sex unions have the same rights as traditional heterosexual marriage or be outlawed? Should embryonic stem cells be cloned to prevent disease, or is such a project the harvesting of human uniqueness for genetic engineering?

The culture of a country is defined by the overt and understood patterns of behavior for those who live in a particular place and time. Every human subgroup has some ideals that are historically derived and are an embodiment of its essential beliefs. At America's founding, many of these original ideals were embodied in the Judeo-Christian ethic, but in the last half of the twentieth century those convictions were redefined or abandoned. The conflict over alternative ideals about America came to dominate politics.

The third premise of the work is that those who win elections in American political campaigns can shape and change the cultural values in the country at large. An election victory legitimizes the claims of one side in the values dispute, and allows that side to set the political agenda. Presidents matter, but so do governors, Supreme Court justices, and legislators. The election of Ronald Reagan and Bill Clinton, the governorship of George W. Bush in Texas, the nomination of Clarence Thomas to the U.S. Supreme Court, and the "Contract with America" all changed the course of politics for the nation as a whole. Their outcome, ratified or rejected in elections, also influenced the cultural agenda for a time.

Almost without exception, election outcomes are the chapter divisions in this book. The most important one was 1980, when Ronald Reagan forged a conservative governing coalition that changed the course of American politics. While every personality discussed in this book had an influence, Ronald Reagan towered over them all. His election and re-election, both by landslide margins, ended a string of five failed presidencies. Just as Lincoln remade the country after the Civil War, and Roosevelt after the Great Depression, Reagan changed America for the new century. His political vision elevated conservative values as an expression of the national will and defended traditional cultural values against postmodern critics. More than any other person, he set the tone for contemporary politics. The cultural, spiritual, and psychological aspects of his presidency influenced his successors, but the ruling majorities were always tenuous.

The title for this book reflects the politics of the twenty-five years that are its subject. Every president worked with a fragile majority. Ronald Reagan used the "boll weevil" Democrats to pass his tax package; the divided government in Washington did in George H. W. Bush and his "read my lips, no new taxes pledge." Bill Clinton had united government for two years; then the GOP took over both houses of Congress for the first time in forty years and the president had to "triangulate" in order to govern. George W. Bush had narrow majorities in Congress for most of his tenure in office.

Ronald Reagan said that "history comes and history goes, but principles endure."[4] The principles are the focus of this book. My specific concern is the concept of *"political culture,"* which I take from the comparative politics literature of political science to mean the "particular pattern of an orientation to politics based on transmitted patterns of conduct."[5] That is a scholarly way of explaining politics as the intuitive notion that people behave in established ways based on the values of what they think is important. In writing this book I relied on a variety of sources, demographic data, election returns, newspaper articles, books, and in a few instances, my own personal experiences.

I dedicate this book, with affection, to my students. They sit patiently under my lectern for semester after semester and ask questions about what happened in their country in the past twenty-five years. If this work has one purpose, it is to tell them about those events in the years before and during their childhood and in the time when they came to college to ask those questions. Alexander Pope has written that old men are like "chronicles that give you dull, but true, accounts of times past."[6] This is one person's version of events, an attempt to understand changes in the nation where the history was experienced in voter outcomes, world events, and subsequent election campaigns. The narrative begins when the author was in graduate school, and it ends when his children are college graduates.

Many people made this book possible. My greatest debt, as always, goes to my wife, Judy, who helped with the research, copyediting, and reading the drafts. She serves as editor, critic, and friend, and it is an understatement to say that this book would never have been written without her. My mother, June B. Woodard, was a special help in proofreading and she offered suggestions as well. A good son always listens to his mother, and I am glad I did this time. The Strom Thurmond Chair of Government at Clemson University allowed me to hire a number of people to assist in the research. Students at Clemson University who helped in various ways were critical to the completion of the manuscript on time. I remember: Rebecca Steadings, Jacob Dawkins, Lindsay Green-Barber, and especially Michael Dobson and Katie Banks, for their contributions. To all these people, my deepest thanks. Any mistakes, errors, or prejudices of interpretation are mine alone.

J. David Woodard
Clemson University
Clemson, South Carolina
November 2005

1

Malaise

Three years after the bicentennial celebration of the world's greatest democracy, on July 4, 1979, President Jimmy Carter sat sequestered in his mountain retreat at Camp David working on a speech for a new national energy policy. The times demanded action, and the nation needed to hear from its president.

That weekend, 90 percent of the gas stations in the New York City area were closed, 80 percent in Pennsylvania, and 50 percent in Rhode Island.[1] Since the fall of the shah in Iran in January and a return of the Ayatollah Ruhollah Khomeini to that country the next month, the mood of the American people had soured. A cutback in foreign oil imports threatened to send the economy into a hyper-inflationary spiral worse than the one six years earlier.[2]

Months before, Carter had called a news conference in response to world events to urge the adoption of voluntary energy conservation measures to cope with a projected 2.5 percent shortfall in oil imports. The energy situation was so tenuous that any disruption, no matter how slight, could lead to a panic in the world markets and rising prices at home. The president had already asked Americans to intensify voluntary conservation: to limit their discretionary driving, shift to car pools and use rapid transit in the cold months of the year. That winter, the thermostats in the White House were set at sixty-five degrees, and offices and businesses across the country followed suit in a national show of resolve.[3]

The warm weather of May showed that voluntary conservation was not working. California residents lined up for hours to buy gasoline; some backups involved more than 100 cars and were eight miles long. The "Golden State," so-named for the optimism it engendered in anyone who lived there, went to an odd/even license plate policy for gasoline rationing. Governor Edmund G. "Jerry" Brown, Jr. accused the oil companies of creating the crisis as a pretense to raise prices and make money. While the controversy raged, dozens of magazine and newspaper articles discussed the advantages of properly inflated tires and the effect a 55 mph speed limit had on fuel consumption.[4]

The country searched its memory to recall the gas rationing on the home front in the years of World War II. The present crisis appeared just as grave, but in a different way. The economic control exercised by the Organization of Petroleum-Exporting Countries (OPEC) was so complete that primitive sultans and dictators in the Middle East ruled like an invading army through the oil markets. All across the country, Americans waited and brooded. Carter proposed a mandatory gas rationing plan, which the House of Representatives defeated by a 246 to 159 vote. Senators and representatives from the western states objected to driving restrictions that limited travel in the vast expanse of their borders.[5] Congressional hearings found that drivers in Texas were the most profligate per capita gasoline consumers in the country, using twice as much as motorists in New York. Cars in the Lone Star State sprouted bumper stickers that read: "Drive 70 and Freeze a Yankee." While the president fumed over legislative inaction, the crisis spread.[6]

Beginning on Memorial Day weekend, local governments in several states posted police at gas stations to direct impatient lines of motorists to the pumps. On June 21, 1979, the odd/even rationing program used in California was adopted for the District of Columbia, Connecticut, Virginia, and Maryland. Filling stations began to close on the weekends, and people started to explore summer outings and vacations that did not require travel.[7] The job of waiting in line to fill the family gas tank fell to women, and some in New York complained that the gas crisis served as yet another example of their exploitation by males.[8] Commuters in the nation's capital rose at 4:00 A.M. to wait in Monday morning gas lines because stations were closed on the weekends. The prospects for an immediate solution were buried under an avalanche of statistics from the pipe-smoking energy secretary, James R. Schlesinger.

The deepening crisis brought out the best and worst in Americans, and their behavior became news. A California driver, upset at waiting in line to buy gasoline for his Rolls-Royce, purchased the San Diego filling station in reprisal.[9] People bought 500-gallon storage tanks and buried them in their back yard so they would have a ready supply in an emergency. In Brooklyn, one man fatally shot another for cutting him off in line at the pump. Avis and National car-rental companies guaranteed only half a tank of gasoline in their cars, while Hertz responded with advertisements guaranteeing a full tank.[10] As long as refineries increased gasoline production, state lawmakers allowed them to use more lead and butane in their processes. The provision flew in the face of common sense and state environmental laws, but the country would do almost anything to lessen its reliance on foreign oil. The talk in coffee shops and around water fountains was of Saudi Arabian sultans, the untapped Alaskan reserves, and using corn in ethanol to supplement the shrinking domestic production.

The pundits had their say about the crisis. James "Scotty" Reston in the *New York Times* declared that the "American people were the most wasteful on

Many gas stations were forced to close their pumps due to gasoline shortages during the 1979 energy crisis. (United States Department of Energy)

earth."[11] In some ways the country had a kind of collective guilt about their predicament that somehow the sins of a profligate lifestyle were finally coming home to roost. Diminishing oil reserves and multiplying misery were the only future available for them. In response to Reston's piece, Walter Dean Burnham wrote that blame for the mess rested not on the populace, but on the nation's corporate and political leaders who benefited from capitalism, more than the individual citizens who were its victims.[12]

In domestic affairs, the nation endured gas shortages, double-digit inflation and interest rates, a growing tax burden, and high levels of unemployment. In foreign affairs, the situation, if anything, was worse. In the late 1970s the roster of countries taken over by Marxist revolution was long and ominous: Vietnam, Laos, Cambodia, Angola, Mozambique, and Ethiopia. Marxist-Leninist regimes were in Nicaragua and Grenada, and El Salvador was threatened with a similar fate. A Marxist leader was installed in Zimbabwe-Rhodesia, and the coup was rumored to be with the tacit backing of the Carter White House. The crescendo of criticism of the president became a roar.

All this bad news came to the president at his Camp David compound on the Fourth of July weekend. In four years as president, Carter went to the retreat sixty-seven times. The rural ambiance was soothing, and it had the positive association of a successful Middle East agreement, concluded months earlier, that remained the single greatest accomplishment of his presidency. A poll the month before found that 70 percent of the respondents did not think the energy problem was as bad as Carter said it was.[13] The main feeling in the country was frustration mixed with disbelief. In the rustic comfort of the mountain retreat, the president greeted visitors and took notes on a yellow legal pad. Carter worked with his wife, Rosalynn, his most trusted political partner and advisor. She had convinced him that the speech on the energy crisis should not cover familiar ground, but had to offer something new for the American people. The president and his first lady were searching for something hopeful to give the nation.

Jimmy Carter saw his administration as an alternative to the "politics as usual" in Washington, and he believed that in a time of need, he had to do something different from what was expected. The president was elected because he was an outsider, who had campaigned on top-to-bottom governmental reorganization along with a promise not to lie to the American people. The energy crisis seemed to be a perfect opportunity for truth-telling in accordance with his pledge.[14] In a remarkable decision, Carter picked up the phone and called the White House to cancel the reserved television time on all networks for the July 5 speech.

Then, for ten days in July, the most public man in America became invisible. He offered almost no explanation, and gave no public rationale for his disappearance. Stories leaked out from the ever-vigilant press, and they hinted of more bad news to come. Columnist Tom Wicker wrote in the *New York Times* that Carter's decision to cancel the speech was the worst mistake a president had made since Richard Nixon's "Saturday Night Massacre," a firing of top officials in the depths of the Watergate scandal that ultimately led to his resignation.[15] He hinted that the same might be in store for Carter. In the days that followed, military helicopters ferried top leaders in the administration to the Camp David Catoctin Mountain resort. Vice-President Walter Mondale emerged to promise "a major address," and said that the president would offer a "bold and forceful" program to resolve America's oil shortage.[16]

The nation watched and waited, transfixed by the delay and anxious about the coming news. On the last day of his self-imposed exile, Carter met with forty visitors in two shifts, including civil rights and labor leaders, businessmen, a half dozen governors, eight mayors, and some New York state legislators.[17] A poll at the time found that the presidential approval rating had dropped from 30 percent, which was the range where Richard Nixon was before he left office, to the nearly uncharted depths of 26 percent.[18] The president was in deep political trouble.

Carter ended his retreat by flying off to meet with some "average Americans." In Carlisle, Pennsylvania, a machinist and his wife, named William and Betty Fisher, received a personal visit. They told the president that "the country is in a downhill spiral with respect to the economy, inflation and gasoline."[19]

Doubtless this was not news, but the visit was made more for symbolic than substantive reasons. The meeting was a tactic developed by the man who upset better known competitors to win the presidency in 1976. Carter won because he was an everyman, someone people could trust, not like the evil Nixon and the arrogant Johnson, who remained isolated in the White House, aloof in a time of trouble. In a time of crisis, the president wanted to visit with people.

On the night before his speech, the president invited some journalists in for a visit. One who was there remembered that Carter asked for a guarantee of confidentiality, and then paced the room in unrelenting self-criticism. The country was in trouble, he said, because as president he had poorly organized the cabinet, the White House staff, and his own legislative priorities. He was guilty of not keeping the nation focused on the most important problems. The whole discussion had the mood of a Southern Baptist altar call, or a funeral service; the only difference was this time the central participant was the president of the United States. One reporter wrote after the meeting that "Jimmy Carter's life was testament to belief in all the cherished virtues—thrift and frugality, hard work and integrity, self-improvement and decency."[20] Yet for all these qualities, he was unable to reduce the intensity of the crisis or improve his popularity in office.

On the evening of July 15, Jimmy Carter seized the bully pulpit of the American presidency and used it to try to inspire the country in what would prove to be a vain attempt to save his presidency. He would be the fifth straight president unable to survive in office to a second term. The Camp David delay served to heighten national anticipation, and people tuned in to watch what he had to say. He began personally, saying that on that very night three years earlier he had accepted the Democratic nomination for president. "I promised you a president who is not isolated from the people, who feels your pain, who shares your dreams, and who draws his strength and his wisdom from you."[21] The words were from the campaign, when Carter pledged not to lie, where he walked down Pennsylvania Avenue holding his wife's hand, and delivered a television address wearing a cardigan sweater.

The president turned to a confession of political sins and read criticisms from the yellow legal sheets taken in the time of his retreat. A southern governor had said, "Mr. President, you are not leading this nation—you're just managing the government." In a comment that was as insightful about the shortcomings of Carter the man as about his presidency, he shared a critique: "Don't talk to us about politics or the mechanics of government, but about an understanding of our common good."[22]

Before a national audience, the president admitted that what he had done about energy was a mistake, and he needed the sympathy and support of the American people for a new start. It was a strange tactic. Presidents acknowledged their shortcomings before, but it was unprecedented to say that their administration was a failure in front of a national audience. Carter turned to a deeper analysis of himself and the nation in the face of the national energy problem. The energy crisis was "a fundamental threat to American democracy," he said, "a crisis of confidence." It was a calamity "that strikes at the very heart and soul and spirit of our national will."[23]

"He was," wrote reporter Haynes Johnson, "holding on to a patch of sand; nothing bound the grains together.... [T]o the country, he appeared irrelevant."[24] Instead of giving the nation a sense of direction and confidence, Carter was showing the same shortcoming that he criticized in the country at large. "We can see this crisis in the growing doubt about the meaning of our own lives and in the loss of unity of purpose for our nation."[25] The 1970s were the "me" decade, a time when Americans were so busy tending to their own needs that they lost faith in themselves and in any interest of the public good. The president was pointing to a real problem, but he was unsure what to do. "The erosion of our confidence is threatening to destroy the social and political fabric of America."

The oil and gas shortages of the 1970s inspired a vast collective end-of-the-universe feeling among Americans and Europeans, a certainty that the good times were over. A popular movie at the time, destined to become a cult classic, was entitled *Mad Max*, with actor Mel Gibson as a motorcycle policeman in a near-future energy apocalypse where the highways of the Australian outback had become bloodstained battlegrounds.[26] The road ahead for the nation was just as desolate as the highways in the movie. "We have always believed in something called progress," the president continued; "we've had faith that the days of our children would be better than our own." But the polls at the time were prophets, and their predictions were worse than any biblical Jeremiah. They showed that "the majority of our people believe that the next five years will be worse than the past five."[27] Although not acknowledged at the time, the public had been dissatisfied with the way their business was being managed for more than a decade. "In a nation once proud of its hard work, strong families, close-knit communities, and our faith in God, too many of us now tend to worship self-indulgence and consumption."[28]

Jimmy Carter echoed the spirit of the times. In post-Vietnam America, guilt was fashionable. History professor Christopher Lasch documented it in his book *The Culture of Narcissism: American Life in an Age of Diminishing Expectations*, writing that "the pursuit of happiness to the dead end of a narcissistic preoccupation with the self"[29] defined the popular culture of the nation. The country was guilty of cultivating violence in the 1960s when John Kennedy, Martin Luther King, Jr., and Robert Kennedy were assassinated. "These wounds are still very deep," the president intoned in his speech, and "they have never been healed." America was guilty for Vietnam, guilty for Watergate, and now guilty for driving cars with V-8 engines. While Germany remained a divided nation thirty years after being defeated by the United States in war and people there paid twice as much for gasoline as American drivers, motorists on the autobahn were able to run their cars at 160 miles per hour. Americans on highways in the 1970s stared down at speedometers with the mandated 55 mph speed limit highlighted for fuel economy and highway safety.

Something did not seem right. But in his speech, Jimmy Carter was not interested in driving faster on the interstates. He was more concerned with cultural values. "As you know, there is a growing disrespect for the government...the churches...the schools, the news media and other institutions." "We remember when the phrase, 'sound as a dollar' was an expression of absolute dependability, until ten years of inflation began to shrink our dollars and our savings."[30] The president was adding fear to guilt. The American vision of the future was not limitless; instead, it was shrinking.[31]

President Carter urged a renewal of faith, "in each other, in our ability to govern ourselves," and in the future of this nation. Carter believed the United States had energy problems because Americans wasted energy. The country was too dependent on foreign imports, he said, and needed a mandatory conservation program. He proposed a domestic synthetic fuel program and a $24 billion transfer program to help the poor pay their energy bills, but he was under no illusion that these measures would awaken the nation from its national energy nightmare. President Carter asked in his conclusion that "Whenever you had a chance, say something good about our country...with God's help and for the sake of our nation, it is time for us to join hands in America."[32]

Americans flicked off their television sets to talk about a bleak future of limits. For the first time they considered what would happen when the world's oil reserves ran out, as they inevitably would some day. What would life be like when the coal mines were empty? The talk was of solar energy, wind power, and battery-operated automobiles. In an echo of World War II's "Meatless Tuesdays," a proposal was made to take every car off the road one day a week. The "America the Beautiful" of spacious skies and amber waves of grain had run out of gas, and many people thought God was no longer shedding his grace on Thee.

The speech by the president was a modest political success: public opinion surveys showed a nine- to eleven-point rise in Carter's meager popularity.[33] The nation gave the president support for at least trying to come to grips with the problem. But any resurgence in popularity was wiped out two days later when Carter asked for the resignation of his entire cabinet and White House staff. The press immediately conjured up the failed Nixon analogy, recalling that he used the same tactic to shake up his administration in 1972. This time the president fired some of his most able cabinet appointments, and the whole experience had the trappings of a political vendetta. Health, Education and Welfare chief Joseph Califano was a personal foe of White House aide Hamilton Jordan, so the secretary was dismissed. The treasury secretary was fired, and the energy secretary and transportation head quit before being asked to leave. Griffin Bell, an old friend of the president, used the opportunity to leave as attorney general and escape back to Georgia.

Carter's governmental reorganization destroyed any self-confidence the country gained from the July speech. In meetings and restaurants around the city of Washington, people talked about the changes and about the results. Washington in the 1970s was a city that loved to gossip. Of course intrigue and secrecy in a nation's capitol were not new. Cicero wrote in 44 B.C., "You cannot imagine the sense of personal dishonor I feel at living in the Rome of today."[34] In a sense, Washington was a new Rome. A conversation overheard in a downtown restaurant might be tomorrow's newspaper headline. Residents of the city remembered that the Watergate scandal had unraveled in living rooms, restaurant interviews, and parking garages around the city.

The metropolitan area filled with lawyers, lobbyists, trade-association representatives, and members of private consulting and research firms. The number of interest groups registered in Washington went from 500 in 1970 to 3,000 in 1980 and nearly 5,000 in 1990.[35] Every day the people who lived there had one subject on their mind: politics. Who was in, and who was out, what was going on at the White House, and who knew someone who could help with something? When they talked about the administration, the natives mentioned their neighbors or friends they knew. In 1979 they talked about the president from Plains and his "Georgia Mafia" who had reorganized the government but were still caught in a crisis they could not control.

A political disaster can wear many masks and come at any time. For Jimmy Carter calamity came on November 4, 1979. "[I]t was a date I will never forget," wrote Carter in his diary. "I spent most of the day, and every spare moment, trying to decide what to do."[36] On that day thousands of people marched through the streets of Tehran to commemorate the shooting of a Tehran University student by the shah's security forces, SAVAK, one year earlier. After a strong anti-U.S. speech by Ayatollah Khomeini, a horde of ragtag revolutionaries overpowered the Marine guards at the American embassy and took the occupants of that compound hostage. Fifty-six American hostages were blindfolded and paraded before the world media.

The takeover came after a controversial decision in the White House allowed the deposed shah of Iran into the United States for treatment of cancer and other ailments. Mohammad Reza Pahlavi had been placed on the throne in 1953 with covert CIA backing. Over the next twenty-five years he became the guardian of U.S. interests in the Persian Gulf. U.S. oil companies profited from Iranian oil and the shah guaranteed a steady supply of it to Israel while the Arab nations exercised a vehement boycott.

The shah's brutal regime was of little consequence to the American government as long as the oil kept flowing. The United States allowed him to purchase whatever weapons in whatever quantities he wanted, and even trained the notorious SAVAK secret police. When deposed, the shah went first to Egypt, but he could not stay there. He was in poor health, and traveled to Mexico. Henry Kissinger and David Rockefeller, two Republicans with White House access, negotiated with the administration to get the shah admitted for treatment in New York City. That event triggered the hostage crisis. After the deposed ruler had gallstones removed from his bile duct, he was set to return to Mexico, but the nation refused to take him. Finally, in mid-December, White House press secretary Jody Powell announced that the shah had secretly left the United States for Panama.

The Iranian students vowed to stay in the embassy and hold the hostages until the shah was sent back to Iran to stand trial for a host of crimes. Three days later Prime Minister Mehdi Bazagan's provisional government dissolved, and Khomeini ordered the Revolutionary Council to take over the government. The new rulers rebuffed American efforts to negotiate the release of embassy personnel. Carter ordered an immediate suspension of oil imports (about 4 percent of U.S. supplies at the time) from Iran, froze Iranian assets in the United States, and ordered two aircraft carrier task forces into the region. Even so, the saber rattling seemed tame.

George F. Will described the administration's sanctions against Iran as ineffectual and guaranteed "to keep the United States immobile... treating the crisis as a media event... [and causing] the erosion of respect for this nation."[37] The seizure of the American embassy provoked an emotional outburst in the United States. Posters were printed across the country showing a raised middle finger forming the "I" in Iran. On college campuses dark-skinned students were singled out for ridicule and abuse. Thousands of Iranian students on visas for study at American universities had demonstrated against the shah for years, usually before a sympathetic student audience. No more. Now they were assaulted and taunted. Attorney General Benjamin Civiletti began to deport Iranian students in the country illegally, and educational visas were not renewed.

Americans were angry and frustrated with the slow pace of events. Within a week of the embassy takeover, Khomeini criticized the pope, called President Carter an "enemy of humanity," and told the students holding the hostages that economic force would be useless. The hostage crisis provoked an emotional outpouring of righteous indignation by the American people, something luxurious after the guilty years of Vietnam. Most Americans believed embassies were off limits when it came to political protest. On December 7, 1941, Secretary of State Cordell Hull had stiffly received the Japanese ambassadors even though he knew their nation had bombed Pearl Harbor. No American citizens stormed the Japanese embassy in reprisal then, and in Washington the Iranian embassy remained calm. But there was no diplomatic reciprocity in Tehran. The United States was made powerless precisely because it was the most powerful country in the world.

The president's strongest vision of the crisis was moral; he was a peacemaker and a reformer who focused his attention on diplomatic strategy.[38] He worked in what one administration insider called "a circular process," moving from meeting to meeting, gathering information and making decisions. The choice of quiet diplomacy meant the administration had to wait on a response before initiating a reply. Most Americans were puzzled; they found it hard to believe that such a sophisticated niceness could solve a crisis when a host of more than 60,000 mullahs in Iran ended Friday prayers by calling for "Death to America." Daniel Patrick Moynihan, a highly respected Democratic senator, criticized the policy by declaring, "You don't negotiate with illegality."[39] Khomeini ordered the students to release women and black hostages from the embassy, and then granted interviews to ABC and NBC News. The criminal act of seizing the American hostages at the embassy was multiplied by endless media speculation and the inability of the world's most powerful military to respond.

The Ayatollah Khomeini would not play by the rules. He said the militants occupying the U.S. embassy were expressing the will of the Iranian people. It was as if the holy man was powerless to stop them. The president sent a private letter to the Ayatollah, and Khomeini promptly read it before the assembled press. In the middle of the takeover, Khomeini ignored his country's disintegration long enough to wage a savage, holy civil war against his own Kurdish citizens, who, he explained, had joined the cults of Satan.

For many observers outside the president's inner circle, Jimmy Carter seemed just as enigmatic as the Ayatollah.[40] The president refused to see the seizure and imprisonment of American diplomats as an act of war that demanded prompt and necessary force. Instead he chose to use diplomacy, and participated in symbolic public events like dimming the Christmas lights at the national Christmas tree in remembrance of the hostages, then praying publicly with the hostage families at the National Cathedral. Presidential advisor Hamilton Jordan convinced Carter to adopt the "Rose Garden" strategy to enhance his stature as president, and at the same time avoid getting mired in the fray of politics. Carter cancelled his plans to go home to Plains, Georgia, for Christmas, and stayed in Washington where he had an excuse to avoid a debate with presidential challenger Edward Kennedy in Iowa.

Like the naval officer he once was, Jimmy Carter remained with his ship, even if it was taking on water. The holiday issue of *Time* magazine that year was entitled "The Cooling of America." The cover showed a family huddled together around a television fireplace with a newspaper headline reading, "Cold Wave Hits: Fuel Prices Up."[41] That winter heating oil sold for ninety cents a gallon, up from fifty-five cents the year before. Wood stove manufacturers and importers said their business was up more than 100 percent from last year, and some legislators were talking about charging them windfall taxes on the their profits because the demand for their product was so high.

In 1980, no event in politics or economics had more importance than the hostage crisis, but it was not alone in causing political turmoil. The issues had more to do with events abroad than at home, and the administration was helpless before both. Foreign policy problems dominated the agenda: the seizure of diplomats in Tehran, the Soviet invasion of Afghanistan, and the revelation that 2,000 Soviet troops were housed in Cuba. The crises stimulated a wave of patriotic fervor.[42] Khomeini's criticism gave Carter a breath of fresh respect, and a second political life. Military recruits looked up to see young men across their desks who cared little about Vietnam, but wanted to avenge the kidnapping of the American diplomats.

In reality, a speedy intervention was impossible. The U.S. military was equipped and trained to fight Soviet forces in Europe, not radical terrorists in the Middle East. The opportunity for revenge and a change in policy came not from the president or the military, but from the deposed shah. His exit from the country allowed the president to consider a military response, an option made more likely since it was an election year.[43]

Following the State of the Union address in 1980, the talk around Washington was of Carter's failing presidency. The longer the hostage crisis dragged on, the less likely it was that he could be re-elected. The president could inspire confidence only at irregular intervals, and he seemed unable to solve the nation's abiding problems. The country wanted action in the Iranian crisis, and Carter gave them quiet diplomacy. They wanted cheaper gas, and he offered them rationing. He did not go where the nation wanted to go. In April of 1980, a *New York Times*/CBS poll found that the president's approval had dropped from a high of 77 percent in December of 1979 to 49 percent in March.[44]

Carter had to do something, and on April 24 he did. Plans for a possible rescue of the American hostages were in the works at the Pentagon within hours of their capture. The standard for such an attempt was established by the Israeli military, who freed 105 men, women, and children from Entebbe, Uganda, on July 3, 1976. The soldiers took the hostages in a lightning attack that killed all eight hijackers of the Air France flight and lasted just one hour on the ground from start to finish. The unexpected daring and impossible logistics made the raid a complete surprise and a popular success.

The American hostage crisis was far more daunting than the Entebbe raid. First, the hostages themselves were being held in the confines of the American embassy. Iranian troops blanketed the streets, and intelligence about their health and whereabouts was almost nonexistent. The second problem was the difficulty of getting to Tehran itself, an isolated city of some 4 million residents surrounded by more than 700 miles of desert and mountains in every direction. A third issue was the deplorable condition of the U.S. military, which had plummeted in size and quality in the seven years since it staged a near-total withdrawal from Vietnam. One of the casualties in the cutbacks was the once-powerful special operations forces that had performed with skill and bravery in Southeast Asia.[45]

The elite Delta unit was a notable exception to this norm. It was founded to combat international terrorism, like an airline hijacking, but was untested in any actual crisis. Commanded by Colonel "Chargin" Charlie Beckwith, the Delta unit was involved in extensive training, but it would have to depend on volunteers in other services to actually get to the operations site. An initial decision was made to find a location in the Iranian desert where helicopters could be refueled, and U.S. intelligence found such a location about 200 miles southeast of Tehran known as "Desert One."

The planned rescue mission was a two-night operation. The first evening, six Air Force planes would carry 132 Delta commandos, Army rangers, and support personnel some 1,000 miles to meet eight Navy helicopters from the aircraft carrier USS *Nimitz* at the remote desert site. After refueling, the helicopters would move the rescue force to a hideout about 50 miles southeast of Tehran. After hiding for twenty-four hours, the Delta force would be driven to the besieged American embassy in vehicles obtained by local agents. Once inside the city, the Delta force would rescue the hostages, then be picked up by the helicopters. Air Force gunships would protect the rescue force from any counterattack, and the whole group would return to the secret base fifty miles outside Tehran to be loaded onto planes. The helicopters would be destroyed and the entire assembly would be flown to a base in Egypt. Such was the plan.[46]

Code-named "Eagle Claw," the plan was daring and complicated. The timing had to be nearly perfect. The risks were high and surprise was of the essence. After five months of planning, organizing, and training with a series of increasingly complex rehearsals, the final decision was left with President Carter. Colonel Beckwith recalled that Carter told them, "I do not want to undertake this mission, but we have no other recourse.... We're going to do this operation."[47] Many things could go wrong, and unfortunately, many did.

By April 24, 1980, forty-four aircraft were poised at six widely separate locations to perform the rescue mission in Iran. The plans called for a minimum of six flyable helicopters to remain out of the eight that left the USS *Nimitz* to reach the remote site at Desert One. Beckwith and his men reached Desert One at 10:00 P.M. on the first night. When the planes landed, the plan was for the Rangers to secure the area and wait for the helicopters to arrive. A short time later, a bus carrying forty-five Iranian civilians blundered into the area. The Iranians were taken into custody. Then a fuel truck and a pickup appeared. The truck was destroyed with an anti-tank weapon, but the driver of the pickup escaped. As a result of these surprises, security was compromised on the mission, and the Delta warriors wondered about their bad luck and the supposed remoteness of the Desert One location. The helicopters were due in at 11:30 P.M., but as the soldiers searched the skies, they realized their colleagues were either lost or missing.

The squadron of eight Sea Stallion helicopters en route to Desert One suffered unexpected problems. One unit lost rotor blade pressure and was forced to land. It was abandoned on the spot, and the crew jumped aboard another helicopter that had landed to help out. Further on, the remaining choppers were struggling with a dust cloud that dropped visibility to yards and sent the cockpit temperatures soaring. Another Sea Stallion lost its gyroscope and had to turn back. The remaining six choppers reached Desert One two hours late.[48]

The mission was down to the minimum six helicopters and behind schedule. As the helicopters struggled to maneuver in the deep sand, one suffered a complete failure of its hydraulic system and had to shut down its engines. That left five choppers—one less that the minimum needed to carry out the rescue. The mission had to be aborted, and the commanders on the ground were left with the unrehearsed job of getting everyone out of Iran at night. Because of the extended time on the ground, one of the planes was running low on fuel and had to leave. In trying to leave, a repositioned helicopter with a flattened nose wheel collided with the plane and the spinning rotors ignited a raging fire. Eight men lost their lives, and others were injured by projectiles flying from the flaming wreckage. Finally, the remaining men were evacuated back to Egypt.

Robat-E-Posht-E-Badam, Iran: One of the U.S. helicopters in the failed attempt to rescue the U.S. hostages in Tehran lies in ruins near this desert oasis. An intact helicopter is seen behind the wreckage. (© Bettmann/CORBIS)

The Iranian rescue mission was a spectacular failure reported by the worldwide press with pictures of burned-out American helicopters being inspected by Muslim mullahs. Initial response to the tragic deaths was restraint in the American press. Then the furor over the failed mission began to surface. Having opposed Operation Eagle Claw from the first, Secretary of State Cyrus Vance resigned on principle. That set off a spate of press speculation over Carter's leadership abilities. *Time* magazine's article, entitled "Debacle in the Desert," asked if the president's "image as inept had been renewed."[49] Joseph Kraft, a columnist for the *Washington Post*, called the rescue mission a "half-hearted, second-best spirit" and called Carter "unfit to be president at a time of crisis."[50] The administration prevailed on a reluctant Charlie Beckwith, the military leader at Desert One, to hold a press conference and dispel rumors that President Carter had lost his nerve and aborted the mission at the last minute.

The Iranian rescue mission went from an undertaking of hope to something tragic. The raid failed, not because of enemy forces, but because of mechanical and administrative problems. The glaring lesson from the mission was that the world's most technologically advanced nation failed in a secret military operation like some two-car collision on a freeway. An investigation by the Pentagon after the fact found that one of the helicopters overheated because a crewman's flak jacket and duffle bag were placed too near an exhaust vent.[51] It was an appropriate metaphor for the Carter presidency—almost a success. A tale of what might have been became a symbol of the administration. The hostages were finally released in 1981, on President Ronald Reagan's inauguration day, 444 days after they were taken.

Had the jacket been moved and a host of later conditions worked, then the rescue might have been a success, and Carter would have doubtlessly been re-elected. The nation indulged in a "what if" scenario, and a "for want of a horseshoe nail" speculation for a time, but short-term conjecture soon gave way to the more persistent legacies of the crisis. The energy predicament, and the failed rescue attempt, made the culture and the geography of the Middle East familiar to every American. After 1979, the politics of the region would dominate the evening news and sit at the top of each security discussion of every subsequent president. The conflict was a disjunction of the realms: the modern, technologically advanced society of the West dependent on foreign oil juxtaposed against the primitive, Islamic fundamentalism of the Middle East.

The failure of the Iranian rescue mission set the stage for American foreign policy for the next thirty years, and revealed three things about international and American politics. The first revelation was that the Middle Eastern states were not intimidated or understanding of the West. In Jimmy Carter's mind, knowledge developed through assimilation and reason. "If an issue was mine," he said, "I wanted to understand it." The president spent hours poring over briefing books assembled by his staff. His strength was knowability, but the Ayatollah Khomeini was inscrutable. Carter wrote in his diary: "Every time one of the Iranian government officials shows any sign of rationality, he is immediately incompatible with Khomeini."[52] The America of incomprehensible military strength was actually weaker for having a modern service economy that was dependent on foreign oil. But it was also weaker for having an inability to understand its opponents. Like Napoleon, who waited in Moscow for the Russians to surrender before realizing he had to retreat, the American president expected Iran to give up when it remained defiant. No image was more abiding from the abandoned rescue than that of Islamic holy men in robes walking among burnt American helicopters. For all its might, America was unable to defeat, intimidate, or even understand the religious ayatollah who labeled their country "A Great Satan."

The second revelation of the conflict was the realization that the United States was unappreciated, in the Middle East and around the world. The "American Century," to quote Henry Luce, was ending with the nation's values under attack from a most unlikely source. The tolerant way of regarding other people's traditions and beliefs conflicted sharply with the intolerant way adversaries viewed American traditions and beliefs. No one in the Middle East remembered D-Day, the European dictators at midcentury, or the Marshall Plan. They did not esteem democracy, desire economic "progress," or understand the cultural values of freedom. In one Middle Eastern country after another, the McDonald's hamburger franchise was despised as much as the American flag. For opponents, America was the corrupt images seen on imported television shows, and the arrogance of technological might built on a shameful culture of self-indulgence.

Finally, the energy and foreign policy crises proved incurable. In time the gas lines went away, but their memory remained. Quiet diplomacy still had its supporters, but most Americans wanted action and not explanations. After 1979, the country learned to walk a tightrope between support of Israel and sympathy for the Palestinians; a desire for economic independence and a reliance on foreign energy supplies. The foreign policy of the United States for the next quarter century was previewed in the events of the Carter presidency.

The failure of the Carter administration led to a Republican president who promised to act boldly to overcome the contradictions of the past. Ronald Reagan took the political initiative away from the Democratic Party and defined a new political coalition. That coalition would not always win elections, or consistently hold together, but it would dominate the way things were done for the next two and one-half decades.

2

1980 Election

The outcome of each election comes from the seeds sown in the one before, and the 1980 result goes back to August 19, 1976. That was the night Ronald Wilson Reagan ended his initial campaign to be president of the United States at the Republican Convention. He lost the nomination by 117 votes to Gerald "Jerry" Ford. The race came in the wake of Richard Nixon's resignation, when the Watergate affair gave the Oval Office to Ford without an election, and Reagan surprised everyone with his strong showing.

More than any president in the twentieth century, Gerald Ford was in office because of his integrity and trustworthiness. His peers in the Congress supported him after the Nixon resignation because he told the truth and kept his word. In his first thirty days as president, he worked diligently to restore confidence in the office, but for all his virtues, Ford was not an exceptional politician. When he pardoned Richard Nixon on September 8, 1974, the new president followed his conscience, and did so to get rid of the whole Watergate cloud of suspicion. In his mind, the idea of a trial over many months with attendant press speculation was more than the country could bear. The nation had been through two years of Watergate, and the domestic unrest needed to end. Ford would say later, "I was absolutely convinced that it was the right thing to do."[1]

The voters were not as forgiving. The timing of the pardon could hardly have been worse. In the 1974 midterm election, Democrats picked up five seats in the U.S. Senate and added forty-nine to their majority in the U.S. House of Representatives.[2] After the pardon, Republican strategists thought the GOP would be in shambles if it failed to win the presidency in 1976, and the unspoken thought was that the party should rally around its besieged president. Gerald Ford declared when he assumed office that he would stand for election in his own right. The announcement improved party morale, but the task of governing as an un-elected president in the minority party remained daunting. Not to run would make Ford a lame duck president, lacking the power to threaten, encourage, or promise patronage in a second administration.

The president expected the support of party loyalists, but he was in for a surprise. When former California governor Ronald Reagan declared for the office, the un-elected president confronted an opponent more formidable than any he could imagine. As a spokesman for the most conservative wing of the party, Reagan had wide appeal, but even those close to him sometimes found his charisma enigmatic and impenetrable. At the time it seemed impertinent for an upstart governor to challenge a sitting president in a time of political crisis. Even the conservatives who admired Reagan feared that his candidacy would harm their cause and the Republican chances for victory in the fall election. Barry Goldwater had turned out to be such a disaster for them in 1964 that conventional political wisdom held that no "true conservative" could be elected president.

The 1976 campaign served to introduce Ronald Reagan's remarkable appeal, and set the stage for his election in 1980. Reagan won the affections of American voters that year because he seemed like such a "regular guy" with whom they could relate. The beginnings of his attractiveness lay deep in the heart of Middle America, in the mythical small-town ideal of wholesome neighborliness depicted in the movie *It's a Wonderful Life* and the stereotype that presidents should be born in log cabins. By birth, Reagan was an everyman, and by accomplishment he was a personification of the Horatio Alger myth and the blessings of simple values in the wholesome places of an America long past and almost forgotten.

Ronald Wilson Reagan was born on February 6, 1911, in the front bedroom of the five-room flat above the general store and bakery where his father worked on Main Street in Tampico, Illinois (population 849).[3] Never an outstanding student, he excelled in high school sports and social activities. For seven summers, beginning in 1926, he worked as a lifeguard at Lowell Park on the Rock River, where he was credited with saving seventy-seven lives. Reagan's college days were spent at Eureka College, a small sectarian institution run by the Disciples of Christ, a place to which he would repeatedly return some ten times after graduation. Once out of college, Reagan was employed for several years as a radio announcer in Des Moines, where as a sports broadcaster he re-created baseball games from a pitch-by-pitch account received by telegraph. The job developed his remarkable imaginative gifts through the work of more than 600 Chicago Cubs baseball games. In March of 1936, he followed the Cubs to spring training in southern California. While there he took a screen test, and abandoned radio to begin a movie career.

Reagan never became a big star in Hollywood, but his performances in several pictures garnered critical acclaim. One reviewer in 1950 said he was "amusingly impatient and blunt" in his portrayal on screen.[4] After World War II, Reagan's film career began to decline, so he made a successful switch to television. As the host of "General Electric Theatre" for several years, and then the announcer for the popular "Death Valley Days," he became a familiar visitor in American living rooms on the black-and-white screen. He had his first taste of politics as president of the Screen Actors Guild (SAG), leading his fellow members in a successful strike to obtain a percentage of profits from television revenues.

Ronald Reagan with his horse "Little Man" at Rancho Del Cielo. (Courtesy, Ronald Reagan Presidential Library)

Reagan's term as president of the SAG from 1947 to 1952 was marked by his cooperation with the FBI in the investigation of people in Hollywood who had attended socialist or communist group meetings. The dealings with labor bosses in these years reinforced his beliefs about capitalism, and Reagan emerged from these experiences as a lifelong economic conservative and anti-communist. He began his career as a partisan Democrat, admiring the legacy of Franklin Roosevelt. His divorce from actress Jane Wyman and subsequent marriage to Nancy Davis renewed his confidence in himself and the basic values of his childhood. The success in Hollywood placed him in the 91st percent marginal income-tax bracket, and made Reagan receptive to free-market economic ideas. He grew conservative with time, returning more and more to the political beliefs of his childhood.

While with the General Electric Theatre, Reagan toured his sponsor's plants, giving pep talks to management.[5] In his original speech, he focused on the virtues of the free market and the benefits of General Electric's products. The standard talk became so popular that he was invited to address trade organizations and civic groups around the country. Later, 1964 Republican presidential nominee Barry Goldwater agreed to have Reagan's speech aired on national television to raise funds and generate support in the last days of the Arizona senator's unsuccessful campaign.

From the time he delivered this national address in 1964 until he won the presidency in 1980, Reagan faced the problem of holding to principles that were out of touch with the prevailing mood of the country. Rather than apologize for his convictions or change them, Reagan became a salesman for economic and political conservatism. His passion came from what Edmund Burke called a moral imagination. "He saw the world through the clear lens of right and wrong . . . [and] firmly believed that however prolonged the struggle, good would eventually prevail over evil."[6]

Reagan believed that the problems facing the country were moral at base, and the foundation for his response was forged in his faith and convictions of childhood. Later in his political life, he echoed beliefs first evident in the speeches he gave in the 1960s. "We're going forward with values that have never failed us when we lived up to them: dignity of work, love of family and neighborhood, faith in God, belief in peace through strength, and a commitment to protect the freedom which is our legacy as Americans."[7]

If one definition of genius is a person's infinite capacity to make use of everyone and everything around him, then the Republican nominee for governor of California in 1966 certainly qualified. Reagan sopped up ideas and material from his aides, audiences, conversations, and summaries that were handed him on cards or articles in local newspapers. Moreover, he used the ideas in his speeches and press releases. He was not a snob, and genuinely valued the opinions of ordinary people. After the Johnson landslide of 1964, and the vision of the Great Society it ratified, he was a lonely voice declaring that the conservative vision of less government and individual responsibility was as viable as ever. Republicans, he said, "represent the forgotten American—that simple soul who goes to work, bucks for a raise, takes out insurance, pays for his kid's schooling, contributes to his church and charity, and knows there *ain't no such thing as a free lunch*."[8] The issues raised in his California gubernatorial campaign of 1966 were addressed to an audience concerned about high taxes, welfare cheaters, and judges who "coddled criminals."

The words came from a man who was warm and genial, not arrogant or overbearing like many politicians. He was handsome, broad-shouldered, and vigorous. Visitors often commented on his size; he was tall, tanned, and trim with bright blue eyes and dazzling white teeth. The face was lined with tiny wrinkles like leather, and he always had a ruddy complexion from working in the sun at his ranch. Undoubtedly his mother's conservative Christian influence left him with a pious deference to others. As governor he had a slight hearing loss, which deteriorated over his time in public office, and he leaned forward to hear questions better. The shortcoming only made him seem more attentive. He was driven by the sense that he wanted "to make America great again," and he was secure, without the oversized ego so typical of others who sought elected office.

Reagan's opponent in the 1966 California gubernatorial race was the popular incumbent governor, Pat Brown, who had defeated Richard Nixon, the GOP presidential nominee four years earlier. Brown saw Reagan as a weak opponent, and his strategy was to portray the former actor as a dangerous reactionary. He tagged Reagan as the "crown prince of the far right," and an amateur in politics.[9] The strategy seemed like a good way to marginalize an opponent. The Democrats defeated Richard Nixon in the gubernatorial race of 1962, and Barry Goldwater in 1964, with this same approach. Reagan was saddled with the approval of fringe groups, like the John Birch Society, an anticommunist association active at the time.

Throughout his political life Ronald Reagan showed that he was an idea man, not an analyst. He surrounded himself with people who knew more than he did, and he let them do their job without interference. His theory of administration was to keep things running, while nudging the whole governmental edifice in a definite direction. Aaron Wildavsky, president of the American Political Science Association and an expert on bureaucracy and budgets, commented that "his ideology kept members of the bureaucracy from sending up trial balloons that would cost more money, and as a result the organizations he led were compliant and under his control."[10] Reagan led by passive resistance, attacking the bloated bureaucracy as the "puzzle palaces on the Potomac," and offering a different vision of smaller government.

His confidence was striking. After he won elective office in California, a group of demonstrators mobilized by the American Federation of Teachers marched on the State Capitol to protest against proposed budget cuts. In the gubernatorial campaign, Reagan was critical of educators, especially those at the university level. His candidacy was opposed by the state education establishment, and they wanted to embarrass him. To their surprise, and against the advice of his top aides,

Reagan confronted the teachers on the steps, where he was greeted by a chorus of "boos." "Ladies and gentlemen," he began with a note of confident irony, "if there are any." His appearance won accolades from both his supporters and opponents.[11]

The theme of Ronald Reagan's 1976 and 1980 presidential campaigns was virtually the same as his bid to be governor: the belief that government, particularly the federal government, had the answer to our ills was false; and this collectivist, centralized approach had created more problems than it solved. The solution was to shrink the size and scope of government, transfer power from the public to the private sector, and move programs from Washington to state and local governments. This was exactly the opposite of the popular trend at the time, which favored centralized government and direction from the top.[12]

On the stump, Reagan was always an actor, always on camera. Andy Busch, one of his biographers, has written, "No matter how Reagan's fortunes waxed or waned in other respects, rhetoric was the one constant."[13] The quick smile, cocked head, and rough-cut good looks captured the audience; even if people had misgivings about his ideas, they still liked *him*. Ronald Reagan was raised to believe that Americans were good people who just needed to be told the truth. That was the message in the Disciples of Christ church of his childhood: "the fields were white unto harvest, but the laborers thereof were few." America was a mission field, and he was the in-gathering evangelist.[14]

After his two terms in Sacramento as governor, Ronald Reagan began his 1976 presidential campaign with a plan that called for him to score a quick win over a faltering Gerald Ford in the early primaries of New Hampshire and Florida, and then glide to the nomination. True to his style, the governor adopted a campaign schedule that kept him away from day-to-day decisions, and let an elite group of managers issue statements in his name. In a prepared speech before a Chicago audience in 1975, Reagan called for a massive transfer of federal programs to the states. After the speech, Gerald Ford's campaign attacked the plan by charging that such a huge transfer would lead to higher state taxes.[15] New Hampshire was a state where taxes were low, and kept that way as a matter of regional pride. The implication was that Reagan was an impractical theorist, who was no match for Ford's long experience in Washington. Ford, who had trailed in the early polls, won the New Hampshire primary by 1,317 votes out of more than 100,000 cast. The president then went on to win in Massachusetts, Florida, Illinois, and Vermont in the weeks that followed.

The opinion was widespread that Reagan was finished after such a poor start with five straight losses. The primary battle was between party moderates who backed Ford and conservative "movement" activists who wanted Reagan but saw the handwriting on the wall. The Nixon resignation and the Vietnam memory hung like a dark cloud over the GOP primary campaign. Republican governors, senators, and mayors urged the California governor to quit in the name of party unity, but even in debt and smarting from Barry Goldwater's endorsement of Gerald Ford, Reagan refused to abandon the field.

With some polls showing him twenty points down, Ronald Reagan went on the offensive. Even though he was a two-term governor without Washington experience, he introduced defense and foreign policy issues into the campaign. He unveiled the surprising charge that Henry Kissinger's State Department had plotted with Democrats to "give away" the Panama Canal, "to Fidel Castro's good friend, General Omar Torrijos." The issue instantly struck a nerve, and Reagan reduced it to an applause line: "We bought it, we paid for it, it's ours and we're going to keep it."[16] He began to move up in the polls, and Ford's managers started issuing press releases asking the governor to get out of the race. Reagan's opponents often mistook his "Mr. Nice Guy" image as a sign of weakness, but the more people pushed to have him leave, the more Reagan dug in his heels.

He borrowed money to purchase television time. Then, with the endorsement of conservative Senator Jesse Helms in North Carolina, he won that state's presidential primary. Reagan trounced Ford in several southern and western states, where his criticism of détente and the Panama Canal resounded with Republican voters. Ford fought back, using all his powers of incumbency. In an unprecedented use of the White House for political gain, the president invited dozens of uncommitted GOP convention delegates to have lunch, cocktails, or dinner with him over at the mansion.

Reagan angrily charged that Ford was misleading the press and the public, not to mention the convention representatives, with his intentions. Unfailingly genial and affable in public, Governor Reagan had a rarely seen temper that could explode like a volcano. In a conference telephone call, he gave Bill Brock, the chairman of the Republican National Committee, "unshirted hell" for refusing to release funds the California governor had raised for the national committee to use for a Panama Canal "truth squad."[17]

Then, on the advice of John Sears, his campaign manager and political strategist at the time, Reagan overreached his burgeoning advantage. He made an overture to have liberal Pennsylvania Senator Richard Schweiker share the ticket as his vice-president.[18] It was an unprecedented move designed to show his flexibility as a politician to a convention skeptical of such a conservative ideologue. It backfired. The right felt betrayed, and the moderate wing felt patronized. In the American political tradition, nominees, not aspiring nominees, picked their vice-presidents at the convention. The Schweiker ploy proved to be a last straw, the remaining uncommitted delegates flocked to President Ford, and the party had its nominee. At the eleventh hour, delegates from several states began a "Draft Reagan" movement on the floor for him to be vice-president, but it fizzled. On the last night of the convention, Reagan made a moving endorsement of Ford that helped to unify the party for the fall election. After the speech, the 1976 campaign for president came to a close for Reagan.

At sixty-five, with two full terms as governor of California behind him, Ronald Reagan seemed headed for political oblivion. In California, he and his beloved wife, Nancy, were financially secure and for the first time in ten years he was not serving in public office or running for election. Reagan spent much of his time working on his Pacific Palisades home, or at the Rancho Del Cielo ("Ranch in the Sky"), a place where he would say, "God really did shed his grace on America [like] the song says." The one-story house with stucco and adobe walls and a red tile roof was a retreat away from the press and public. Reagan would drive up the narrow winding road into the Santa Ynez Mountains to clear brush and ride horses on the more than six hundred acres. "The people who came to the house always described it the same way: humble, simple, plain, unpretentious... like him."[19]

In the fall of 1976, Jimmy Carter was elected the thirty-ninth president of the United States, with 297 electoral votes, beating Gerald Ford's 240. The Carter presidency opened on a high note when the president stepped out of his limousine on the slopes of Capitol Hill and walked down Pennsylvania Avenue, with his wife at his side, exulting in the cheers and the sunshine. The euphoria did not last long. Beginning in 1977, Cuban soldiers took up positions in Ethiopia. While Carter insisted that America had nothing to fear from communism, a pro-Marxian faction took control of Yemen on the tip of the Arabian Peninsula. Vietnam, Laos, and Cambodia fell and a Cuban-backed group took power in Grenada in the Caribbean. In Nicaragua, a guerilla army known as the Sandinista National Liberation Front (FSLN) gained strength.

The Soviet successes and Carter's inept responses pushed Ronald Reagan out of any considered retirement and back into the political fray. He renewed his candidacy for president by maintaining a vigorous travel schedule, speaking to audiences around the country, meeting with visitors, and reaching thousands of listeners with a weekly radio commentary. His box of notes and clippings was from popular sources like the *Los Angeles Times*, *National Review*, and *Reader's Digest* along with memorable lines from his favorite movies. Journalists loved to catch him in mistakes, but they did not realize that when Ronald Reagan spoke with earnest intensity, the audience believed in *him* more than in anything he was saying. He understood the power and value of talking to voters about America as a bastion of freedom; whether or not he had all the necessary facts was less important than his passion for the country.

Radio was an ideal medium for the discussion of values, and he knew it. During the 1930s Reagan, just like Roosevelt before him, learned that with the right tone of voice and choice of words, a radio personality could develop intimacy with the audience. The descriptions and stories he told on air stimulated the human imagination and had the effect of endearing the listener to the speaker. After his failed presidential bid in 1976, Reagan wrote dozens of five-minute radio broadcasts himself. The commentaries were later transcribed for newspaper columns. In 1978, Reagan estimated the broadcasts were heard on 286 radio stations, and the columns appeared in 266 newspapers to reach an audience of 20 million people each week. Few people realized that the actor known for his voice and good looks was a voracious reader and writer as well. William P. Clark, who served as chief of staff to Governor Reagan in California and followed him to Washington as national security advisor, recalled, "Yes, he was a writer...insisting that the top of his desk be clear at the end of each day."[20]

What did candidate Reagan talk and write about in the years before the 1980 presidential election? He talked a lot about communism: "Castro has some 15,000 troops *stirring up trouble in Africa*...[and] it is unrealistic for us to fail to recognize the Soviet Union has opened a new stage to achieve strategic dominance over Africa with all its mineral riches." He talked about Southeast Asia, and America's exit from region. He was comforting and affirming at the same time, calling for a new foreign policy. "Possibly Vietnam was the wrong war, in the wrong place at the wrong time [but] there is one message that needs to be sent to all nations of the world...there will be no more abandonment of friends by the United States of America." The disgrace of Vietnam was not a deterrent for Reagan, and he was willing to rattle the saber of American military intervention. In 1977 he wrote, "The troubles in Nicaragua bear a Cuban label."[21]

When the federal government declassified secret documents on the Truman administration's Cold War strategy, Reagan read them and over the course of two radio broadcasts emphasized the theme that "the Cold War is a real war, and the survival of the free world is at stake." Reagan believed that the Soviet Union was no colossus, and in his columns and radio commentaries, he hammered home the theme that the USSR was weak and vulnerable because the ideas of communism were antithetical to the nature of human beings.

One of the abiding legacies of the 1980s is the way Ronald Reagan forged and energized a new political coalition on behalf of conservative ideas. But at the beginning of the decade, no one thought a political breakthrough by conservatives was possible. In the words of one commentator, "The Republican Party stood for nothing and antagonized everybody."[22] Even after Nixon resigned and the two years of the Ford presidency, Republican party identification remained in decline, going down from 26 percent to 18 percent. Ford continued to follow Nixon's liberal policies, with Nelson Rockefeller as vice president, liberal ministers in the cabinet, tax increases as a solution for budget shortfalls, and détente with the Soviet Union.

The Reagan vision was different. He saw détente as pandering, tax increases as crippling, and liberalism as exhausted. Nowhere was the failed philosophy of the past more apparent than in foreign policy. The nation reeled under the words of Iran's foreign minister, Sadegh Ghotbzadeh, who announced that his country was prepared to keep the American hostages "more or less forever."[23] Many Americans asked themselves how it was that a small country in the Middle East could hold the world's greatest superpower at bay. American economic and military power was a liability. By the late 1970s, the economy remained caught in "stagflation"—with high unemployment coinciding with high inflation—rendering the likelihood of any recovery remote.

Even with these problems, it seemed unlikely that Carter would be defeated. Incumbent presidents who chose to run seldom lost. Carter had beaten Ford, of course, but Ford had not been elected. The last time a voted incumbent lost was 1932, and Franklin Roosevelt needed the Great Depression to do it. The polls uniformly showed Carter comfortably ahead of Reagan, and with the country in crisis—regardless of who was responsible—the electorate equated American patriotism with loyalty to the occupant of the White House.

Across the country that year, the 1980 election had an effect on some people who were destined to become America's next generation of leaders. American history is the story of a succession of crises, and for later leaders, the decade of the 1970s and Reagan's reaction to events in that time shaped them.

A glance at the names is useful. In 1980, George W. Bush was helping to raise money for his father's presidential bid from oilmen he knew as a businessman and neighbor in Midland, Texas.[24] Bill Clinton, the youngest governor in the United States in four decades, would become at the age of thirty-four the youngest defeated governor in American history.[25] Some consolation was provided in that his wife, Hillary Rodham (she would not take his name), had given birth to a baby girl, Chelsea, earlier in the year. Al Gore was just finishing his first term as congressman from the 4th district of Tennessee. John Kerry was serving as district attorney in Middlesex County, Massachusetts. Donald Rumsfeld capitalized on his appointment to Gerald Ford's cabinet to become the CEO of G. D. Searle and Co., a worldwide pharmaceutical company.[26] Colin Powell had attained the rank of major general, and assisted his boss, Frank Carlucci, in advising President Carter on the hostage crisis.

The leaders-to-be had to wait until the nation changed course, as it was about to do in 1980. The polls that year showed that voters had questions about Reagan, but their concern over the economy and foreign policy put Carter's job approval in freefall. The dominant event of the election was the hostage crisis that froze Jimmy Carter in indecision and rescue failure. When the president presented himself as a victim of events beyond his control, Ronald Reagan urged voters to hold the president responsible for the condition of the country. No event in the election, with the possible exception of the economy, had more importance for Reagan than the one of American indecision in the face of crisis, and he consistently drove the point home in his speeches and press releases.

Four years earlier, Carter had lost a huge lead over Gerald Ford, but came back to narrowly beat the incumbent president. The Democrats around Carter at the time believed one reason for Ford's defeat was his poor use of the powers of his office. In 1980, the Carter administration promised a vigorous defense of its policies, and an unabashed "Rose Garden" incumbent strategy when it came to the election campaign.[27] Two Democrats opposed the president. Ted Kennedy, the heir to a family legacy that stretched back twenty years and gripped the heartstrings of the American electorate like few politicians in the nation's history, was a sentimental favorite. The early polls that year showed him with 62 percent of the Democratic support, compared to Carter's paltry 24 percent. The other candidate was Jerry Brown, the governor of California and the son of the man Ronald Reagan defeated for office in 1966. To Democratic primary voters, the Brown name suggested another West Coast family legacy and a personality that believed nothing totally and at the same time saw some truth in everything. Against these two party rivals, Jimmy Carter played the powers of his office to perfection, skipping a debate in Iowa and using the White House news-making machine to dominate the daily agenda with the Iran crisis.

The hostage emergency frustrated Carter's Democratic opponents, but proved no hindrance to Reagan. There were six GOP candidates that year. George Herbert Walker Bush was a man of impressive origin and accomplishment, the scion of a wealthy, eastern Republican family, a millionaire and independent oilman who had been director of the Central Intelligence Agency, ambassador to the United Nations, and special envoy to China. The third major candidate in the race was John Bowden Connally, a former governor of Texas and secretary of the Treasury and Navy who characterized himself as a wheeler-dealer with experience. The trailing pack consisted of John Anderson, Bob Dole, Phil Crane, and Howard Baker.

The Reagan message was tailored directly to the indolence of the Carter era. Michael Barone would later write that "he spoke the language of Franklin Roosevelt," meaning that Reagan was gushing with enthusiasm, confident, cheerful, theatrical, and larger than life.[28] The condition of the country, Reagan declared, required a new, bolder approach of lower taxes and less government wedded to a strong national defense. With the exception of the military buildup, it was a familiar tactic that worked when the former actor ran against Pat Brown of California in 1966, and it still worked fourteen years later. Reagan argued that he was the perfect person by experience and conviction to lead the transition, just as he led the Golden State years earlier. In an act of pragmatism and party unity— which would affect American politics for three decades to come—Ronald Reagan chose George H. W. Bush as his running mate at the Republican convention.

While Republicans found a champion, the Democratic president fended off competitors from his own party. When told that Ted Kennedy was going to challenge him for the nomination, Jimmy Carter gave one of the more memorable election year lines: "I'll whip his ass!"[29] The Carter campaign took electioneering seriously, and even without an appearance by the president, beat Ted Kennedy by a two-to-one margin in Iowa. No matter how hard he tried, Kennedy was never able to resurrect the glories of his family's past to defeat the incumbent president. Carter easily won renomination at the Democratic Convention.

Jimmy Carter developed a concept called the "misery index" in his 1976 campaign against Gerald Ford. It was defined as the sum of inflation and unemployment. Ronald Reagan brought up the index, which was around 13 percent under Ford and was more than 20 percent under Carter, as a central campaign issue. On the stump, Reagan hammered away at the incumbent president: "A recession is when your neighbor loses his job, a depression is when you lose your job and a recovery is when Jimmy Carter loses his job."[30]

With the economic crisis as a backdrop, Reagan ran a campaign of upbeat optimism. He directed his comments to blue-collar workers despite their union leaders' efforts to keep them locked in the Democratic fold. Only twice in the twentieth century, 1930–1939 and 1970–1979, did Americans end the decade poorer, on average, than they began it.[31] In January 1980, consumer prices were rising at a 17 percent annual clip, and the working-class families of the country were feeling the pinch. To these families Ronald Reagan would say: "The way to fight inflation is to whittle down the size of the federal government, remove the layers of fat, and then cut the income taxes across the board for everybody in this country."[32]

But issues in the election went deeper than economics, and Ronald Reagan was prepared to address them. On the back of his campaign biography, *Why Not the Best?*, Carter described himself as a former governor of Georgia, farmer, engineer, naval officer, nuclear physicist, Christian, and American.[33] Early in the book Carter recalled his growing up years in Plains, Georgia, "and each Sunday we attended Plains Baptist Church, where my father was a Sunday school teacher."

The incumbent president from Georgia was not retiring about his religious beliefs, and many "born-again" evangelical Christians expected him to oppose abortion and the Equal Rights Amendment when elected. Carter did not. The fact that Jimmy Carter, a Southern Baptist, born-again Christian, had not objected to these trends in his presidency heightened the growth of a movement destined to be called the "New Right," or "Christian Right" or "New Religious Right." It was more widely referred to as the "Moral Majority," after the fundamentalist political action group formed by the Reverend Jerry Falwell. However, its membership and influence went far beyond this one group.

The members of the Religious Right worked on a number of related fronts, and much of their geographical base was in the South. The movement was originally a loose and poorly articulated collection of television evangelists, renegade mainline clergymen, coordinating committees, and conservative political activists. A clear organizational structure emerged from three organizations: Christian Voice, a coalition of several pro-family groups on the West Coast led by author-lecturer Hal Lindsey and actor Pat Boone; Religious Roundtable, a group of prominent Southern Baptist pastors and related evangelicals, who sponsored a number of workshops for pastors; and Moral Majority, founded by Jerry Falwell, which was a collection of independent, fundamentalist, and mainline ministers concerned about the drift of the country. All three groups were active in fund-raising, campaign mailings, and the establishment of opposition research and position papers in the 1980 election.

The movement began as a meeting in a hotel near the Dallas-Fort Worth airport where leaders like Billy Graham, Charles Stanley, Adrian Rogers, Pat Robertson, and Rex Humbard met to discuss the need for a united response to address the crisis in government and its cultural marginalization of evangelicalism. The decision was made to hold a series of training sessions for pastors, who would in turn go back to their congregations. One minister after another took a microphone in the meeting to complain about the Carter presidency and its effect on life in their community. Newspaper columnist Bob Novak attended a "Campaign Training Conference" for ministers in Georgia and concluded that "Jimmy Carter's goose was cooked because I saw the intensity of these people."[34] As late as 1965 Jerry Falwell had castigated his fellow clergy for taking part in the march at Selma, Alabama. Now ministers, who had earlier disdained politics, took the lead in educating their congregations about the evils of "secular humanism" and the responsibility Christians had to be active in the public arena.

Francis Schaeffer, a pastor who wrote extensively during this period, authored a best-selling book entitled *A Christian Manifesto* that argued: "The State must be made to feel the presence of the Christian community."[35] In the late 1970s it did. Members of the Christian Right believed their moral attitudes were closer to the preferences of the majority of Americans, and more mainstream than those in evidence on movie screens, on television sets, and in classrooms of state universities. They believed that a liberal elite controlled the federal government, the national media, and the great research universities. This combination of secular humanist values and concentrated power was thwarting their conservative agenda.

Ronald Reagan seemed an unlikely hero for the New Christian Right. He was divorced and remarried, his performance as a parent was suspect, and he won fame and fortune in the movie and television industries, regularly vilified for their contribution to moral decay. As governor of California he signed into law a liberal abortion statute, he was not a regular churchgoer, and his tax return showed that he contributed less than 1 percent of his income to charitable and religious causes. Reagan was taciturn about his Christian beliefs. When asked if he was "born again" he responded by giving his church affiliation and asking the questioner to pray for him.[36]

What Reagan did have was a feel for his evangelical constituency that Carter lacked. Maybe it was his Disciples of Christ churchgoing background, or his mother's legacy of regular instruction from the Bible. Whatever it was, Reagan was the one candidate who seemed able to speak directly and effectively to the newly empowered born-again constituency. While all three men in the presidential race—John Anderson, Ronald Reagan, and Jimmy Carter—claimed to be Christians, only Reagan could offer a conservative economic agenda, complete with a "standing tall" foreign policy, and convictions similar to the evangelicals on the crucial social issues. To sympathizers across the land, Ronald Reagan had policies to go along with his public witness.

The Republican platform that year reflected the conservative ideologues in public display and the influence of the New Religious Right. Gone was earlier support for the Equal Rights Amendment, and in its place was a plank supporting a constitutional amendment to outlaw abortion and a recommendation that opposition to abortion be a prerequisite for any federal judgeship. In contrast to earlier GOP conventions, this one had few ideological victims bleeding in the aisles after votes on the new platform. The Reagan campaign team constantly played the role of healer and party unifier among diverse groups, and while many thought the final platform too conservative, the party as a whole easily united behind the nominee. The new tenor of presidential politics was set at the end of Reagan's acceptance speech, when the newly selected standard bearer asked for a moment of silent prayer, and then closed with a benediction, "God Bless America."

Ronald Reagan was comfortable singing about God's anointing, because he believed the Almighty had poured out blessings on the nation at large, and on him in particular. From the time he stepped from the baptismal tank of the First Christian Church at 123 S. Hennepin Avenue in Dixon, Illinois, in 1922 until he died in 2004, Reagan was motivated by a belief that Christians were "enjoined by Scripture to resist and attack evil." When faced with what he saw as the darkest force in his lifetime, Soviet communism, he met it with not only political but also spiritual beliefs. In private statements Reagan disclosed that he thought God had chosen him for a special purpose. After an assassination attempt in 1981, Reagan would write in his diary: "Whatever happens now I owe my life to God and will try to serve him every way I can."[37]

When candidate Ronald Reagan ended his acceptance speech he was not a man with a broad grin, but a man of grave conviction. He linked his personal religious convictions to his party's political destiny. Any lingering doubts about Ronald Reagan's membership in, and support from, the religious right vanished when he came to Dallas's Reunion Arena on August 21, 1980, to address the Religious Roundtable. Seventeen thousand people filled the seats, along with millions of television viewers, who gathered to hear the speech by the then nominee destined to be called the Great Communicator. Reagan opened by stating the obvious: "I know this event is non-partisan, so you can't endorse me, but I want you to know that I endorse you."[38] To an audience used to hearing fiery evangelists, Reagan warmed their hearts with an endorsement of tuition tax credits, his complaint that the Supreme Court had expelled "God from the classroom," and his observation that everybody in favor of abortion had already been born. At the end of the speech Reagan invoked his legendary storytelling ability to say that if shipwrecked on an island and able to choose but one book to read for the rest of his life, he would choose the Bible. The speech brought thunderous applause in Dallas, and established the GOP nominee as the candidate with values like those of conservative white Christian voters.

Other groups were warming to Reagan as well. One month before the election, he appeared in predominantly Democratic Hudson County, New Jersey, before a working-class flag-waving audience. Reagan promised to restore American prestige at home and abroad, and the hard hats in the audience responded with cheers.[39] Carter began to lag behind traditional Democratic voters in crucial states like Michigan, Pennsylvania, and New Jersey, while Reagan made dramatic gains among Jews, Roman Catholics, and ethnic blue-collar minorities.

In the last weeks of the campaign the Democrats sought to exploit the "fear factor" about Reagan by raising the likelihood of nuclear war if he was elected president. After the October 29 debate, President Carter said his daughter, Amy, felt that the most important issue was the control of nuclear arms. But the man on television did not appear scary; instead, Ronald Reagan was a familiar television figure, humane, vulnerable, and sincere.

To pro-life voters in Philadelphia, Reagan said, "The American people today... are ready to shelter and protect the least protected among us, and I believe that specifically includes the unborn."[40] The stance was in direct contrast to other candidates, who tried to mute criticism on their abortion stand by taking some middle position or avoiding it altogether. On defense, Reagan promised a 600-ship navy and a revitalization of American military power worldwide.

In the week before the election, voters expressed dismay about Carter's indecisive nature, but they were also apprehensive about Reagan's policies. Reagan never led in the polls until after the last presidential debate on October 29. A fifty-state survey of top campaign strategists hours before the election found Reagan with 235 electoral votes, and Carter with 145.[41] As Carter's poll numbers continued to slip while Reagan's rose, the president accused Reagan of using the hostage crisis as a "political football" to win the election.

The contrast with Carter could not have been greater. The president gamely defended his policies abroad and promised economic improvement at home, but the country was in no mood to wait or listen to the Georgian's explanations. They were weary from the disquiet of two decades of change, and wanted someone to inspire them. Reagan did. Baby boomers saw Reagan as a reassuring parent, when he called for a "moral and military rearmament."

In the end, Jimmy Carter's attacks came too late. Reagan promised a curb to "big government," a restoration of economic health through supply-side economics, and a renewed respect for U.S. foreign policy. Although his candidacy was burdened by the third-party effort of John B. Anderson, a moderate Republican who ran as an independent, the twin issues of the economy and the hostage crisis favored Reagan.

Polls the night before the voting still had the outcome a toss-up, but in the end Reagan won a landslide victory, and the Republicans also gained control of the U.S. Senate for the first time in twenty-five years. The Reagan conservative coalition and its legacy would define politics in the country for thirty more years. The Republican president garnered 489 electoral votes to Carter's 49. Reagan was elected with a sweep of all but six states and the District of Columbia. John Anderson, the third-party candidate, won no electoral votes, but had over five million popular votes.

The extent of Reagan's victory was more apparent when the nation's media markets were analyzed. In the 1980s the country was becoming a land of urbanized cities where Democrats held sway downtown and Republicans flourished in the burgeoning suburbs. A media market has always been defined as an urban broadcast area where the three major networks once competed against one another for viewers. Cable changed the nature of the rivalry, but the

A. C. Nielsen rankings for every city count the number of television households in each market. The media market is a good measure of the political importance of each urban place, and their allegiance explains voting outcomes. Campaigns poll and place advertising based on media market surveys. The nation has over 200 media markets, and they frequently cross state borders, and take in viewers in neighboring states. The demographics vary, but one fact remains: half the country's population live in the top thirty markets. In 1980 Ronald Reagan won twenty-four of these markets.

The "inside-the-Beltway" crowd was shocked. Ronald Reagan got 51 percent of the vote compared to incumbent Jimmy Carter's 41 percent and John Anderson's 7 percent. "It was the biggest repudiation of an American president since Herbert Hoover lost in 1932, and perhaps the most stunning too."[42] Republicans gained 13 Senate seats, winning all the close races and defeating liberal icons like Frank Church of Idaho, who had defined the agenda of American politics in the 1970s.

The election of 1980 was a key turning point in American politics. The earlier political rhetoric of civil injustice and political equality was replaced with new words of economic expansion and military might. Reagan's success led to a new party realignment with liberal Republicans and conservative Democrats changing party affiliation in the 1980s and 1990s. It signaled the new electoral power of the Sun Belt suburbs as political power shifted from the North to South and Sun Belt.

3

I, Ronald Wilson Reagan

For the first time in recorded history the presidential swearing-in ceremony was held on the West Front of the Capitol. Previous inaugurals were behind the marble building in the shade overlooking a dull parking lot. This one was different. The view was spectacular, a vista framed by libraries and museums stretching down the Mall to the Washington Monument. The West Front accommodated some 32,000 official visitors, with thousands more assembled in the grass and down sidewalks cordoned off by police. It took a month to build the scaffolding, painted white to reflect the bright sun of January 20, 1981.

The night before the formal ceremony, at a gala in Landover, Maryland, actor Jimmy Stewart appeared on stage with General Omar Bradley, the nation's oldest living five-star general. Bradley was in a wheelchair, and together the two men stopped in front of the president-elect and saluted. In a response his wife says surprised her, Ronald Reagan stood and returned the salute. Then, when he sat down, the next president leaned over to whisper, "I think it's finally sunk in."[1]

Reagan was preparing to take office amid the greatest sense of political and economic uncertainty since Franklin Roosevelt arrived in Washington almost fifty years earlier. The question on everyone's mind was what his brand of conservatism—"Reaganism" as it was called—would look like. Most people thought he would moderate in office. That was what Nixon and Ford had done, and Reagan's record in California suggested he would change course if he had to. Economic problems dominated the public discussion, and it was by no means clear that any of his ideas would take root.

The next day at the inauguration itself, the weather was 55 degrees, the warmest on record for such an event. The president wore a club coat, striped pants, and a gray vest, and Nancy wore a red dress and coat by Adolfo. Chief Justice Warren E. Burger administered the oath of office on the Reagan family Bible, in which his mother had once inscribed this thought for the day: "You can be too big for God to use, but you cannot be too small." "It [the Bible] was old and crumbling," wrote Nancy Reagan in her memoir, "and taped together, and it seemed just right for the occasion."[2]

With the sun in his face, Ronald Reagan spoke down the sweep of the Capitol steps and into history just before noon. "In this present crisis," he said, "government is not the solution to our problem, government is the problem."[3] He wrote much of the twenty-minute speech himself, with the avowed purpose of shedding the politics of past despair and getting the country to believe in itself again. The sixty-nine-year-old former actor brimmed with a can-do confidence and a dewy-eyed nostalgia, but his proposals were longer on vision than on planning. The inauguration spirit captured no less a personality than *New York Times* columnist James "Scotty" Reston, who declared that the speech was a theatrical triumph, and one of the best ones in recent memory.[4] The country needed reassurance, which he said Reagan provided, but no one was certain what would happen next.

The inaugural was more emotional than most because at the moment Reagan took the oath of office, the American hostages were being loaded aboard a Boeing 727 and flown out of Tehran's blacked-out Maharabad Airport. Between the election in November and Inauguration Day, a flurry of negotiations had ensued with the Iranians for the release of the hostages. Reagan took the oath of office almost at the exact moment when American hostages were being released. The yellow ribbons tied to trees around the nation as a symbol of remembrance began to come down, and the 444 days of the long national nightmare were over. The president spoke only of his relief that the hostages were home, but in the years after the crisis it became clear that the new Iranian leaders were as unsure about the trigger-happy cowboy reputation of the new president as American voters had been in the election campaign.

President and Mrs. Reagan traveled from the Capitol to the White House down Pennsylvania Avenue in an open-top limousine as people stood ten deep to wave and cheer. That night Nancy Reagan set tongues wagging with an inaugural wardrobe said to cost around $25,000, prompting critics to say her extravagance was out of place in a time of economic hardship.[5] A seven-foot-tall, 3,000-pound inaugural cake, baked in six sections in Quincy, Massachusetts, arrived in Washington too soft to be reassembled and too big to fit through the Kennedy Center doors. The whole thing had to be taken to the Army and Navy Club, where it was consumed by generals and admirals.[6]

Ronald Reagan's first official act upon moving into the White House was to take out the solar water heating panels on the roof placed there by Jimmy Carter. Eight days later he ended oil price controls. The changes were more symbolic than anything else, but they sent a message: the days of talking about limits were over; the new philosophy was captured in the spirit of the times. It was the 200th anniversary of the Constitution, the 100th anniversary of the Statue of Liberty, and as the president said on the first day he went to the Oval Office, "those who say they don't believe in heroes, just don't know where to look."[7] The skeptics thought it impossible, but the new president was determined to prove them wrong.

The country's population in 1980 was a little more than 227 million, just about double what it was in the Great Depression years when Nelle Reagan scribbled that thought for the day in her Bible. Demographers wondered if it would get much larger, since more and more women were working and couples were consciously deciding not to have children. Eighteen percent of births were outside of marriage in 1980; the number of singles in the population, along with the number of couples living together without bothering to marry, was on the rise.[8]

The Gross National Product was about $3.0 trillion. The Dow Jones Industrial average drifted back and forth around the 900 mark. It would reach a low of 776 in August of 1982.[9] America's economy was, in the words of the time, "soft"; but for most people that word was a misnomer. The country was in a recession, and it seemed insoluble. The federal budget was usually around $500 billion, with the Defense Department taking the largest chunk, at $134 billion. Still, it was not enough, and the government was constantly either borrowing money or asking for a tax increase. The average salary was $24,500, and in more and more families both spouses worked to pay the bills. Movie tickets cost $2.69, a Burger King burger cost $1.40, and *Time* magazine sold for $1.75 at the counter.[10]

The press called it "Reaganomics." George H. W. Bush, when running as a contender for the GOP nomination earlier in the 1980 campaign season, derided the recovery plan as "voodoo" economics. By whatever name, Reagan's economic proposal was the most ambitious reform effort of American capitalism since the New Deal. The four key parts of it were income-tax cuts, new expenditure priorities, monetary restraint, and regulatory reform. Without a doubt the most controversial part of the package was the tax cuts. Historically the government did not cut taxes in a time of recession; it cut them in times of budget surpluses. The problem was the country had not had one of those since the Eisenhower administration. The Reagan proposal was unique. It suggested that when taxes were cut the money they generated for business and upper-income groups would be used for capital investments. The economy would recover, and the tax losses would be reclaimed by the resultant expansion. This approach, variously called trickle-down or supply-side, would reinvigorate spending and consumption. The expectation was that fiscal cuts, along with a diminished role for government in the system, would end what Reagan criticized in his inaugural: "a tax system which penalizes successful achievement and keeps us from maintaining full productivity."[11]

For the program to work, a delicate balancing act was required. The "Reagan Revolution" set the spending priority for the military, not social programs. Monetary policy had to be tightened enough to bring down inflation, but not so much as to create a recession. Regulation had to be cut to boost productivity, but without eliminating public support for the controls which caused their enactment in the first place. Taxes had to be cut, but without raising the specter of bulging deficits. The confidence of the president guided the whole plan, but the details remained murky. In March he presented a budget proposal to Congress that called for spending cuts totaling some $48.6 billion.

To pass the program, Reagan cobbled together a coalition of Republicans and conservative Democrats. Allies came from a region that was once synonymous with the Democratic Party: the South. The new conservatism in Washington was political capital that could be spent in any state south of the Potomac River. For example, Reagan carried Texas by 600,000 votes, while Democrats won nineteen of twenty-four congressional districts. Democratic loyalty was suspect in other parts of Dixie as well, where in 1980 the GOP carried every state in the region with the exception of Jimmy Carter's native Georgia.[12] In Washington, James Baker worked sixteen-hour days courting congressmen. "During the first hundred days of his presidency, Reagan held sixty-nine meetings with 467 members of Congress, prompting some of them to say that they had seen more of Reagan in four months than they had of Carter in four years."[13]

By June the work paid off, and Congress passed Reagan's budget without major alterations. It was the largest tax cut in American history, and most of the press concluded that with it, Reagan had ended fifty years of liberal government.[14] The *Wall Street Journal* editorialized about the "spectacular tax victory."[15] More importantly, Reagan had shown a sophisticated grasp of the issues and the legislative process. He knew how to use television, and his personal popularity, to get what he wanted. It was becoming clear that he would stick to his convictions, and not moderate under pressure.

The coalition of conservative Democrats, called "boll weevils" (because many of them came from the South, and their abandonment of the Democratic party had a debilitating effect on the majority party in Congress), and Republicans formed again in August to enact a series of tax reductions on individual incomes that amounted to 25 percent over a three-year period. It also lowered the tax on estates and provided for Individual Retirement Accounts (IRAs), in the hope that the proposed reductions would lead to more savings, diminished consumer spending, and less inflation. In passing this legislation, Ronald Wilson Reagan changed the economic philosophy in Washington, and altered the course of American politics.

At the time, the president's critics believed that his popularity came more from his personality than his programs, but an event in the making would erase that sentiment. Reagan had been president for seventy days on March 30, 1981, when he went to speak before 3,500 members of the AFL-CIO's Building Workers Union at Washington, D.C.'s Hilton Hotel. He was confidently defending his budget cuts, and at the same time urging support for his economic plan. As the only president ever to be an AFL-CIO member, he knew from the campaign that he would get a warm reception from what was usually a hostile audience for Republicans. After the speech, Reagan exited the hotel by the VIP entrance, where a black Lincoln limousine awaited him, and police stood at a rope barrier restricting reporters, onlookers, and cameramen. In the crowd lurked twenty-five-year-old John W. Hinkley, Jr., carrying a .22-caliber Rohm RG-14 revolver loaded with Devastator bullets designed to explode on impact.[16] In a bizarre attempt to live up to his family's expectations, and at the same time impress actress Jodie Foster, Hinckley had decided to kill the president.

As Reagan raised his arm to wave at the crowd, six shots rang out in rapid succession. Press Secretary James Brady collapsed with a bullet to the head. Secret Service agent Timothy McCarthy and policeman Thomas Delahanty were also hit. Agent Jerry Parr pushed President Reagan into the limousine, slamming his head on the doorjamb in the process. The president fell onto the car's transmission hump and did not believe that he had been hit, even though he felt an acute pain in his chest. "Jerry, get off, I think you've broken one of my ribs."[17] Paar noticed that blood was coming out of the president's mouth and he ordered the limousine go directly to George Washington Hospital.

Reagan, ashen-faced, complained of difficulty breathing on the way, but when the limo arrived at the emergency room he walked into the hospital without assistance—only to collapse inside. He faced two hours of surgery as doctors removed a .22-caliber bullet that struck his seventh rib and lodged less than an inch from his heart. The president had a partially collapsed left lung and received eight units of blood. Dr. Dennis S. O'Leary of the hospital staff said he was "right on the margin" of death, losing about 40 percent of his blood volume.[18] Four days later the president's temperature soared to 102 degrees. More bad news waited. Although the White House wrapped the twelve-day hospital stay in optimism, Reagan had a secondary infection that was as serious as his initial gunshot wound.

News of the shooting traumatized the country. Television coverage was live, but the news reached others third and fourth hand, from a passing stranger, or a telephone call, or a waiter in a restaurant. Nancy Reagan recalled the "scenes of Parkland Memorial Hospital in Texas and the day President Kennedy was shot."[19] Michael Deaver, the president's aide, believed that President Reagan was not in any real danger, until "I ducked into the room where the president had been taken . . . [and saw] my president, was stripped to the skin and one of the doctors was holding his coat up to the light, evaluating the tiny bullet hole under the left sleeve."[20] Around the nation, people wanted the news to be false. They gathered around televisions and car radios and talked to strangers in bars. The unspoken fear was that the shooting continued a string of national disasters stretching back to the 1960s and signifying some sort of decline in American exceptionalism and the unraveling of society.

That did not happen. Reagan's quick recovery, more remarkable given that he was seventy years old, was seen as symbolic of a revitalized national spirit. His job approval rating rose to 73 percent, and his courage and humor earned him the admiration of the nation. "Honey, I forgot to duck," he lightheartedly told his wife when she came into the emergency room; and he quipped, "Please tell me you are all Republicans" to the doctors when he was wheeled into the operating room.[21]

In the next few months, the stamina and determination of a still-recovering Ronald Reagan was put to the test. That August, the 13,000 members of the Professional Air Traffic Controllers Organization (PATCO) decided to go on strike until their demands for reduced workloads and higher salaries were met. As federal employees, the controllers were violating a written pledge in the no-strike clause of their employment contract. Unlike a walkout of automobile workers or coal miners, this one was less a threat to the economy than to the safety of the nation's airline passengers.

In the White House Rose Garden, the president responded with an ultimatum that was clear: return to work within forty-eight hours or face termination. The demand was awkward because PATCO was one of the few unions that supported Reagan's candidacy in the 1980 election. To the surprise of the PATCO strikers, and labor union loyalists in the Democratic Party, the public sided with the president and had little sympathy for the controllers. When the federal employees did not show up for work, Reagan fired them, and directed Transportation Secretary Drew Lewis to hire replacements.[22]

Lane Kirkland, president of the AFL-CIO, joined a picket line with members of the striking air traffic controllers. In Toronto, three controllers were suspended for showing sympathy in refusing to clear flights to the United States. PATCO appealed for other unions in the United States and abroad to honor their strike and boycott sending planes to American airports.[23] The press and union leaders openly speculated that airplanes would crash when they were directed by inexperienced workers. If there had been an accident, of course, then the consequences for Reagan would have been catastrophic, but no accidents happened. For the new president, fresh from victories in Congress and a remarkable recovery from an attempt on his life, a new principle was now at work in Washington declaring that people should be held accountable for their oaths. The decisive way Reagan handled the PATCO strike convinced many Americans that he was, in the words of Haynes Johnson of the *Washington Post*, "the kind of leader the country longed for and thought it had lost: a strong president."[24]

The city of Washington was finding out more about the president in bits and pieces, and discovering that he was very different from his predecessors. For example, he was not the type of leader to consult polls to guide his decisions. Instead, he used public opinion to find out what people were thinking, and then summoned his powers of persuasion to get them to change their minds. In September before he took office, 60 percent of those surveyed by the Gallup poll thought that the high cost of living and inflation were the most important problem facing the country. No respondent had even heard of tax cuts as a solution for the budget crisis. In the fall of 1981, Gallup found that 87 percent of Americans had heard of the administration's tax cut program, and 59 percent favored it as a solution. Not all of this was Reagan's doing, of course, but much of it was.[25]

Despite his success using the bully pulpit of the presidency, the former actor and his wife remained strangers to the established rituals and folkways of official

Washington. Every administration was migratory, of course, but Washington usually found ways to be welcoming in any circumstance. When John Kennedy was president, the country exulted in his drawl and good looks, while hostesses learned to serve clam chowder at parties. When Jimmy Carter arrived as a professed outsider, the city made his administration comfortable with grits and southern hospitality.

To understand politics in the United States, it is necessary to know something about the nation's capital city. The population of Washington began to explode in the World War II years, when the metropolitan area mushroomed from 621,000 in 1930 to well over a million by the end of 1941. "Seventy thousand new people," wrote David Brinkley of those times, "arrived the first year after Pearl Harbor alone."[26] The city filled with military officers and civilians who carried briefcases with government contracts, encrypted instructions for invasion plans, and military assessments. World War II was won because of secrets: the Allies had the Enigma machine that read Hitler's plans as soon as his field officers did, and the "Purple" code that allowed Americans in the Pacific to know what the Japanese were doing before the battle of Midway. Washington was the nerve center for secrets. The ultimate confidence at the time was the Manhattan Project, a work so privileged that it produced the atomic bomb and ultimately ended the war without anyone knowing about it.

"Not many fortunes were made in Washington, but a great many made elsewhere were spent there."[27] In the years of World War II, public and private social affairs in the city took on the air of a covert, shadow government by invitation only. Casual meetings and conversations, or a guest list of invited prominent people to a Georgetown dinner party, could signal a major change in policy. For example, on a cold and rainy January 19, 1942, while the Russian armies pushed the Germans back to Mozhaisk, sixty miles west of Moscow, there was a half-mile-long traffic jam on Foxhall Road as the entire Washington establishment turned out for what *Life* magazine called the "city's biggest blowout since the war began." Marjorie Merriweather Post Close Hutton Davies, heiress to the Post-Toasties cereal millions, and her husband, Joseph E. Davies, former ambassador to Moscow, hosted the new Russian ambassador. While a string quartet played Russian music, the Secretary of State's wife, Mrs. Cordell Hull, poured coffee from a golden pot into gold-rimmed white teacups made in czarist Russia. What mention was made of whether the United States should increase its support to the Russian army engaged in an offensive in the snow? Only the invited guests knew, and they were not talking, but the implications were clear. No wonder that Franklin Roosevelt called the city's social elite "parasites," but the natives had another name for themselves and their activities: "parties with a purpose."

The Cold War saw the birth of the CIA, and intrigue and subterfuge became a staple of government service in the city. Federal employees in social situations learned to say they worked "for the government" and left it at that. Informal contacts were vital. In 1962, the Soviet response to John F. Kennedy's move in the Cuban missile crisis came from a discussion at a diplomatic party, where ABC State Department correspondent John Scali relayed a message from a KGB embassy official that broke the deadlock.[28] *Washington Post* reporter Bob Woodward had late night meetings with his contact "Deep Throat," named for a pornographic movie at the time, in a parking garage. Their meetings were arranged when Woodward moved a potted plant on the balcony of his apartment, then opened his home-delivered *New York Times* to find a secret notation calling for a meeting in a way the reporter still does not understand.[29]

That is the way things were done in Washington, and anyone who lived in the city learned to play the game. The federal government offices spread like water splashing out of a tub, and soaking "Washington" into the Virginia and Maryland suburbs. The new residents came for jobs, first in Roosevelt's New Deal, then in John Kennedy's New Frontier, and later in Lyndon Johnson's Great Society. The people who lived there had "access," meaning they knew legislative staff, reporters, undersecretaries, and friends who worked around the city. They could "get something done," and became a part of the permanent government with a new name—"Inside the Beltway." The interstate highway that circled the city and the inner suburbs of Virginia and Maryland came to represent a permanent ruling class in the nation's capitol.

Where you were from was less important than whom you knew. Presidents came and went, but the perpetual residents of the city and the civil servants in the bureaucracy remained. The incestuous relationship multiplied through marriages, divorces, and remarriages, past working relationships, and previous administrations. After an election defeat the appointed officials, be they Democrat or Republican, simply decamped to universities, think tanks, law offices, and consulting firms to keep doing what they did on the public payroll. They worked on K Street. The difference now was that they were outside rather than inside the government, but in many ways they could be just as effective, and a lot better paid.

In no institution of government was permanent power more concentrated than in the Congress of the United States. Democrats on the Hill, and their staffers on the permanent committees, enjoyed the privileges once reserved for royalty at a medieval court. Between 1930 and 1980 the Democrats controlled the House of Representatives every year but four, and had ruled unchallenged since 1955. The majority in the House was like a baseball team that always played at home and changed the ground rules for each game.[30] Residents in Hollywood learned to manufacture fame, and the Americans of the Midwest took pride in their land, but in Washington the currency of the realm was power. The government kept growing in the 1970s, and the permanent members of the community kept finding new opportunities in the change.

Life in Washington came at a price. In *The Decline and Fall of the Roman Empire*, Edward Gibbon recalled the lament that "the rich acquired...the ground which they covered with palaces and gardens; [but] the poorer citizens...might purchase in the little towns of Italy a cheerful, commodious dwelling at the same price which they annually paid for a dark and miserable lodging."[31] Washington was the same way: it experienced a boom that made the city not only the world's most powerful, but also the most expensive.

The 1970 census showed that professional households in Montgomery County in Maryland and Fairfax County in Virginia had the highest growth rates of any major metropolitan area in the country. The economy was special because it was virtually recession-proof, and the city became a haven for hundreds of thousands of two-income families. The demographics were impressive: more than a quarter of Washington's adults had college degrees, and 15 percent had done postgraduate work. The metropolitan area had more lawyers and more single people than any other city in the country.[32]

In the first few years of the 1970s, metropolitan Washington became the number-one retail market in the United States, with eleven new shopping centers in the area. Bloomingdale's, Neiman-Marcus, and Lord & Taylor joined Hecht's and Woodward & Lothrop in centers that joined intersections off the Beltway. Real estate costs were tied to commuting time. Congressional wives went to work as realtors and outstripped their husbands' salaries in a summer of selling. One longtime realtor said the city "had more real estate agents than houses."[33]

The impression official Washington had of the new president in 1981 was initially unfavorable. Clark Clifford, the silver-haired Brahmin of the nation's political establishment, who had served presidents across half a century and prided himself on political access, pushed for a meeting in the first weeks after Reagan's inauguration. Michael Deaver reluctantly acquiesced to the request. That evening at the house of another Washington institution, Pamela Harriman, Clifford declared Reagan to be "an amiable dunce."[34] Nicholas von Hoffman of the *Washington Post* said it was "humiliating to think of this unlettered, self-assured bumpkin being our president."[35] Tip O'Neill, the venerable Massachusetts Democrat, opined, "He knows less that any president I've ever known." Anthony Lewis of the *New York Times* claimed he had only a seven-minute attention span.

What the insiders did not understand was that Ronald Reagan connected with the American people in a way few of them—regardless of their experience—could fathom. The president realized that the spirit of the nation was more important than any monthly statistics measuring economic progress, or poll results showing presidential popularity. Reagan's job was to inspire confidence in the future and reassure the country that things were going to work out. The optimism was not a trivial quality; instead, it was an essential approach to life that had carried him from Dixon, Illinois, to Hollywood and the White House. With him as actor the country was one vast stage. He translated the complexities of a postindustrial economy into phrases and stories that people could understand.

Often the stories, while compelling from a political standpoint, were pure fiction. Reagan confused scenes from movies with real events. The most famous of these gaffes was a story he used in the 1976 and 1980 campaigns, and repeated in 1983 at the annual convention of Congressional Medal of Honor winners. The setting was World War II Europe. During the course of a bombing raid over the continent a B-17 bomber was hit by antiaircraft fire. The ball-turret gunner was severely wounded, and the other crew members were unable to get him out of the turret. As the B-17 continued to lose altitude the commander ordered the men to bail out. "And as the men started to leave the plane...the boy knowing that he was left behind to go down with the plane, cried out in terror." The last man out was the commander, who took the boy's hand and said, "Never mind, son, we'll ride it down together." The Congressional Medal of Honor was posthumously awarded.

The story caused Lars-Erik Nelson of the *New York Daily News* to do some research. The reporter went through 434 citations of the Medal of Honor, and could find no such award. He wrote a column about the speech and Reagan's fictional storytelling. A reader responded that the story reminded him of a scene from the 1944 movie *A Wing and a Prayer*. Another reader believed the story had appeared in an issue of *Reader's Digest*, and Nelson found the account there about a Flying Fortress base in England. Yet he could find no verification for the story. The best he could do was determine that the apocryphal incident had become almost a legend around the base, but no one confirmed it had any basis in fact.[36]

It mattered little to Reagan if the stories he told were invented or real; what mattered was their effect on the audience. For an actor the effect of storytelling was measured in the response of the listeners, not the accuracy of the tale told. When informed of the Nelson article, Reagan justified the story by saying that he wanted to rebuild the military, and just as important as the hardware was the military's morale. The president had an arsenal of emotional stories that he used with great effect. The press was constantly sniping at him for their accuracy, and official Washington made them the stuff of cocktail circuit conversation, but they missed the point. Hollywood was America's dream factory, and Reagan was a part of that manufactured culture. He incorporated fiction into political rhetoric to fit his own needs.

His favorite story was about two little boys, and it symbolized his approach to his job as president. One little boy was a dour pessimist and the other one an extreme optimist. They were both taken by their parents to a psychiatrist because the parents wanted to encourage the pessimistic son and make the optimistic boy more conscious of the obstacles in life. To accomplish this, the pessimist was placed in a room with shiny toys and the optimist in a room containing horse manure. When the parents returned, the pessimistic boy was crying. He had refused to play with the toys out of fear that he would break them. The parents found the optimistic child happily shoveling through the fertilizer. He told them, "With this much manure around, I know there's a pony in here somewhere."[37]

When Reagan was not telling jokes or stories, he was resting. Washington was, and remains, a city of compulsive twelve-hour days and workaholics who measure themselves by how many hours they put in. The president, with the most powerful and demanding job in the city, worked relatively short days from nine to four. Carter was known as a man who took briefing books home and studied them late into the night upstairs in the residence. Reagan had no such schedule. When the press poked fun at him, he joked, "It's true that hard work never killed anybody, but I figure why take the chance at this late age."[38]

What Reagan did enjoy was the time-consuming ceremonial part of the job. Anyone who standardly invited the president to an event might suddenly be shocked to find out that he accepted. In Washington, where socializing and access were part of the job, Ronnie Reagan was not one of the boys. He thought that parties and dinners were for fun, not work. In most social situations he preferred to tell stories, and when asked how he was bearing up under the strain of the office he would invariably tell a joke. He loved to hear the band play "Hail to the Chief," and Reagan grasped something Carter never did. Americans wanted their president to be a ruler. As Frank Reynolds, the ABC News correspondent, said of the American electorate, "They *want* to look up to the president... [and] they don't like it when he goes on television wearing a sweater" (as Jimmy Carter had done).[39] Ronald Reagan never disappointed anyone when it came to respect for the office of the president.

Reagan's principal oddity, of course, was that he was a conservative ideologue in a city full of liberals, relativists, and compromisers. The last avowed conservative in town was Richard Nixon, and official Washington exposed him as a fraud and drove him from power. Denizens were suspicious of the new actor president, but he showed them in the years to come that he was tough, fair, and above the criticism. In the give-and-take of political compromise he could be resolute and unyielding. Reagan came to the office with a short "to do" list: he had a clear idea of what he wanted to accomplish and he never wavered from it.

Humor was Ronald and Nancy Reagan's secret weapon, and one they used with devastating effectiveness when under relentless public criticism. In the spring of 1982, Nancy used her stage skills to ingratiate herself to skeptics and surprise the natives in a way no couple had before, or since. If there is any merit to the old proverb that opposites attract, then extroverted presidents usually marry introverted wives. After a year in office, the press was snapping at Nancy Reagan and she was feeling the pain. To the "inside-the-Beltway" crowd she was a frivolous socialite who hobnobbed with the idle rich and dressed in designer gowns with mink as an accessory. She set tongues wagging when the Reagans tapped private sources for $800,000 in fix-up expenses at the White House, and an additional $200,000 for new china. Nancy Reagan was said to be too much "Hollywood," enamored with the glitz and wealth of tinsel town.

First ladies always came in for some press scrutiny in Washington. Bess Truman and Mamie Eisenhower were criticized for their dowdy clothes, and while Jackie Kennedy was the epitome of glamour, she paid for her popularity with a lack of privacy. Betty Ford was treated well by the press, especially after her bout with breast cancer, but Rosalynn Carter was mocked for taking an interest in the policy issues that preoccupied her husband. In a 1981 poll by

Nancy Reagan. (Courtesy, Ronald Reagan Presidential Library)

Good Housekeeping, Nancy Reagan did not even make the ten "most admired" women on the list.[40]

The First Lady's Washington-wise secretary, Sheila Tate, suggested that she use the annual Gridiron Dinner in March of 1982 as an opportunity to surprise the locals and change her image. The event was a coveted ticket around town, a white-tie dinner held every spring for 600 invited guests. The program was always the same: members of the press performed clever and funny skits poking fun at both Democrats and Republicans. The skits were followed in turn by two speakers, one from each party. The evening ended with a brief toast to the president, followed by his response. Everything was "off the record," but the evening could be memorable for barbs, laughs, and the way people handled criticism.

In 1982, the word was out that the press was going to do a skit poking fun at Mrs. Reagan's fashion tastes. Sheila Tate thought it would be good if Nancy Reagan appeared in her own skit, in a surprise role. But Nancy Reagan, a former MGM actress, had more than a bit part in mind. "Would you sing?" Tate asked. The former stage actress turned first lady said she would. "Would you dance?" Another nod of agreement followed the question. Someone suggested that Mrs. Reagan attack the press in her parody, but she knew show business better than the Washington insiders. "I'm not willing to attack the press.... If I'm going to do this at all, I think I should make fun of myself."[41]

A White House speechwriter put together a routine based on the old show tune "Second Hand Rose," and Mrs. Reagan rehearsed without telling the president. When the night arrived, and the Gridiron chorus did a version of "Secondhand Clothes," mocking the extravagance of Nancy Reagan, she stepped away from the head table for the ladies room. Some in the room thought her leaving was a sign that she was visibly upset at the parody, but the whole place was stunned a few minutes later to see her burst through a rack of clothes on stage wearing an aqua skirt, with red and yellow flowers held together by safety pins, a floppy hat and feathered boa.

On stage, the old Fanny Brice hit from the 1920s got new lyrics:

> Secondhand clothes,
> I'm wearing secondhand clothes.
> They're all the thing in spring fashion shows.
> Even my new trench coat with fur collar,
> Ronnie bought for ten cents on the dollar,
>
> The china is the only thing that's new
> Even though they tell me that I'm no longer queen,
> Did Ronnie have to buy me that new sewing machine?
> Secondhand clothes, secondhand clothes.
> I sure hope Ed Meese sews.[42]

For a minute the act was greeted by thunderous silence, then the audience rose and yelled for an encore. Amid a standing ovation she repeated the routine. Gone was the image of a self-absorbed socialite, replaced by one of a politician's wife who cared what other people thought, and showed it.

After a year in office it was hard to tell whether Reagan created the times or whether he was a product of them. Either way, he was presiding over a dramatic transformation of American life and politics. For most of the previous fifty years his party had been out of power; now it was governing again, this time with a fragile coalition of conservative Republicans and defecting Democrats and a new political style. From the time of Franklin Roosevelt politicians had sought to lift the sprit of the nation *with* government; now Reagan was accomplishing the same thing by saving them *from* government. The private sector was where the action was, and Americans turned to revitalize their own economy in the face of recession and the Soviet challenge.

In the 1960s and 1970s, the pulse of the country was taken on college campuses. Incidents at one university had a way of escalating rapidly and attracting television coverage for copycat imitations elsewhere. By 1980, the mood changed, and the vast majority of undergraduates were, if not right minded, then at least better behaved. A study by UCLA and the American Council on Education found that college freshmen were more interested in status, power, and money than at any time in the previous fifteen years.[43] The most popular major on campus was business management, and political activism was replaced by a resurgent interest in ballroom dancing.

College students of the time wanted marketable skills, not political visibility. The language on campus changed, and a new generation emerged to say: "Like my time was the eighties, and it was awesome, like totally the best ever, you know?" College tuition was within reach of most Americans, and their children went to college, even if they did not graduate. Female students knew that a degree was necessary, since marriage and childbirth meant two incomes in families. New majors proliferated on campuses and enrollments surged. Night classes and weekend degree programs were targeted to full-time employees who needed more education in the increasingly complex marketplace.

The combination of Nancy Reagan's opulent elegance and British Princess Diana's love of fashion stimulated a return to more luxuriant clothing styles. The standard was set by Linda Gray, who portrayed "Sue Ellen" in the popular television show *Dallas*. The look was one of power, bold colors, diamonds, and dresses with padding in the shoulders. Women were seen as rivals or partners, and not revolutionaries. The miniskirt made a comeback and denim became an acceptable fabric for dress occasions. Anne Klein, Perry Ellis, and Calvin Klein were popular designers of the time.

The glitz extended to movies, where Steven Spielberg and George Lucas earned reputations as "blockbuster" directors. *The Empire Strikes Back* (1980), *Raiders of the Lost Ark* (1981), *ET: The Extra-Terrestrial* (1982), and *Return of the Jedi* (1983) had appeal for both adults and children.[44] Americans stayed at home and watched movies on their new VCRs. In 1982 actress Jane Fonda, dressed in a striped leotard and leg warmers, released a workout video that proved more popular than her movies. CNN, cable news, and MTV, the music video network, began broadcasting in these years, and now the country could watch politics and musicians all day long.

It is said that the book *Frankenstein* was written about the effects of the Industrial Revolution on European society. In the early 1980s a new horror book could be published about an innovation destined to change American life more than anything since the invention of the automobile: the home computer. The microcomputer became affordable because the mass production of the silicon chip–based microprocessor made smaller technology affordable. Home computers were mostly 8-bit microprocessors, and the market was soon flooded with Apple IIs, Kaypros, and Commodore 20s, the latter being the first computer in the world to pass the 1 million mark in sales.[45]

In many ways the early 1980s mood was upbeat and nostalgic for the optimism of the 1950s. In the White House, Ronald Reagan was a throwback to the swagger the country had after World War II. The only difference was this time the economy was not cooperating. White House operatives, who in 1981 envisioned a Republican congressional majority in the approaching elections, were wondering if the president would be re-elected. At a campaign fundraiser in Minneapolis, Minnesota, before the midterm elections, Reagan emerged from his limousine to be greeted by a banner proclaiming, "Welcome President Hoover."[46] On Election Day in 1982, more than 9 million Americans were out of work, and the jaunty optimism of the inaugural ceremony was beginning to fade.

None of this bothered Ronald Reagan, or at least he did not show it. The key to his presidential personality was an unshakable conviction that everything would turn out fine if everyone would just "stay the course." It became a mantra for the GOP in 1982, even in the face of the disappointing statistics and dropping poll numbers. The president believed he could smash Democratic strongholds among working people and minorities, and establish his party as the majority one—provided he was blessed with that greatest of political assets: luck. Reagan interpreted his landslide victory as a mandate for change, almost any change, but the results would take time.

At the end of 1982, the Russians were bullying abroad, opposing any deployment of the Pershing II missiles, and unemployment at home was greater than at any time since 1940. The Republicans lost twenty-six seats to the Democrats in the midterm election, but the conservative "boll weevil" majority governing coalition survived. By the end of 1982 only 41 percent of Americans said they approved of Reagan's leadership, and in early 1983 that figure would drop to 35 percent. His was the lowest midterm figure for any president in forty years.[47] From this nadir he would surge to win re-election by a landslide in 1984. How did he do it? Reagan's political triumph came from three things: first, an expanding economy that continued to grow into the next decade; second, his mastery of divided government and acceptance of budget deficits; and third, Soviet belligerence and hubris.

On the economic front, the problem was not that Reaganomics was not working; it was that it was having mixed results. Inflation fell dramatically in the first year the new president assumed office. Decreases in the costs of various goods, especially oil, helped stabilize an economy that had been in freefall. Gone were the gas lines that haunted his predecessor, replaced by a belief that the economic pie must be increased, not simply sliced differently. The conviction of growth was fundamental to supply-side, Reaganomic doctrine. The administration believers wanted an expanding economy, and by 1983 they were beginning to see signs that the indicators were turning up. But there was a down side as well; the costs of entitlement programs like Social Security, Medicare, and Medicaid soared. To cover the shortfall, government borrowing went to record levels.

Reagan campaigned in 1980 by rashly promising a balanced budget and huge reductions in federal spending as a cure for the nation's economic woes. But he also promised an increase in defense spending, and an economy in the doldrums meant decreased tax revenues. In 1981, Reagan sent to Congress a $695.3 billion budget for fiscal year 1982. At the time, he predicted that this would generate a $45 billion deficit. Congress approved a $695.5 billion budget, almost the exact amount requested by the White House. However, the real deficit ended up being $128 billion, nearly three times larger than predicted. Talk of a balanced budget disappeared. The difficulty of borrowing made businesses wary of new capital investment, despite the tax cuts. Foreign competition, especially from Japan, added to domestic uncertainty.

In December of 1981, Reagan's director of the Office Management and Budget (OMB), David Alan Stockman, was quoted as saying the budget numbers did not "add up." Stockman had hoped that Reagan could win larger cuts in domestic spending, but Congress refused to cut Social Security spending, so the OMB director admitted in a widely read interview published in the *Atlantic Monthly* that the deficit would grow.[48] The man most to blame for this, Stockman alleged, was Ronald Reagan, whom he described as a nice man but no revolutionary economic thinker. As a consequence, Stockman abandoned his supply-side convictions and went from being a believer in tax cuts to favoring tax increases. Conservatives were outraged at Stockman's interview and many called on him to resign. "Had it been up to me," said Nancy Reagan, "Stockman would have been out on the street that afternoon."[49] But President Reagan stood by his budget director, and at the same time did not abandon his economic beliefs.

Every year he was in office, Reagan submitted budgets to Congress that were larger than the previous year's, and every one contained sizeable budget deficits. Reagan's impressive victory in 1980 and his repeat in 1984 failed to crack Democratic hegemony in the U.S. House, though the Senate early went the way of the presidency. In modern times high budget deficits have occurred in times of divided government, when different parties control the executive and legislative branches of government. Economists generally accept that 3 percent or more of the Gross National Product (GNP) is a telltale sign of unacceptably high deficits. From World War II until 1980, the offensive deficits the country had occurred only during a time of divided government. Not surprisingly, in the years from 1981 to 1987, when Democrats controlled the House and Republicans the Senate and White House, deficits were the rule.[50]

This meant that Ronald Reagan, the champion of fiscal restraint and conservative government, was driving the country into bankruptcy. Nowhere was the uneasiness more apparent than in the U.S. Senate, where majority leader Howard Baker had to deal with thirteen GOP freshman senators implacably opposed to budget deficits, government growth, and raising the national debt ceiling. Before a crucial vote to allow more government borrowing, Baker rounded up the freshmen and put them around a conference table. Then he brought in Republican Senator Strom Thurmond. The senior senator from South Carolina epitomized tight-fisted austerity and fierce independence. He stood against federal intervention as a staunch segregationist, and held the Senate record for filibuster, twenty-four hours and eighteen minutes. In the meeting, Thurmond affirmed that he had never in his whole career voted to increase the debt limit. "But I've never had Ronald Reagan as president before ... and I'm going to vote for the debt-limit increase ... and so are you."[51] The incident captured the mood of the times; if the economy recovered, then no one would remember the deficits.

That is exactly what happened. Economic conditions improved markedly after the midterm elections. The Dow surged from its 1982 low of 776 to a high of 2,722 in August of 1987, a gain of more than 250 percent. Federal programs affecting the general welfare were cut in the expectation that people would be working instead of applying for governmental assistance. The howl from what David Stockman called the "social pork barrel" was shrill and unending. When Reagan was elected, programs for the poor made up about 10 percent of the federal budget. To shrink welfare spending, Congress passed Reagan's Reconciliation Act of 1981, which reduced the budgets of 212 federal programs. The cuts included 11 percent in food stamps, 28 percent in child nutrition programs, 13 percent in Aid to Families with Dependent Children (AFDC), 25 percent in student financial aid, and 28 percent in fuel assistance for the poor.[52]

A group called the Committee for Creative Nonviolence set up an outdoor soup kitchen across from the White House, and named the place "Reaganville," in memory of the "Hoovervilles" of the Great Depression.[53] The administration was accused of being insensitive to the less fortunate, and turning a deaf ear to those in economic need. As inflation plummeted, unemployment rose, from 7 to nearly 11 percent. Homeless men and women, many of them alcoholics and drug addicts unable to take care of themselves, began appearing on the streets of major American cities.

Critics pointed to them as evidence of Republican selfishness. Actually, homelessness in the 1980s had its origins in 1972, when the U.S. Supreme Court handed down its decision in *Papachristou v. City of Jacksonville*. The decision overturned the convictions of several persons on vagrancy in Jacksonville, Florida. Justice William O. Douglas, writing for the majority, rationalized that "persons 'wandering or strolling' from place to place have been extolled by Walt Whitman and Vachel Lindsay."[54] The new vagabond poets of America congregated on park benches and public buildings, asked for handouts at rest stops beside interstate highways, and pushed their belongings in shopping carts on the sidewalks of major cities. The government could not detain or remove them.

Another court case, also from the 1970s, aggravated the situation. In 1975, the Supreme Court ruled in the case of *O'Connor v. Donaldson* that the mentally ill could not be confined unless they could be shown to constitute a danger to others or were incapable of living on their own. The decision accelerated the emptying of state mental hospitals and sanitariums.[55] The mentally ill found shelter in deteriorating old buildings converted to slum hotels. They paid rent with the help of federal programs that recognized schizophrenia and other severe mental illnesses as disabilities and paid pensions to those suffering from them.

The court cases, and their surprising redefinition of rights, meant that local governments found it impossible to remove vagrants from parks, sidewalks, bus terminals, libraries, and public amenities. The bad publicity that followed efforts to evict people from public facilities meant that mayors and local politicians allowed the problem to get worse, despite complaints from commuters and residents. New York Mayor Ed Koch asked city and community boards to suggest buildings that could be used to shelter the homeless in an approaching winter.[56]

When Ronald Reagan came into office he cut the Housing and Urban Development (HUD) budget in fiscal 1981 from $34.2 billion to $16.6 billion. This was a cut in authorization, not outlays. Such an authorization was a spending limit, much like a Visa or Mastercard account sets a personal credit limit, but revealed nothing about the amount of money spent. The actual amount of HUD outlays went up in the Reagan years, but this fact was drowned in the tide of political fallout that came from the initial budget authorization cuts. The visible homeless on city streets were taken as the symbol of Reaganomics in action for administration critics. Former antiwar activist Mark Snyder declared in 1982 that some 2.2 million were homeless and that "the number of homeless people in the United States could reach 3 million or more during 1983."[57] A report to the HUD Secretary on the Homeless and Emergency Shelters (1984) concluded that the number of homeless was much less, and probably ranged from 250,000 to 350,000 nationally. The emergency shelters, far from bursting at the seams, were only about two-thirds full.

The truth was less interesting than the urban legend. CBS television aired a documentary entitled *People Like Us* during this time. The show added a personal side to the recession by showing the effects of the economic policy on everyday Americans. Bill Moyers, the narrator, described an Ohio man with cerebral palsy who had been dropped from the welfare rolls. The argument was that there was no one to protect him and thousands of others. Americans have always looked for scapegoats in adversity, and the president was the obvious target. On July 20, 1982, CBS correspondent Dan Rather reported that the drop in housing starts showed that the economy was at the bottom and staying there, but "the Reagan administration was said to dislike such gloom."[58]

Deregulation, another of the legacies of Reaganomics, came in for as much criticism as budget cutting and deficits. Reagan promised to "curb the size and influence of the federal establishment" in his inaugural address.[59] Upon assuming office he announced his intention to cut 37,000 federal jobs, and the PATCO strike took care of some 13,000 in one fell swoop. He instituted a freeze on new regulatory programs and staffed existing ones with members whose background and points of view frequently reflected the interests of the industries they were supposed to regulate.

No issue of deregulation was more controversial than that of the Environmental Protection Agency (EPA). Though founded in the years of the Nixon administration, the agency had become a haven for environmentalists and others opposed to business and real estate expansion. When Reagan appointed Anne Burford to head the EPA, critics accused her of failing to clean up toxic waste and coddling business interests. She cut the EPA funding and transferred enforcement responsibility to the states. Amid the controversy, Burford resigned after only twenty-two months on the job.

The criticism then shifted to James Watt, the secretary of the Interior, who was part of the so-called Sagebrush Rebellion among western business leaders who wanted to reverse the tradition of strong federal protection of the nation's public lands and native resources. Among Watt's more controversial proposals was one to sell 35 million acres in the public domain. Environmentally conscious individuals and groups like the Sierra Club fought Watt's efforts, and Watt did not help himself by comparing his opponents to Nazis and communists and making statements like: "We will mine more, drill more and cut more timber."[60]

In 1983, the final year in which the Reagan tax cuts went into effect, the U.S. economy went on a biblical march, with "seven fat years" of uninterrupted growth. It was the biggest peacetime economic boom in U.S. history. The gross domestic product expanded by a third in real terms, and the median family income grew by 15 percent in constant dollars.[61] The recovery took Reagan's critics in the media, and experts on campus, by surprise. Television coverage continued to focus on the fears, not the accomplishments, of the economy. Along the Great Lakes and throughout the Midwest, the strengths of steel, chemical, and automobile industries began to erode as new growth shifted to the flourishing Sun Belt. CBS reporter Dan Rather reported a story entitled "The American Farmer: Plowed Under" that detailed an economic crisis for American farmers caused by high interest rates, low crop prices, and weather.[62] An NBC story earlier in 1984 compared small business failures with the years of the Great Depression, and warned of returning inflation. But the media could not alter the realities. Reagan quipped that "the best sign that our economic program is working is that they don't call it 'Reaganomics' anymore."

It is impossible to understand Ronald Reagan, or his presidency, without an appreciation of his aversion to communism. It was a struggle that consumed him and touched the very center of his personal and political life. From the time he was president of the Screen Actors Guild through his rise with General Electric to elected office, he was a devoted anticommunist. As a consequence, his foreign policy, just like his economic policy, was in defiance of the way Washington treated the Soviet bloc.[63]

The conventional wisdom was that communism would collapse because of the erroneous economic presumptions at its core, and that a meltdown was inevitable. The assumption that people worked under compulsion for others in defiance of their own self-interest was bound to fail. The bipartisan foreign policy of containment, initiated in the Truman administration, declared that the United States would support peoples resisting subjugation by the USSR, but not intervene or directly confront the Soviets. The policy could be described as one of wait and watch; it allowed communism to collapse from its own weight.

In the meantime, the United States discouraged Soviet aggression by building up a large stockpile of nuclear weapons. The idea behind the policy was that present fears were less than horrible imaginings. If the Soviet Union knew a confrontation would end hopelessly with bombs and rockets hitting Moscow, then the chances for peace would be greater, or so the theory went. John Foster Dulles, the Secretary of State under Dwight Eisenhower, called the policy "massive retaliation." Later it would become "mutually assured destruction," with the more fitting acronym MAD.

Ronald Reagan had lived through World War II and the Cold War. He was opposed to this policy, which had been pursued by both Democratic and Republican presidents with the Soviets. American presidents dating back to 1969 were of the belief that if the United States waited and played its cards right, it could have security on the cheap without war or confrontation. This was called détente. Reagan believed the USSR was in the last throes of life, and he despised the policy. "It was a conviction that Reagan himself deeply believed was born not out of reality, but of political pathology at home: defeatism, pessimism and appeasement."[64]

The Reagan policy was in defiance of accepted conventions; he wanted to challenge the communist ideology at its base and force the Soviets to roll back their expansionist plans. In one of the most significant speeches of his presidency, delivered to the National Association of Evangelicals on March 8, 1983, Reagan described the Cold War as a "struggle between right and wrong, good and evil." He asked the audience to pray for those who lived in totalitarian darkness, and then he concluded about the governments that "they are the focus of evil in the modern world."[65] The "evil empire" phrase was a subject of scorn at the State Department and on college campuses, but Reagan kept using it in his speeches and it kept working on his audiences.

The president enjoyed reading intelligence reports about life in the Soviet bloc after he was elected. The briefing books were more detailed and based on better information than the newspaper clippings, special reports, and verbal accounts he relied on in his pre-presidential days. He loved the intelligence the CIA had given him at his home in Pacific Palisades after he was elected. In his first year in office, Reagan chaired fifty-one meetings of the National Security Council, more than one a week. "He particularly enjoyed information about the economic troubles they [the Soviets] were experiencing," recalled David Wigg, the CIA liaison to the White House.[66] The president's plan was to expand the American economy, then increase American military spending and squeeze the Kremlin. He believed Moscow could not grow its military budgets because its consumer economy was already on a starvation diet. The Russians could afford neither guns nor butter. Reagan reasoned that if the United States went forward with an arms race buildup, then the communist system would collapse. In short, the defense buildup was as much about economic warfare against the Soviets as it was about restoring American military power.

The "evil empire" speech captured Reagan's views, and he used it in numerous speeches and conversations. Since he saw the conflict between East and West as fundamentally moral, he regarded his first duty as president to be the affirmation of values in the American political system. As president, he believed one system was basically good, and the other one was fundamentally evil. He repeatedly said the West did not have to fear communism, and Ronald Reagan did not fear it either.

Others did, and they attacked the administration without pause. Anthony Lewis of the *New York Times* had a hard time finding words to describe the policy: "sectarian," "terribly dangerous," "outrageous," and "primitive."[67] Historian Arthur Schlesinger returned from a trip to Moscow in 1982 and found "more goods in the shops and more food in the markets" than on any previous trip. He dismissed the Reagan policy of confrontation as misguided.[68] Lawrence I. Barrett, in his book *Gambling with History: Ronald Reagan in the White House*, argued that the president made a mistake in management, and "relied too heavily, too long on his subordinates... [who] were the general [managers] of national security affairs."[69] Massachusetts Institute of Technology economist Lester Thurow praised the Soviet economic achievements and declared it a mistake to think that the people of Eastern Europe were miserable.

The establishment thinking of the time was in agreement with the sentiments of Messrs. Lewis, Schlesinger, Barrett, and Thurow. The belief was that the United States and the Soviet Union were both superpowers based on different systems; neither one nor the other was inherently superior. In this view, the United States should avoid saying or doing anything that Moscow might view as "provocative" or "destabilizing." Above all, it was foolish to try to roll back Soviet advances; instead, the West should try to moderate the designs of communism.

Almost alone, Ronald Reagan had an alternate view of the alleged power and virtue of the Soviet system. He knew that any state-planned economy that dictated individual decisions and regulated consumption was bound to fail. For him the Soviet Union was a "sick bear," and the question was not if it would perish, but when. As he said to the graduates of his alma mater, Eureka College, at their commencement in May 1982, "The Soviet Empire is faltering because rigid centralized control has destroyed incentives for innovation, efficiency and individual achievement."[70] What was out of the ordinary is that Reagan saw communism not just as incompetent, but as evil. The blight of the idea and its effect on human beings was the focus of the president's ire.

In 1983, the Soviets presented the world with an example of their wickedness and confirmed Reagan's policy at the same time. Korean Airlines Flight 007 was one of the more than 125 international flights that left New York's JFK Airport on August 31, 1983. The Boeing 747 jumbo airliner lifted off carrying 244 passengers, including Congressman Lawrence McDonald, known as a virulent anticommunist and scheduled to attend the thirtieth anniversary celebrating the end of the Korean War. After refueling in Anchorage, Alaska, the flight headed to Southeast Asia.

Radar operators with the Soviet Air Defense force picked up KAL 007 over Sakhalin Island and identified it as a hostile invasion of domestic airspace. They instituted a state of emergency that included scrambling jet interceptors, with instructions to make visual contact with the intruder aircraft. A few moments later, the pilot of the Sukhoi-15 (SU-15) fighter informed ground control that he could see the airliner and fired warning bursts from his cannons to slow the plane down. Time was crucial for what happened in the next few minutes. The SU-15 pilot was low on fuel and the Soviet air defense commander had only minutes to decide what to do about an intruder aircraft that would soon be in international airspace. Standing border-integrity regulations were to order interlopers to land—and shoot them down if they failed to comply.

On orders from his base, the SU-15 pilot dropped back eight kilometers and fired two missiles when the plane was ninety seconds from international airspace. In the bureaucratic language familiar to anyone in the military, the pilot radioed back to his base: "The target is destroyed." A heat-seeking missile struck one of the 747's four engines and Flight 007 remained aloft another twelve minutes before crashing into the sea, killing all aboard.[71]

President Reagan insisted from the beginning that the Soviets knew they were firing at a civilian airliner, and he called it a "barbaric act." After days of sullen silence the Russians charged that the airliner had been conducting a "spy mission" over Sakhalin Island. In the U.N. Security Council, the U.S. representative said the Soviets were "lying—openly, brazenly and knowingly. It is the face of a ruthless, totalitarian state." The tragedy presented the Reagan administration with a dilemma. In the previous months they had worked to relax tensions, signing a new multiyear grain agreement with Moscow, agreeing to the sale of pipeline equipment to the Soviets, and preparing for new arms limitation talks.

In the end, the United States chose moderation, and the rhetoric was the strongest response in the crisis. The administration orchestrated mild economic sanctions and Reagan called for a national day of mourning in a televised address. Most Americans polled at the time thought the president's response was not tough enough, but there was now international exposure and condemnation of the Soviets as a by-product of the crisis.

The Reagan strategy from the outset was to confront the Soviet Union and its minions on a number of fronts. The plan was multifaceted: a military buildup, the deployment of Pershing and cruise missiles, the Strategic Defense Initiative, the familiar doctrine of assistance to anticommunist guerillas, and a global crusade to promote democracy and capitalism. These policies capitalized on a rare consensus in American peacetime politics which favored substantial increases in military spending in 1981.

In its first two years in office, the Reagan administration faced a serious challenge regarding the deployment of nuclear weapons in Europe. The Western allies had agreed to station 108 Pershing II missiles and 464 Tomahawk cruise missiles to counter a Soviet buildup. The peace movement in the United States, France, and Germany arose to excoriate the United States for deploying the weapons and escalating the arms race. Jonathan Schell's bestselling book *The Fate of the Earth* (1982) declared: "We hold this entire terrestrial creation hostage to nuclear destruction, threatening to hurl it back into the inanimate darkness.... The machinery of destruction is complete, poised on a hair trigger."[72]

The statistics on nuclear war were frightening. The U.S. stockpile reached its peak in 1967 with more than 32,000 warheads of thirty different types; the Soviet stockpile reached its peak of about 33,000 warheads in 1988. The human mind could barely comprehend their effects. The nuclear weapon detonated in Hiroshima was the equivalent of 12,000 tons of TNT, and the combined effect of the blast killed 300,000 people. Most of the bombs in the two superpower arsenals would have about ten times the force of the Hiroshima blast. The effects of a full-scale nuclear exchange were incalculable. A thermonuclear explosion produces blast, light, heat, and varying amounts of fallout. The concussive force of the blast itself takes the form of a shock wave that radiates from the point of the explosion at supersonic speeds and can destroy any building within several miles.

The intense white light of the explosion causes permanent blindness to people gazing at it from a distance of several miles, and the heat sets combustible material afire, creating huge fires that might coalesce into a firestorm. Then the fallout contaminates air, water, and soil for years after the explosion. All these effects are from just one nuclear weapon. Life after a nuclear exchange would be, in the words of Jonathan Schell, "a republic of insects and grass."

The antinuclear demonstrations were directed squarely at Ronald Reagan, in the hope that by applying pressure in the streets, he would make concessions at the bargaining table. The effect was to get average Americans, who were genuinely concerned about the prospect of a nuclear exchange, to agree to the concept of a nuclear freeze. Reagan opposed such a policy because it would codify what he saw as the existing imbalance of power between the United States and USSR. Yet in numerous city councils, state legislatures, and even the U.S. House of Representatives, the idea of a freeze was endorsed. Even the president's daughter, Patti Davis, favored the idea, and went so far as to have supporters of it meet with her father.

Reagan remained obdurate. He agreed to cut the U.S. program if the Russians would make corresponding reductions, but they refused. In the give and take at the bargaining table, Paul Nitze, the top negotiator for the United States, asked Reagan what he should say to the Soviets after the administration rejected a proposal. "Well, Paul," said the president in his best Hollywood humility, "you just tell them you're working for one tough son of a bitch."[73]

He was. When the date for the scheduled Pershing and cruise missile deployment arrived in October of 1983, more than 2 million people took to the streets of Europe in protest. Reagan did not budge an inch. ABC television aired a docudrama entitled *The Day After*, about a mythical nuclear attack on the United States. The ABC executives chose to broadcast the show in prime time nationwide, three days before deployment of the first Pershing missiles. The movie plot followed a group of characters in Kansas and Missouri and the effect nuclear weapons had on their lives. The most chilling scene was when America's Minuteman missiles were launched, their rocket-fuel trails providing the only indication to a horrified civilian population that nuclear war was underway.

In a final gambit to win in the court of public opinion, the Soviet Union threatened to withdraw from all arms negotiations if the missiles were made operational. The peace movement ratcheted up the demonstrations, declaring that the opening scenes of the movie *The Day After*, when East and West break off negotiations, was coming true. The president directed U.S. negotiators to make no new concessions and allow the Soviets to leave if they wanted to. Reagan knew that the Soviets needed the Americans as a foil to stay in power, and any withdrawal by them would only be temporary. The president, along with British Prime Minister Margaret Thatcher and West German Chancellor Helmut Kohl, led the West in seeing to it that the missiles were operational.

The struggle over missiles in Europe sent relations between the two superpowers to unplumbed depths. The constant confrontations with the USSR and the resulting tension led Reagan to embrace an alternative to the MAD philosophy that had guided American policy throughout the Cold War. When he was governor of California, Reagan visited the facilities of Lawrence Livermore Laboratory, where Dr. Edward Teller, the father of the hydrogen bomb, showed him the work his students were doing on space-based lasers. Teller told the then-governor that the lasers could be used to destroy nuclear missiles fired at the United States. Not surprisingly, when the Joint Chiefs of Staff met privately with Reagan on a snowy day in December of 1982 to discuss an alternative to MAD, they found him receptive. National Security Advisor Robert C. McFarlane recalled that the president sat quietly and listened to the military proposals. "It was clear from his demeanor that he was convinced it could be done."[74]

Reagan had long been concerned that the United States had no defense against Soviet missiles. "We have spent all that money," he said to presidential advisor Martin Anderson after a briefing, "and have all that equipment and there is nothing we can do to prevent a nuclear missile from hitting us."[75] The president had confidence in American ingenuity dating back to his days as a spokesman for General Electric. Even though he had no fixed idea about what the system would look like, Reagan decided to announce the beginning of research and development of the program.

In March of 1983, the president gave a major foreign policy address calling for a system to defend the nation against nuclear attack. He asked, "Wouldn't it be better to save lives than avenge them?"[76] The president knew that ordinary Americans wanted some protection from nuclear extinction. The idea was to set up a large number of space satellites that would detect the launch of an enemy missile and then shoot it down. The satellites would form a protective shield over the country. Behind the policy was Reagan's belief that it was immoral for a nation to ignore an antimissile defense and leave its citizens helpless against a Soviet nuclear attack. The system had huge technical complexities, but it was far better than what was in its place—which was nothing.

The Strategic Defense Initiative, known as SDI, was consistently opposed by many, including numerous Democrats in Congress. They labeled it "Star Wars," and criticized the high cost, the supposedly insurmountable technological challenges, and the fact that the United States would have to withdraw from the 1972 Anti-ballistic missile (ABM) treaty to deploy the system. Haynes Johnson wrote that the whole idea just propped up defense firms in California's Silicon Valley that did highly classified work for the federal government.[77] The critics declared that SDI would actually lead to nuclear proliferation since the Soviets would have to send up more missiles in the hope that some would penetrate the shield. What was more, the antimissile system was almost impossible to test or employ in space.

These antagonisms did not worry Ronald Reagan, who knew that some shield, no matter how porous, was better than none. He dismissed the faultfinders with his usual humor. "Star Wars" was one of his favorite movies, and in the end good triumphed over evil, and that was all that mattered to him. SDI supporters also promoted the moral and legal superiority of defense over the obsolete notion of nuclear superiority associated with the MAD doctrine. Destroying an enemy attack before it killed millions was better than allowing the attack to happen and then retaliating against an opposing country.

Shrill domestic criticism was muted by Moscow's reaction, which was a mixture of shock and anger. SDI posed the most serious threat to the Soviet Union's position as superpower that it had encountered in the Cold War era. The program forced the Soviets to develop a new antimissile system, when they could barely afford their present budget. A month after Reagan's speech, 200 Soviet scientists wrote a letter published in the *New York Times* criticizing the Reagan administration initiative. The letter sent a firestorm of controversy around the country, and comfort in the White House.

Ronald Reagan may not have anticipated the ferocity of the debate, but he remained unflappable in the midst of it. His determination to stand by SDI was legendary in Washington. In retrospect, the program was ingenious from a political point of view. It destroyed the logic of the nuclear freeze movement because Reagan showed himself to be more committed to protecting American citizens than destroying the Soviets. In one sense, SDI was disarmament through technology, rather than signed documents. Soviet leadership treated SDI as a real threat and returned to the bargaining table. The program would become one of the reasons for the collapse of the USSR in 1989.

An opportunity to test the resolve of the new policy of confrontation with communism fell in the administration's lap in October of 1983. Eugenia Charles, prime minister of Dominica and chair of the Organization of Eastern Caribbean States, sent a communiqué to Washington requesting U.S. intervention. The situation in Grenada, a small island in the region, was precarious, and Charles was concerned that the Marxist government of Prime Minister Maurice Bishop was allowing Cuba to gain influence in Grenada, especially in the construction of a military-grade airport with Cuban military engineers.

On October 13, the Grenadian army, under the control of former Deputy Prime Minister Bernard Coard, seized power in a bloody coup. Maurice Bishop was held under house arrest for six days and then murdered. The severity of the violence, along with Coard's hard-line Marxist ideals, moved Washington to action. The conflict involved the United States and its Caribbean allies on one side, and Fidel Castro's Cuba, the Sandinista government in Nicaragua, and various Marxist guerilla armies in the region on the other. Reagan saw Grenada as a timely opportunity to eliminate a communist government and at the same time embarrass Fidel Castro.

A call from the neighboring Caribbean nations expressing alarm was all Reagan needed as an invitation for an invasion. At Camp David the president huddled with his advisors on the phone where he concluded that immediate military action was needed. Although the invasion officially started on October 25, Navy Sea, Air and Land Teams (SEALS) entered Grenada two days earlier. U.S. Marines landed at Pearls Airport and U.S. Army Rangers parachuted into the uncompleted runway at Point Salines. The initial assault consisted of some 1,200 troops, who met stiff resistance from the Grenadian army and Cuban military units on the island. In two days the American force grew to some 5,000 troops, and gradually they subdued the air and ground forces.

The United States was immediately assailed for its invasion decision by Mexico, Nicaragua, Guyana, and a host of former State Department lawyers, who said the action was inconsistent with international law. Fidel Castro contended that the great majority of Cubans on the island were construction workers, technicians, and medical personnel, not soldiers. But Reagan's confrontation strategy was vindicated when the invading force found a cache of weapons that could arm 10,000 men—automatic rifles, machine guns, rocket launchers, antiaircraft guns, and armored vehicles. Of the approximately 800 Cubans on Grenada, fifty-nine were killed and twenty-five wounded, and all were returned to Havana after the victory. The Defense Department concluded that the great majority of Cubans in Grenada were military and formed two combat battalions while posing as construction workers. Forty-five Grenadians died, with 337 wounded. The United States suffered nineteen killed and 119 wounded. Some 1,000 medical students at the St. George School of Medicine were rescued and repatriated to the states.[78]

Criticism did not die down about the Grenada operation after it was complete. For some, the invasion was nothing more than a mask for the disappointment of a terrorist bombing in Lebanon. For others, the Grenada invasion was proof positive that the United States was willing to confront communism and take the heat for the decision. Grenada was the nation's first military victory since Vietnam, and it sent a message across the Caribbean and Nicaragua that any expansionist plans on the part of communist nations would be met with an American military response.

The Reagan policy of confrontation with communism was having success, but in the Middle East the administration's foreign policy was just as confused and frustrated as at any time in the Carter administration. The focus was on Lebanon, a country the size of Connecticut, beset with virtually every unresolved dispute afflicting the people of the region. American intervention in Lebanon was influenced in part by historical precedent; in 1958 President Eisenhower landed Marines in Beirut. The presence of some 14,000 troops at that time allowed U.S. policy makers to calm a civil disturbance, select the next president of Lebanon, and extract the force in three months without significant incident or casualties.

The Lebanon of 1982 was, however, significantly different from that of 1958. Nearly 100,000 persons in the nation of 3 million people had died in hostilities that began with a violent civil war in 1975. Another problem was that the administration itself was divided over what to do, and friction between Secretary of State George P. Shultz, Secretary of Defense Caspar Weinberger, and National Security Advisor Robert C. McFarlane exacerbated the problem. Fourteen years earlier, George Shultz had come to Washington to assume a cabinet post in the Nixon administration. When the Office of Management and Budget was created in 1970, Shultz was named to head it and Weinberger was picked as his top deputy. The two men clashed from the very beginning, when Weinberger resented Shultz's imperial manner. After leaving the Nixon administration, Shultz became president of the giant Bechtel Corporation, with Caspar Weinberger as its general counsel. When Reagan was elected, Weinberger lobbied to become secretary of state, but the job went to George Shultz instead. Weinberger had to settle for the Department of Defense, which was a post much closer to Reagan's heart and one from which the secretary could influence foreign policy.[79]

The seeds of American involvement in Lebanon were sown in April of 1981, when the Syrians bombarded a town in the Bekaa Valley. Lebanon was a country beset by factions: sympathizers with the Palestinians, the Israelis, the Syrians, Lebanese Christians, Muslims, and other partisans. At one time the administration counted twenty-six different groups contending for power in the besieged nation. Their zealous pursuit of conflicting goals destabilized the political situation. Washington and Moscow both had their surrogates in the region, and one crude indicator for identifying the loyalties of local fighters was to note whether they carried AK-47 or M-16 rifles.

In July of 1982, Secretary Shultz proposed sending the U.S. Marines into Lebanon as part of a multinational force to bring stability to the troubled region. Philip C. Habib, the president's special envoy in the Middle East, recommended the action in conjunction with a cease-fire to allow the departure of Yasir Arafat and his PLO (Palestine Liberation Organization) fighters from the country. Defense Secretary Weinberger, along with the Joint Chiefs of Staff, opposed the deployment. "It would be very unwise, wrote General John W. Vessey as chairman, "for the U.S. to find itself in a position where it had to put its forces between the Israelis and the Arabs."[80] Their anxiety was heightened when the diplomatic agreement stated that "the United States will provide appropriate guarantees of safety...[but] the American force will not engage in combat."

Reagan was impressed with the argument that the U.S. commitment would end the fighting among the factions, so he overruled the Joint Chiefs and ordered in the troops. On August 25, the Marines went ashore in Beirut, four days after the French troops arrived. The decision was in keeping with what was done in 1958, but this time the stakes were much higher, and the outcome less sure. The PLO evacuation was completed without significant incident, and the Marines redeployed to their ships on September 10.

They should have stayed at sea. To all intents and purposes, the multinational force had been a success, but events in the Middle East do not embrace peaceful accomplishments for long. The assassination of President-elect Bashir Gemayel on September 14, along with the murder of an estimated 700–800 Palestinian civilians in the Sabra and Shatila refugee camps in Beirut as the Israeli army watched, forced a second military deployment. Some in the administration were convinced that Weinberger's premature withdrawal of the Marines created the conditions for the assassination and massacre. The secretary of defense responded that his first allegiance was to the troops. On September 20, Ronald Reagan, still horrified about the civilian slaughter, announced the formation of a new multinational force with France and Italy to restabilize the region. Once again Defense Secretary Weinberger advised against American involvement in the tribal warfare of the region, and the Joint Chiefs advised that unless the United States had clear rules of engagement and a clear advantage in force, their presence was pointless. Once again they were overruled by Reagan and Shultz, along with National Security Advisor Robert McFarlane.

The bloodiest event of Ronald Reagan's first term was born of good intentions. The new mission of the Marines was to be an "interposition force" in one of the most dangerous and faction-ridden places on earth. The hope was that a strong government would return to Lebanon, bolstered by a well-equipped military, and all foreign forces would leave. Unfortunately this hope was just another name for fear. Violence returned on April 18, 1983, when a delivery van filled with explosives detonated on the grounds of the U.S. Embassy on Beirut's waterfront, killing sixty-three people, including seventeen Americans.

The administration's public demeanor remained firm: the U.S. troops would remain to fulfill their mission. Some encouragement came the next month when Lebanon and Israel signed an agreement ending the state of war between the two countries and providing for a phased Israeli withdrawal. The catch was that Israel would leave only when Syria and Palestinian forces did, and no one had bothered to obtain Syrian assent. The stalemate continued, and the multinational force soldiered on into a hot Beirut summer.

By late August the Marines were caught up in firefights with armed elements in the predominantly Shia suburbs of South Beirut. U.S. ships of the Sixth Fleet responded with naval gunfire, and the fighting between U.S. Marines, Lebanese armed forces, and militia groups intensified. Although congressional support remained, skepticism was increasing. In testimony before the Committee on Foreign Affairs, Secretary of State George Shultz said the Marines "are an important deterrent, a symbol of the international backing behind the legitimate Governor of Lebanon, and an important weight in the scales." So the Marines were a "deterrent," a "symbol," and a "weight"—but they were also a target.

The critical point was reached in the fall, when Muslim forces launched an attack on the Lebanese government's army. U.S. Navy ships off the coast went into action again with artillery and air assaults on Muslim strongholds. Reagan would later say that he was under the impression that the Navy attack was to defend the land-based Marines. To the Lebanese Muslims the shelling of their villages was proof that the United States was now intervening against them. Because of the role the United States had in training the Lebanese Army and U.S. naval bombardment, groups like the Druze, the Amal, the Palestinians, and their Syrian supporters saw the American Marines as props for the minority Lebanese government. Hezbollah and other pro-Iranian factions in Lebanon were now dedicated to revenge and the destruction of Americans.

Their retaliation came at 6:22 A.M. on October 23, 1983, and it was devastating. A young man drove a yellow Mercedes truck into the four-story concrete headquarters building where 350 members of the 1st Battalion, 8th Marine Regiment were sleeping. During the next six and one-half hours, 234 Marine bodies would be recovered, and seven more would die in the next days, bringing the total to 241.[81] At the same time a similar explosion blew up a French military barracks a few kilometers away, killing fifty-six French troops.

Years later, Reagan would remember the time as the "saddest day of my presidency, perhaps the saddest day of my life."[82] It was the worst tragedy to befall the military since Vietnam. The president addressed a grieving nation to affirm the policy, saying, "If we are driven out of Lebanon, radical rejectionist elements will have scored a major victory." Though defensive, there was nothing to do but declare publicly that the Marines would remain in Beirut.

Two days after the bombing in Beirut, the U.S. military invaded Grenada. While the two events were unrelated, the success in the Caribbean helped mute the failures in the Middle East. In the months that followed, the Muslim terrorists continued their war by abducting Americans and holding them hostage in Lebanon. The debate over how to respond triggered renewed conflict between Weinberger and Shultz. The secretary of state favored military strikes against suspected terrorists, while Weinberger and the Joint Chiefs said no military action should be undertaken without the support of Congress and the American people. The disputes were not confined to terrorism; they quarreled over arms control, the relations with the Soviet Union, and the European Union.

In January of 1984, with polls showing a majority of the populace wanting to withdraw the Marines, new hearings were held in Congress. The administration continued to insist that it would not be forced to withdraw from Lebanon, but the tide at home was clearly going out. Things were no better in Beirut. After the success of Grenada, Reagan chose to retaliate in Lebanon. Twenty-three aircraft from the carriers *Independence* and *Kennedy* attacked the Sheik Abdullah Barracks in Baalbek, but two aircraft went down and one pilot was killed while another was captured. In February, the Lebanese army attempted to move into West and South Beirut against diverse Muslim militia forces supported by Syria. U.S. naval gunfire supported them, but the fighting showed that the Lebanese army, upon which the administration had lavished much praise, equipment, and training, was inadequate to the task. On February 7, President Reagan announced that he had ordered the Marines to "redeploy" to ships offshore.

Across the Potomac River in Arlington National Cemetery, a Cedar of Lebanon tree was planted over a small memorial. The cedar marks the graves of more than 300 American military, embassy, and civilian personnel who were killed in Beirut in the 1980s. The following October 23, the date of the Marine Corps bombing, a remembrance service was held. The tree and the service were just the first of many to commemorate the miscalculations the United States would make in the Middle East.

── 4 ──

A Rising Tide

The Reagan Revolution, as the times came to be called, followed the economic growth in real income from 1983 through the end of the president's second term in 1988, to the recession that concluded the Bush presidency in 1992. During this time the gross domestic product (GDP) doubled.[1] In the expansion through the two Reagan terms, "real-after-tax income per person rose by 15.5 percent, [and] the real median income of families, before taxes, went up 12.5 percent."[2] Measured in constant 1990 dollars, the percentage of families earning between $15,000 and $50,000 fell by 5 points, and the percentage earning more than $50,000 in constant dollars rose by 5 points. Millions of families moved up the ladder from the lower class to the middle class. America had gone from "stagflation" and the highest prices in thirty years to galloping capitalism, and everyday citizens were investing in the stock market.

The middle-class market sought the deposits of ordinary savers and young people just beginning to accumulate assets. Wall Street had previously ignored these customers, but now it sought them out. Prudential-Bache, an aggressive firm, was quoted in *Barron's* as saying it "sees its clients as the $40,000-a-year young professional on the fast track."[3] As the market expanded, more individuals placed their money in funds to balance risk and profit. Suddenly the stock market report was of interest to everyone.

Stockbrokers assured investors that their money was safe, but in late 1987 they discovered the real meaning of risk. The market was doing quite well for the first nine months of the year; it was up more than 30 percent and reaching unprecedented heights. Then, in the days between October 14 and October 19, the market fell off a cliff. On October 19, subsequently known as "Black Monday," the Dow Jones Industrial Average plummeted 508 points, losing 22.6 percent of its total value. This was the greatest loss Wall Street had ever suffered on a single day, even worse than the crash of 1929. It took two years for the Dow

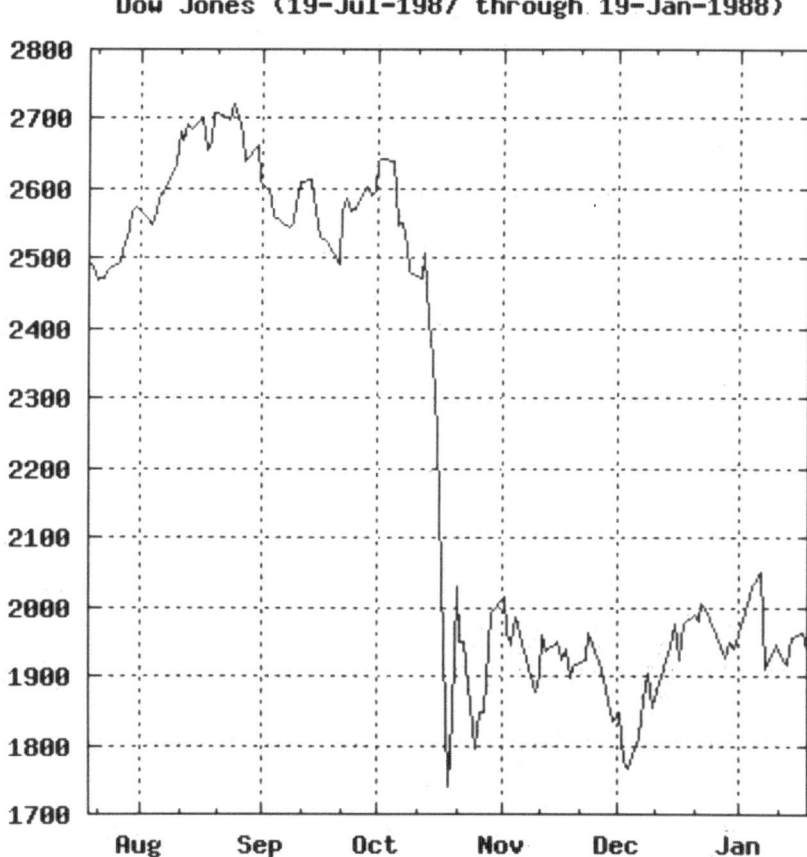

Black Monday: The Stock Market Crash of 1987. (Courtesy, Edward Betts)

to recover completely; not until September of 1989 did it regain all the value it lost in the 1987 crash.

One important lesson came out of the crash: investors who sold took a bath. Those who held on and continued a disciplined and systematic program received rewards. The American economy continued as the greatest wealth producer the world had ever seen. The consequence of all this was a standard of living beyond the comprehension of the rest of the world, and a cause for envy by peer nations. While $200,000 was enough to make the top 1 percent of American income in 1980, a family might need well over $300,000 to be in that category a decade later. The Congressional Budget Office estimated that it would take more than $550,000 to be in the top 1 percent in 1992. No sooner had a survivor of the 1970s comprehended what was happening than he became obsolete.[4] Reagan's supply-side ideas unleashed a wave of entrepreneurial and technological innovation that transformed the economy and restored the country's self-confidence. Economic prosperity had been the impossible dream of youth, and now it was everywhere.

The vast majority of the population experienced substantial gains in real income and wealth. With millions of people earning more money, much higher incomes were required to make it to the top 5 percent, or the top 1 percent of the nation's income bracket. At the time, the rising tide of economic prosperity lifted at least 90 percent of the American family boats. For those who lived through it, the 1983–1992 period would be remembered as an uncomplicated golden time, mourned as lost, and remembered as cloudless.

The spending began at home, where people purchased new homes and remodeled older ones. Declining interest rates made mortgages affordable, and the number of single-family homes expanded each year from 1980 to 1988. Consumers also had more cars to drive as the two-income, two-car family became the norm. From 1980 to 1988, the number of new car models increased by half, the most popular being the minivans for suburban families. Lower air fares and discount packages allowed passengers to travel to previously unheard-of places, and the number of people flying overseas rose by 40 percent during the 1980s.

Much of this expense for the new lifestyle was charged to credit cards. Americans took three-, four-, and five-day trips and the amount of credit card debt more than doubled. Specialty chain stores like the Gap, Limited, and Banana Republic targeted upscale, professional customers who wanted to take advantage of their new standing and credit to add the latest styles to their wardrobes. Shopping malls proliferated in suburban settings, and the consumption ethic gave birth to Wal-Mart, destined in the next decade to become the nation's largest company. While American life was becoming more affluent, it was also becoming more complex.

Of course there were critics, and for them the era was never that splendid; it was derided for its inbred conformity, flatulent excesses, and materialistic binges. The "me" decade of the 1970s turned into the "my" decade of the 1980s. The faultfinders saw the surge of abundance as a joyless vulgarity. In 1987, filmmaker Oliver Stone released the movie *Wall Street*. The story involved a young stockbroker, Bud Fox, who becomes involved with his hero, Gordon Gekko, an extremely successful, but corrupt, stock trader. In the most memorable scene of the movie, Gekko makes a speech to the shareholders of a company he was planning to take over. Stone used the scene to give Gekko, and by extension corporate America at the time, the characteristic trait of economic success.[5]

Gekko: Teldar Paper, Mr. Cromwell, Teldar Paper has 33 different vice presidents, each making over 200 thousand dollars a year. Now, I have spent the last two months analyzing what all these guys do, and I still can't figure it out. One thing I do know is that our paper company lost 110 million dollars last year, and I'll bet that half of that was spent in all the paperwork going back and forth between all these vice presidents.

The new law of evolution in corporate America seems to be survival of the unfittest. Well, in my book you either do it right or you get eliminated.

In the last seven deals that I've been involved with, there were 2.5 million stockholders who had made a pretax profit of 12 billion dollars. Thank you.

I am not a destroyer of companies. I am a liberator of them!

The point is, ladies and gentlemen, is that greed—for lack of a better word—is good.

Greed is right.

Greed works.

Greed clarifies, cuts through, and captures the essence of the evolutionary spirit.

Greed in all its forms—greed for life, for money, for love, knowledge—has marked the upward surge of mankind.

And greed—you mark my words—will not only save Teldar Paper, but that other malfunctioning corporation called the USA.

Thank you very much.

The same theme was addressed in literature. In 1990, one of America's foremost writers, Tom Wolfe, released a blockbuster bestseller entitled *The Bonfire of the Vanities*.[6] The book dealt with what Wolfe called the "big, rich slices of contemporary life," in this case the heady materialism of the 1980s. The plot followed the life of Sherman McCoy, a prodigiously successful bond trader at a prestigious Wall Street firm. One night Sherman, accompanied by his mistress, fatally injures a black man in a car accident. As a result of this accident, all the ennui of metropolitan life, race relations, instant affluence and gratification, and the class structure of the city afflict the lead character.

As a member of the new ruling class, Sherman McCoy and other bond traders were allied with opportunistic politicians in speculative excesses. Sherman was supremely confident that he would escape his fate. The 1980s were critiqued as the epitome of American decline and the triumph of finance capitalism spurred by Wall Street bond and stock manipulators, like McCoy's employer, Eugene Lopwitz. Sherman McCoy had to pay for his greed and irresponsibility; he lost his job, his wife and his child, his mistress, his home, and his class standing. But in the end he lied to escape prosecution, and got even with every institution—the courts, the media, and the economic system—which were also built on a foundation of lies.

American capitalism, and its excesses, had long been a topic of intellectual and literary criticism. Theodore Dreiser wrote the novel *An American Tragedy* in 1925 as a critique of business practices at the time. The story followed a bellboy who sets out to gain success and fame, only to slip into murder and death by execution. Dreiser declared that the materialistic society was as much to blame as the murderer himself.[7] What was new in the *Bonfire* plot was that the perpetrators escaped capture and conviction. In the new world people could be evil and—if they had enough money—bear no consequences for their actions.

During the 1980s, the power and influence of American corporations expanded to exorbitant heights. General Motors had revenues greater than 90 percent of the world's nations.[8] The Reagan administration eased restrictions on the stock market and on antitrust laws so some of the more massive corporate takeovers in American history happened in the decade. The largest one was between R. J. Reynolds, the tobacco company, and Nabisco, the maker of cookies, crackers, and cereals, for $24.9 billion.[9]

Other companies were taken over in what was known as a leveraged buyout, where investors joined forces with the managers of a company to buy it. The funds came from the managers themselves, but most were borrowed. The money for takeovers was raised through the sale of so-called junk bonds. Junk bonds were high-risk investments by securities rating agencies, such as Standard and Poor's and Moody's, marked as such because they had a potential for higher yield and failure. If the people who bought the bonds were successful in the takeover, then they were handsomely rewarded; but if they failed, then there was the possibility that the bonds would not be repaid.

Companies with low debt loads were attractive targets for leveraged buyouts, which meant that successful businessmen found themselves the object of "corporate raiders." Benjamin Franklin's age-old virtues of thrift and frugality resulted in business success, so much so that the entrepreneurial founders lost control of their companies. Sometimes, to prevent these unwanted effects, recently acquired companies bought back their stock at higher than market prices—in effect, paying raiders to go away. The practice was known as "greenmail," for its resemblance to blackmail. More than $12 billion in greenmail was paid by corporations such as Texaco, Warner, and Quaker State in the first few months of 1984.[10]

The business of mergers required dozens of brokers, lawyers, and bankers. A new class of business people known as "young, urban professionals," or "yuppies," emerged as experts in the takeover game. They were stereotyped as college-educated men and women, who dressed well, lived in expensive apartments, drove expensive cars, exercised in gyms, and worked twelve-hour days. "An MBA (Masters of Business Administration), a condo and a BMW" became the mantra of the age. One woman interviewed on television unabashedly declared, "I aspire to materialism." "Big spender" became a term of approbation. A writer at the time described it this way: "People saw money as power...[they went to] 'power lunches' while wearing fashionable 'power suits'...designer fashions bloated egos and fattened the cash registers of swank stores."[11] The spenders were living on credit and buying on margin, but they did not seem to mind. Spending and mergers were fueling the boom, and any tendency to go slow was seen as alarming.

Leveraged buyouts were risky, but legal, transactions. As in any business, a few successful corporate raiders operated outside the law. On May 12, 1986, Dennis Levine, who had made $12.6 million on insider-trading deals, implicated two well-known Wall Street traders: Michael Milken and Ivan Boesky. Both men were charged with violations of federal securities law. Boesky agreed to pay $100 million in forfeitures and penalties, and Michael Milken admitted to six felonies and agreed to pay $600 million in fines. The amount of the fines was staggering, but more revealing was the corporate raider lifestyle the investigations uncovered. In the early 1980s Milken was reportedly making $550 million a year.[12]

Overall, the freeing of the market for corporate control had important benefits for women in the workforce. College-educated women moved into fields like business, engineering, medicine, and law. "The result was that women as a whole, whose average earnings had been 58 percent of those of men in 1979, earned 68 percent ten years later."[13] Professional women began moving into managerial positions where they soon faced the problem of how to combine motherhood and career. In the 1980s work itself was changing. The computer and instant communication enabled more people to work at home, and women soon learned that part-time, or maternity leave, arrangements allowed them to close the income gap with their male counterparts.

The boom arose from numerous springs: the new government economic philosophy, technological innovation, an altered world economy, and a changing labor market. The latter trend would have political consequences well into the next century. For example, immigration had a dramatic influence on the labor pool and the expansion of entry-level jobs. In the 1970s, 4.5 million immigrants were legally admitted into the country, and many more came illegally.[14] In the 1980s legal immigration swelled to 7.4 million, with additional millions of illegal entrants. The vast majority of immigrants from Central and South America, who made up about half the total, had considerably lower levels of schooling than native-born Americans. Their presence resulted in higher wages for college graduates and depressed wages for those who had lower levels of schooling.[15]

The immigration trends caused increases in wage and income inequality, because of the demand for skilled labor due to technological changes and new trade patterns. Sophisticated new technologies flourished in the aerospace, defense, electronics, and computer industries. Sprawling scientific complexes raised the standard of living for millions of Americans. Research funds for technology, or R & D (research and development), which were practically insignificant in the 1950s, amounted to an estimated $100 billion a year at the end of the 1980s. Americans were making money with their minds, and not on the assembly line.[16]

Little of this was new. Sociologist Daniel Bell wrote in 1973 that there was a natural progression from a traditional society, based on agriculture, to an industrial one based on manufacturing. Then there was a subsequent transition from an industrial to a postindustrial society, which culminated in a service economy. This progression to a postindustrial society occurred when the emphasis on the production of goods was overtaken by a service economy. The postindustrial society meant an extension of scientific rationality into the economic, social, and political spheres. By the late 1970s only 13 percent of American workers were involved in the manufacture of goods, whereas a full 60 percent were engaged in the production of information.[17] The new "knowledge society" was run by university-trained employers. In this society technical skill was the base of power, and education the means of access to power. Individuals who exercised authority through technical competence, called "technocrats," dominated society.

The birth years of the postindustrial society were in the 1950s, but it came to fruition in the 1980s. The 1950s saw great technological developments such as the atomic bomb and the digital computer, but the character of knowledge itself began to change thirty years later. Workers had to be taught how to think, not how to do routine tasks. Change was so prevalent that knowledge of any specific task was quickly washed away by a new wave of innovation. Theoretical knowledge of abstract principles was central in the postindustrial society, and the key organization of the future was the university, along with think tanks and research centers.

During the 1980s the academy itself was changing. The number of professors at American universities in 1980 was four times what it was in 1960. As faculties grew, so too did the specialization of their disciplines. Student enrollments in fields like business, computer science, engineering, and mathematics soared, while the liberal arts and social sciences lost out in comparison. It was the age of the computer chip, which made everything smaller and faster.

Universities were only the tip of the iceberg of culture producers that included not only the creators of the new society, but also its transmitters. Labor in the postindustrial context involved those in journalism, publishing, magazines, broadcast media, theater, and museums and anyone who was involved in the influence and reception of serious cultural products. The growth of cultural output was a fact in the knowledge industry. Consider what happened to those Daniel Bell called "the cultural mass" of art producers. New York had only a handful of galleries in 1945, and no more than a score of known artists; by the 1980s the city had some 680 galleries and more than 150,000 artists.[18] Add to these artists producers of books, printers, serious music recordings, writers, editors, movie makers, musicians, and so forth and the size of just one part of the mass culture was exposed.

Bell argued that the postindustrial society would change politics, as well as culture and economics. In his view, government would increasingly become instrumental in the management of the economy; less control would be left to market forces. Instead of relying on the invisible hand, Bell saw that the postindustrial society would work toward directing and engineering society.[19] He could not have been more wrong. The spirit of the 1980s was against the command decision views of Daniel Bell. Conservatives had long denounced Keynesian economics as a fraud, and expanding government as a threat, but their ideas were unpopular in the period of post–World War II prosperity. When liberalism's troubles began to mount in the 1970s, free market alternatives re-emerged.

Milton and Rose Friedman effectively rebutted the government as manager thesis, and replaced it with the free market–rational actor model. Their book, *Free to Choose,* was as clear an exposition of free market economics as anything since Adam Smith, and it showed how good intentions in Washington often had deplorable results in practice. Friedman made conservative economic ideas available and attractive to the mass public. To quote their thesis on the power of a free market idea: "If an exchange between two parties is voluntary, it will not take place unless both believe that they will benefit from it," or "the price system is the mechanism that performs this task without central direction, without requiring people to speak to one another or like one another."[20] This was the book that explained how freedom had been eroded, and prosperity undermined, by the runaway spending and growth of government in Washington. *Free to Choose* was very influential on the thinking of Ronald Reagan and millions of ordinary Americans.

As strange as it may seem, by the 1980s the modern postindustrial society was itself becoming old fashioned. The period after World War II was characterized by three things: (1) the power of reason over ignorance, (2) the power of order over disorder, and (3) the power of science over superstition.[21] These features were regarded as universal values, and were inculcated into the fabric of American culture. They were also the basis for Ronald Reagan's view of the world. His time with General Electric convinced him that American technology was second to none, and he wedded that faith to the national experience. After he left office he said, "There are no such things as limits to growth, because there are no limits on the human capacity for intelligence, imagination and wonder."[22]

In the decade of the 1980s, the faith in reason, order, and the power of science, so dear to Reagan, was coming in for criticism. The command and control center for the criticism was the universities, the very postindustrial leaders Daniel Bell had identified years earlier. Much of Reagan's initial political success in his California gubernatorial race was based on criticism of antagonistic college students and their teachers, and his belief that America was a nation of technological might that outproduced and advanced knowledge to win a rightful place on the world stage. For example, Reagan regularly recalled American production in World War II, and his belief that the nation was a "bastion of freedom," and "a city set on a hill."

The problem was that universities were questioning everything Reagan said and stood for. The best known of these criticisms was labeled as deconstruction, a French import that questioned rationality and definitions. Deconstruction held that written words could never have fixed meanings, and, as a result, any text revealed ambiguities, contradictions, hidden meanings, and repressive political relationships. The modern world, according to these new thinkers, had expanded industrial capitalism and scientific thinking, but it also brought the world Auschwitz, the possibility of nuclear war, the horrors of Nazism and Stalinism, neocolonialism, racism, and world hunger. The critics believed that modernism had run its course, and society had entered a new age—the age of postmodernism.

Postmodernism is a complicated term because the concept appears in a wide variety of disciplines and areas of study, including art, architecture, music, film, literature, fashion, and technology. In general, postmodernism rejects the uncritical acceptance of the power of reason, order, and science. According to postmodernists, the assumption that there is such a thing as objective truth is at base a modern fallacy. For them there is no linear progress in society, no ideal social order, and no standardization of knowledge. Instead the world was a picture of fragmentation, indeterminacy, and chaos. Postmodernists held that culture should affirm this fragmented reality, and consider order to be only provisional and varying from person to person.[23]

The contrast between modern and postmodern is seen in a comparison of professions. In several of them, such as medicine, law, and engineering, mastery of a specific body of knowledge and the application of an intrinsic logic led to something known as progress. When a doctor diagnosed and treated a disease, or when an engineer designed a bridge, their work assumed a rational understanding of the world and a logical means of dealing with it. In short, these professions presupposed an objective order in existence. Different medical doctors, using the same objective science and trained in a standard methodology, could examine the same patient and arrive at an identical diagnosis and course of treatment. They exemplify modernism.

A host of new professions arose by the 1980s that had no universally recognized body of knowledge, and no generally accepted methods, although they invoked the jargon of science. The social sciences were shining examples of new postmodern professions. For example, someone in need of "mental health" could be treated by a Freudian, a Jungian, a humanist, or a behaviorist. A political scientist could be a behaviorist, a formal theorist, one trained in classical political thought, or an area specialist with no training other than language skills, and then there were those who believed politics could not be a science. The philosophies behind the psychological analysis and the political analysis, were incompatible, and the methodologies conflicted and were oftentimes incomplete and sometimes untested. They exemplify postmodern professions.[24]

The conflict between modern and postmodern surfaced in Reagan's appointment of William Bennett as chairman of the National Endowment for the Humanities. Bennett had a Ph.D. in philosophy from the University of Texas and a law degree from Harvard. He was a conservative academic who spoke movingly about the threat deconstruction and postmodernism posed to the teaching of the Western classics. "We must give greater attention to a sound common curriculum emphasizing English, history, geography, math, and science ... [and] we have to understand why these subjects were thrown out or weakened in the cultural deconstruction of our schools of the last twenty-five years."[25] The very thing Bennett warned against was taking place at one of America's premier universities. The curriculum of Stanford became an issue in 1988, when the faculty voted to reform the Western Civilization course away from a "European-Western and male bias." The revision became an issue for discussion not only on college campuses, but also in newspapers and television talk shows across the country.

The education debate was part of a national one on the modernist/postmodernist divide. The society had not moved beyond modernity; there were still plenty of people who thought America was the hope of the world and believed in its technological future as well. But there were others who had their doubts, and they delighted in the period of transition. The character of the change was seen in the new pop culture.

The baby boomers, usually defined as those born between 1946 and 1964, left the world a legacy of rock and roll. In the 1980s "rock became a reference point for a splintered culture."[26] The most important outlet for 1980s music was MTV, or Music Television, that began broadcasting on August 1, 1981. It brought music videos into American homes, and criticism of the dominant modern culture to a new generation. Some immediately saw that the new medium, which exulted in "fast cuts, slow motion, and artsy black-and-white photography—all selling sex and violence—defined the visual style of the decade, spreading to movies, prime time series, advertising and magazines."[27]

The end of the peace and love generation of music came on December 8, 1980, when John Lennon was shot seven times outside the Dakota, an apartment building where he lived in New York City. Lennon's murder, by twenty-five-year-old Mark David Chapman, was made more horrifying because the assassin was a self-confessed fan. The paranoid fear by pop stars of their audiences was epitomized in Lennon's death, which was a prelude to the era's approaching fragmentation and cult of personality.

Michael Jackson was the most important pop rock star of the decade. When Jackson recorded *Off the Wall* with Quincy Jones as producer in 1979, it sold 6 million copies. That achievement made it the best-selling album ever recorded by an African American. His next album, *Thriller*, entered the Billboard Top Ten on January 3, 1983, where it stayed for seventy-eight weeks, remaining at number one for thirty-seven weeks. At the end of the decade, *Thriller* had sold over 40 million copies, making it the best-selling record album of all time.

By the mid-1980s, African American artists dominated the Top Ten music list. Lionel Richie, Tina Turner, Rick James, Billy Ocean, and Stevie Wonder all had number one hits in 1984. The most flamboyant artist of the time was Prince Rogers Nelson, whose shocking lyrics on the album *Dirty Mind* (1980) led Tipper Gore to form the Parents Music Resource Center in 1984 to protest sexually explicit lyrics. That protest would eventually result in "Parental Advisory" labels on album covers. Prince's flamboyant style led to questions about his personal life, especially if he was gay or bisexual. His response was classically postmodern: "Who cares?"[28]

The popularity of rock music, and musicians, became a global experience in the 1980s. Renowned rock figures embarked on world tours, and the performances were experienced through enormous video screens and television broadcasts. Technology blurred the distinction between live events and reproduced videos and recordings. "From rock music to tourism to television and even education, advertising imperatives and consumer demand are no longer for goods, but for experiences."[29] A rock music concert became the ultimate postmodern experience, proof with manufactured reality that all claims to truth—and even truth itself—were socially constructed.

In July 1985, one of the biggest events in rock history, the Live Aid concert, was held simultaneously in London and Philadelphia. The concert was attended by 160,000 fans while another 1.5 billion watched it on television or listened on the radio in 130 countries. The two simultaneous all-day concerts involved pretty much anybody who was anybody in the rock-and-roll world, and Phil Collins caught the supersonic Concord to play in both cities on two different continents. Hundreds of thousands of people raised their voices together to end the show by singing, "We are the World." The Live Aid concert raised over $80 million in foreign aid that went to seven African nations: Ethiopia, Mozambique, Chad, Burkina Faso, Niger, Mali, and Sudan.

MTV opened opportunities for women to flaunt their personality and sexuality on the screen in ways, and at an age, their parents could never have imagined. Tina Turner, Cyndi Lauper, and Madonna Ciccone emerged as singing, sexual icons of the time. The latter's album *Like a Virgin* created a stir when she took the woman-as-sex-object ploy to new public heights. She found herself singing to prepubescent audiences dressed in layered gypsy blouses, bangled necklaces, and an exposed midriff. In true postmodern style, Madonna changed her public image many times, going from dance queen to "boy toy," to the "Material Girl," to trashy on-stage exhibitionist. Each time, she influenced popular fashion and the style of pop music.[30]

Rock music was becoming an index of cultural capital, and a telltale revelation of social change. Older Americans, who had invented the youth culture, stood by speechless as their children adopted rebellious fashions at increasingly younger ages. Girls as young as eleven or twelve found themselves on the cover of beauty magazines. A 1989 article in the *New York Times* described a new marketing drive of cosmetics for little girls, six years old, "painted to the hilt."[31] Preadolescent dieting was rampant in the fourth and fifth grades, and in a survey of schoolgirls in San Francisco, more than half described themselves as overweight, while only 15 percent were so by medical standards.[32]

American adolescence in the 1980s was prolonged, enjoyed, and catered to by a host of advertisers offering instant gratification. None of this was new, but the scale of the assault was unprecedented. The television suggested a morality far different from what most Americans were used to. Little girls wore leg warmers and wanted to be like Jennifer Beals, the dancing heroine in *Flashdance*. Patrick Swayze crossed the line from courtship to seduction in *Dirty Dancing*. The top movie in 1986 was *Top Gun* starring Tom Cruise as Lt. Pete "Maverick" Mitchell, a U.S. Navy fighter pilot who seduces his flight instructor. At some time every kid saw, or played with, a *Ghostbuster* product. The 1984 science fiction comedy starred three parapsychologists who were fired from New York University and started up their own business investigating and eliminating ghosts.

The 1980s were a time when the "Cola Wars" between Coke and Pepsi reached new heights—or lows, depending on your perspective. Coke was losing market share to its competitor, so on April 23, 1985, "New Coke," a sweeter variant on the original, was released with great fanfare. By the middle of June, people were saying "no" to New Coke. The reaction was nationwide, with the recent product called "furniture polish" and "sewer water." Within weeks "Coke Classic" returned to the market, and the company stock jumped 36 percent. Only in America could a marketing disaster turn into company profit. For entertainment, Americans fooled with Rubik's Cube, a plastic square with its surface subdivided so that each face consisted of nine squares. Rotation of each face allowed the smaller cubes to be arranged in different ways. The challenge, undertaken by millions of addicts, was to return the cube from any given state to its original array with each face consisting of nine squares of the same color.

Kids still rode bicycles around the neighborhood, swam in local pools, and used little CB radios to talk to each other. Schools were discussing twelve-month sessions, but summer for most was still from Memorial Day to Labor Day. They did not yet have 100 channels to flip through on television, or cell phones to flip open, email, or instant messengers. If they wanted to visit with friends they still went home and gave them a call.

Television aired a number of shows with black stars, the most successful of which was the *Bill Cosby Show*. It was the top-rated show of the decade, and showed African Americans as economically successful, middle-class professionals. *Miami Vice* made a star of Don Johnson. *The Golden Girls* made its premier in 1985 and featured stars well into their fifties and sixties. The best night on television from 1984 to 1986 was Thursday, when *The Cosby Show*, *Family Ties*, *Cheers*, *Night Court*, and *Hill Street Blues* dominated. *St. Elsewhere*, along with shows like *Hill Street Blues*, *L.A. Law*, and *Thirtysomething* were a result of demographic programming at a time when cable television was experiencing spectacular growth. The shows earned comparatively low ratings, but were kept on the air because they delivered highly desirable audiences of young affluent viewers whom advertisers wanted to reach. In 1987, a fourth network, Fox, went on the air to compete with CBS, NBC, and ABC. Before the end of the decade, 90 percent of American homes were able to tune into Fox.

Talk shows flooded onto the airways in the 1980s. David Letterman got his start in 1982, and by 1989 Oprah Winfrey, Geraldo Rivera, Sally Jessey Raphael, Pat Sajak, Arsenio Hall, and Larry King hosted popular shows. The Reagan appointees on the Federal Communications Commission (FCC) revolutionized broadcasting when they voted to abolish the agency's long-standing fairness doctrine, which required broadcasters to provide a balanced presentation of public issues. With FM radio stations given over to rock and country music, older, more conservative listeners turned to AM radio, where right-wing hosts like Rush Limbaugh, Pat Buchanan, and G. Gordon Liddy entertained them with criticisms of women, liberals, Democrats, and environmentalists.[33]

In the burgeoning suburbs, kids collected and traded Garbage Pail Kids, and had to have as many Cabbage Patch Kids as possible. They wore Swatch watches and Izod shirts, and spent time in shopping malls where they found their every need: music stores, clothing stores, fast food courts, movie theaters, and all their friends. On their first kiss they heard "Take Your Breath Away" on the radio, they danced like an Egyptian, and they did the "moonwalk." The Challenger explosion was broadcast live, and a viewer never heard a curse word used on television.

The combination of technological change and more consumer outlets led to a growth in pornography. Cheap video technology allowed the industry to grow to an estimated $7 billion in 1984, as three-quarters of the nation's video stores carried the tapes for rental. In May of 1985, Attorney General Ed Meese appointed a commission to study the effects of pornography and suggest ways to control it.[34] The recommendations had little effect because the individualistic ethic of the time valued choice and consumption over any standard of government control of cultural morality.

For most Americans, the return of economic prosperity was tacit proof that an improvement of black and white relations was imminent. An expanding economy meant gains for everyone. Discussions of race revolved around the place of affirmative action, but the nation was occasionally treated to sensational stories of scandal, and introduced to new leaders. In November 1987, a black teenager covered in dog excrement with racial slurs written on her body was discovered crawling in the garbage of a town south of Poughkeepsie, New York. The girl, Tawana Brawley, was soon represented by the Reverend Al Sharpton of New York City and two lawyers.[35] Sharpton had no congregation, but did have a reputation as a community activist and spokesman for dissident causes. Brawley claimed to have been abducted by several white men who held her for four days and repeatedly raped her while in captivity. The Sharpton team turned the sensational incident into a national media feeding frenzy.

Before the press, Sharpton claimed that Brawley was the victim of a racist judicial system, and the legal team recommended she not cooperate with the police conducting the investigation. Eventually, Tawana Brawley's story fell apart, and an official examination found that she had never been assaulted and had smeared the excrement and written the epithets herself. Once the truth came out, the two lawyers were subject to legal discipline, but Al Sharpton suffered no repercussions and continued his race-baiting activities. He ran for the New York Senate seat in 1992 and 1994, for mayor of New York City in 1997, and for the Democratic presidential nomination in 2004. Throughout his career he never apologized or explained his activities in the Tawana Brawley case.

The Brawley case showed the power of the new mass media. The "age of publicity," as Louis Kronenberger called it, began in the 1920s when flagpole sitting and goldfish swallowing became ways to get attention. Conspicuous ballyhoo became fashionable after World War II, when couples took their marriage vows on carnival carousels and spent their honeymoons in department store windows. As television grew, so too did the Barnum spirit. World records were set for domino toppling, frankfurter eating, and kazoo playing, and all of it was seen on television. The problem was that no one could predict what was likely to become news or why it would occupy public attention or for how long. More importantly, fame in America not only lasted for just fifteen minutes; it often left devastating results in its wake.

In October of 1987 the country fixated on the rescue of "Baby Jessica" McClure, who fell down an eight-inch-wide, twenty-two-foot-deep hole in her backyard in Midland, Texas. For the next fifty-eight hours the country watched spellbound as rescuers left jobs and worked nonstop to save the baby. On the evening of October 16, paramedics Steve Forbes and Robert O'Donnell wriggled into a passageway drilled through rock to save "Baby Jessica."[36]

When it was over, the gifts sent to her would provide a million-dollar trust fund. Twenty years later, hardened West Texas roughnecks would wipe tears from their cheeks as they talked about the rescue and the media coverage it inspired. The child's parents, Chip and Cissy McClure, subsequently divorced, and one of the rescuers, Robert O'Donnell, killed himself in 1995. His brother, Ricky, said O'Donnell's life fell apart because of the stress of the rescue. In the new media age fame was fleeting and suffocating at the same time.

In 1941 Henry Luce wrote an article for *Life* magazine entitled "The American Century." Luce was the most powerful and innovative mass communications person of his era, and the purpose of his essay was twofold: (1) to urge American involvement in World War II, and (2) to put forth the idea that the American principles of democracy and free enterprise would eventually come to dominate the world. The idea of American preeminence was dangerous in the eyes of some, but the basis of the piece bespoke what most people acknowledged whether they liked Luce's formulation or not.

"We have some things in this country which are infinitely precious and especially American," wrote Luce, "a love of freedom, a feeling for the equality of opportunity, a tradition of self-reliance and independence."[37] Forty-two years later, the editors of *Time* magazine, the sister publication to *Life*, updated Luce's vision with an essay entitled "What Really Mattered." In the essay the *Time* editors evaluated the meaning of America and what values were most precious to its citizens in 1983. They concluded the fundamental idea America represented was freedom, but it was different from what Luce had in mind: "America was merely free: it was freed unshackled.... To be free was to be modern: to be modern was to take chances.... The American Century was to be the century of unleashing."[38]

During the 1980s the limits of freedom were explored in the political, social, and personal realm. In the 1930s, scientists freed the atom, and fifty years later doctors were trying to free the body from its genetic dictates. Could organ transplants, sex change operations, and genetic manipulation make us immortal? Could the nation be free of superstition, so that Americans could indulge their passions for personal peace and affluence? Freedom was one of the prime conditions of postmodernity, and the cultural preoccupation with it a prelude for change. The advent of a global communications system meant that the world was coming together at one level, and falling apart at another. At the end of the decade the United States was the world's only superpower, yet it would be held captive by countries with only a fraction of its political power, but united by television to worldwide religious followers across the globe.

Postmodernism came of age in this climate in the decade of the 1980s. The election and re-election of ex-actor Ronald Reagan put a new gloss on the possibility of politics shaped by images alone. The convictions of the president were a throwback to an earlier time, but his style of image politics, carefully crafted and orchestrated for mass consumption, was of a newer era. The world was changing, and the older language of genres and forms was becoming obsolete.

―― 5 ――

Morning in America: The Second Term

Democrats watched the calendar with a mounting sense of anticipation throughout the spring of 1984. For them the victories in the 1982 midterm elections, and each new development in the 1983–1984 political season, brought them closer to an end of what Richard Reeves called "the Reagan detour."[1] Their bright expectation was that the next presidential election would be the occasion for a rebirth of the ruling Democratic coalition in both the U.S. Senate and the White House, and an end to the former California governor who had cast them into outer political darkness.

The Republicans were counting the days to the election as well. For them the improving economy and the personal popularity of their man in the White House was a harbinger of hoped-for success in the fall. They expected that the supply-side solutions would invigorate the economy, and signs were that it was working. But they also knew that Republicans had a long history of being a minority party. Neither Eisenhower nor Nixon was able to translate a presidential victory into a governing majority for the GOP, and Reagan might prove no different.

Throughout his first term in office, President Reagan was aided by a legislative consensus and an executive staff that showed remarkable, if fragile, ideological and personal unity. The president got around the problem of an uncooperative Congress by winning over the country, which then put pressure on its elected representatives. The "boll weevil" Democrats and the Republicans united to barely pass the conservative economic program and affirm the growth in military spending. But the victories came at a partisan cost. The legislative order of battle "found 99 percent of the Republicans lined up against 89 percent of the Democrats."[2] Even with this loyalty, the governing consensus was frail, and a GOP victory in the fall election was not going to be easy.

Republicans campaigned in 1980 on the slogan "Vote Republican—For a Change." That was because 40 percent of the electorate identified themselves as Democrats that year, as opposed to 22 percent holding Republican affiliation. The only way the GOP could win was to get Democrats and/or Independents to cross over on election day. By 1984, the persuasive president had skimmed some 4 to 5 percent of those voters in the country who claimed an alternate allegiance, but to win, the GOP still had to attract more attention from self-identified "Independents." These were voters who liked to say they voted "the man and not the party."[3] Despite economic and political problems in the midterm elections, the only question in the mind of party loyalists was whether the 73-year-old man in the White House would run again. If he did, and won, he would be the oldest president to be sworn into office.

Reagan did not keep them waiting for long. On January 29 he formally announced that he would seek re-election with a five-minute nationally televised speech. We have "made new beginnings," he said, but that work "was not finished."[4] Polls at the time showed that a majority of Americans backed Reagan's policies, and the president was seen as a confident, decisive leader. Clearly, Reagan had a style that the electorate liked. He enjoyed people and was unfailingly polite and courteous to them. Even opponents did not find a confrontation with him personally uncomfortable. The problem was that he was prone to rambling and incoherent responses when caught unprepared. Reagan's tight circle of White House advisors and political strategists vowed to keep him under wraps, and away from any impulsive revelations and the criticisms of a prying press.

A packed Democratic field lined up to take on the incumbent. The favorites were Walter Mondale, Carter's vice-president and an old Washington hand; John Glenn, who usually did well in hypothetical races against the president; and Colorado Senator Gary Hart, whose movie actor good looks and idealism were reminiscent of the McGovern campaign which he managed in 1972. Five other candidates enlivened the race: Alan Cranston of California, George McGovern as a liberal nominee retread, and Jesse Jackson, who became the first African American given a serious chance of winning the nomination. The trailing two candidates were Reubin Askew of Florida and Ernest "Fritz" Hollings from South Carolina.

Mondale was the early favorite. He recognized the importance of interest groups in the Democratic Party and won the endorsement of the American Federation of Teachers, the National Organization of Women, the AFL-CIO, and the National Federation of Labor. He also led in the contest for "super-delegates," meaning Democratic senators and congressmen, as well as mayors and governors, given convention seats by new party rules. In spite of these endorsements by established party regulars, polls repeatedly showed that Democrats were looking for a different face. Walter Mondale had all the things Democrats wanted in a candidate, but he touched their heads and not their hearts. In straw polls, John Glenn and Gary Hart often did better against Reagan than the frontrunner, even though they were not as well known.

At the center of the nomination process for the Democrats were the primaries and caucuses, all regulated by a new set of guidelines that led to front-loading the early primaries, a proportionate and bonus delegate selection system for the convention, and an expanding number of contests. Within the party itself, labor, black, and women's groups clamored for attention, and their demands joined the chorus of Hispanics, homosexuals, environmentalists, nuclear-freeze advocates, and Jews. Mondale appeared as the champion of them all, a fact that caused John Glenn to grouse, "Will we offer a party that can't say no to anyone with a letterhead and a mailing list?"[5]

Despite criticism, Mondale remained dominant in the weeks leading up to the Iowa caucuses. John Glenn opened a $2.5 million line of credit with four Ohio banks, but his prospects as a serious candidate were fading, and Jesse Jackson was coming under increasing criticism for a series of anti-Semitic remarks and campaign blunders.[6] Mondale had been cultivating Iowa for two years from over the border in Minnesota. On television the Minnesota senator took the high ground, and praised his colleagues' comments refusing to indulge in petty political combat with anyone except Ronald Reagan. On election night his strategy was rewarded with 49 percent of the vote. In a national poll taken the following week, Mondale was the preferred candidate of 57 percent of the polled Democrats.

To all outward appearances, the former vice-president seemed to be on his way, but even in victory problems were evident in his campaign, and the press was not reluctant to point them out. For one, Mondale was not popular with younger voters, and while he was well known, he was not especially well liked. In their search for a contest in an otherwise dull political year, the media focused on the surprising showing by Gary Hart in Iowa (16.5 percent) and the contrastingly poor performance of John Glenn (5 percent). Suddenly Hart was a serious challenger in New Hampshire, the only state where he had a serious grassroots organization.

With the media, and the candidate himself, suddenly exaggerating the results in Iowa, Democrats looking for an alternative to Walter Mondale fixed on Gary Hart. The low tax mentality of New Hampshire, and Hart's openness to free market solutions for the nation's economic woes, led him to a 37 percent to 28 percent victory over Mondale in the Granite State. Hart woke up to find himself on the cover of news magazines, sought out for television interviews, and carrying the label of "frontrunner." All this attention was attributable to a mere 12,000 votes in New Hampshire.[7]

Still, the triumph was substantial enough to carry the Colorado senator to successive victories in the Maine and Wyoming caucuses and in the nonbinding Vermont primary. Television stories following the New Hampshire primary were bereft of harsh criticism and much unflattering analysis of Hart. The trailing candidates were neglected, and Askew, Cranston, and Hollings withdrew. The focus shifted to the "Super Tuesday" primaries of March 13, when nine states would choose delegates. All of a sudden, the newly ordained

Democratic leader had warts, and the once fawning press found inconsistencies in his record, ranging from issue positions to his last name and correct age.[8] Mondale rebounded smartly from his disappointment in New Hampshire to win the Alabama and Georgia primaries, opposite Hart's victories in the larger states of Massachusetts and Florida. A week later, Mondale defeated Hart and Jackson in Illinois. As Glenn and McGovern withdrew, a series of debates allowed voters to fill in the blanks for the contenders and Mondale inched ahead. Despite some later Hart victories, including upsets in Ohio and Indiana as well as California, the Mondale victories in New York, Pennsylvania, and a host of smaller states together with his substantial "superdelegates" convention numbers worked to give the former vice-president the nomination.[9]

Political conventions have long since ceased being deliberative bodies; instead, they are media dramas designed to showcase the candidate before a national television audience. The problem in San Francisco in 1984 was that Mondale was overshadowed by two speakers, New York Governor Mario Cuomo and Reverend Jesse Jackson, who were spokesmen for traditional Democratic constituencies he was supposed to represent. Convention keynoter Mario Cuomo described the plight of "thousands of young people without jobs or an education giving their lives away to the drug dealers every day." His "Tale of Two Cities" theme was a contrast to Reagan's "City Upon a Hill" optimism of 1980. The "other" America Cuomo described was populated by millions who did not benefit from the Reagan recovery.[10]

Jackson's address was a primetime public apology confessing error and asking forgiveness for remarks made during the campaign. His stirring rhetoric to delegates, especially African Americans, declaring "Our time is come," drew a larger television audience than Mondale's acceptance speech later in the week.[11] When Mondale came to the rostrum, he tailored his remarks to the groups in the hall, and offered the arm of the federal government in assistance. He tried a gambit that he thought would be bold because it illustrated his transparency as a candidate, but in the end it backfired.

"By the end of my first term," Mondale declared in his speech of July 19, 1984, "I will cut the deficit by two-thirds." "Let's tell the truth. Mr. Reagan will raise taxes, and so will I. He won't tell you. I just did."[12] The Reagan strategists could not believe their ears. Politicians do not win elections in America when people have to vote themselves a tax increase in the voting booth. Mondale left the convention behind in the polls, while the Reagan campaign took a public pledge the next week not to raise taxes.[13]

Democratic unity at the convention came more from a shared disdain for Ronald Reagan than any enthusiasm for their candidate, and this lack of loyalty showed up in the vice-presidential nomination. Mondale undertook a very public process of interviewing candidates, more to placate interest group constituencies than to really choose someone he actually wanted as a running mate. In the end, party activists intruded and helped make his decision for him. Half the delegates to the convention were women, many of them committed feminists who threatened a floor fight if the nominee did not put a female on the ticket. After a time, Mondale chose New York congresswoman Geraldine Ferraro, a decision which pleased his constituency but added almost nothing to the national ticket.

Ronald Reagan's lack of an opponent allowed him to build a war chest and voter registration operation second to none. On June 6, 1984, he appeared in Normandy, France, for the fortieth anniversary of the D-Day Invasion. Even though it was the end of the primary season for the Democrats, it was Republican Reagan who garnered the lion's share of television coverage for his trip.[14] The president read the letter of a daughter of one veteran who recalled her father's sacrifice before he died, and the camera panned an audience as tears filled many eyes. "These are the men who took the cliffs. These are the champions who helped free a continent. These are the heroes who helped end a war."[15]

The D-Day commemoration recalled one of America's greatest triumphs, and Reagan's moving speech would be excerpted as a commercial in the approaching campaign. In his book *Our Country*, political historian Michael Barone says that Reagan's re-election was assured after just this one appearance because the president was able to reach the electorate better than any of his Democratic rivals.[16] Clearly Reagan had advantages beyond incumbency; he was an exceptional speaker who could reach the hearts, as well as the minds, of his audience.

The fall election matched two candidates from opposite ends of the ideological spectrum. Not since Lyndon Johnson trounced Barry Goldwater in 1964 were voters presented choices that differed as markedly as those of incumbent President Ronald Reagan and former vice-president Walter Mondale. Unlike 1964, this time the rout would be on the conservative side. Reagan's "Morning in America" theme tapped into a powerful need many Americans had to forget the struggles of the past, and redefine what had happened in a way that pleased a nation grown weary of its own conflicts.

The paid advertising for the campaign was destined for immortality. This was the election when Walter Mondale mimicked a Burger King commercial to ask Gary Hart, "Where's the beef?" about the content and credibility of his ideas. But the lasting legacy was Reagan's own; his message that "everything is okay again" was embodied in the theme Morning in America. Two commercials remain as vivid and effective today, more than two decades after they were aired, as when they were used in 1984.[17]

The first commercial was entitled "Ronald Reagan: Prepared for Peace." It featured Reagan's voice over thirteen separate images with visuals like a guard holding up a large picture of the Ayatollah Khomeini, tanks rolling down a rural, dirt, jungle road, and a burning American flag. It ended with a shot of President Reagan delivering a speech:

This was America in 1980, held in contempt by foreign nations. Across the world, people were losing their freedoms. So many countries thought America had seen its day, but we knew better. So we stopped complaining together and started working together. Today America is strong again. We are looking to the future with confidence and pride. America's best days, and democracy's best days, lie ahead.

Another commercial in the campaign was entitled "President Reagan: Leadership That's Working." This spot, just like the other one, featured a narrative over a montage of images, but this time the speaker was not President Reagan. A man with a deep, warm, reassuring voice talked with upbeat music as a backdrop. The spot opened with a boat sailing in an urban harbor, the first rays of the rising sun reflected in the water. The next scene was of a man in a suit stepping out of a taxi, a man on a tractor, and a young person delivering a newspaper in a suburb. The spoken narrative conveyed the theme:

It's morning again in America. Today more men and women will go to work than ever before in our country's history. With interest rates at about half the record highs of 1980, nearly 2,000 families today will buy new homes, more than at any time in the past four years. This afternoon 6,500 young men and women will be married, and with inflation at less than half of what it was just four years ago, they can look forward with confidence to the future. It's morning again in America, and under the leadership of President Reagan, our country is prouder and stronger and better. Why would we ever want to return to where we were less than four short years ago?

The advertisement presented an idealized view of a successful middle-class life in America. As the newspaper delivery boy rode out of the picture, a man got in a car just as the speaker said: "work than ever before in our country's history." The economic recovery guided the visuals in the commercial. The next pictures were of a wedding in a church, the couple kissing, and final shot of them bounding down the steps while the attendees threw rice at them. The spoken narrative was of inflation, marriage, and looking forward with confidence to the future. The images dissolved into a shot of the U.S. Capitol as the underlying music rose to a brief crescendo, and the next few images were of flags being raised. The montage ended with a prolonged shot of the American flag and the question "Why would we ever want to return to where we were less than four short years ago?"

The country was not going back. The images associated with the Morning Again in America theme implied, and in some cases stated, that Ronald Reagan was the reason why things were better, and that he was responsible for turning the nation around and bringing it out of darkness into light. Even though the candidate did not appear on film, the music by stringed instruments was in a simple, lilting mood which signified optimism and hope. The viewer had an emotional connection between the positive images of America, with the flags, workers, weddings, and Ronald Reagan. The president was comfortable with this approach; after all, it was what Hollywood did every day. However, the critics were less charitable; they found the ads misleading and vacuous in content. The irony of the whole media campaign was that Reagan's approval ratings were so strong that no special paid advertising was really necessary. The Morning Again in America theme successfully encapsulated the mood of the country in a way no other presidential campaign had, or would again.

Reagan also benefited from the Olympic Games being in Los Angeles, in the golden California sunshine. The Russians boycotted the events that year, in reprisal for America's refusal to go to the Moscow games in 1980. The televised events produced a harvest of gold medals that contributed to the exuberant mood and feeling that the United States was a better and happier place than at any time in the recent past. The euphoria carried over into the fall campaign, but it came to an abrupt end on October 7, when the two candidates debated in Louisville, Kentucky.

The president fumbled and repeated himself, his recall of statistics was unclear, and at one point he said he was "confused" by the format. "I was just awful," Reagan confessed after it was over.[18] Suddenly the campaign became a pitched battle. Internal polls in the Reagan campaign showed the president dropping 13 points, and while still comfortably ahead nationally, the gap closed in major states like New York, Pennsylvania, and California. Reagan's top advisors changed tactics. They went over the schedule and concluded that their candidate was over-prepared, so the campaign team focused on restoring his confidence. Almost everything, from the number of debate preparations to his stump speech, was changed.

At the next debate in Kansas City, the president was more relaxed and confident. Henry Trewhitt of the Baltimore *Sun* asked if Reagan, the oldest president in U.S. history, was up to the job. He continued, "Is there any doubt in your mind that you would be able to function in such circumstances?" Reagan remained calm, glancing down at the podium in his best straight man style, and answered, "Not at all, Mr. Trewhitt, and I want you to know that I will not make age an issue in this campaign. I am not going to exploit, for political purposes, my opponent's youth and inexperience."[19] Everyone laughed, including Mondale, and the quip surged the president back into a comfortable lead.

It is impossible to find a turning point in an election that led to a forty-nine-state landslide. Michael Barone might be right; maybe the election was over in June. What Reagan understood is that the American people craved something bigger in their history and national memory than Gerald Ford's evacuation of Saigon or Jimmy Carter's malaise speech. When the fifty-six Americans were held for ransom by Khomeini's Iran, the press said it was "America held hostage." By contrast the D-Day story was about America as ferocious liberators, not backroom barterers.

Almost half the voters had made their decision at the beginning of the election year, and only one-fourth waited for the televised debates to decide.[20] Reagan gained 59 percent of the popular vote, a record 525 electoral votes, losing only Minnesota and the District of Columbia. The previous record for a landslide in American politics was 523 for Franklin Roosevelt in 1936, and 520 for Richard

Nixon in 1972. The victory was all the more remarkable given that Reagan was mired in very low approval numbers just two years earlier.[21] In winning, he garnered more votes for his Republican presidency than had ever been cast for a U.S. politician, and again took twenty-four of the top thirty media markets. But that enthusiasm did not extend to the Congress, where Republicans lost two seats from their majority in the Senate, and made only a modest gain of fourteen in the House. The fragile governing coalition would continue.

The first inaugural for Ronald Reagan was the warmest on record; the second was the coldest. The day dawned sunny, but bitterly cold. The estimated noontime swearing-in temperature was seven degrees Fahrenheit, with wind chills from the minus ten to minus twenty degree range. Because January 20, 1985, fell on a Sunday, the public Inauguration ceremony was scheduled for Monday, January 21. A private ceremony was held in the White House at the bottom of the Grand Staircase. The swearing-in was witnessed by about eighty-four people, mostly family and cabinet officials. The public inauguration was moved indoors to the rotunda, and became a semiprivate ceremony. In his abbreviated inaugural address, Reagan said the nation was "poised for greatness" in his second term. "Let history say of us, 'These were golden years— when the American Revolution was reborn, when freedom gained new life, when America reached for her best.' "[22]

Over the years, official Washington had become used to cabinet changes in the second term of a president. In fact, changes had been the rule rather than the exception. But the city had never seen anything like what happened in January of 1985. Chief of Staff James Baker swapped jobs with Treasury Secretary Donald Regan. Edwin Meese became attorney general and Chief of Staff Michael Deaver resigned to go into private business. The swaps set off a chain of cabinet-level changes.[23] The history of second terms for American presidents is that they are usually not as successful as first terms because the cabinet and staff are less enthusiastic, more prone to mistakes, and not as loyal as the initial appointees. The most glaring example, of course, was the Watergate scandal in Richard Nixon's second term. But Sherman Adams, Dwight Eisenhower's chief of staff, was also caught up in a gift-giving scandal in the second term. All the maladies of past presidents would return to haunt Ronald Reagan, when extreme measures were taken in pursuit of personal goals, or with good intentions, but without an understanding of the consequences.

The first crisis began as part of a well-intentioned plan to observe the fortieth anniversary of V-E Day, May 8, 1945. Reagan was scheduled to attend an economic summit in Bonn that week in 1985, and West German Chancellor Helmut Kohl saw an opportunity to demonstrate the strength of the friendship that existed between the two men and the nations they led. Kohl appealed to Reagan in November of 1984, in a visit to Washington, to join him in appearing at a German military cemetery to symbolize the reconciliation between the former foes. Reagan agreed. As he later told an aide, he felt he owed Helmut Kohl, who despite considerable public and political opposition had stood with the president on the deployment of Pershing missiles in West Germany a few years earlier.

In February of 1985, White House Deputy Chief of Staff Michael Deaver made an advance trip to plan the visit to Kolmeshohe Cemetery in Bitburg, a quaint little town in the Eifel hills where nearly 11,000 Americans attached to a nearby airbase lived in harmony with about the same number of Germans. Deaver was suffering from alcoholism, and was not the public relations maestro he had been in two political campaigns and as an aide to Reagan since his gubernatorial days. He failed to discover that forty-nine *Waffen SS* Nazi soldiers were buried at Kolmeshohe, and West German officials did not mention this fact either. When asked later, the White House said both German and American soldiers were buried in the cemetery, but reporters found out that all U.S. soldiers had long since been removed from German soil. The White House began to backpedal. To add to the embarrassment about the incident, the handful of interred *Waffen SS* had been the combat branch of the Third Reich's elite guard, the *Schutzstaffel*, created in 1923 to serve as Hitler's personal bodyguards, and later as guards at concentration camps.[24]

The itinerary was announced in April, and immediately it created a firestorm of controversy. Jewish leaders like Elie Wiesel asked, "May I implore you to do something else, to find another way, another site." Nancy Reagan agreed, but Director of White House Communications Pat Buchanan argued that the president should resist the pressure from the Jewish lobby and the liberal media and go to Bitburg. Buchanan had a powerful ally, Helmut Kohl, who called to urge the president to keep his commitment. A poll in West Germany found that 72 percent of West Germans thought the visit should go forward as planned despite the controversy.[25]

Suddenly Reagan's visit, made almost as an afterthought, assumed vast moral significance. The White House was quick to point out that the president had scheduled a ceremony at the site of the Bergen-Belsen concentration camp on the same visit. No matter. The International Network of Children of Jewish Holocaust Survivors, the American Legion, the Union of American Hebrew Congregations, decorated World War II American veterans, fifty-three senators, and 257 U.S. representatives all urged the president to cancel the trip. Polls at the time showed that a majority of Americans, both Democrats and Republicans, opposed the scheduled trip.[26]

Reagan would not budge, and neither would Kohl. The president had a stubborn character trait that once something was in the script, it stayed put. "His beliefs were as inerasable as the grooves of an LP.... The only reliable way to recognize the approach [was] to listen for signal phrases: 'As I've said many times...'" White House aide Robert McFarlane would say after the controversy, "Once Reagan learned that Kohl would really be badly damaged by a withdrawal, [Reagan said], 'We can't do that, I owe him.'"[27]

President Reagan spent only eight minutes at the Bitburg Cemetery, along with Kohl, ninety-year-old General Matthew Ridgway, who commanded the

82nd Airborne in World War II, and Luftwaffe ace General Johannes Steinhoff. There were almost no protestors at the site, and the rally at the nearby American airbase was spectacularly successful. Reagan told his deputy chief-of-staff, "History will prove I'm right.... If we can't reconcile after forty years, we are never going to be able to do it."[28]

Lost in the flames of the controversy was the moving speech Reagan gave at Bergen-Belsen before going to Bitburg. Summoning his exceptional rhetorical skills, the president said, "All these children of God under bleak and lifeless mounds.... Here they lie, never to hope, never to pray, never to live, never to heal, never to laugh, never to cry ... beyond the anguish, the pain and suffering, and for all time, we can and must pledge: Never Again." One reporter who covered the trip said, "It was a striking example, of which there have been many in Reagan's life, when he was rescued from poor judgment by a successful performance."[29] In the weeks after the event, the president showed another habit: he forgot what happened and never looked back.

The Bitburg fiasco had lingering consequences, but it was more important for what it showed about the way things were being done in the White House than for any immediate political fallout. It would take another incident, a far more serious one, before the problems would surface again. There was a word for the more extreme measures being used by individuals in pursuit of their private agendas in the administration: scandal. It was about to acquire a synonym: Iran-Contra.

The stage for this most disastrous of self-inflicted calamities to strike the Reagan presidency was set by an awful terrorist act. On June 14, 1985, TWA Flight 847, from Athens to Rome, was hijacked with 153 passengers and crew aboard, including 135 Americans. The pilot was forced to fly from Beirut to Algiers, and then back to Beirut where the hijackers brutally beat and then shot to death a U.S. Navy diver. After refueling, the plane was flown back to Algiers and again to Beirut, where most of the passengers were released. In the final terror-filled odyssey, thirty-nine American passengers and crew members were herded off TWA 847 and held captive in Lebanon. Ultimately they were released through diplomatic pressure and the intervention of Syrian President Hafez Assad, but the hijacking itself made a mockery of Reagan's tough talk about swift and effective retribution against terrorism. What is more, hostage-taking became a means of foreign policy in the region.

About a year later, in July of 1985, a delegation of visitors from Israel met with National Security Advisor Robert "Bud" McFarlane with a proposal to help free hostages. They proposed to act as an intermediary by shipping 508 American-made TOW anti-tank missiles to Iran in exchange for American hostages being held by Iranian sympathizers. Once the exchange was made, the United States would ship replacement missiles to Israel.[30] At first the proposal did not sound like an effective way to defeat terrorism or rescue its victims, but the pressure to do something about hostages was unrelenting.

Back in 1979, when fifty-six Americans were being held at the U.S. embassy in Tehran, one of Jimmy Carter's first reactions was to impose an embargo on arms shipments to Iran. Reagan won the election of 1980 with a promise to be tougher on the Iranians than his predecessor. The Israeli proposal was in violation of American law, policy, and proclaimed rhetoric. Even so, it had an appeal that went beyond principle.

The hostages provided an emotional motive to open secret negotiations, and the opportunity of building a relationship with moderates operating within the Khomeini government gave the plan credibility that it would usually not have had. "On balance my interests are to see our larger interest in establishing an entrée to someone in Iran," wrote Robert McFarlane. Reagan was recuperating from surgery to remove a malignant tumor from his intestine, and did not hear of the plan for a month. When he was told, he found Secretary of Defense Weinberger and Secretary of State Shultz in rare agreement that the proposal was outrageous. But the president was cheered by the prospect of getting hostages out of Lebanon, and he approved it in principle. The transfer of arms took place over the next two months.

In retrospect, the outcome of the first round of negotiations with the hostage-takers was not good for the United States, and did not justify the risk, but the promise was that these first steps would lead to a breakthrough. The Israelis informed McFarlane that they could not deliver all the hostages, but only one. It was up to McFarlane to decide which one. After some delay, the Muslims released Benjamin Weir, a Presbyterian missionary who had been held sixteen months. To some in the administration, his freedom was tangible proof that the policy, no matter how daring, had some beneficial effects.

The captive whose fate most concerned the administration in Washington was William Buckley, who had been the CIA station chief in Beirut. Because of the sensitive nature of his mission, Buckley was especially vulnerable, and intelligence reports indicated he had been cruelly tortured by his Muslim captors.[31] The Israelis were vague about Buckley's status; in reality he had been brutally murdered and was not even available for a hostage exchange. Concern over the captives led to another round of negotiations, even though there was no evidence that earlier efforts had been effective. This time the Israelis proposed to ship 500 Hawk anti-aircraft missiles in exchange for the release of all remaining American hostages. During this second round of negotiations, McFarlane was working to prepare Reagan for a summit meeting with Mikhail Gorbachev, so he entrusted the details of the assignment to his deputy, Oliver North. North was a Vietnam veteran with a Bronze Star, a Silver Star, two Purple Hearts, and a Navy Commendation Medal. He was zealous to succeed in his covert mission, even though he admitted later that he was largely unfamiliar with what was being done.

While Israel and the United States worked in the same direction on Iran, officials from both countries had long since joined paths in Central America. As early as May 1983, Washington and Tel Aviv developed an arrangement for the Defense Department to buy Soviet bloc weapons captured from the PLO in Lebanon. The arms were transferred to the Contras, from the Spanish word *contrarrevolucionario*, the CIA-backed rebels battling the Cuban-backed Sandinista regime in Nicaragua. The new proposal in 1985 allowed an American intermediary, rather than Israel, to sell arms to Iran in exchange for the release of the hostages, with profits funneled to the Contras. The proceeds from the arms sales were diverted by Colonel Oliver North, still working in the White House but now as an aide to U.S. National Security Advisor John Poindexter.

Ronald Reagan's determination to eradicate communism worldwide focused on the Sandinistas in Nicaragua, who were backed by the Soviet Union and Cuba. The Sandinistas also supported left-wing rebels against the government in El Salvador, which had received substantial U.S. support and was the scene of a destructive civil war throughout the 1980s. The president saw the whole of Central America as under a communist threat. In 1985, the Sandinista movement won in elections validated by some international observers as fair and free, but rejected by the Reagan administration as fraudulent. A determined and unyielding Reagan told National Security Advisor Robert McFarlane about the situation in Nicaragua, "I want you to do whatever it takes to help these people keep body and soul together."[32]

Probably Reagan's aides took his general plea as a carte blanche to do everything necessary to achieve that end. The president had become frustrated at his inability to secure the release of the American hostages being held by Iranian terrorists in Lebanon, and Congress had recently passed a law to tie his hands on giving military aid to the Contras. The hatred Ronald Reagan had for communism led him into temptation. "He was the guy that knew the Iranians had rubbed Jimmy Carter's nose in it.... Now all of a sudden he's got the same situation, and he's responsible for it.... Ronald Reagan eats his heart out over this."[33]

In January of 1986, Reagan allegedly approved a plan whereby arms would be sold to Iran in exchange for the release of the hostages, with profits funneled to the Contras. With the marked-up income of the exchange being some $10 million in the administration's pocket, the Contras could be supplied without asking Congress for more money. Meanwhile, in the Middle East, the Iranians captured new hostages as soon as they released the old ones. This was the end of the arms-for-hostages deals, but the United States continued to ship weapons and spare parts to Iran from May to November.

With or without the president's knowledge, the diversion plan continued, and Oliver North was at the controls. He had opened negotiations for a third round of arms sales to the Iranians, even though the released hostages were merely being replaced in what Secretary of State George Shultz would later call "a hostage bazaar." The problem was that on the one end the Americans were being swindled by the Iranians, and on the other the U.S.-supported rebels were floundering on the battlefields of Nicaragua. All the while, the public posture of the administration was that the United States did not negotiate with terrorists and was resolute in its determination to rid the world of the international evil.

In the midst of this charade, the Reagan administration had a public opportunity to act against, instead of just denounce, the terrorists. The most blatant public face of terrorism in the world was Colonel Muammar el-Quaddafi, the ruler of Libya. Quaddafi was an outlandish personality who allegedly had a private fetish for wearing women's clothing and makeup. But behind the façade, Libya was an active state sponsor of terrorism. Early in April of 1986, terrorists blew up a discotheque in West Berlin which was a hangout for U.S. servicemen. Two Americans and a Turkish woman were killed, and 230 others were injured. Evidence pointed to Libya as the culprit. Reagan would later declare that the United States had proof of a direct Libyan role, and that a raid on that country would cause Quaddafi to "alter his criminal behavior." At last, the administration had an opportunity for Reagan to back up his public rhetoric with military action.

On April 14, U.S. Air Force and Navy bombers based in England dropped ninety 2,000 pound bombs on the Quaddafi compound of Tripoli and Benghazi. The bombs killed Quaddafi's adopted two-year-old daughter and wounded two of his sons.[34] Quaddafi escaped injury because he was sleeping outside the compound, but scores of civilians were killed. In the wake of the raid, Secretary of State Shultz declared that the raid was the beginning of a more militant policy by the Reagan administration toward terrorism. The public face of the policy was affirmed, but no one knew about what was going on behind the scenes.

The secrecy was beginning to take its toll. Robert McFarlane resigned his position in the White House, leaving John Poindexter and Oliver North at their posts. Then on October 5, 1986, an antiquated cargo plane was shot down over Nicaragua by a surface-to-air missile. The lone survivor, Eugene Hasenfaus of Marinette, Wisconsin, was captured, and his haggard photo was soon on the television and the front page of every newspaper.[35] Half a world away, Lieutenant Colonel Oliver North was in negotiations with Iranian government representatives for yet another hostage exchange. The next month, the first public allegations of the weapons-for-hostages deal surfaced on November 3, when the Lebanese magazine *Ash-Shiraz* reported the United States had been selling weapons to Iran in secret in order to secure the release of American hostages in Lebanon.

For most Americans, the two events were unconnected, and played out at opposite ends of the globe. But back in Washington, Oliver North and his secretary, Fawn Hall, began shredding documents implicating them and others in the arms-for-hostages arrangements. On November 25, President Reagan and Attorney General Edwin Meese shocked the country by disclosing that the two operations were in fact intertwined. When Attorney General Meese found a so-called "diversion memo," which North wrote in the spring of 1986, detailing the scheme to skim money from arms sales to the Contras, he went directly to the president. "He [Reagan] decided that we should immediately make a complete disclosure of our findings, and this resulted in a full-scale press conference the following day at noon."[36] For this offense, North was fired and his superior, National Security Advisor John Poindexter, who knew and approved the plans, was allowed to resign.[37]

The subsequent press conference did little to relieve the pressure on the administration, but the political effects were dramatic. "When the scandal broke in late 1986...it had a devastating impact [on] Reagan's approval ratings [which] dropped precipitously from nearly 70 percent to around 35 percent."[38] The public outrage over the Iran-Contra revelations were partly to blame for GOP reversals in the 1986 midterm elections, where Republicans lost control of the U.S. Senate for the first time in Reagan's presidency. Ultimately, documents and testimony produced during subsequent investigations showed that North and Poindexter were part of a much larger group within the administration circumventing the law and misleading Congress. These machinations involved many foreign governments, including Israel, Saudi Arabia, South Africa, China, Taiwan, Panama, Costa Rica, Guatemala, El Salvador, and Honduras.

Faced with mounting pressure, Reagan appointed a Special Review Board headed by Senator John Tower to look into the scandal. The president claimed he had not been informed of the operation despite an entry in his own diary stating otherwise. The review board implicated North, Poindexter, and Weinberger, but could not conclusively determine the degree of Reagan's involvement. In the final Tower Commission report, Reagan was rebuked for not having a firm control on his national security staff.[39]

A partial explanation for presidential mismanagement rested with his wife. After the attempted assassination of her husband, Nancy Reagan began regular consultations with an astrologer, Joan Quigley, whose charts helped set the president's schedule.[40] Ronald Reagan was casual in his superstitions, but Nancy Reagan became convinced that Quigley's advice had protected her husband from repeated assassination attempts. Real and imagined dangers led the White House to defer final acceptance for any event until Mrs. Reagan had approved. Much of the Bitburg fiasco was attributable to Nancy Reagan's superstitions, and the world will never know how much of the Iran-Contra mismanagement was a consequence of Nancy Reagan and her astrologer.

Congressional hearings into the Iran-Contra affair, and the criminal trial of North and others, were just as inconclusive. After months of speculation, the highlight came on July 7, 1987, when ramrod-straight Marine Lieutenant Colonel North appeared in the Caucus Room of the Russell Senate Office Building to testify before the committee. The comparisons with Watergate by the press were inevitable, but Oliver North was no conspirator and he would be no scapegoat. "I had faith and belief in the goodness of my country and what democracy and freedom meant.... I thought, if I could convey those feelings, then the American people would understand.... I didn't think it was wrong, I thought it was a neat idea."[41] North's candid testimony, laced with throat-clutching patriotism, gradually turned the national audience to his side. He did what he did not for money or power, but out of loyalty to his president and the country.

Speculation about the involvement of President Reagan, Vice-President Bush—who would face questions about Iran-Contra as he ran for president—and other administration officials continued for the next eight years. Fourteen people were charged with crimes. In the end, North's conviction was overturned on a technicality and President Bush issued six pardons, including one for Robert McFarlane, who had already been convicted, and one to Caspar Weinberger before he stood trial.

In 1988, a report by the Senate Subcommittee on Narcotics, Terrorism and International Operations concluded that various people in the Contra movement were involved in drug trafficking. The World Court ruled in favor of the Nicaraguan Sandinistas and charged the United States to pay restitution fines to the government, which it refused to do. The U.N. General Assembly passed a similar resolution, which the United States similarly ignored. Finally, the Sandinistas lost power in fresh elections in February of 1990, following a decade of U.S. economic and military pressure.

One year after taking the presidential oath for a second time, the president was called to the role of counselor and comforter, this time for the most dramatic failure in U.S. space science history. Americans had grown used to technological triumphs in outer space. The lunar landing in 1969 was witnessed by the largest television audience ever, but by the 1980s interest in space research was fading. The public was told that the possibility of failure was small, and the launches and recoveries seemed routine after a time.

NASA's space shuttle program began in the 1970s to create reusable craft for transporting cargo into space. By the 1980s, four shuttles were in the fleet. The launch of space shuttle *Challenger*, set for January of 1986, would be the twenty-fifth mission for the program. *Challenger* had flown nine successful times and the only thing unusual about this mission was that Sharon Christa McAuliffe, a New Hampshire high school teacher, would be the first teacher in space.

Earlier in the year, space agency officials worked feverishly to prepare the space shuttle *Columbia* for launch only to encounter weeks of frustration and a record seven postponements. The *Columbia* astronauts were twenty-five days late going up, and its landing was postponed twice because of bad weather. At the same time, insurance companies began to shy away from the space program because since 1968 insurers had paid out $500 million in claims for failed or lost communication satellites. All in all, the glint was off the NASA rose.

From the beginning, the *Challenger* mission was plagued with problems. The flight was originally set for January 22, but had been rescheduled five times. The launch was the first one from a new pad, this one closer to the viewing public, and many in the audience would say later that it was the loudest and most stunning lift-off ever. *Challenger* left the launching pad at 11:38 A.M. Eastern Standard Time. That morning the countdown went smoothly, despite freezing temperatures. The flight administrators would later say, "There was absolutely no pressure to get this particular launch off."[42] Later, an investigation showed that substantial pressure was brought by NASA on dissenting engineers to approve the launch in the face of questions they had about the weather.

The *Challenger* explosion, January 28, 1986. (Courtesy, NASA)

A great spurting spout of yellow-white flame erupted from the three engines as the cameras showed the shuttle held on the launch pad for four incredible seconds. About one minute thirteen seconds after launch, as students across the country watched on live television feeds, the shuttle exploded, killing all seven crew members. Apparent in the pictures of the accident was evidence that the shuttle was a potential bomb that carried 385,000 gallons of liquid oxygen at liftoff, and any leak was like a blasting cap.

The *Challenger* disaster sparked national mourning on a scale not seen since the assassination of President John F. Kennedy. President Reagan watched the explosion on television at the White House in "stunned silence." At 4:00 P.M., he addressed the nation.[43]

> The crew of the space shuttle *Challenger* honored us by the manner in which they lived their lives. We will never forget them, nor the last time we saw them, this morning, as they prepared for the journey and waved goodbye and "slipped the surly bonds of earth" to "touch the face of God."

World leaders expressed shock and sorrow over the explosion, and newspapers around the world cut their domestic coverage to provide details about the disaster. On the day of the launch, 505 journalists were accredited to cover the mission from the Kennedy Space Center in Florida, and just thirty were at the Johnson Space Center in Houston, Texas. Within three days, 1,467 reporters and broadcasters were on site at the Cape, and 1,040 were stationed in Houston.

As the press converged on the NASA facilities in Florida, the agency public affairs officers struggled to cope with a flood of questions. Within hours of the explosion all videotape of the launch was impounded.[44] The *New York Times* and United Press International speculated on causes of the disaster, and refused to surrender film evidence of the accident. Jesse Moore, associate administrator for spaceflight at NASA, gave the official line on the day of the explosion: "It's too early for us to speculate.... We clearly don't want to zero in on something prematurely and say that's it and not get the prime cause."[45]

The next time the agency spoke again was on February 13; by then the media was guessing that an external tank or fuel line failure triggered the disaster. Press speculation came from the black color and dense composition of the smoke puffs that suggested a joint insulation or rubber o-ring in the joint seal was being burned by the hot propellant gases. The official report on what happened to the *Challenger*, officially labeled STS-51-L, was issued on June 9, 1986. The comprehensive 225-page report by the fourteen-member Rogers Commission documented the technical and managerial factors that contributed to the accident.[46] Much of what they had to say was already public knowledge by the time it was published. The technical analysis implicated the SRB-o-rings, which failed as a result of inadequate inspection and low temperatures at launch time. The problem went beyond the o-rings, to the procedures NASA used to approve a launch. The investigation and corrective action following the *Challenger* tragedy caused a thirty-two-month halt in shuttle launches.

Throughout his presidency, Reagan had ample opportunities to comfort the country. Among them were the shooting down of the Korean airliner, the Beirut hostage victims, the war in Lebanon, the invasion of Grenada, the murder of the American ambassador to Pakistan, the terrorist bombing in Beirut, airline hijack victims, and the *Challenger* explosion. Reagan's age and life experience all made him able to fill the role of all-knowing, wise father figure to the country. Even the crusty Tip O'Neill, Democratic Speaker of the House and inveterate White House opponent, dabbed his eyes after the president's remarks on the *Challenger* disaster and said, "He may not be much of a debater, but with a prepared text he's the best public speaker I've ever seen."[47]

The great turning point in the Cold War tension between East and West coincided with Ronald Reagan's second term and the first four years of Mikhail Gorbachev's leadership of the USSR. The prelude was set by the deaths of Soviet leaders Leonid Brezhnev in 1982, Yuri Andropov in 1983, and Konstantin Chernenko in 1984. These three leaders were old men who adhered to the Marxist-Leninist ideology in spite of the suffocating effect it had on their own nation and the rest of the world. At home and abroad the Soviet system was regarded with increasing cynicism, contempt, and ridicule.

Ronald Reagan was chief among the accusers. He specialized in collecting jokes about the inefficiency and cruelty of the Russian system, but beneath the humor was an abiding belief that communism was fatally flawed and on the verge of collapse. The Soviets recognized the president's disdain, and during the 1984 presidential election attacks from them and the American left regularly stressed that Reagan's foreign and defense policies were pushing the world to the verge of nuclear war. Averill Harriman, a former ambassador to the Soviet Union and an advisor to five presidents, wrote that under Reagan's policies, "if permitted to continue, we could face not the risk but the reality of nuclear war."[48]

The nuclear prospect constantly haunted Reagan, who was awed by the biblical prophecy of Armageddon, which he imagined as a nuclear hell. The opportunity for change came in September of 1984, when Soviet Foreign Minister Andrei Gromyko met with Reagan. Nicknamed "Grim Grom" in the White House because of his inflexible and hard-line manner, Gromyko had become ambassador to the United States in 1943, and was a familiar mouthpiece of bad news for American administrations. The president sensed from Gromyko's complaints that instead of pushing the world to the brink of war, his defense expenditures were really exposing an inherent weakness in the Soviet economy. Just as Reagan prophesied, the USSR was unable to maintain a rapid growth in defense spending and at the same time satisfy demands for consumer goods and services. If the United States engaged in a military buildup, the president believed Moscow would not be able to keep up.

Economists at the U.S. Treasury provided Reagan with an estimate that a $5 drop in the price of a barrel of oil on the world market increased the GNP of the country by 1.4 percent.[49] The friendship between the United States and Saudi Arabia was an economic weapon that Reagan exploited to force the Soviets into a defensive posture. Lower oil prices also reduced the U.S. trade deficit. In the summer of 1985, the Saudis opened the oil spigots and the domestic economy boomed.

That expansion spelled trouble for the Soviet Union, with its Afghanistan incursion and multiplying problems at home. The new leader, Mikhail Gorbachev, came from a family of peasants who suffered under Stalin's ruthless effort to drive farmers off their private land onto collectivized farms. He was not a deep believer in communism. As an agricultural minister he knew the limits of a command economy, and at age fifty-four he was no dyed-in-the-wool cold warrior either. Instead, Gorbachev was an idealist in a sea of guardians, a change agent in a room full of bureaucrats. He had a magnetic personality and almost limitless confidence. Once at the top of the Soviet hierarchy, Gorbachev declared, "We have to awaken society from its lethargy and indifference as quickly as possible and involve the people in the process of change."[50]

Reagan immediately dispatched Secretary of State George Shultz and Vice President George Bush with a letter to the Soviet premier inviting him to a summit. The date was set for mid-November in Geneva. Between them, Gorbachev and Reagan would have four historic summits (Geneva, Reykjavik, Washington, and Moscow), and exchange more than a dozen personal letters between visits. In the end they would ratify the Intermediate Nuclear Forces (INF) Treaty, which banned all intermediate nuclear missiles, and conclude the outline of the Strategic Arms Reduction Treaty (START) that dramatically reduced long-range nuclear forces. In short, they would change the world and bring about the ultimate end of the Cold War.

Before 1985, U.S.-Soviet relations were at an all-time low. The downing of KAL-007 and the deployment of missiles in Europe resulted in the Soviet Union walking out of arms control talks. From the beginning, the Soviet premier had two problems: the first was the need for military disarmament, and the second was the Afghanistan invasion. Gorbachev needed disarmament to revive the Russian economy and an honorable way to get out of the war. For his part, Reagan was not about to give Gorbachev either one. The president fervently defended the Strategic Defense Initiative (SDI) and signed a security order that sent 10,000 rocket-propelled grenades, 200,000 rockets, and 200 Stinger shoulder-fired anti-aircraft missiles to the rebels in Afghanistan.

Amid this tension, Gorbachev arrived at the Geneva summit unable to conceal the failures of the communist experience from the Soviet people. He hoped to open up Soviet society ("glasnost") and restructure its economy ("perestroika"). The summit took place from November 19 to November 20, where the two men engaged in three private meetings and four plenary meetings. Prior to the meeting, Gorbachev initiated a moratorium on nuclear testing, and proposed a 50 percent reduction in previously installed long-range strategic missiles.

Reagan felt prepared and "up" for the summit after months of preparation, much as actors do before a big performance. As he stepped out of Chateau Fleur d'Eau and into the icy air blowing off nearby Lake Geneva, the president wore no coat, hat, or scarf. Gorbachev stepped out of a limousine dressed in a charcoal-gray hat and matching scarf and wrapped in a heavy overcoat. A surprised Gorbachev shook Reagan's hand and asked, "Where is your coat?" "It's inside," said Reagan, leading the visitor in by the elbow.[51]

Reagan and Gorbachev understood that all the problems between the United States and the Soviet Union could not be resolved in two days; what they both seemed to believe was that a frank exchange would allow them to establish a foundation for a permanent peace later on. The talks were blunt, and little progress was made at first, in part because of contention over the SDI. At one point the two leaders met at a pool house near the shore of Lake Geneva before a roaring fire, one that would give the meeting its name: "the fireside summit." After rambling through several topics, Reagan looked into Gorbachev's eyes and told him: "I do hope for the sake of our children that we can find some way to avert this terrible, escalating arms race." Then he paused, and Gorbachev, thinking Reagan was finished, opened his mouth to speak, but the president was not through: "because if we can't America will not lose it, I assure you."[52]

President Reagan and Soviet General Gorbachev at the first Summit in Geneva, Switzerland, November 19, 1985. (Courtesy, Ronald Reagan Presidential Library)

Reagan continued staring into Gorbachev's eyes while the Russian interpreter translated his words.

Moscow was receptive to a gradual reduction in arms but believed that "arms reductions must be viewed through the interrelationship to space weapons." In short, Gorbachev demanded that reductions be linked to a ban on the "Star Wars" SDI. It was on the way back from the pool house that Reagan proposed the most substantive accomplishment from the first summit, that being the agreement to hold future summits. The Soviet offer to cut nuclear weapons was historic, and remained on the table, but to Reagan SDI was no bargaining chip. The president believed SDI could make nuclear weapons obsolete, rendering the Kremlin's most powerful asset, their missile technology, obsolete. The Geneva summit ended without substantial progress, but both sides showed flexibility and—something unheard of between the two countries—trust.

Five months after the first summit, a catastrophe transformed world attitudes about Soviet intentions and heightened nuclear fears worldwide. On April 25, 1986, the worst nuclear power accident in history occurred at Chernobyl, a nuclear power plant located about eighty miles north of Kiev. The plant had four reactors, and the fourth exploded at 1:23 A.M., creating a fireball that blew off the reactor's heavy steel concrete roof. The accident killed more than thirty people and resulted in high radiation and the immediate evacuation of 135,000 people.[53]

Reagan was convinced that the Chernobyl explosion damaged Gorbachev's leadership at home and made him more receptive to the need for arms reduction. When Gorbachev proposed a preparatory meeting with Reagan in a private letter before the second summit, the president quickly accepted. The formal agenda was unclear, saying it was just to discuss "unresolved issues." So on October 11 and 12, 1986, at Reykjavik, Iceland, Gorbachev and Reagan met a second time. While the leaders labeled it a "presummit," the session very nearly produced a radical agreement and set the stage for ultimate bilateral superpower disarmament.

From their earliest discussion, it was clear to Reagan that Gorbachev was under tremendous pressure at home and abroad, and was anxious to deal with the West. The president proposed the elimination of all offensive ballistic missiles within ten years, and Gorbachev reciprocated by proposing to eliminate the even larger category of *all* strategic weapons—period. The sticking point was Gorbachev's insistence that Reagan confine SDI to the laboratory, and not move to test and deploy it in space. Again, Reagan said he would not go back on his promise to make the system operational in fact, and not just in theory. When the Soviet leader refused to continue talking until SDI disappeared, Reagan closed his briefing book and stood up, effectively ending the summit. "The meeting is over," he said. "Let's go, George (Shultz), we're leaving."[54] Gorbachev was stunned, and the Reykjavik meetings, which were supposed to last another day, collapsed.

The world expressed grave disappointment at the outcome. Their remorse matched that of Secretary of State Shultz and Ambassador Gromyko. The diplomats backpedaled before the cameras, and the criticism was that Reagan went to the presummit unprepared. Nevertheless, a *New York Times*/CBS poll showed an eleven-point jump to 72 percent of Americans who thought the president was successfully handling relations with the Soviet Union. The legacy of Reykjavik was hope, and it came as much from Gorbachev as from Reagan. "We have reached agreements on many things," said the Soviet General Secretary. "We have traveled a long road."[55]

The spirit of disarmament continued after the summit in various meetings with representatives of both sides, but Reagan was mired in the Iran-Contra revelations and on the political defensive through much of the spring and summer of 1987. Like presidents before him, Reagan sought solace by traveling abroad, even though at his age trips were a strain. In June, he made a ten-day tour of Europe, capped by a visit to West Berlin. There, before a worldwide audience, he challenged the Soviet Union to make good on its proposals for world peace. "If you seek liberation: Come here to the gate! Mr. Gorbachev, open this gate! Mr. Gorbachev, tear down this wall!"[56] The speech was the most impressive since John Kennedy confronted the Soviet Union at the same place, but this time the United States stood poised to vanquish its adversary.

Reagan seemed to have the momentum in negotiations as well as rhetoric, but in the Washington summit that December, it was Gorbachev who was the media star. After meeting with Nikita Khrushchev in Vienna, President John F. Kennedy described him as "rude and savage," with a "vicious and sneering manner."[57] That was the stereotype of Russian leaders until Gorbachev came to Washington. The Soviet leader campaigned like a candidate running for elective office, driving the Secret Service and the KGB mad by stopping his limousine on Connecticut Avenue in the city so he could get out and shake hands with well-wishers. In staid Washington they called it "Gorby fever."

The epidemic produced results; both sides signed the Intermediate Nuclear Force (INF) treaty that would lead to the immediate destruction of 859 U.S. nuclear missiles and 1,836 Soviet nuclear missiles with a range between 300 and 3,400 miles. This was the first treaty of any kind between the United States and the Soviet Union to provide for on-site verification of arms destruction. Asked by the press if he resented the attention given Gorbachev in Washington, Reagan replied, "I don't resent his popularity. Good Lord, I co-starred with Errol Flynn once."[58]

Before the final summit, Gorbachev improved his popularity in the United States by withdrawing Soviet forces from Afghanistan. The U.S. policy of helping the rebels proved successful. At a summit discussion in Washington, Reagan interrupted to tell Gorbachev, "What you are doing in Afghanistan is burning villages and killing children. It's genocide and you are the one to stop it." By the time the two leaders came to Moscow in the spring of 1988, Reagan was less interested in securing diplomatic agreements than in pushing for human rights. On May 29 he found himself the recipient of popular attention when crowds lined the street to welcome him. Reagan met with Jewish refuseniks, Pentecostals imprisoned for their faith, and human rights activists, and he even visited a monastery which was a spiritual oasis for the faithful in Moscow. The next day he spoke on free markets beneath a gigantic white bust of Lenin at Moscow State University. When he finished, the president was greeted with wild applause. "It was not the Reagan we expected," said one of the students. "There was nothing old fashioned or stale about him. He seemed so lively, active and thinking."[59]

If there is one aspect of the national character that the Reagan years showed, it was that the present is a final restoration of an unreconstructed past. After two decades of instability and self-examination, the country wanted a father figure for comfort, and Ronald Reagan filled the bill. When he took office, the economy was in shambles, the nation's armed forces were demoralized, and democratic capitalism was in retreat worldwide. Reagan supported freedom movements worldwide, rebuilt the armed forces, cut taxes, and deregulated the economy. His economic reforms put the United States on a new path, and his international leadership led to an end of the Cold War.

Every presidential term opens or closes the doors of change in American society. Reagan's presidency signaled a major shift from Democratic to Republican Party dominance in political life. For most of the 1930s through the 1960s, the Democrats were preeminent, controlling the principal elective institutions in Washington and the states. In the 1970s, Democratic hegemony came in for scrutiny. By 1980, the Democrats' seemingly commanding posture began to unravel. Reagan won two elections, the GOP captured control of the Senate, and the conservative message began to trickle down to the state level.

In his last address to the American people, Ronald Reagan asked a rhetorical question about the "shining city" that was the American political experiment. "And how stands the city on this wintry night? More prosperous, more secure and happier than it was eight years ago." Ronald Reagan not only changed the country, he changed the world. He showed in his rhetoric and character that the centuries-old ideas of the founders of the American republic were as relevant as at any time in the past.

As *Newsweek* put it, Reagan embodied "America as it imagined itself to be—the bearer of traditional Main Street values of family and neighborhood, of thrift, industry and charity instead of government intervention."[60] The nation could neither repeat its past nor leave it behind. After intervening in foreign conflicts, the country turned inward, seeking comfort from middle-American values with a dash of California cool. "So we beat on against the current," wrote F. Scott Fitzgerald at the end of his novel about another age in America, "borne back ceaselessly into the past."

6

A Thousand Points of Light

The Twenty-Second Amendment to the U.S. Constitution stipulates that no one can be elected president more than twice. Since its adoption in 1951, the prohibition has been used only on generally well-liked Republicans, first Dwight Eisenhower in 1960 and then Ronald Reagan in 1988. An effect of the amendment is that it renders the president a "lame duck" in his last two years in office. Official Washington knows that the president's days are numbered, and so the permanent residents are less inclined to cultivate good will or displeasure from the White House. The lame duck syndrome afflicted Ronald Reagan's last two years in office when a combination of the term limitation and the Iran-Contra scandal drained the lifeblood out of his presidency.

Democrats regained control of the U.S. Senate in 1986 and joined their colleagues in the U.S. House to dictate the domestic agenda to the White House. The president had to accept legislation he would have preferred to veto, like the plant-closing law that required companies to give sixty-five days' notice to their workers before shutting down a facility. The law was a slam on the laissez-faire capitalism and free market idealism so dear to the heart of the GOP. In 1988, Congress overrode Reagan's veto of the Civil Rights Restoration Act. The president called it a "quota bill," but in suffering a veto override he further alienated African Americans from the party of Abraham Lincoln and the Emancipation Proclamation. The political initiative shifted from the White House to Congress, and it became harder for Reagan's nominees to high administrative offices to be confirmed.

The zenith of this conflict, which was institutional as well as personal, came in September of 1987, when Justice Lewis Powell announced that he would retire from the Supreme Court. Reagan had already elevated William Rehnquist to Chief Justice, and appointed Sandra Day O'Connor and Antonin Scalia to the high court. Powell was a "swing vote," often casting the deciding vote in 5-to-4 decisions.[1] To tip the balance of power in favor of the conservatives, Reagan nominated Robert Bork, a District of Columbia federal appeals judge known for his articulate and outspoken convictions. If confirmed, Bork would be the nation's 104th Supreme Court justice and a reliable vote for strict interpretation. The nomination set the stage for one of the biggest political battles of the decade.

Robert Bork was born in 1927; he earned a law degree at the University of Chicago, and subsequently taught at Yale Law School. There he became one of the best-known conservative jurists in the country, opposing abortion and gay rights while favoring the death penalty. His writings and legal decisions made him one of the most articulate critics of the Warren Court and of the liberal drift of the judiciary. Bork served as solicitor general of the United States, the lawyer representing the United States before the Court, and was called upon by President Richard Nixon to fire the Watergate special prosecutor. His record inspired either passionate devotion or vitriolic disdain.[2]

Democrats Edward Kennedy and Joe Biden immediately announced their opposition to Judge Bork.[3] As his confirmation hearing approached, liberal and conservative groups spent an unprecedented $20 million in a campaign to either disparage or laud the nominee.[4] If his appointment had come one year earlier, at the time of the Rehnquist promotion and Scalia nomination, Bork almost certainly would have been confirmed. Because of Iran-Contra, Reagan no longer had the solid support, either among the general public or on the Hill, that he enjoyed earlier. From the time the Senate Judiciary Committee began its hearings in mid-September until the final vote, opposition to Bork gathered strength.

In five days of televised testimony, which was the longest since public hearings on judicial nominees began in 1939, Bork did not do a great deal to help his case.[5] He seemed to equivocate from his position of "original intent." According to this doctrine, courts can protect only those liberties guaranteed as rights under the Constitution; all other liberties are subject to limitation by the legislative branch. Throughout his career, Bork was highly critical of the judicial activism of the Supreme Court in cases involving abortion, affirmative action, and civil rights. The courts, he said, should not thwart the will of popularly elected lawmakers. For example, Bork had written that the Fourteenth Amendment should apply only to race, and not to gender issues. Yet in his testimony, the judge said equal protection should apply to women.[6] As he tried to moderate some of his positions to be acceptable to Democrats in Congress, Judge Bork alienated his supporters and further infuriated his detractors. All parties acknowledged that Robert Bork was one of the most astute legal scholars in the country; the American Bar Association gave him its highest rating, "exceptionally well-qualified." But the credentials did not endear him to the Senate majority.

After weeks of testimony, the Judiciary Committee voted 9 to 5 against confirming Bork. Most observers expected the judge to withdraw after the vote, but Bork decided to soldier on. Though he was disappointed in his wavering support in Congress and at the White House, Judge Bork thought that a crucial principle of judicial independence from politics was at stake. On October 23, 1987, the Senate voted 58 to 42 against the nomination of Robert Bork to the U.S. Supreme Court.[7]

The day after Bork's repudiation by the Senate, President Reagan vowed, "My next nominee for the court will share Judge Bork's belief in judicial restraint."[8] That nominee, Douglas H. Ginsburg, had to withdraw after he admitted smoking marijuana as a member of the Harvard Law School faculty. The third candidate, Anthony Kennedy, was a moderate who easily won confirmation given the carnage from earlier nominations.

Watching this congressional savaging from the sidelines was Vice-President George Herbert Walker Bush, who first came to Washington in 1966 as a congressman from the seventh district in Houston, Texas. Since that time, he had been ambassador to the United Nations, chairman of the Republican National Committee, chief liaison of the U.S. Office in China, director of the Central Intelligence Agency, and as vice-president, heir apparent to the Reagan legacy. The hauteur of Democratic questions to Robert Bork was familiar to him. In the entire time he had been in Washington, the Democratic Party was dominant in the U.S. Congress, and Republicans succeeded only when they compromised and cooperated with the majority. Bush's tenure as chairman of the Republican National Committee coincided with the Watergate scandal, and he was faced with the unenviable task of rebuilding morale in the dispirited party after the scandal.

The same month Robert Bork was rejected, George Bush made his announcement to run for president. As a high school band played "The Yellow Rose of Texas" at the Hyatt Regency Hotel in Houston, the candidate took the podium to declare that he had no plans to go off in "radical new directions." He affirmed that his candidacy offered the country "steady and experienced leadership."[9] From the beginning, the Republican nomination was Bush's to lose. In the months leading up to the announcement, the vice-president enlisted more big-name supporters, raised more money, and built a national organization. He also hired a thirty-three-year-old campaign manager named Lee Atwater, who would subsequently be characterized by *Esquire* magazine as "all blood on the floor and don't look back."[10]

In spite of the hype, something was still not right for the Bush campaign. Bush's candidacy was less about abstract principles and ideas than about loyalty and honesty. For conservatives enamored with Reagan's soaring rhetoric and ironclad convictions, the vice-president seemed to come up short. *Newsweek* followed up Bush's announcement with a cover story entitled "Fighting the Wimp Factor." "Bush suffers from a potentially crippling handicap—a perception that he isn't strong enough or tough enough for the challenges of the Oval Office."[11] Conservative columnist George Will went even further by calling the newly announced candidate "Ronald Reagan's lapdog." The criticism, along with the widening Iran-Contra controversy, took its toll.

Five candidates besides Bush declared for the GOP nomination in 1988. Congressman Jack Kemp from New York and former Delaware governor Pierre DuPont IV declared themselves to be the leaders of the "ideological" conservatives, while Pat Robertson led the "religious" conservatives. Former secretary of state Alexander Haig and Bob Dole, senator from Kansas, were national leaders with high visibility. Dole was the more formidable opponent. He ran as Gerald Ford's vice-presidential running mate in 1976, and briefly entered the Republican presidential primaries in 1980.

The first test for all the candidates came in Iowa, and from the beginning the Bush campaign was in trouble. Farmers were struggling with low prices and bankruptcies, and the candidate's connection with Reagan was a liability. Bob Dole, on the other hand, was from nearby Kansas and campaigned under the slogan "I'm one of you." At his announcement for the presidency in his hometown of Russell, Kansas, Dole declared that he would be "sensitive to the needs of the left-out and the down-and-out in our society."[12] He privately jabbed at Bush, declaring that, unlike the vice-president, he was not the silver-spoon candidate in the field.

Then, as so often happens in American politics, an unexpected event changed the whole campaign. CBS anchorman Dan Rather approached George Bush about doing a "candidate profile" for the evening news broadcast. The two had known each other since the 1960s, and Rather had even been a guest in the Bush home. The relationship between the two men was cordial and Bush agreed the exposure would help. But word soon leaked back to the Bush campaign that Rather's intentions this time were malevolent; he wanted to paint the candidate with the brush of the Iran-Contra scandal. Media advisor Roger Ailes recommended Bush go ahead with the interview, but prepped him on how to handle the questions.

The vice-president sat for the on-camera interview at his desk in the Dirksen Senate Office Building. One of the conditions of the appearance was that it be done live, so CBS could not edit any of the comments. As an introduction, CBS aired a background piece alleging that the vice-president was not being truthful about how much he knew of the Iran-Contra arms-for-hostages meetings. CBS anchorman Dan Rather opened the interview by pushing questions that accused Bush of being present at discussions where the Iranian arms deal was discussed. Rather jabbed, and Bush responded. "It's been looked at by the Tower Commission," Bush said, and then he mentioned he had been "totally vindicated" in sworn testimony. But the CBS anchorman demanded, "Let's talk about your record."[13]

Questions followed on Bush's activities, and finally the accusations aroused his ire. He flashed a question back to the anchorman: "How would you like it if I judged your whole career by those seven minutes when you walked off the set in New York?"[14] The question left Rather in a pained silence. Several months earlier, when the anchorman was on location in Miami, the newscast was delayed by the U.S. Open tennis championships, and Rather stormed off the set in anger for more than seven minutes. The CBS newsman tried to shake off the comment, but the damage was done. George Bush, World War II veteran, successful businessman, and appointed government official was no "wimp"; instead, he was the man who vanquished Dan Rather.

The exchange boosted Bush's campaign, particularly among conservatives who despised the mainstream media and Dan Rather in particular. Yet the CBS interview did not have an immediate effect in Iowa. On February 8, the final tally read 57 percent for Dole, 25 percent for Robertson and his "invisible army" of conservative evangelical Christians, and 19 percent for Bush.[15] Iowa was a state where the vice-president defeated Ronald Reagan in 1980; eight years later he failed to take a single one of the state's ninety-nine counties. Moreover, the idea that George Bush was Ronald Reagan's unanointed successor went without notice by Iowa's voters.

In New Hampshire, Bush was helped by the experience and guidance of that state's governor, John Sununu, as well as the negative campaign ads of Lee Atwater and Roger Ailes. One of the more devastating ads was entitled "Straddle," for its two-faced image of the senator and its audio message that Dole had waffled on defense, oil-import fees, and the raising of taxes. Polls showed that the contest was close between Bush and Dole, so in the last week the vice-president received important endorsements and campaign help from Barry Goldwater. On February 16, Bush swamped Dole 38 percent to 28 percent. Robertson followed his surprising Iowa second-place finish with a disappointing fifth.

After the victory, Bush made a live split-screen appearance with NBC anchorman Tom Brokaw and Senator Robert Dole. When asked if he had anything to say to the man he had just beaten, Bush responded, "No, just wish him well and meet him in the South." Brokaw then turned to Senator Dole and asked if there was anything he wanted to say to the vice-president. "Yeah," Dole said, his eyes flashing with anger, "stop lying about my record."[16] The dark side of Bob Dole emerged to create a ripple effect in the subsequent primaries. The interview revived a reputation for nastiness that the Kansas senator had tried to live down. Dole scored his last two victories in South Dakota and Minnesota, but they were inconsequential because of Bush's triumph in South Carolina, and then across the South. On April 26, George Bush locked up the nomination by winning the Pennsylvania primary.

The race for the Democratic presidential nomination in 1988 was a story of who was not running and who managed to stay in the competition to the end. Three of the Democrats' best candidates, New York Governor Mario Cuomo, Senator Sam Nunn of Georgia, and Senator Ted Kennedy of Massachusetts, all chose not to run. The frontrunner label fell to former Colorado Senator Gary Hart. In his first try in 1984, Hart won more than 1,200 convention delegates, and spent the next three years cultivating ties to traditional Democratic constituencies like organized labor and issuing a host of major policy statements. Gary Hart, age fifty, announced his quest for the presidency on April 13, 1987, at the foot of the Rocky Mountains with a promise as lofty as the backdrop. His campaign would be to revive a sense of national purpose: "All of us must try to hold ourselves to the very highest standards of integrity and ethics."[17] Immediately he was beset by a host of angry creditors who complained that he was late in paying off his campaign debts from four years earlier.

Hart began as the frontrunner with everything in his favor. Polls showed him not only winning the Democratic nomination, but even beating George Bush in a hypothetical matchup.[18] Seven other Democrats entered the fray. Along with Hart were Washington politicians like Joseph Biden, the senator from Delaware; Richard "Dick" Gephardt, House leader from Missouri; Al Gore, senator from Tennessee; and Paul Simon, senator from Illinois. Two governors, Bruce Babbitt from Arizona and Michael Dukakis from Massachusetts, were in the race, along with the Reverend Jesse Jackson.

On the day Gary Hart formally announced for the presidency, a profile of him in *Newsweek* magazine made passing reference to his troubled twenty-eight-year marriage to his wife, Lee, and to rumors of infidelity. "The Hart marriage has been a long but precarious one, and he has been haunted by rumors of womanizing."[19] When confronted with the hearsay that he was unfaithful, Hart challenged reporters to follow him around, declaring that they would be "bored." Within days, reporters at the *Miami Herald* received an anonymous phone call from a woman who said, "Gary Hart is having an affair with a friend of mine."[20]

The newspaper subsequently sent reporters to Washington on a tip that Senator Hart was having a rendezvous with a woman other than his wife. The *Herald* reported on May 3 that Hart hosted Donna Rice, a twenty-nine-year-old model and actress, over the weekend while his wife was in Colorado. Hart protested that he was a victim of inaccurate reporting, and maintained that he had done nothing immoral. Instead, he challenged the paper's ethics in publishing the story without proper verification. But it was too late; other media began to raise questions about Hart's credibility, and on May 8, 1987, the Colorado senator quit the race. He would return in December of 1987, but without effect. The damage to his reputation was too much for him to overcome.

Hart's departure left the Democratic race without a frontrunner, and the remaining candidates were disparagingly labeled the "seven dwarfs" by the now-vigilant press. Shortly afterward, Joseph Biden's campaign was under scrutiny when he was found to have plagiarized a speech from British Labour Party leader Neil Kinnock. The investigation revealed that Biden had earlier been guilty of a similar type of plagiarism when in law school. These misrepresentations resulted in his withdrawal.

Biden's exit was engineered by John Sasso, the campaign manager for Massachusetts Governor Michael Dukakis. Sasso provided the media with videotaped copies of Biden's plagiarism, and then lied about doing so. Later, the campaign manager resigned for his indiscretions, and the whole affair had the collateral effect of shining the spotlight of public attention on the Dukakis campaign. The

Massachusetts governor benefited from the exposure. Michael Dukakis was the son of Greek immigrants, and as a two-term governor, he had executive experience and a television persona his competitors lacked. He took credit for his state's economic comeback, the "Massachusetts Miracle," and presented his points in a calm, credible way that recommended him on important issues.

All the Democratic candidates migrated to Iowa with the exception of Al Gore, who declared that the caucuses there were unrepresentative of primary voters nationally and volunteered that his campaign would focus on primaries in the South. The favorite in Iowa was Dick Gephardt, from nearby Missouri, who appealed to labor and farm voters. He won with 31 percent of the vote, narrowly ahead of Paul Simon's 27 percent and Michael Dukakis's 22 percent. In New Hampshire, Dukakis capitalized on his regional appeal to take a 36 percent to 20 percent victory over Dick Gephardt. "Although Iowa and New Hampshire got the Democratic race off to a muddled start, there were hints soon afterward that Dukakis and Jackson would be the two finalists," since each ran either first or second in the pre-"Super Tuesday" primaries of Minnesota, Maine, and Vermont.[21]

The Super Tuesday contests involved states from New England to Hawaii, including the crown jewels of the South: Texas and Florida. To the chagrin of Al Gore, who hung his candidacy on winning the southern states, Jesse Jackson ran strongest in the region. Dukakis won the most delegates on that day, and the most states; but at sunset, no clear winner appeared. Three candidates, Dukakis, Gore, and Jackson, maintained momentum as other candidates fell back or quit the race. When the candidates moved north into the industrial Midwest, Dukakis appeared to have the inside track, but he lost two big states (Illinois and Michigan), and for the first time, Democrats seriously considered that they might nominate the nation's first African American for president.[22] Jesse Jackson was exceeding expectations, even though he was seen largely as a protest candidate. Before the Wisconsin primary on April 5, Jackson found himself under intense press scrutiny for comments he had made about New York Jews and writing a letter of support to embattled Panamanian leader General Manuel Noriega. On primary day, Dukakis won all but one county in Wisconsin in a decisive 48 percent to 28 percent victory over Jackson. When the Massachusetts governor followed this up with a convincing victory in New York and Pennsylvania, the nomination was his.

At the convention Michael Dukakis received the endorsement of all his former opponents, Paul Simon, Dick Gephardt, and Bruce Babbitt—but not Jesse Jackson. Reverend Jackson demanded rule changes on the selection of delegates, the party platform, and serious consideration for the vice-presidential slot before he would pledge allegiance to the party's nominee. Jackson won some concessions on the first two issues, but none on the last. On July 12, Dukakis selected Lloyd Bentsen of Texas as his running mate, something Jesse Jackson learned about secondhand from a reporter.

The 1988 general election contest was compared to that of 1960, when Massachusetts Senator John F. Kennedy ran with Texan Lyndon Johnson against

Republican Vice-President Richard Nixon. The rematch was Massachusetts Governor Michael Dukakis with Texan Lloyd Bentsen against Republican vice-president George H. W. Bush. The "Boston-to-Austin" connection inspired Democrats once again, and for the first time since the convention, Dukakis was in the lead. He would not stay there very long.

The headlines from the August 15–18 Republican convention could not match the Democrats for drama. The main surprise for the GOP was that George Bush passed over better-known prospects to choose Dan Quayle of Indiana as his vice president. Quayle's Vietnam draft deferment came in for early scrutiny, but he had the virtue of having a solid, conservative voting record that delighted long-time supporters of Ronald Reagan who were concerned about Bush's tepid ideological convictions.

To reassure his critics Bush began using a phrase in the New Hampshire primary, and throughout the campaign, not to raise taxes. In his acceptance speech at the convention, a passage penned by his leading speechwriter, Peggy Noonan, was destined for immortality.[23]

I'm the one who will not raise taxes. My opponent says he'll raise them as a last resort, or a third resort. But when a politician talks like that, you know that's one resort he'll be checking into. My opponent won't rule out raising taxes. But I will. And the Congress will push me to raise taxes and I'll say no. And they'll push, and I'll say no, and they'll push again, all I can say to them is: "Read my lips, No new taxes."

The phrase, delivered with seemingly great conviction and passion, became one of the most prominent sound bites played by the media after the convention. It would return to haunt George Bush as president.

In another part of his acceptance speech at the Republican convention of 1988, the nominee explained the GOP's difference with the Democratic Party in a memorable metaphor. The American tradition, he asserted, emphasized participation in community and voluntary associations, rather than relying on government. The tradition of "the Knights of Columbus, the Grange, Hadassah, the Disabled American Veterans...the union hall, the Bible study group...a brilliant diversity spread like stars, like a thousand points of light in a broad and peaceful sky."[24] Bush's well-crafted speech solidified his reputation and moved him into a clear lead in the polls, which he never relinquished.

After any political campaign is over, it is easy to see that a number of mistaken assumptions and small decisions made early in the process determined the outcome. For Michael Dukakis there were three miscalculations in 1988 that led to his defeat: (1) he underestimated his opponent, (2) he failed to respond adequately to the Bush attack ads, and (3) he failed to raise issues that could have led to his victory in the fall.

Next to Ronald Reagan, the Democrats saw the vice-president as a humbler politician, who looked very much like a man of straw. They saw him as a man with a good résumé, but without election experience. Lloyd Bentsen, the vice-presidential candidate for the Democrats, defeated Bush for the U.S. Senate in 1970, and the thinking was that the pair would do the same thing eighteen years later. The objective of the Bush campaign team was to counter this image of their man. They did so under the direction of Lee Atwater, the hard-driving political consultant from South Carolina who updated the art of attack politics, and Roger Ailes, the man who made television ads memorable. Voters seemed to accept the negative campaign ads as long as the subject was the candidate's record and not his person, but even personal attacks were permissible if they related to presidential roles. For example, filmed footage of Michael Dukakis circling the lot of a General Dynamics plant with a helmet on his head as he waved from the turret of an M-1 battle tank was turned into a GOP attack ad that pointedly declared: "And now he wants to be our commander-in-chief."[25]

Another ad panned the littered and polluted waters of Boston Harbor, explaining that Michael Dukakis was responsible for the mess. The voiceover of pictures showing a procession of men in regulation prison outfits moving through a revolving gate declared that the governor had vetoed the death penalty and given furloughs to "first-degree murderers." The policy of furloughing prisoners left the most lasting impression on the electorate. In the hands of the Bush team the copy of the "Revolving Door" was devastating.[26]

As governor, Michael Dukakis vetoed mandatory sentences for drug dealers. He vetoed the death penalty. His revolving-door prison policy gave weekend furloughs to first-degree murderers not eligible for parole. While out many committed other crimes like kidnapping and rape. And many are still at large. Now Michael Dukakis says he wants to do for America what he's done for Massachusetts. America can't afford that risk.

Prison furloughs would leave the most lasting legacy after the election was over.[27] The Bush media team found out about an African American Massachusetts prisoner named Willie Horton, who had been convicted for the murder and dismemberment of a teenage gas station attendant. Sentenced to life for first-degree murder and ineligible for parole, Horton was one of four prisoners given weekend furloughs in the first two terms of Dukakis's governorship. While out, the convict made his way to Oxen Hill, Maryland, where he held a twenty-eight-year-old man captive with repeated beatings and stabbings, and then assaulted and raped the victim's fiancée. The fact that Horton was black made the ad devastating and controversial, but it was also effective in debunking Dukakis's record.

The Republicans, not the Democrats, began to fill in the gaps of voter knowledge about Michael Dukakis. The picture was not pretty. He was a "card-carrying" member of the American Civil Liberties Union, identified as the group opposed to prayer in public schools.[28] He vetoed a Massachusetts death penalty bill. He used the First Amendment to justify stopping a legislative bill that required school children to recite the Pledge of Allegiance. As he explained his Pledge of Allegiance veto decision on television, with members of the Harvard

Law School faculty behind him, a grizzled Democratic campaign veteran was heard to mumble, "He's won the votes from fifty constitutional lawyers, and lost them from fifty million Americans." Dukakis supported gun control and had a weak record on defense spending.

On the stump, Bush took to the attack. Amid a sea of red, white, and blue flags, he said he was the only candidate who "believes in voluntary prayer in the schools" and "in the sanctity of human life." The experience in his own extended family was that "adoption was better than abortion." He traveled to Boston to receive the endorsement from that city's Police Patrolman's Association, saying, "Let's get tougher on criminals" and not "take away the guns of innocent citizens." He visited a flag factory in New Jersey and said he was proud to say the Pledge of Allegiance, unlike the "card-carrying" Dukakis.[29]

Before the election, experts were confident about which issues would surface in the campaign. They thought that "day care, parental leave and elder leave" would dominate. Others believed that "fairness" of the Reagan economic policies would be an issue. The post–Iran-Contra scandal should have been an important issue for debates, as well as continued funding of the Contra guerillas in Nicaragua. The defense budget for SDI, or "Star Wars," could have been an issue. None of these issues figured in the outcome. All the speculation resulted in "issues that weren't."[30] Instead, the talk was of "flags, the national guard and the pledge of allegiance."

Negative campaigning was not George Bush's style. He was a man known for being likeable, and all his life his success was due more to his manner, which instilled loyalty in others, than for any slashing style. Noblesse oblige, defined as the inferred responsibility privileged people have to act with generosity to those less privileged, has a long history in American politics, traceable back to George Washington, Thomas Jefferson, and Teddy Roosevelt. George Bush was part of the legacy. He came from old money, prep school at Andover, and college at Yale. As a young man, he had two prized virtues: athletic ability and the reputation for being a "regular guy." The last trait would always be with him, and with his style and popularity he was an easy person to like and follow.

Few saw that behind the shy manner and the easygoing style was some steel. This was a son who went against his father's advice to enlist in the Navy in 1942 after prep school, and that father, Prescott Bush, would later become a U.S. senator from Connecticut. The son was a man whose record upon discharge from the service included 1,228 hours of flying time, 126 carrier landings, and 58 wartime missions. This was a businessman who financed his first house of 800 square feet with an FHA (Federal Housing Administration) loan, and made his money as a high-risk independent oilman in Texas. This was a politician who won elective office as a Republican in Lyndon Johnson's and Sam Rayburn's Democratic state, and then went on to build the GOP into the majority party. In short, George Bush was hard working, fair, and loyal; and as vice-president he was criticized for that allegiance.[31]

In a meeting at the family home in Kennebunkport, Maine, Bush indulged in some self-analysis. "I have to become more like Ronald Reagan," he told his staff, "but I can't go all the way.... I can't surrender it to [others] like Reagan did."[32] The campaign which emerged from that meeting was the most slashing since "Give 'em hell, Harry," Truman's 1948 campaign against the "do nothing" Eightieth Congress. Bush improved as a candidate, but the most memorable moment of the fall campaign came not from the Bush campaign, but from Dukakis himself.

In the second presidential debate at Pauley Pavilion on the campus of the University of California at Los Angeles (UCLA), any remaining hope Dukakis had of winning the election was lost when he answered one question. The moderator, CNN's Bernard Shaw, had the first query for the Democratic nominee: "Governor, if Kitty Dukakis were raped and murdered, would you favor an irrevocable death penalty for the murderer?" In a detached and cold way, as if reciting an answer from a briefing book, Governor Dukakis said he did not favor the death penalty for the crime. The image of him rattling off statistics as he avoided the question persisted in the minds of the electorate.[33]

On November 8, voters elected George Bush by a 53 percent to 46 percent margin. Turnout was low, indicating that many people were disinterested in both candidates, but Bush still won forty states. The margin could be described as "convincing," but it was less than the two Reagan landslides. The Republican presidential candidate won eighteen of the top thirty media markets, and split evenly with the Democrats in four others. The Democrats gained seats in both houses of Congress, while losing the presidency, and the phrase "divided government" entered the permanent vocabulary of every political commentator.

It might have seemed that the election of George H. W. Bush was a third term for Ronald Reagan, but from the beginning the new president made it clear that he did not intend to operate in the shadow of the former one. Chief of Staff John Sununu announced to the press in December of 1988 that the new administration would have "a limited agenda," but even so Bush was determined to have a "kinder and gentler" approach to governing.[34] He opened his administration to press scrutiny. During the transition he held more press conferences than Reagan had in the previous two and one-half years. He also let it be known that Reagan appointees would not be automatically reappointed to their former jobs.

The Bush administration began on Friday, January 20, 1989, on the 200th anniversary of the inauguration of George Washington. The new president took the oath of office with his hand on the same Bible the first president used, as well as the Bush family Bible. He wore a business suit instead of the formal morning coat of his predecessor. Foreign policy drove the new administration almost from the beginning. The words in Bush's inaugural address proved prophetic. "A new breeze is blowing, and a world refreshed by freedom seems reborn.... The day of the dictator is over.... The totalitarian era is passing."[35]

Within six months of taking the oath of office, the Soviet Union began to unwind and communism worldwide began to collapse.

Lech Wałesa led Solidarity's triumph in Poland in June. Hungary's decision to open its border with Austria in the summer led to East Germans leaving in droves. Just one year earlier, Erich Honecker, the leader of Communist East Germany, stated that the Berlin Wall would be standing for another "fifty or even one-hundred years."[36] Few questioned his statement, but on November 9, 1989, jubilant Germans surged to the wall. "We are trying to read very cautiously and carefully the change in East Germany," said the new president, but Chancellor Kohl was more emphatic. On the phone with Bush he described the events going on in East Germany. "It has the atmosphere of a festival.... Without the U.S. this day would not have been possible.... Tell your people that!"[37] The stampede set the stage for a public collapse of communism and German reunification on October 3, 1990.

Czechoslovakia's "Velvet Revolution" began on November 17, 1989—fifty years to the day after Czech students held a demonstration to protest the Nazi occupation of their country. The latent protest began as a legal rally, but riot police stopped the students halfway in their march, and 167 people were injured in the ensuing melee. Workers' unions joined the students' cause, and groups began to demand the resignation of the communist government. Massive demonstrations of almost 750,000 people in Letna Park in Prague on November 25 and 26 and a general strike on November 27 proved fatal for the communist regime, and it collapsed without major bloodshed.[38]

As the winds of change blew over Eastern Europe, the people of Romania despaired of any revival in their land. Nicolae Ceausescu had successfully resisted all pressures for liberal reforms and adhered closely to communist orthodoxy and centralized administration at home. His secret police, the "Securitate," maintained rigid controls over free speech and the media allowing no internal opposition. In December 1989, Ceausescu ordered armed and security forces to the city of Timisoara, where demonstrators were chanting, "Down with Ceausescu," "Down with communism," and "God is with us." The protests spread to Bucharest, and on December 22, the army defected to the demonstrators.

The Ceausescus tried to flee to a waiting helicopter, but they were captured by the armed forces. All across the nation news of the collapse of the government spread, and people came out of hiding to celebrate. According to press reports, the charges against the couple included "genocide" of 60,000 people, destroying the country's economic and spiritual values, and trying to flee to claim $1 billion reportedly hidden abroad.[39] On December 25 the couple was hurriedly tried, convicted, and shot by a firing squad at Targoviste. Millions of Americans, off for Christmas holidays, watched as the bodies were displayed on television for the entire world to see.

The most remarkable images of the decade were associated with freedom in places where it was unthinkable just years before. Yet the collapse of communism was no well-ordered script, especially in the world's most populous country—China. One of Bush's first trips after his inauguration was to the People's Republic of China in March of 1989. The visit was supposed to be a sentimental return by the new president to remember a time when he headed the twenty-four-person U.S. liaison office after Richard Nixon opened negotiations with China. It did not turn out that way. Fang Li Zhi, a prominent dissident hated by the Chinese leadership, was inadvertently invited to a banquet hosted by Bush. The deputy vice premier mentioned this fact to the president in the limousine on the trip in from the airport. Bush expressed genuine diplomatic regrets, but explained that to change the guest list at such a late date would make for a far bigger issue. The incident showed that the Chinese were nervous about the burgeoning protests for democracy in their country.

There were many causes for complaints in the world's largest communist nation, including government corruption and a lack of citizen freedom. The precipitating event for an international crisis was the death of a beloved government official, Hu Yaobang. Most bureaucratic leaders in China were despised by the populace, but this one man was associated with generally popular policies, and for that reason his passing was a cause for grief. In late April 1989,

A Beijing citizen blocks tanks on the Avenue of Eternal Peace in Beijing during the crushing of the Tiananmen Square uprising. (© Reuters/CORBIS)

100,000 sign-waving protestors began to gather in Tiananmen Square to mourn Hu Yaobang's death and attend his funeral.[40] Soon their sorrow turned to rage. At first, mostly students occupied the square, but they were soon joined by people from all walks of life: teachers, doctors, factory workers, judges, and even police officers and soldiers.

Chinese television viewers were treated for three hours to the extraordinary sight of a government official being interrogated by ordinary students. The questions were on sensitive subjects, like corruption, beatings, deployment of troops, and isolation of the nation's top leaders from public accountability. Defiant and enthusiastic crowds of more than 100,000 marched through Beijing to demand more democracy, and smaller demonstrations spread to other cities. In the shame culture of China, the protests were a worldwide public humiliation for the government.

Deng Xiaoping, the mercurial leader of China, denounced the protestors as "counter revolutionaries" on April 26, but his sobriquet only had the effect of making the situation worse.[41] Hundreds of students began a hunger strike, wearing headbands that read "Starving for Democracy" and in full view of the world press. Soviet leader Mikhail Gorbachev's promise of openness and reform had a collateral effect in the world's largest communist nation. The ripple in China began to grow into a wave when Gorbachev arrived on May 15 for an official state visit. The students marched in Tiananmen Square carrying his picture and screaming their support for perestroika (restructuring). After Gorbachev left, the students stayed in the square to protest. As a result, on May 19, the government declared martial law to deal with the situation.

The army moved in to clear Tiananmen Square on June 4. Thousands of soldiers and tanks surrounded the protestors and then moved in firing submachine guns at those who refused to leave. Chinese students in the United States reacted with outrage at the news of the army's attack on pro-democracy demonstrators. When it was over, the estimate was that over 7,000 demonstrators may have died, and thousands more were wounded. The Chinese government hid the bodies so the actual death toll would never be known, but the images of the conflict were seared on the world's conscience. The picture of a single student dissident standing before a column of tanks to signal them to stop became a worldwide symbol of resistance to domestic tyranny.

The talk in Washington was of cutting the budget at home as the bills of the Reagan years came due with a vengeance. The U.S. budget deficit was $2.7 trillion, and service on the debt itself was $200 billion a year. The business of the 101st Congress revolved around the federal budget and its deficit. The red ink cast a pall over any attempt to articulate a domestic or social agenda. Instead, the discussion always returned to the deficit and its effect on the economy.

Publicly, President Bush refused to even discuss the possibility of a tax hike. In the face of red ink, he asked for a 50 percent cut in the capital gains tax in hopes of stimulating growth "Reaganomics" style. But unlike during the

Reagan years, when the president was able to win bipartisan support for some of his policies, George Bush found no cooperation across the aisle this time. He found that the Democrats, who regained control of the Senate in 1986, were in no mood to cut deals with the new Republican president.[42] The fragile coalition disappeared, and the legislature was unable to pass a crime bill, health care reform legislation, or any measure to address campaign finance reform. The budgets continued to foster huge controversy, with each political party blaming the other for the crisis.

The new president was able to keep his pledge of no taxes that first year by following the bipartisan tactics of the 1980s and extracting a promise from Dan Rostenkowski (D-Illinois) to wait a year before proposing a tax hike. As a result, Bush's first budget passed in record time. During his presidency, President Bush would use his veto forty-one times, with only one override. Oftentimes the threat of a filibuster by Republicans was enough to cause the Democrats to back down. But the budget impasse involved more than partisanship; the growing power of special interest groups contributed to the gridlock as well.

In the end, the budget battle had to be postponed—not resolved. If the economic picture continued to darken, then a second brokered budget would be impossible. By the year's end, the Democrats began to lay down markers for the upcoming round of negotiations. Democratic leader George Mitchell made it clear he would not entertain any proposals for cuts in the capital gains tax, and New York Senator Daniel Patrick Moynihan called for eliminating the Social Security tax, making reasonable budgets impossible. Overshadowing all this financial maneuvering was the prospect of an expensive bailout of the nation's badly mismanaged savings and loan industries.

The savings and loans (S&Ls), or thrifts, were financial institutions that invested most of their depositors' money in home mortgages. In the Reagan years, the thrifts were deregulated, and when the market in real estate boomed, especially in the southwestern United States, the S&Ls garnered huge profits for their clients. After 1985, S&Ls began to show signs of trouble and many began to fold. One of them, Silvarado Savings and Loan in Denver, Colorado, was associated with Neil Bush, the son of the president. In October of 1986, Neil Bush had extensive loans with Silverado, and he knew that the company had multiple big loans going sour and a credit rating so bad it could not even issue junk bonds on Wall Street.[43] To raise cash, the Silverado executives devised a scheme to loan money for real estate developments at prices for more than what the property was worth, with the investors buying Silverado stock with the excess.

In the fall of 1989, the Federal Deposit Insurance Corporation (FDIC) took over more than a billion dollars' worth of assets from Silverado Savings and Loan. The company was in freefall, and even though Neil Bush had resigned from the board of the S&L in 1988, the scandal lapped at the door of the Bush family residence in Washington, D.C. The president promised to stand by his family and not comment on the situation. "His [Neil's] whole problem," Barbara Bush wrote in her diary, "is that he is our son."[44] The S&L scandal became a political issue, and the Bush bailout scheme was personalized by the press when Neil Bush was called before a congressional committee. More importantly, no one seemed to know how much it would cost to fix the S&L problem.[45]

The satisfaction of watching communism collapse around the world was diluted by problems in the American hemisphere. This time the issue was Manuel Antonio Noriega in Panama, a ruler who celebrated President Bush's inauguration by publicly burning an effigy of Ronald Reagan.[46] The Central American dictator had been working with the CIA since 1967, but the crisis began some twenty years earlier when a military associate of Noriega accused the general of involvement in drug trafficking and the assassination of political opponents. The rumor was not without substance, and the prospect of humiliation made Noriega a dangerous adversary. President Ronald Reagan tried to oust Noriega through economic sanctions after two Florida grand juries indicted him on drug smuggling and racketeering charges. It did not work.

The general wore many hats. He was a huge operative in the Latin American drug trade, and was also being used by the United States to funnel arms to the Contra rebels in Nicaragua. Noriega had dealt with Cuba as well as Washington, and seemed to be loyal only to whoever paid him last. A badly kept secret was that for years the CIA, and policy makers in both parties, had winked at Noriega's drug dealing because they needed him as a conduit to pursue other policies in the region.

On May 7, 1989, Noriega nullified the results of an election that effectively ousted him.[47] International observers and journalists in Panama confirmed, the day after the voting, that intimidation, theft, and fraud were used by the government to control the results. Fundamental to George Bush's understanding of the world was his World War II experience of liberating the world from dictators. The president saw Manuel Noriega as yet another despot in need of chastening. On May 10, an opposition demonstration in the old sector of Panama City was halted, and members of Noriega's personal police force waded into the demonstrators with clubs and iron bars. Later Gillermo Endara, the opposition presidential candidate denied office by Noriega, showed reporters the stitches in his battered scalp. He spoke to the press from his wheelchair: "I blame Noriega for everything bad that has happened in the Republic of Panama."[48] He was not alone. The grisly scene had an effect on President Bush, who ordered more U.S. troops into the region to protect the Americans living in Panama and told the Joint Chiefs of Staff to put together a plan to invade Panama and oust Noriega.

President Bush followed a cautious path through diplomacy in the crisis which won praise from liberals and conservatives alike for his skill. By gradually increasing pressure on Noriega, the president redefined the issue as a conflict between democracy and dictatorship, rather than one of the superpower United States versus undermanned Panama. In an interview with the *Washington*

Times, Bush could barely contain his rage at the Panama leader. "You've had an election that was stolen right out from under the eyes of the people and the eyes of the world... you have 40,000 American citizens and quite a few American troops in Panama... and we have the vital interests of the Canal."[49]

In December, when a twenty-four-year-old U.S. Marine was shot at a roadblock and another American officer was beaten and his wife molested by Panamanian troops, Bush gave the word to invade. The invasion was set for one o'clock on the morning of Wednesday, December 20. Operation "Just Cause" took twenty-four hours, with the loss of twenty-four lives. The only problem in the operation was that Manuel Noriega could not be found. Finally, the papal nuncio Monsignor Sebastian Laboa announced that Noriega, wearing blue Bermuda shorts and a T-shirt, had asked for asylum. Television images of U.S. troops playing exceedingly loud rock music in front of the Vatican's embassy in Panama City to drive Noriega from his refuge and force him to surrender did little to improve the image of the United States as a bastion of freedom. After days of high-visibility negotiations, Noriega gave up, and by dawn on January 4, 1990, he was in a cell in Miami.[50] Less than two months later, news came from Nicaragua that Daniel Ortega and his Sandinista rebels had suffered a stunning setback at the polls. Democracy had been restored to both Panama and Nicaragua.

Among the more unpleasant aspects of life in 1989, given that the tension in the world had subsided, was the weather. In the middle of September, millions of people throughout the Caribbean and the United States watched in profound amazement as Hurricane Hugo traveled thousands of miles in undiminished intensity. At midnight on September 21 it slammed into Charleston, South Carolina, with peak wind gusts between 155 and 165 miles per hour and tides twenty feet above the mean sea level.[51] It was the most intense hurricane to strike Georgia and the Carolinas in 100 years. Almost 200 miles inland, Hugo still had 100 mph wind gusts as it roared through Charlotte, North Carolina, and into Virginia. At the time, Hurricane Hugo was the most expensive tropical storm to ever strike the United States, and caused the death of seventy-five people.

The next month, as the nation prepared to watch Game Three of the World Series between the San Francisco Giants and the Oakland Athletics, an earthquake measuring 7.0 on the Richter Scale rocked the San Francisco Bay area. The quake collapsed a portion of the Bay Bridge and a three-quarter-mile, double-decked section of the Nimitz freeway. It resulted in sixty-three deaths and nearly 14,000 injuries. Because of the World Series television coverage, millions of people watched what was happening in real time, with reruns and live coverage from the site. Property losses amounted to over 1,000 homes lost and nearly 14,000 damaged.[52]

For years experts had warned that such a catastrophe was inevitable, and their analysis of this one was not comforting. The epicenter for the quake was some fifty miles south of the heavily populated San Francisco and Oakland area. Had it been in the urban area, the results would have been devastating. In less than fifteen seconds of ground-shaking in an earthquake, the country was reminded that the worst was yet to come.

The earthquake was only one of several afflictions San Francisco bore. The decade of the 1980s was becoming known as the AIDS (Acquired Immune Deficiency Syndrome) decade. In 1981 the country had 100 AIDS cases; by the end of the 1980s it had 1 million infected. Some of the disease was among drug users and heterosexual couples, but most of it afflicted gay men. The devastation was part of a worldwide plague, with Africa suffering the most. The disease struck all ages and all social classes.

Unfortunately for George Bush, the most riveting problem in Washington remained the cost of government domestic programs. The issue remained divided government, and by 1990 it was clear that the Democrats on the Hill were in no mood to compromise on the budget. Hanging over the negotiations that year was the Gramm-Rudman-Hollings Act of 1985. The law mandated automatic budget cuts in case Congress was unable to meet targets. Although most provisions of the law were declared unconstitutional by the Supreme Court in 1986, members of Congress sought to live up to the spirit of the bill by meeting its targeted estimates. The problem was that forecasts for the fiscal 1991 budget deficits were twice, or more, than those mandated by the Gramm-Rudman-Hollings Act. Government spending for the world's largest democracy was at a standstill. The Democrats wanted Bush to raise taxes, and the White House wanted the Congress to cut spending.

In the ensuing clash, the president's disavowal of new taxes placed negotiations in a deadlock. The other abiding issue was the S&L crisis, which was growing into an economic catastrophe that had no equal in U.S. history. Approximately 1,000 S&Ls failed between 1980 and 1991, most of them at the end of this period. As the bills came due, the cost of bailing out the thrifts was estimated to be some $500 billion, and the federal budget deficit would soar as the government adopted a strategy of not allowing the largest banks to go under. The budget negotiations went forward under a cloud of uncertainty and mistrust.

On May 6, the congressional leadership in the budget negotiations met with the president and select members of the GOP leadership and White House staff in the president's living quarters.[53] The intimacy of the meeting was intentional in hopes of coming to an agreement. Democratic Senate Majority Leader George Mitchell asked Bush if he was prepared to negotiate on taxes, and the president replied that he was. The White House immediately issued a press release that declared that budget talks would begin "with no preconditions." The Democrats agreed to a continuing series of meetings, with the number of participants varying from the eight in the room at the residence that evening to as many as twenty-six in some of the negotiations. But the "no preconditions" agreement meant a tax increase was practically inevitable, and as a result the negotiations immediately went into a panic of finger-pointing.

On June 26, President Bush retreated from his "no new taxes" pledge. The agreement proposed increasing gasoline taxes by 12 cents a gallon, and cutting Medicare by almost $60 billion. Republicans objected to the tax hike, and Democrats criticized the cuts in Medicare. In September, with the deadline of October 1 as the beginning of the fiscal year looming, the negotiations entered the final stage. Bush delivered a personal televised plea for a compromise budget plan, but the situation became worse without agreement. Congress passed emergency appropriations measures that eventually led to a compromise agreement. In the final proposal, the top income bracket was raised from 28 to 31 percent, limited tax deductions for the wealthy were eliminated, the tax on gasoline was raised by five cents a gallon, and Medicare was cut by some $42.5 billion. Bush reluctantly accepted the plan.

In a subsequent interview, years after the storm of the agreement was past, Bush said that breaking his promise on taxes "played right into the hands of the opposition," as well as the conservative critics in his own party.[54] Republicans saw Bush's compromise decision as an ultimate act of betrayal, and confirmed for them that he was an illegitimate heir to the Reagan legacy. Some conservatives subsequently claimed that the tax hike caused the recession of the early 1990s, while others countered that the economy was already in a slide before the crisis. One thing was sure: the political fallout was devastating. Bush was sky-high in the polls after the Gulf War, so high that he was thought invincible for re-election in 1992. But his popularity began a decline in the face of the recession and the rebellion in the Republican ranks over his decision to go back on his tax pledge.

The legacy of Ronald Reagan was that a promise not to raise taxes had supplanted anticommunism as the rallying point for conservatives. The ideological party members saw the Bush decision as an incredible betrayal, instead of a necessary political compromise given the situation of divided government. The White House thought it was better to enter the election of 1992 as the bearer of tax hikes rather than as the architect of an economic recession. Unknown to all concerned was that George Bush would bear both burdens in the upcoming presidential election.

7

From a Distance

The defining event in George Bush's presidency came as a result of yet another dictator, this one much more dangerous than Manuel Noriega and destined to leave a larger legacy. Saddam Hussein had been a fixture in the bloody and unpredictable politics of Iraq since the early 1960s. He would provide not only President Bush but the entire host of Western democracies with their greatest crisis since Vietnam. The word most frequently used to describe Saddam, whose name means "one who confronts," was "brutal." Of the many examples available to illustrate this trait, one will suffice.

On July 18, 1979, five days into his new presidency, Saddam Hussein called a meeting of over 300 Baath Party senior leaders. Dressed in his military uniform, and smoking a Cuban cigar, Saddam listened as an announcement was read to the assembled group declaring the discovery of "a painful and atrocious plot" to overthrow the new leader. Hussein himself then stepped to the rostrum to introduce the plot's instigator, who appeared in person after a visit to the party torture chamber. "The people whose names I am going to read out should repeat the slogan of the party, and leave the hall."[1] He began to read, stopping occasionally to disclose part of a name, then light and relight his cigar without finishing. As Saddam went down the list, guards escorted the identified individuals outside. The fear in the room was contagious. Some wept, and all wondered if they were identified on the paper the Iraqi dictator held in his hand. Finally, the reading ended with some sixty-six names, and as Saddam continued to speak, he had to suddenly dab his eyes with a handkerchief. Fear gripped the room in a panic, and the assembly broke into loud sobbing.

At once members of the audience rose as one to shout, "Long Live Saddam," and declare that the dictator was being too lenient to the traitors, and should search out other conspirators. The wave of relief in the room was mixed with drenching wonder as to what would happen next. In the days that followed, everyone present would learn a new definition of loyalty. Saddam obliged senior party members and government officials to join him as they personally executed their former colleagues.

The effect of this, and similar incidents, was a mind-numbing fear throughout the country of Iraq. Silence was preferred; the averted glance replaced the straight stare. The savagery of Saddam's methods was supposed to make him invincible, and the terror worked with Machiavellian efficiency. The mere mention of his name inspired awe, and when mercy was granted—which was not often—Saddam's behavior could even engender a strange kind of gratitude. Only a very few brave Iraqis said anything, and their comments often earned them a spell in a camp for their pains. News of how awful the camp experience was rippled out from the families who suffered, resulting in an efficient, private compliance. The key to Hussein's power was the way the regime implicated ordinary people into the workings of the Baathist state. A European diplomat stationed in Baghdad once told a reporter from the *New York Times* that "there is a feeling that at least three million Iraqis are watching the eleven million others."[2]

Saddam's ruthlessness was the result of many things, some personal and some cultural. His rise to power capitalized on the centuries-old Sunni-Shia split, the Arab versus Persian religious and ethnic disputes, and the personal animosity Saddam Hussein had for Ayatollah Khomeini in neighboring Iran. While the Iraqis were led by fear, the Iranians had a divine reverence for Khomeini. Khomeini's ouster of the shah and leadership of the Iranian revolution of 1979 led to a protracted war between the neighboring countries from 1980 to 1988, dubbed the Iran-Iraq War.

In the fighting between contiguous states, Baghdad planned for a quick victory over Tehran. Saddam wanted oil, and he expected that when his armies invaded, the people in the Arabic-speaking area of Iran would respond by rising against Khomeini's fundamental Islamic regime. It did not happen that way, and after a time Iraq found itself bogged down in a stalemate of its own making. To avoid defeat in the conflict, Hussein sought out every possible weapon, including significant quantities of chemical weapons. From April to August 1988, the Iraqis used the iniquitous weapons to defeat the Iranians in battle. When the war was over, both sides suffered grievous losses. Estimates of casualty figures were unreliable, but the best ones suggest that more than one and a half million casualties resulted from the war between Muslim neighbors, and millions more were made refugees. The Iraqis suffered an estimated 375,000 dead and wounded, with another 60,000 troops taken prisoner. The Iranians had at least 300,000 dead, with 500,000 injured.[3] At the time of the war, Khomeini was said to have had a "martyr complex," with no qualms about sending his followers, including young boys, zealous for martyrdom, off to their deaths for his greater glory.

When it was over, the Iran-Iraq War settled none of the issues which precipitated the conflict. The borders and living conditions in the two states at the beginning of the war remained virtually unchanged. A cease-fire arranged by the United Nations put an end to the fighting, but it left the two sides open to pursue an arms race with each other and with nations in the region. By 1990, Saddam Hussein had the fourth largest military in the world, guarding the second largest deposit of ready oil reserves in the world.

Iraq is a large nation, approximately the area of the state of California, with a 1990 population of sixteen and one-half million people. After the Iran-Iraq War, Saddam faced a foreign debt of some $80 billion. He saw the solution to his economic dilemma, as well as one of its major causes, in his neighbor to the south. The emirate of Kuwait was first delineated by the British, who drew a line over the sands of the old Ottoman Empire without any inkling of the oil under the desert sands. In 1990, Kuwait was a nation with a land mass the size of New York State and a population of 1.7 million. It was little more than a gigantic oil well, which provided over 94 percent of the national revenue and resulted in no need for anyone to pay taxes.

Saddam Hussein opened his offensive against Kuwait by renewing a historic border dispute, declaring that he needed access to the oil fields and the islands of Warbaad Bubiyan. He charged that the Kuwaitis were "slant-drilling" into the lush Rumaylah oil field, the majority of which was in Iraqi territory. Saddam used the twisted logic of the Middle East to say that oil production was "a kind of war against Iraq," and when added to the $10 billion he borrowed from Kuwait for the Iran-Iraq War, the two excuses together justified his belligerence. On July 15, 1990, the U.S. Defense Intelligence Agency confirmed that a division of the elite Iraqi Republican Guard troops had begun moving to the Kuwait border. Within four days, some 35,000 Iraqi troops and 2,000 tanks from three divisions were within ten miles of the Kuwait border.

In 1990, Saddam Hussein commanded a splendid army. It numbered more than 1 million men under arms, with 5,000 battle tanks and more than 6,500 armored personnel carriers with 3,000 towed artillery and 500 pieces of self-propelled artillery.[4] When it invaded Kuwait, Iraq succeeded in surprising the entire world, but a careful reconstruction of events showed that Saddam had been bellicose for some six months before the invasion. The previous April, he announced that Iraq had advanced chemical weapons and would not hesitate to use them. "We will make the fire eat up half of Israel, if it tries to do anything to Iraq," he said.[5] The words had racial and religious overtones, reminiscent of threats Hitler made about the Sudetenland in the spring of 1938. In that earlier crisis the prize in Czechoslovakia was the same as Kuwait: oil. Saddam followed this rhetoric with another speech denouncing Kuwait, Israel, and Western imperialism.

Every time the Iraqi dictator said or did something provocative, Western experts counseled their governments not to overreact. The resulting hesitancy was construed in Baghdad as weakness. So on August 2, 1990, Iraqi military forces invaded and occupied Kuwait in twelve hours, almost without resistance. The emir fled the country in his Mercedes, making calls to world leaders along the way. The next day, Kimberly Ann Elliott authored an Op-Ed piece in the

New York Times that again counseled caution. She argued that broad-based economic sanctions by the world community would achieve an Iraqi withdrawal from Kuwait, and that any unilateral action by the United States would fail.[6] In the diplomatic parlors of New York, the tactful response was to wait him out. Saddam expected as much: some protest, but no real reaction. This time he was wrong.

Reports of human rights abuses by Iraqi forces reached the outside world almost as soon as troops occupied Kuwait City. The most sensational story was a September 5 report that the Iraqis were taking hospital equipment, turning off the life-support systems of patients, and removing babies from incubators. From the time this report reached the Western press, it became almost a truism for rallying support for war.[7] Journalists later called the accuracy of the stories into question, but their veracity could only be known after Saddam was driven from Kuwait. From the time of the occupation, Amnesty International reported widespread torture of persons in custody, the imposition of the death penalty, and execution of hundreds of unarmed Kuwaitis fleeing the country.

Saddam had taken a gamble, and confusion seemed to be the result. When President Bush received an eleventh-hour request from the emir of Kuwait for aid, he could offer no immediate help. Attempts to replace aggression with international understanding had a long history of failure in the Middle East, and this time was no different. Bush kept in touch with his ambassador at the United Nations, the Pentagon, and other world leaders most of that night. The next morning, the administration began to stir; it ended a policy, in place since the Iran-Iraq War, of accommodating Hussein. The president declared that he would settle for nothing less than total Iraqi withdrawal from Kuwait. But that night after hearing the invasion news, he wrote in his diary, "the country at this juncture doesn't really care."[8] Outrage from around the world gradually followed, and the United Nations passed the first of an eventual twelve resolutions condemning the invasion.

George Bush's preference for personal diplomacy sent him to the phone. In the five days after the invasion, he made a series of some four dozen calls to leaders around the world. He spoke to every national leader in the Western alliance, and to many in the Middle East. Fear was apparent from the outset; most of Saddam Hussein's neighbors were afraid they were next. No one nation had the will, or the military might, to oppose the Iraqi dictator. The American president vowed to defend Saudi Arabia and its oil reserves, speaking in Texan words reminiscent of the Alamo, that "a line has been drawn in the sand."[9] Bush met with British Prime Minister Margaret Thatcher in Aspen, Colorado. The lessons of the 1930s, with the failure to stop Hitler early and the accompanying policy of appeasement by Neville Chamberlain of the dictator, were very much on both their minds. Together, the two leaders worked out a plan to: (1) keep Israel away from the conflict, (2) persuade the Soviet Union to support the coalition, and (3) convince Saudi Arabia's King Fahd to invite Western military units into the region.

George H. W. Bush participates in a Gulf War briefing led by General Colin Powell. (Courtesy, George Bush Presidential Library)

Israel immediately agreed to keep a low profile unless it was attacked. The second part of the puzzle, support from the Soviet Union, proved surprisingly easy. By 1990, the economic situation in Russia had grown desperate, and Gorbachev had no choice but to ask Bush for aid just to keep the food situation from collapsing. Mutual need made for an immediate strong alliance. A joint declaration from Foreign Minister Eduard Shevardnadze and Secretary of State James Baker called for "an international cutoff of all arms supplies to Iraq" after "its brutal and illegal invasion."[10]

The Saudis proved more of a problem. When the shah of Iran fell in 1979, Jimmy Carter promised to send F-15s to Saudi Arabia as a show of support. He sent the planes, but left them unarmed. In discussions at the Pentagon with Prince Bandar, as a representative of the royal family, Secretary of Defense Dick Cheney presented impressive photographic evidence of Iraqi forces on the border of the Royal Kingdom of Saudi Arabia. Cheney said the United States was ready to help the Saudis "defend yourself from Saddam." The response from the prince was immediate and to the point: "Like Jimmy Carter did?"[11]

Bush and Cheney had access to unheard of intelligence. Saddam's military machine was partly a creation of the Western powers, and the United States knew its limitations. They also knew that Saudi and Egyptian leaders were eager to see an end to the dangerous Iraqi regime. The administration had some cards of its own, and Cheney began to play them. Saddam Hussein had lied to Saudi King Fahd, and Bush had a good personal relationship with the king, going back to his days as CIA director. Within the week, Saudi Arabia asked for help for its own reasons. As Prince Bandar said at the time, "He who eats Kuwait for breakfast is likely to ask for something else for lunch."[12] On August 7 the first U.S. forces, F-15 strike Eagle fighters from Langley Air Force Base in Virginia, landed in Saudi Arabia.

The president addressed the nation the next day. Bush had to walk a fine line between belligerence and appeasement, but his convictions were firm. Earlier in the week, when his aides were considering a number of options, Bush disembarked from his helicopter to address the waiting press. The choices, he explained with a wrinkled brow, were "wide open," but then he added grimly, "This will not stand, this aggression against Kuwait." In his public pronouncements on August 8, the president ruled out an immediate invasion of Kuwait, saying he would give economic sanctions imposed by the United Nations time to work, but he remained firm in saying that America sought the "immediate, unconditional and complete withdrawal of all Iraqi forces from Kuwait."[13]

Americans yearned for a diplomatic solution, and there was almost no debate over whether Saddam threatened national security. He did not. What he menaced was international stability and economic permanence. Europe and Asia were in greater jeopardy than the United States, so the president had to cut his cloth to fit the public mood. Any military deployment would be defensive, but no matter how low-keyed it was, the political significance was prodigious. American troops stationed on foreign sand meant war was imminent. Where Saddam had his adoring public, George Bush faced a fragile coalition in Congress and a hostile press. The differences were significant.

The military deployment was called "Desert Shield," and by the end of August, 80,000 allied coalition troops were in Saudi Arabia. The presidential phone calls resulted in a coalition of thirty-four nations, with the United States supplying about 85 percent of the military personnel. Defending the Kingdom of Saudi Arabia was a job for ground forces, not airpower, and each side moved to reinforce itself in the sand. Saddam Hussein raised the number on his side to 200,000, and Bush responded by calling up 40,000 reservists.[14] It was the first call-up of reserves in the United States since the Tet Offensive of 1968, and the criticism of administration policy was reminiscent of that bitter conflict. "This [decision] makes me doubt that you have either the courage or the character to meet the challenge of finding a diplomatic solution to this crisis," wrote one person to the *New York Times*.[15] Andrew Kopkind, the acerbic critic writing in *The Nation*, declared, "All Bush is doing is asserting America's post–Cold War role as the unopposable, nuclear-tipped world cop, enforcing rules of its own making for its own narrow, short-term interests."[16]

Across Pennsylvania Avenue, in Lafayette Park, signs and protestors decried the "blood-for-oil" buildup. In the executive mansion itself, the president worked at a frenetic pace. His personal physician described Bush as a "workaholic," and at age sixty-six he was busy as long as he was awake. He had arthritis in his shoulders, so nurses trained in physical therapy worked on the muscles of his neck and upper body at various times to relieve the stress. He seemed to gather strength as more countries shared the outrage he had for the injustice in the Middle East, but the domestic criticism was shrill and unending. Despite what he said about the "cancer" of deficits, they continued to grow, and in his own party Bush faced Republican dissenters who complained about his reneging on the no new taxes pledge. In the 1990 midterm elections, the Republicans lost one seat in the Senate and eight in the House. The elections, the deficits, and Middle East politics were inextricably intertwined.

The critics were still calling for sanctions in Iraq, but Bush had already told his advisors in private that he was not going to put half a million men and women "sitting on the sands of the desert waiting for sanctions to work."[17] In the weeks that followed the presidential announcement of a coalition deployment, both sides hardened their positions. By Thanksgiving 1990, Saddam Hussein had a ground contingent of approximately 680,000 men. The United States had 500,000 "boots on the ground," and with its allies, the numbers were about even.

The difference was in the technology and skill of the two armies. While the Iraqi military was hardened from years of battle, some of it practically hand-to-hand with the Iranians, it was suspect in other ways. The Americans relied on their training and the sophistication of their weapons. Not everyone thought the American approach would survive in actual combat. In 1981, James Fallows, who had been a speechwriter for Jimmy Carter, wrote a book entitled *National Defense*. Fallows argued that the nation's military was in danger of being borne away by a belief in complex and expensive technology that would prove unpredictable in combat.[18] Along with other critics, Fallows thought that all the computerized weapon systems would be useless in the blowing dust and burning sands of the desert. American military leaders were confident, but most of the tanks, helicopters, planes, and artillery—not to mention the men and women who operated them—were unproven in combat.

In early November, President Bush announced that the defensive military buildup now provided an offensive option, and "Operation Desert Storm" was in effect. The new strategy was to force Iraq out of Kuwait. Former secretary of Defense and later vice-president Dick Cheney recalled the mood at the time: "Diplomacy was easy in those circumstances."[19] Contributions to the coalition forces ranged from Singapore's thirty-man medical team to 45,000 troops, nine ships, and five tactical fighter squadrons from Britain. The United Nations passed Resolution 660, which authorized the use of "all necessary means" if Iraq did not withdraw.

With international public opinion behind him, George Bush turned to the U.S. Congress for final support. He wrote a letter to the leaders of both houses asking

President Bush and King Fahd participate in an Arrival Ceremony in the Royal Pavilion in Saudi Arabia and discuss the situation in Iraq. (Courtesy, George Bush Presidential Library)

for a resolution backing the war. The months of televised international debate gradually generated popular opinion at home in favor of intervention. On the television screen, Saddam Hussein's visage showed dark eyes set deep beneath an overhanging brow, a mustache and the countenance of a man untrustworthy. The Democratic-led opposition reluctantly followed suit after a fierce debate. Tom Harkin, a Democratic senator from Iowa, argued that "the reasons for us being there seem to change as the winds change," and that "sanctions will take time to have their full intended effect."[20] The supporting resolution passed the Senate by a 52-to-42 margin, while the House backed the president by a more convincing 250-to-183 margin. The joint congressional action was approved on January 12, 1991.

Among Americans there was considerable ambivalence about going to war. One legacy of a superpower is that it can prevail in battle and then suffer defeat in the court of world opinion. Americans in 1991 remembered that military victories in Vietnam were obliterated by protests at home. Their last memory of a wartime commander-in-chief was Lyndon Johnson being contradicted by reporters showing a different war in the field from the one being described in

Washington. The press used words like "quagmire" and "bogged-down" to warn the viewing public about the commitment, and the prospect of a protracted struggle haunted every Pentagon and White House briefing. The U.S. military buildup in Saudi Arabia was the largest deployment of American troops and supplies since Vietnam, and in terms of powerful weapons, it may have had no equal in all of military history—including the Normandy invasion. War was a last resort, and the proportionality of what the United States was about to do worried citizens, war planners, and the U.S. president. On the night before the invasion, George Bush invited the Reverend Billy Graham to stay in the White House. Before retiring, the president wrote in his diary, "Oh, God, give me strength to do what is right."[21]

The winds of Operation Desert Storm began howling across the sands of Kuwait and Iraq at 3:00 A.M. Baghdad time on January 17, 1991. At that hour the first two, of 100, cruise missiles targeted for the Iraqi capitol that night arrived in force. Fifty minutes later, fast-flying decoy drones reached Baghdad where the air defenses opened up on them firing indiscriminately. An armada of American planes appeared and followed radar beams back to their emission point and destroyed the hostile radar and missile facilities. After a time, the Iraqis took down their air defenses and did not turn the radar back on. Several weeks before the invasion, U.S. intelligence agents had successfully inserted a computer virus into Iraq's military to help disable Baghdad's air-defense system.

In the middle of the chaos, F-117 Nighthawk bombers appeared, and their first target was the twelve-story, antenna-tipped structure the Iraqis called the International Telephone and Telegraph Building in downtown Baghdad.[22] The building was the command-and-control center for the Iraqi military. The first 2,000-pound bomb penetrated the roof, and then two more Stealth bombers dropped two more 2,000-pound high-blast bombs through the holes, obliterating the building's top two stories. That first night, allied aircraft hit five command centers and presidential palaces throughout the country.

As the first bombs and missiles went off, the sky over Baghdad lit up with anti-aircraft fire. After Moscow, the Iraqi capital had the heaviest concentration of air defenses of any city in the world. Yet in fifteen minutes each F-117 pilot delivered his bombs precisely on target without incident.[23] One hour and twenty minutes behind the first ten F-117's, a second wave, twice as large, flew toward Baghdad on the moonless night. The planners used aerial photographs from spy satellites with image resolution so good that they could identify air ducts and other details on the targets. The Stealth pilots pinpointed not just rooftops, but the exact place on the roof where they wanted the bombs to hit. The bombs did not always cooperate, but most of the time the targeting was deadly. In the first three hours of Desert Storm, more than 400 combat planes, along with the 100 cruise missiles, hit targets across Iraq and Kuwait.

Now the media began to show their worldwide power and substantial reach. In Room 906 of Baghdad's al-Rashid Hotel, CNN correspondents Bernard Shaw, Peter Arnett, and John Holliman were seeing it all. They were the only

American network able to broadcast live during the bombardment, and they gave an exclusive and uncensored view of the war from behind enemy lines.[24] CNN ratings topped those of the three major networks and more than 200 U.S. affiliates dropped their network coverage to go live to the CNN feed. The filmed footage of bombs exploding in Baghdad and anti-aircraft fire futilely chasing drones, cruise missiles, and stealth aircraft in the night sky became the signature image of the war.

By dawn, the key parts of Saddam Hussein's military infrastructure were in shambles. Television coverage in Baghdad was constricted to one window of the al-Rashid Hotel, but the CNN broadcast showed columns of smoke rising from a number of buildings against the vast expanse of the sky. Morning television shows in America gathered reports from the Pentagon, State Department, and White House. Viewers watched briefings by military and civilian officials, and the press asked questions before an audience of millions. The mood could be described as one of "guarded optimism." In one glimpse, a sleep-deprived George Bush opened the door behind a reporter to say, "It's going well, the first reports are good," and then retreated back into a meeting.

To minimize casualties, U.S. General Norman Schwarzkopf pursued a strategy of continued air attacks for more than five weeks. The air war targeted a multitude of strategic sites as well as "targets of opportunity" on the ground. Like any war in American history, this one had its special sights and sounds, to be remembered in later years in a kind of blurred kaleidoscope of selections to stir the emotions. Because CNN had a dedicated line before the shooting started, the network was able to send back live pictures throughout the conflict. With instant satellite coverage for television and CNN's round-the-clock news service, there was nothing print journalists could do that television had not already done. The daily television fare became video footage of correspondents standing in front of their hotel in Dhahran, planes taking off and landing, and generals with pointers and maps.

The images came in waves. There were the blossoms of Quonset huts, ringed by camouflaged supplies. The nighttime sounds of aircraft landing behind reporters were mixed with the "thumbs up" signs of encouragement from the ground crews in the daylight hours, as fearsome-looking aircraft taxied for take-off. The print medium inserted more graphics of pictures, charts, and diagrams in a shameless imitation of their television counterparts. The result was visual over stimulation of a war that was increasingly antiseptic from the air. The weapons resembled something from a science fiction movie, with bombs programmed to sweep in windows, come in through air shafts to bunkers, and take out not just a bridge, but the crucial center span of the structure that rendered it permanently inoperable.

The weapons were called "smart bombs," and they seemed somehow appropriate for the world's reigning superpower. The aircraft that delivered them were so secret that the U.S. military denied their very existence for years before the war. Airplanes like the British Tornados and the F-117A Stealth fighters gave the 1,800 land- and carrier-based planes of the coalition force an advantage

The F-117 Stealth Fighter. (Courtesy, U.S. Air Force)

unmatched in previous conflicts. During Operation Desert Storm, F-117s flew approximately 1,300 sorties and scored hits on 1,600 high-value targets, most of which were in downtown Baghdad. When the cruise missiles worked in concert with the bombers, the effects were devastating and dramatic.

To protect the troops poised on the border in Saudi Arabia, the American military revealed yet another remarkable new weapon: the Patriot missile. The box-like, tubed missiles were designed to detect, target, and destroy incoming missiles that might be no longer than ten or twenty feet in length. Within hours of the start of the war, the Iraqis launched Scud missiles at Tel Aviv in Israel. Television viewers saw civilian casualties, emergency ambulance workers, and women with children wearing gas masks. The riveting question of whether the government of Israel would respond in kind, and risk fracturing the delicate alliance so cautiously constructed by President Bush, captured the viewing public. When the Israelis held off, Bush mollified them with the promise of Patriot missiles. Neither the civilian casualties nor the pounding he was taking at the hands of the U.S. coalition seemed to bother Saddam Hussein. The dictator predicted that the stealth aircraft would "be seen by a shepherd in the desert as well as by Iraqi technology, and [the Americans] will see how their stealth falls just like ... any [other] aggressor aircraft."[25]

The shepherds were about to get their chance. With complete air superiority, coalition forces disabled all of Iraq's command and control centers within two weeks. In the dazed aftermath of the bombing, Iraq had no communication between commanders in Baghdad and troops in the field. Allied forces pummeled airfields, aircraft bunkers, ammunition depots, oil dumping stations, and supply lines linking Baghdad with troops in southern Iraq and Kuwait. American intelligence officers who interviewed more than 1,400 Iraqi prisoners of war discovered that the dug-in forces at the front were demoralized and bitter at President Saddam Hussein for waging the war.

On Thursday, February 21, the world awoke to find that the Soviet Union was offering to mediate the conflict.[26] In a phone call between Bush and Gorbachev, the U.S. president declared that the Soviet plan was "unacceptable." The deadline for Saddam to leave Kuwait was set for 8 P.M., Baghdad time, on February 23, Day 38 of Operation Desert Storm. Earlier, a Brookings Institution military analyst had presented figures that implied the coalition forces would suffer casualties of between 32,000 and 48,000 troops.[27] The news media picked up on the number, and the country braced for the worst. Iraq's infantry was dug in behind a ten-foot-high berm along the border, with the elite 125,000-man Republican Guard in southeastern Iraq and northern Kuwait. The American troops treated their enemy with respect; after all, the Iraqis were experienced from the Iran-Iraq War in the use of chemical and biological weapons. One artillery executive officer recalled, "We knew they outnumbered us in tubes by six to one...[and] they followed the Soviet doctrine in artillery, which included the principle that the primary target for artillery was the enemy's artillery."[28] The most poignant memory for many soldiers was the unbearable tension of waiting for the operation to begin.

The "liberation of Kuwait," or "G-Day" for the troops, began on February 23 and lasted 100 hours. Marines crossed the border into Kuwait and the left flank of the U.S. Army invaded southern Iraq. General Schwarzkopf feigned a frontal attack by using a large number of forces to launch an amphibious attack and hold the Iraqi army in place, then moved the bulk of his forces west and north in a major use of helicopters and tanks to attack the Iraqis from behind. The five weeks of air attacks had greatly demoralized the Iraqi front-line troops. An Iraqi lieutenant's war diary reflected the way he felt during the air attacks. "Death was yards away from me...the missiles, machine guns and rockets didn't let up...one of the rockets hit and pierced our shelter...one tank burned and three others...were destroyed...time passed and we waited to die."[29]

Experts predicted that Iraq would use nerve gas against American troops, and retired officers on television warned viewers of the weather, morale, and unknown factors of the battle. The American troops were eager to prove to the world that their confidence in themselves, their estimation of the enemy, and the chances of victory in approaching battle were justified. "Oorah, let's do it sir." "This is it." "Let's kick some ass." As one participant recalled, "we just figured that the closer we got to Kuwait, the sooner the fight would start...the sooner we could kick Saddam's butt... and the sooner we did that, the sooner we could all go home to enjoy warm showers, cold beer, wives and girlfriends."[30]

Within three hours of the start of the ground war, the reports coming in to General Schwarzkopf's headquarters were both encouraging and harrowing.[31] The encouraging part was the 1st and 2nd Marine divisions were making far better progress than expected, and they had already taken more than 1,000 prisoners of war. The news in Kuwait City was less sanguine; Iraqi troops were torturing and killing civilians before leaving the city. The Iraqis were displaying a genius for bad publicity. They not only committed atrocities, but they advertised them and left a record.

On the battlefield, American soldiers showed ferocity reminiscent of their forefathers. This time they had the best equipment and training of any army on the field. Tank commanders in the 3rd and 1st Armored Division found that their M1A1 Abrams tanks could see, identify, and shoot the Iraqis far beyond the Iraqi tank-gun range. The front-line enemy forces were quickly killed or surrendered. After the war, the House Armed Services Committee estimated that the Gulf War air campaign killed 9,000 Iraqis and wounded another 17,000. The guess was that as much as 30 percent of Saddam's troops simply deserted. The numbers did not matter, because the Iraqis were no match for the motivated Americans and their allies. Servicemen took thousands of Iraqi prisoners, ultimately totaling 80,000, many of the prisoners chanting "M-R-E" when they surrendered. The acronym was military slang for "Meals Ready to Eat," and it was not unusual for mobile American forces to give food and water to the Iraqis who stood beside the road with their hands in the air, and then move on. Lieutenant Colonel Keith Alexander, of the 1st Armored Division, declared on the first day of the war, "We were the New York Giants scrimmaging the Jayvees from some high school called the Iraqi 26th Division."[32]

Americans sat on their couches and chairs to watch twenty-four-hour coverage of the events on their television screens, with the dazzling technology of live, color broadcasts by satellite. The immediacy was almost addictive, and so was the scope. The networks covered Iraqi envoys, and then switched to pictures of American airbases and troops moving into position. Editors mixed the images into a musical collage, with the lyrics of a popular song, *From a Distance*, by Bette Midler in accompaniment.[33]

Around the world it was clear that everyone was watching the events in the Middle East from a distance. The viewers saw oil wells on fire, and the effort of Saddam Hussein to create an ecological disaster by dumping oil into the Persian Gulf. They also saw thousands of Iraqi soldiers surrendering. Although Saddam Hussein's regular troops were giving up, and more were in retreat, the elite Republican Guard divisions were not running away. They had been kept behind the lines and were well fed and determined to put up a counterattack.

In the opening hours of the war, several Iraqi units were destroyed by the huge American armored divisions in the far west. Baghdad realized the Republican Guard was in danger of being enveloped by the "Left Hook" strategy of the

George H. W. Bush riding in an armored Jeep with General Schwarzkopf in Saudi Arabia, November 22, 1990. (Courtesy, George Bush Presidential Library)

American-led coalition. Despite extensive damage to their communications capabilities, Saddam's generals sent their best armored divisions to block the allied advance. The result was several tank battles between the best tanks the engineers in the United States could devise and their counterparts in the Soviet Union. The American troops had been told that the Russian-made T-72 tank was almost unbeatable, but in actual combat it was no match for the M1A1 Abrams. Early in the morning of February 26, 1991, Lieutenant Colonel Pat Ritter's battalion encountered one of the best Republican Guard units at a map location known as 73 Easting. The Americans took hits on their lightly armored Bradley fighting vehicles, and some of it was later shown to be "friendly fire" from American units. But the Iraqis suffered casualties like in a horror movie. After the battle, the Americans found fifteen T-72 tanks, eleven armored fighting vehicles, an anti-aircraft gun, and four tanks all burning from direct hits.[34]

After several such encounters, Saddam issued a general retreat order to save as much of his army as fast as he could. When U.S. commanders heard that the enemy was pulling out, F-15 planes turned the road from Kuwait City to Basra into "the highway of death." The American troops were on course to trap and destroy the entire Iraqi army, and all of the carnage could be seen on television.

Viewers heard freed Kuwaitis tell of being questioned, beaten, and tortured by Iraqi secret police during the occupation. They saw people of Kuwait City line the streets in jubilation wearing Kuwaiti flags, flashing victory signs, and chanting "Bush, Bush, Bush" while crying and kissing members of the allied forces. The joyous din was punctuated by sporadic automatic weapons fire from the airport where troops were still meeting light resistance. One grateful Kuwaiti woman named her newborn son after a newspaper correspondent, who was the first American she met during the recapture of her country by allied forces.[35]

At 1:00 P.M. Washington time on February 27, General Schwarzkopf held a press conference to declare, "We almost completely destroyed the offensive capability of the Iraqi forces in the Kuwait theatre of operations."[36] On television screens in the United States, networks were showing the first pictures of the "highway of death." The lurid setting of burning oil wells and sandstorms produced bizarre pictures of enemy casualties. The television showed dozens of burned-out vehicles, and the reporters described the nighttime attack on fleeing vehicles. Correspondents interviewed tank and artillery commanders who mentioned that when they fired on the Iraqis, they saw only infrared images, and the enemy never knew what hit them. In daily briefings, khaki-clad generals rolled tapes of bombs entering the smallest of openings with deadly accuracy. The Pentagon emphasis on high technology was vindicated. The president, and his advisors, realized that the scenes showed a slaughter, almost for slaughter's sake. George Bush quietly asked, "How do we end it?"[37]

The high moral ground of the engagement, with the United States throwing an invading bully out of Kuwait, was being eroded by the magnitude of the rout. In spite of the battle victories, the commander of the enemy still remained in power, and a decision was made to try to take him out. On the final night of the war, within hours of the cease-fire, two U.S. Air Force bombers dropped specially designed 5,000-pound bombs on a command bunker fifteen miles northwest of Baghdad in a deliberate attempt to kill Saddam Hussein.

President Bush terminated the ground war at midnight on February 28, 1991. The decision was popular at home and in the White House, such that there was no "sloppy muddled ending," to quote the president, which he feared in the court of world public opinion. The U.S. central command believed that the Republican Guard was largely destroyed, the lines out of Kuwait sealed, and the American troops further in their pursuit of the enemy than was actually the case at the time. When asked by General Colin Powell if the American forces should stand down, General Schwarzkopf responded, "I could live with that." American casualties stood at 148 combat deaths, and 145 non-battle deaths.[38] Put simply, when faced with a choice between further bloodshed and ending the war immediately, all concerned did not hesitate to stop the war.

Later, when spy photographs and satellite imagery could be deciphered, it became clear that total victory had eluded the Allied coalition. Only three of the eight divisions deployed to Kuwait by Saddam had been destroyed. A fourth had lost half its strength, but managed to escape. The exits from the Kuwaiti theatre

As Iraqi military personnel and their families fled Kuwait, they came under attack by coalition forces. The result was miles of destruction lining a major road in northern Kuwait. (© Peter/Turnley/CORBIS)

were not cut off; at least two Republican Guard divisions were over the Euphrates River, and racing to defend the capital when the war ended. Even the much-televised "slaughter" on the "highway of death" turned out to be wrong, since the majority of Iraqis fled their vehicles when the first aircraft appeared. Only about a dozen bodies were found among all the charred vehicles.

On the day the United States called a halt, the majority of the Iraqi army was in a planned retreat, and they managed to evacuate some of their best T-72 tanks along the way. Saddam Hussein was still alive and very much in control; neither of the two giant, laser-guided bombs hit him, nor had the air attacks destroyed his chemical warfare stocks of sarin nerve gas, mustard gas, and possible biological agents. Seven Iraqi generals, but not Saddam, met with General Schwarzkopf to formally sign the permanent cease-fire.

Within hours after the war was over, Iraqi Shiites in Basra rose up against Baghdad's rule. This, too, was part of the hoped for Allied victory plan. Military defeat, coupled with domestic insurrection, would destabilize the Iraqi government. In northern Iraq, the Kurds began a violent rebellion, driving the Iraqi garrison out of the city of Kirkuk. Saddam quickly redeployed the Republican Guard to quell both insurrections. The T-72 tanks, so vulnerable to the American

Abrams tank, were impervious to the rocks and bullets of the nearly defenseless Kurds and Shiites.

At home, the country was undergoing an altering of its essence and view of itself. On television shows, in newspaper articles, and on talk radio, the battleground of ideas about the country, foreign policy, and the world community was waged. The most obvious result was a rebirth of confidence. Americans had placed little yellow ribbons on trees, posts, and their lapels to remember the troops overseas during the Gulf War. In March the ribbons came down, the celebrations began, and confidence remained.

George Bush had approval ratings in the high eighties. Gallup had him at 89 percent, higher than Harry Truman on the day the Nazis surrendered.[39] Republicans in Congress bragged about having backed the president on the war, and they rubbed their patriotism in the face of their Democratic colleagues. Early skepticism was forgotten amid an orgy of patriotism, parades, and flag waving not seen since the end of World War II. On March 6, the president addressed a Joint Session of Congress, and in a dramatic moment turned to face the Kuwaiti ambassador in the House gallery to say, "Kuwait is free!"

All in all, it was a fine and lovely spring. The troops came home and air travelers bought them lunch and snacks in airports as a way of showing appreciation. The prevailing mood was upbeat, but behind the self-congratulation were recurring problems, and they would return to haunt the president who was running for re-election. For one thing, Saddam was still punishing Shiites in southern Iraq and chasing the Kurds in the north. America's great Gulf War victory was turning pyrrhic.

There was some concern over personal problems, like the president's fitness. Ever since the end of the war, George Bush felt tired, and his sleep patterns were erratic. At first his doctors thought it was the stress of command, but on Saturday, May 4, Bush developed shortness of breath while jogging at Camp David. The physicians determined that the president suffered from atrial fibrillation related to a thyroid disease. Later, the diagnosis was changed to Grave's disease, something both the president and his wife contracted within a year of moving into the White House.[40] Bush's style of leadership was energetic and hyperactive, and the illness slowed him down.

The mood was somber as the White House began to prepare for the 1992 election. The press even carried speculations that the president would not seek a second term, a rumor immediately quashed by the administration. White House Chief of Staff John Sununu had managed to alienate most of the people who worked with him, and he was on the way out. The death of Lee Atwater at age forty left the Republican National Party's major political operation without a leader. Then, in June, Justice Thurgood Marshall retired from the Supreme Court. As the first African American to be appointed to the Court, Marshall epitomized the ideal of leadership in the legal fight for civil rights. Amid all the staff turmoil, the president faced a Supreme Court appointment fight reminiscent of Robert Bork.

The president's choice for the Court was a forty-three-year-old, conservative African American from Pinpoint, Georgia, named Clarence Thomas. Immediately the liberal NAACP, the National Organization of Women, and the Urban League opposed the nomination. The battle was shaping up to be as vicious as any story from the Gulf, and it was all carried on television. Questions were raised about Thomas's lack of experience since he only served two years as a federal judge. The Senate Judiciary Committee hearings were relatively uneventful, but the senators still split 7 to 7 on the nomination. Finally, they voted to send it to the full Senate without recommendation.

When the appointment reached the floor of the Senate, the Thomas nomination took a sudden and dramatic turn. Anita Hill, a law professor at the University of Oklahoma, came forward with accusations that Clarence Thomas had sexually harassed her. Hill had worked for Thomas years earlier, when he was head of the Equal Employment Opportunity Commission.[41] She charged that Thomas mentioned inappropriate sexual acts and pornographic films after she rebuffed his invitations to date. Even though polls showed that most blacks supported Clarence Thomas, the debate which emerged on television pressed the case that the judge was little more than a servile agent for Republican white racism. The hearings brought the nation explicit revelations, and numerous countercharges, but largely unsubstantiated evidence of harassment.

Then the Thomas hearings became a media circus. Republican Senator Alan Simpson appeared on ABC's *Nightline* program brandishing Thomas's telephone records showing that Hill kept in touch with Thomas long after she resigned from the EEOC. There were explicit, and detailed, discussions about "Long Dong Silver," pubic hair on Coca-Cola cans, and the double entendre of phone calls. When the nominee testified before the Senate Judiciary Committee about Hill's allegations, he called the inquiry "a high-tech lynching for uppity Blacks." The incident became a match of one person's word against another's, with the television audience as umpire. In the end, the Senate voted 52 to 48 to confirm Clarence Thomas to the Supreme Court.

Even though the evidence was not clear at the time, the mangled process of choosing and confirming a Supreme Court justice in the charged media atmosphere wounded the Bush administration. Conservatives were not endeared, many women were alienated, and blacks were angry. The controversy obliterated the positive view the public had of President Bush from the Desert Storm war. The approval ratings for the president began to turn down, and they portended a bitter harvest in the fall.

8

Don't Stop Thinking About Tomorrow

In the new decade, streams of past history began to merge. The world was very different in 1991 from what it had been just four years earlier. In a sense, George Bush had spent the political capital accumulated by Ronald Reagan. The Berlin Wall was gone. Americans and Russians were busy destroying their intercontinental missiles, instead of aiming them at each other. The two old rivals were even cooperating in space travel and trade. Eastern Europe was independent; the Soviet Union was no more, and Germany was united for the first time since 1945.

The time was a lacuna, an unfilled period between the end of the Cold War and the beginning of a new war against terror. The threat of nuclear war was practically nonexistent, and the fading glow of Operation Desert Storm kept alive optimism about an enduring peace in the Middle East. Arabs and Israelis were engaged in direct talks, and while history was against them, hopes were high for some permanent resolution of tension in the region. The hiatus was the spring of optimism, and postwar babies who had come of age in the Vietnam War years again found themselves the beneficiaries of historical circumstances not of their making.

As America grew into the 1990s, the vanguard of the biggest, richest, and best-educated generation America had ever produced was in its forties. By gaining their political consciousness in the late 1960s and early 1970s, the baby boomers developed an iconoclastic frame of reference and were prone to be more self-indulgent and politically independent than their parents.[1] The divorce rate peaked in 1981, and the new decade saw the advent of the term *single mothers*, where women liberated from being called housewives reached "glass ceilings" at work and faced surly teenagers at home. The country reveled in emerging social distinctions, as wine-drinking became fashionable and the president declared that he did not like broccoli. In the 1990s, the century was ending, and many Americans preferred to think about life as it would be, rather than what it had been.

Presiding over all this was a sixty-eight-year-old president, who was a World War II hero and father figure. George H. W. Bush told his staff that he was a president who, given the partisan divide, could be most effective with Congress by avoiding political conflict. "I want to postpone politics, 1992," he said, and all in the room knew what he meant.[2] In spite of their presidential success, Republicans were still a minority on Capitol Hill and in the allegiance of most Americans. They won political victories by forging alliances, not dividing loyalties and attacking opponents in an election campaign. Unfortunately for the president, politics would not wait. The window of his popularity, and the opportunity for advancement created by the Gulf War, was closing. As in most elections, foreign policy was regarded as less important than domestic issues. The collapse of the Soviet empire removed the threat of communism and eliminated national security as an important issue in the minds of voters. The two issues had been instrumental in attracting "Reagan Democrats" to the Republican banner and building winning coalitions in previous elections, but they were unavailable in 1992.

At home the country faced a familiar problem. The nation was in its deepest recession since the early 1980s. The setback was relatively mild by historical standards, but it came at a bad time for an incumbent president. This time the job losses were among white-collar workers in the new knowledge-based economy, as well as the familiar blue-collar workers in the manufacturing sector.[3] On election day, 60 percent of the voters would list the economy as the most important issue in deciding their vote, while only 9 percent would say that foreign policy was that influential in their decision.[4] Throughout 1992, the public perception was that business was bad and getting worse. Even Bush's accomplishments, like the North American Free Trade Agreement (NAFTA), which eradicated most trade tariffs within ten years, were used as an anti-reelection rallying cry. Democrats argued that the free-trade agreement would result in the relocation of American industry and jobs overseas, and in the midst of a recession, their arguments began to strike home.

The main problem seemed to be George Bush himself. His staff, and the people who saw him every day, wondered if he was fully over his health maladies and was really all that eager to campaign. On September 14, the president's doctors said he had fully recovered from Grave's disease and no longer required medication to regulate his heartbeat.[5] He had gained back the fifteen pounds he lost earlier, and appeared ready to face the cameras. When it came to campaigning, George Bush saw politics in personal terms of loyalty and cooperation more than allegiance to a core set of principles. Bush confidant James Baker wrote after leaving office, "Friendships mean a lot to George Bush...his loyalty to friends is one of his defining personal strengths."[6] After the triumph of Desert Storm, Bush had poll numbers to support a domestic program of political consolidation. But he had no desire, or any agenda, for legislation. As

John Sununu, the former Chief of Staff, told a conservative audience in Washington before leaving town, "There's not another single piece of legislation that needs to be passed in the next two years.... If Congress wants to come together, adjourn, and leave, it's all right with us."[7]

The leisurely timetable for the president's re-election upset many conservatives, and they took the occasion to abandon Bush in droves, citing a long list of disappointments. In December 1991, the flagship conservative publication *National Review* formally broke with the president.[8] George Bush was becoming a victim of what some people called the "Churchill syndrome." The sentiment of the electorate for Bush, like that for British prime minister before him, was: "You're a wonderful global leader, but you don't understand our problems here at home."[9]

The fury of conservative wrath was embodied in the presidential candidacy of Patrick J. Buchanan, a television commentator and columnist who had served in communications positions in the Nixon and Reagan administrations. Buchanan was best known as co-host of CNN's nightly *Crossfire* television show, and he used his prime-time pulpit to blast "King George" on everything from his support of free trade to his mishandling of the economy. When he resigned his television job to go on the campaign trail, the venom became personal. While the White House dithered, Buchanan spent a month and a half in New Hampshire accusing Bush of violating the tax pledge and doing nothing about an economic situation that was devastating the Granite State. The television commentator, who had never held elective office, explicitly offered himself as a protest candidate, declaring: "Send them a message." In the New Hampshire primary, the voters did just that. Buchanan finished a startling second, garnering 37 percent of the vote to the president's 53 percent. "Over half of the Republican electorate in New Hampshire disapproved of Bush's performance, and only one-third of Buchanan voters said they would vote for Bush in November."[10]

The Republican race for president now entered a second, and more serious, phase. No one was more earnest about the business at hand than the president. Bush attacked Buchanan's isolationism on trade and unwillingness to intervene in the Persian Gulf, and declared that votes for a protest candidate could only risk a liberal Democratic victory in the fall. The Buchanan campaign responded by attacking Bush for signing the 1991 Civil Rights Act (a "quota bill"), for public funding for the arts—including a film supporting homosexuality—and giving in to the "Jewish lobby" on the Gulf War.[11] The next two weeks of campaigning were hard fought, but the president gradually overwhelmed his challengers, both former Klansman David Duke and Pat Buchanan. Together the two could only muster about one-third of the Republican vote, but the damage was still done. The primary attacks left some voters with the impression that the president was rich, indifferent, and out of touch with them. The rebuke that he was guided by no core beliefs was especially stinging, because Bush believed he was an effective vice-president precisely because he supported Reaganism. In spite of all this, Bush won the Michigan primary in the middle of

March and effectively ended the primary race for the nomination. The winner-take-all rules for delegate selection to the GOP convention put an end to upstart campaigns, and Bush coasted to victory.[12]

The Democrats were having their own problems. In the middle months of 1991, with the Gulf War a warm memory and when potential presidential candidates would "test the waters," George Bush seemed invincible. For this reason Tennessee Senator Al Gore, Senate Majority Leader George Mitchell, Reverend Jesse Jackson, House Majority Leader Dick Gephardt, New York Governor Mario Cuomo, and Senator Sam Nunn of Georgia all declared themselves out of the race. On television talk shows and in news interviews, the Democrats had a grim, hammered look about them as they discussed the upcoming race. There were feeble signs of animation when they talked about people like Ted Kennedy and the long-gone glory days of the Democratic Party, but they knew they were grasping at straws, and inside they were preparing for a fourth straight defeat.

That August, in Little Rock, Arkansas, the nation's senior governor with twelve years' experience at age forty-five was anything but downcast. He was born in tragedy—his father died in a car wreck before he arrived—so William Jefferson "Bill" Clinton learned optimism at an early age. From a childhood in provincial Hot Springs, Arkansas, where he learned a talent for politics and careful networking, Clinton used the American educational system to rise to unimagined heights. As a delegate to Boys Nation he met President John F. Kennedy, and then graduated fourth in his high school class to excel in the study of politics, and its practice, at Georgetown University. One classmate would recall meeting Clinton, "and him telling me within forty-five minutes that he planned to go back to Arkansas to be governor or senator and would like to be a national leader someday." Some thought him manipulative; others said he was "down to earth."[13] Whatever the description, the memories were that he was ambitious and likeable and loved to be surrounded by people who talked as much as he did.

Wherever he lived, his room became a kind of floating seminar where people gathered to talk about the issues of the day. An Oxford don remembered that while Clinton was a Rhodes Scholar in England, he learned "that politics consists of making use of people you can trust who really are very clever." A fellow Democrat would describe him publicly as "an unusually good liar—unusually good."[14] He took it as a compliment. The energy and intelligence of other people seemed to flow through him. He was a big and burly man with thick curly hair and a fresh-scrubbed face. His mother contributed immeasurably to his inner drive, but he drew most of his strength from meeting and working with other people. He had a confidence that was striking. At Yale Law School he immersed himself in politics, and pointed his efforts toward helping the Democrats in the 1972 presidential race.

Twenty years later, he spoke at Harvard University, where he attacked the Reagan-Bush years, saying, "America spent too much time and money in the

1980s on the present and the past, and too little attention and money on the future."[15] He was all about what would happen next, as a Georgetown student, Rhodes Scholar, graduate of Yale Law School, the nation's youngest governor, and then aspiring president; he was always focused on what was yet to come. The problem was that Clinton was little known outside of Arkansas, and the reputation he did have was not auspicious. In 1988 he moved to the national stage when he introduced presidential nominee Michael S. Dukakis to the Democratic convention. Unfortunately, he gave an interminable thirty-two-minute televised speech, drawing applause only when he said, "In closing..." Four years later, Clinton was the leader of the Democrats' second tier of candidates, a group that included Governor Douglas Wilder of Virginia, Senators Tom Harkin of Iowa and Bob Kerry of Nebraska, former senator Paul Tsongas of Massachusetts, and former California governor Jerry Brown, who was back after failing to win twelve years earlier.

When he declared for office in October 1991, Bill Clinton found himself at the top of a weak field, instead of at the bottom of a strong field. Others said that if he ran well, then more seasoned and powerful first-tier Democratic candidates would come into the race and take the nomination from him. In private, Clinton himself admitted as much, and said that he expected Governor Cuomo to enter the race, and that the New York governor would be the odds-on favorite to win the nomination should he run. But with each passing week, Governor Clinton showed he was exceptional in one important aspect of presidential politics: fundraising. By the end of the reporting period he had 40 percent more money than his nearest rival, and he was gaining momentum.

Clinton was also honing a message. If he won the nomination, his candidacy would be the most conservative since 1976, and he had always been a cautious defender of the establishment. In Arkansas he attacked organized labor and courted corporate interests when it served his purpose to do so. He had supported the death penalty since his 1976 race for attorney general.[16] As a founder of the Democratic Leadership Council (DLC), he pushed the party to the center, but to win primaries, Clinton had to appeal to liberal party activists. The Arkansas governor ripped Republican domestic policies, and promised to restore the American dream for the "forgotten middle class" at his announcement.[17] In a Georgetown speech, he presented a broad vision with a specific plan. "In a Clinton Administration," he said, "we'll cut income taxes on the middle class... [but] the deficit won't go up—instead those earning over $200,000 per year will pay more."[18] The plan was a New Democratic slant on an old-line liberal solution, taxing the top 5 percent to cover the middle class, but it made the Arkansas governor more appealing to the party's rank-and-file membership. He said something, somewhere, sometime that almost any Democrat would like; and the more people heard him, the more they liked *how* he said it as well.

The traditional campaign season in American politics began, as usual, with two crucial dates: the Iowa caucuses and the New Hampshire primary. In 1992 Clinton discounted Iowa because favorite son Senator Tom Harkin was in the race. One month before the vote, the Arkansas governor held a sizeable lead in New Hampshire, but he began to falter for two reasons. First, Paul Tsongas weighed in from neighboring Massachusetts with a "call to economic arms" proposal that challenged Clinton's middle-class tax cut. Five of the state's seven major banks had failed, and home values were down 30 percent over the previous two years. The Tsongas attack declared that the Clinton plan was the creation of a political strategist and would give the average person less than a dollar a day refund.

The second reason was more sensational. On January 23, *The Star*, a supermarket tabloid, published a charge from an Arkansas woman who said she had a twelve-year affair with Bill Clinton. The allegations included a copy of an abortion receipt allegedly paid for by the governor, details of various romantic meetings, and taped phone calls of a cover-up denial. Gennifer Flowers even went on television to give a tearful rendition of the affair. On the heels of the infidelity charge, the *Wall Street Journal* ran a story on February 6 about Clinton's attempts to manipulate the draft laws in 1969 and avoid military service in Vietnam. The two charges were devastating, and all at once the front-running campaign was in meltdown in the face of the shattering revelations.

Clinton gathered his campaign staff together in the East Conference Room of the Little Rock Governor's Mansion. The candidate had the flu, with a cough and a raging fever. He went through a cursing tirade, spewing out venom and declaring that the campaign would not be about his personal life and he would not quit. Then his wife, Hillary Clinton, took the floor to declare, "We're going to fight like hell, to fight like we do in Arkansas."[19] Around the room the pep talk began to take effect, the mood lifted, and everyone went back to work convinced that Bill Clinton would not be driven from the race like Gary Hart had been when he was exposed for sexual infidelity four years earlier.

The next day, new ads aired in New Hampshire, a state one-sixth the physical size with one-third the population of Arkansas. Clinton threw himself at the people of the state with a punishing schedule. He appeared on CBS's *Sixty Minutes*, along with his wife, and in general terms acknowledged that he had "caused pain" in his marriage. For her part, Hillary Clinton pledged to trust her husband, and evinced the attitude of, "If it doesn't bother me, why should it bother you?"[20] Together they declared that they were being held to an unfair standard of marital perfection that a divorced candidate (e.g., Ronald Reagan) did not have to meet.[21]

On February 18, 1992, Bill Clinton received 25 percent of the New Hampshire vote, finishing 8 points behind Paul Tsongas. He immediately labeled himself the "comeback kid" and the frontrunner. Almost single-handedly, by reversing the attacks, blaming the press and the "Republican attack machine," Governor Clinton pulled himself back from the edge of political oblivion. The media focus on Pat Buchanan's upstart showing in the Republican primary and President Bush's troubled political fortunes allowed Clinton to escape scrutiny of his nearly 20-point drop in the polls two weeks before election day.[22]

The New Hampshire primary showed something about the new nature of American media politics. The public's short attention span to political matters, coupled with the now-developing twenty-four-hour news cycle, meant that candidates could reinvent themselves on a daily or weekly basis. In the words of one political scientist, politics had become postmodern, "all text and no content, all rhyme and no reason.... Crossing the line from intellectual to anti-intellectual discourse has altered the ways in which we (are forced to) understand and participate in politics."[23]

Clinton grasped this, while his opponents did not. With his natural charisma and comfort before the camera, the Arkansas governor was able to withstand revelations of marital infidelity, marijuana indiscretions, draft dodging, and voter manipulation by offering easy-to-grasp slogans and an "aw shucks" personality. The favorite medium of communication for the Clinton campaign was "popular culture," with venues like the Don Imus radio show, the Arsenio Hall late night television show, *Larry King Live*, and a ninety-minute *Rock the Vote* program on MTV. In the "War Room" of the campaign headquarters, which was a place plastered with paraphernalia, the feeling was that Clinton was barely hanging on. James Carville, the Louisiana consultant, wrote four words on a white blackboard for Bill Clinton to repeat every time he went out to speak: "It's the economy, stupid." As the lyrics to Fleetwood Mac's "Don't Stop Thinking About Tomorrow" echoed in the background, the Clinton campaign rolled on.[24]

Two days after the New Hampshire primary results were certified, the presidential race was thrown into turmoil by the entry of an independent candidate. Historically, the most important third parties have been those that represented disaffected elements of one of the two dominant parties. But in the 1980s and 1990s, the media-saturated electorate was attracted to candidates who promised to break the monopoly of both the Democrats and Republicans. The prospects of ending "politics as usual" in Washington was such that many voters were attracted to any candidate, regardless of his chances of success.

The new mimetic personality was H. Ross Perot. He was a billionaire Texas entrepreneur who initially made headlines by making well-publicized trips to Vietnam to rescue American POWs held after the war was over and sending mercenary soldiers to rescue some of his employees during the Iranian hostage crisis of 1979. The story of the rescue, told in a 1984 book *On the Wings of Eagles,* was later made into a television movie. Perot's reputation, implicit in his actions, was that he understood loyalty and succeeded where the U.S. government failed. "While they just talked, he acted." He was a Nike man, a "just do it" kind of guy who got things done.[25]

On February 20, 1992, right after Pat Buchanan had humiliated George Bush in New Hampshire and after Bill Clinton had weathered numerous attacks on his character, Ross Perot appeared on CNN's *Larry King Live* talk show. "If voters in all fifty states put me on the ballot—not forty-eight or forty-nine states, but all fifty—I will agree to run." What was more, Perot was prepared to spend up to

$100 million of his own money in the campaign.[26] The self-funded Texan agreed to bypass parties, conventions, and the nomination process itself, accepting only a draft by voters. "If the volunteers say, 'Ross, it's a dirty job but you've got to do it,' I belong to them."[27]

The response by the public to Perot's announcement was impressive. In the polls he soon surged to 20 percent support, a figure he would double in the summer months of June. At one point, when Perot set up a toll-free number for voters to call to offer assistance and support, a spokesman said the Texan was receiving 2,000 calls an hour. After a time, polls showed him ahead of the leading candidate nominees of both major political parties.[28]

By March, it was clear that for the first time in American history, three southerners would vie for the presidency in the fall election. Zell Miller of Georgia characterized the upcoming campaign as one with "an aristocrat (Bush), an autocrat (Perot), and a Democrat (Clinton)." After two months, the rules of the nomination process took over, and the opinions of the voters began to harden. The Democratic policy of proportional representation kept alive the campaigns of Paul Tsongas and Jerry Brown, but gradually the defeated candidates saw their ratings fall and their sources of funding dry up. The winner-take-all features of the Republican Party meant that George Bush could relax until the convention because trailing candidates were unable to gather delegates or speak to the assembly.

For his part, Ross Perot went public, and that would prove to be his undoing. The honeymoon of his candidacy was over, and journalists began to provide in-depth biographical sketches of Perot's private life. They wrote of his fascination with the military, dress codes at work, and a penchant for hiring private investigators to check out employees as well as political enemies. Gradually, a dark side of Perot emerged in the press accounts, and the candidate began to drop in the national polls, just when the major parties headed to their conventions. Criticisms of his management style, contributions to political campaigns, "insider" business deals, and involvement with the Nixon White House all brought Perot back to earth.[29] In a live broadcast on ABC, Perot contended that Citibank was insolvent, and the next day he confronted homosexual protest groups who wanted him to retract a statement saying he would not name a gay or lesbian to a cabinet-level post. Newspapers carried stories of Perot's investigation of Richard L. Armitage, the Pentagon officer, over POW issues in Vietnam.[30]

The candidate responded that Republican "dirty tricks" underlay the revelations in the news, and he personally blamed George Bush for his predicament. In the polls, widespread support for his candidacy began to evaporate. On July 11, Ross Perot addressed the National Association for the Advancement of Colored People (NAACP) meeting in Nashville, Tennessee. From the lectern he characterized members of the audience as "you people." He was roundly criticized for racial insensitivity, and this time the press declared he was "culturally out of touch" with African Americans.[31] In an abrupt response, which seemed to confound his followers and confirm his critics, Perot withdrew from the presidential race on July 15.

That same week, the Democrats met in convention in Madison Square Garden in the heart of New York City. "We had a good five weeks," said Bill Clinton, "while Bush and Perot fought with each other."[32] Just a week earlier Clinton selected Senator Albert Gore, Jr., forty-four, of Tennessee as his running mate. The convention keynote was delivered by Representative Barbara Jordan of Texas, and delegates heard Mario Cuomo emotionally declare that "the nation cannot afford another Democratic defeat." Unlike some earlier Democratic conventions, this one was well planned and run as a prime-time extravaganza of short speeches and coordinated messages. The nominees boarded buses and headed for campaign stops in New Jersey, Pennsylvania, West Virginia, Ohio, Kentucky, Indiana, and Illinois after adjournment. The tour was designed to take the candidates to small towns and rural areas not visited by candidates in modern, media-driven campaigns. The hope was that the excitement and momentum of the convention city would continue in the heartland. It did. As a result of a successful convention, the Clinton-Gore ticket received one of the most significant "bounces" in the polls of any ticket in American history. Clinton caught, and then surpassed, President Bush, running ahead by some 27 points in some polls.[33]

The Republicans could only wait and watch until August 17 when they gathered at the Astrodome in Houston. Once convened, the delegates heard an opening night speech from Pat Buchanan, who declared that a "religious war" was taking place in the United States between believers and secularists. One spokesman for the GOP told the press that "we are America, they are not America."[34] Republicans vowed to make homosexual rights a major issue in the campaign, and that threat overshadowed Ronald Reagan's presence and stirring address.[35]

The Clinton campaign was quick to highlight the rhetoric, and the media also gave it prominence.[36] Even with the bad publicity, which Republicans said was undeserved, the Bush-Quayle ticket garnered a boost from the convention. On Labor Day the Republicans still trailed the Democrats by 7 to 10 points. Clinton entered the fall in the lead, but the outcome turned on two crucial events beyond the control of either major political party.

The first came on October 1, when Ross Perot re-entered the presidential race. While the pundits declared that Perot's support came in equal amounts from both major candidates, the suspicion was that he hurt his fellow Texan much more than the Arkansas governor.[37] The second moment of change came during debate week, October 11–19, when four debates, three presidential and one vice-presidential, were packed into one week. Ross Perot worked to separate himself from the other two candidates, and his vice-presidential candidate, James Stockdale, did the same, but their collective effect was to increase loyalty to the two major candidates. Perot gathered some momentum, and even Bush looked better in the last debate, but the youth, confidence, and energy of Bill Clinton outstripped his rivals. The Democratic campaign surged ahead based on the theme of "change," while the Republicans floundered on the mantra of "experience and trust."[38]

Confronted by a superb campaigner in Bill Clinton and a united Democratic party, along with a superbly financed third-party candidate, George Bush went down to defeat in November of 1992. He received only 37.4 percent of the popular vote, and never topped 40 percent in any of the final polls. Clinton carried thirty-two states and the District of Columbia, and won 370 of the 538 electoral votes. He won twenty-one of the top thirty media markets, including the six largest (New York, Los Angeles, Chicago, Philadelphia, Boston, and San Francisco). Ross Perot took 19 percent of the vote and won no electoral votes, but Republicans believed that his candidacy cost their candidate re-election. Clinton won a plurality among independents, and did well in the suburbs, where Republicans had historically built up huge margins to offset central city losses.

Instead of having the usual Inauguration Day in 1993, Bill Clinton chose to have an "Inauguration Week." A number of events were planned, including a two-hour outdoor concert with hundreds of thousands of people crowded onto the Mall for a free concert. The schedule featured entertainers such as Aretha Franklin, Michael Bolton, Tony Bennett, Bob Dylan, Diana Ross, and the rapper L-L Cool J. While Latin pop star Ricky Martin entertained on Friday, 1970s superstars—and campaign anthem artists—Fleetwood Mac were special guests for a number of events. The inauguration used high-tech pageantry, red, white, and blue fireworks over the Potomac River, and Hollywood celebrities at Washington social events to set a new tone in the capitol city. The total price tag was put at some $25 million for the extravaganza.

The inauguration events showed the new first couple in a glamorous light, and it was immediately clear that they stood in dramatic contrast to their predecessors. Gone were grandparents, and in their place were Bill and Hillary Clinton, who represented all the undisciplined indulgences and spoiled wants of the postwar generation. Their activist politics sprang from a determination to teach the world the error of its ways, and was founded on a belief that government could be made more meaningful. Hillary Rodham Clinton appeared in *Vogue* magazine, and was held up as a model of the modern woman who could be all things: wife, mother, and influential politician.[39] The Clintons had a "partnership marriage," one for mutual convenience without the necessary requirement of fidelity. Bill Clinton had a history of obsessive philandering, while his wife seemed to have a mothering instinct. From the opening round of their courtship, they were "an evenly matched romance and a fair fight."[40] The two were a traveling soap opera on the campaign, with public fights and arguments. Together they were about to treat the nation to a soap opera display of marital relations on a public stage before a captive national audience.

Bill Clinton took the oath of office as the forty-second president on January 20, 1993. The sun was bright and the crowd stretched down the Mall as Maya Angelou became only the second poet in U.S. history to have the honor of writing and reciting original work at the Presidential Inauguration. At the other end of Pennsylvania Avenue, the new president faced a Congress led by a dwindling Democratic majority, and an insurgent GOP that wanted a revival of the Reagan Revolution. The two branches were destined for a rocky and divided engagement. Evident from the beginning was the role Hillary Clinton would play in the new administration. Initially, she wanted to be the top White House domestic policy advisor, and when that failed, she demanded an office in the West Wing of the White House. Traditionally, first ladies had offices in the East Wing, where they were involved in issues like roadway beautification and children's reading programs. Not this time. Hillary Clinton wanted a top policy job, and finally she settled for a project to supervise. Within the first week of his taking office, the president appointed his wife to chair the Task Force on National Health Care Reform.[41]

Once in office, the new president overestimated his ability to propose and enact sweeping policy changes when he earned less than a majority of votes. The public wasted little time in making up its mind about him. When the president took action on two controversial policies, the removal of abortion restrictions and the endorsement of homosexuals in the military, opinions hardened for and against him. After two weeks in office, only 16 percent of the public had no opinion on the president's job performance—compared with the approximately 40 percent of the populace who withheld judgment at the same time in the Reagan and Bush administrations.[42]

Health care and the economy were the two big issues facing the new administration. The most immediate need involved reconstituting the budget to the business cycle. During the campaign, Bill Clinton promised a middle-class tax cut, an investment program in America's infrastructure, health care reform, a stimulus program of fast-track spending, and deficit reduction. The Omnibus Budget Reconciliation Act of 1993 was designed to accomplish all these purposes. In reality, it served up a huge helping of the status quo with familiar remedies. Vice President Albert Gore broke a tie vote on August 6, 1993, to pass the measure in the Senate, and the president signed the law four days later.[43]

Republicans charged that Clinton promised a middle-class tax cut and delivered "the largest tax increase in American history" instead. Both sides were partially right. A promise to increase taxes on the affluent was a central feature of the plan. Almost two-thirds (63 percent) of the projected tax increase hit high-income couples (over $140,000 a year) and individuals (over $115,000 a year). Aside from an increase in the top income-tax rate, money for the increase came from taxes on business, primarily a rise in the corporate tax rate and new limits on deductions for entertainment expenses. The plan included more Medicare payroll taxes on top earners, an expansion of the Earned Income Tax credit for low-income workers, a gas-tax increase, and an increase in the minimum tax all workers must pay.

Democrats declared that they had reversed twelve years of Republican "trickle-down" economics and would turn the largest deficit in American history into the largest budget surplus in history. Republicans countered that the administration plan was a flea on the raging bull of the 1990s economy; it did not cause interest rates to fall, nor did it reduce the deficit or expand the economy. The marvelous economic boom of the decade came as a result of corporate restructuring and downsizing in the 1980s and early 1990s and the fantastic rise in new technology, especially computer and communication innovations. Virtually none of the growth was attributable to government. Yet, even Republicans would subsequently give Clinton credit for getting out of the way of the free market. The president was generally a free trader; he let Alan Greenspan and the Federal Reserve Board keep inflation in check while he signed a "tax increase on the rich."

While her husband tended to the economy, Hillary Clinton held closed-door meetings to address the long-standing health care problem. Every poll showed that the public wanted reform, and the political situation on the Hill favored the Democrats. The major problem was the dramatic increase in health care costs, from 9 percent of the GDP in 1980 to 14 percent in 1993, with estimates as high as 19 percent by 2000. The ad hoc advisory staff eventually included 500 participants, drawn from the executive branch, congressional staffs, the research community, and the private sector.[44] They worked in secret, and effectively limited leaks to the press.

Candidate Clinton had promised to recommend a national health insurance plan within the first 100 days of his presidency, but the deficit reduction politics took precedence, so the package did not get to Congress until September of 1993. When it arrived, the rhetoric for passage was wrapped in indignation. The most quoted statistic was that 37 million Americans, living in the world's most prosperous nation, had no health insurance, and tens of millions more had inadequate coverage.[45] The Clinton solution was to guarantee coverage for all Americans. Early on, the administration signaled a willingness to negotiate almost every element of its plan, save one: any alternative must cover everyone. George Mitchell, the Senate majority leader at the time, declared, "[Clinton's] plan will assure security.... The American people will have health coverage that can never be taken away."[46] After its introduction, Mrs. Clinton demonstrated a dazzling command of the details of the legislation in a historic appearance before cameras and the key congressional committees. Before the Senate Labor Committee, she declared that health reform was an issue beyond partisan politics, and before the Senate Finance Committee she said the new program would streamline costs. Mrs. Clinton's presence on Capitol Hill awed both Democrats and Republicans, so much so that they asked few penetrating questions.[47]

The plan for health care reform was popular at first. A Gallup poll in September of 1993 showed public support for the proposal by nearly a 2-to-1 margin.[48] Liberals favored a health care plan like Canada's that would be regulated and financed by the national government. The political effect of such legislation was impressive, strengthening the Democratic Party's base among lower-income working-class voters who had no coverage and middle-class voters fearful of losing what they had. Republicans had traditionally objected to big government and expanding social-welfare programs, but they were initially stunned by the popularity of the president's program and its presentation in Congress. Bob Dole, Republican senator from Kansas, opined that "Republicans want to cooperate with the Clinton administration on health care."[49] The "go-slow" strategy by Republicans was designed to give the opposition time to regroup. It worked.

The health care industry was not interested in compromise or in joining forces with either political party on the issue. Instead, the industry launched an independent campaign arguing that health care was not in crisis, and that the Clinton plan was little more than a blatant grab for power by the Democrats. The Health Insurance Association of America (HIAA) was composed of some 271 midsized and small insurance companies who would be out of business if the legislation passed. They were determined to stop it. Irving Kristol, a conservative strategist and Republican advisor, echoed this criticism when he declared that the health care bill was a "serious *political* threat to the Republican Party," and might "revive the reputation of ... the Democrats ... as the generous protector of middle-class interests."[50] The private health insurance industry extended a united and strong front against the Clinton health reform initiative. From September 1993 until the summer of 1994, HIAA spent some $14 million to $15 million on ads, dubbed by the press as the "Harry and Louise" commercials. The spots featured a couple agonizing over the details of the Clinton plan with exchanges like this one:[51]

Louise: This plan forces us to buy our insurance through these new, mandatory government health alliances.
Harry: Run by tens of thousands of new bureaucrats.
Louise: Another billion-dollar bureaucracy.
Harry: You know, we just don't need government monopolies to get health coverage to everyone.
Louise: Congress can fix that.
Harry: And they will, if we send them that message.
TELEPHONE NUMBER FOR THE FACTS YOU NEED TO SEND CONGRESS A MESSAGE.

The campaign was reinforced by mailings and phone calls. Soon the press picked up on the "Harry and Louise" criticisms, and found that the "increasing government role" theme was connecting with voters. By the homestretch, the Gallup poll showed that 53 percent of Americans surveyed said they would be relieved, more than angry, if Congress did not pass comprehensive health care.[52]

With each passing month, opponents were able to redefine the Clinton plan as a welfare-state scheme to benefit the uninsured at the expense of the already-insured middle class. Democrats in Congress were divided on the issue, which spurred the Republicans to new heights of unity in opposition. In the course of the battle the debate became personal. Critics labeled the plan "HillaryCare," and tied feminist stereotypes of demanding women to the legislation, and to the First Lady who spoke for its adoption.

The president tried to refocus attention on the issue in his 1994 State of the Union address, and he laid down the gauntlet to the Congress. In the most dramatic moment of his speech, the president threatened to veto any legislation that did not guarantee health insurance to everyone.[53] The opponents took up the challenge, and won. On August 11, 1994, House Democratic leaders announced that health care legislation would be delayed, and about the same time, their counterparts in the Senate admitted that the votes were not there to ensure passage. The whole effort came to an ignominious end on September 22, almost exactly one year after its introduction, when bipartisan Senate supporters of a weaker compromise plan finally admitted they could not salvage a vote on the floor.

In the end, the supporters of the health care initiative were out-financed and out-finessed by their opponents. Big businesses opposed it, and from the beginning it was a burden on small businesses. The "Harry and Louise" ads were devastatingly effective. From them, voters learned that they could not choose their own doctors and would be subject to government mismanagement. The health care fiasco showed that Bill Clinton believed in government, even big government, in a post-Reagan era. He was a minority president who seemed not to be in tune with the times.

Three months after entering the White House, the president faced another crisis of how much government intervention is enough, or too much. Early in the year, four agents from the Bureau of Alcohol, Tobacco and Firearms (BATF) were killed, and sixteen injured, in a confrontation with a Texas religious cult. The Branch Davidians had lived outside Waco, Texas, since the 1930s, but they were lately suspected of illegal firearms violations and subsequently incurred an early morning raid from the BATF. The sect's thirty-three-year-old messianic leader, David Koresh, had an almost hypnotic hold on his followers and an arsenal of weapons to boot. A standoff ensued after the February raid, and for the next fifty-one days the situation in Waco dominated the daily news cycle.

On Sunday night, April 18, Attorney General Janet Reno met with the president to get his approval for an FBI raid on the compound to apprehend Koresh and his followers. After some hesitancy, Clinton agreed to the raid. The next day, just after 6:00 A.M., two specially equipped M-60 tanks began to punch holes in the buildings to insert gas in an effort to flush the Davidians out. Over the next six hours, four Bradley armored vehicles joined the tanks, firing 40 mm canisters of gas through the windows. Around noon, smoke was seen coming from the second-story windows, and within minutes the thin frame building was engulfed in an uncontrollable fire, fanned by gusty winds.

The entire scene was carried live to a national audience and seen around the world on television. When it was over, more than seventy-four people were dead, including twenty-five children. The Waco operation was a tragedy, and critics declared that the government overreacted. Although it was not known at the time, the incident was a prelude to further domestic terrorism. President Clinton had personal regrets: "I was furious at myself, first for agreeing to the raid against my better judgment, then for delaying a public acknowledgment of responsibility for it."[54]

Like most presidential candidates, Bill Clinton had spoken in only the most general terms about the diplomatic course he would follow if elected. A principal concern about his candidacy was a lack of foreign policy experience, but he had an opportunity early in office to dispel any lingering suspicions about his talents. On September 9, Yitzhak Rabin, prime minister of Israel, called the White House to announce that Israel and the Palestine Liberation Organization (PLO) had reached an agreement for the autonomy of the Gaza Strip and the West Bank. The agreement was achieved in secret talks between the parties in Oslo, Norway. The terms fulfilled a process begun by the Madrid Treaty in 1991, and brought an end to the intifada, or mass uprising, of Palestinians that had cost the lives of thousands since 1987.

President Clinton with Prime Minister Yitzhak Rabin of Israel and Palestine Liberation Organization Chairman Yasir Arafat on the South Lawn. (Courtesy, William J. Clinton Presidential Library)

Most of the work of structuring the peace lay in the future, but both parties agreed to come to Washington within the week to sign a Declaration of Principles on the South Lawn of the White House. The president jawboned both leaders into attending the ceremony, saying that no one would believe they were fully committed to the peace process unless they both came in person. It was a gamble for both Rabin and Yasir Arafat, chairman of the PLO, to come, since neither of them knew how their people would react to the signing. On the morning of September 13, the atmosphere around the White House fairly crackled with excitement as more than 2,500 invited guests filed in. The president introduced the two leaders to the crowd, which included former presidents Jimmy Carter and George Bush, as well as all former secretaries of state and national security advisors. At the signing itself, Israeli Foreign Minister Shimon Peres and his Palestinian counterpart inked the document. Then, when the signing was complete, the President shook hands with Arafat, then Rabin, and stood back to spread his arms to bring the two adversaries together. Arafat lifted his hand to a hesitant Rabin. The handshake was the first ever in public between the two arch enemies. Rabin addressed the crowd in English, saying, "Enough of blood and tears...enough!" Then Arafat said, "The decision we reached together was one that required great courage." The President then closed the ceremony saying, "Shalom, go as peacemakers."[55]

Not all foreign policy endeavors were as successful as this one, especially when the venue was unfamiliar, overseas, and hostile. In December of 1992, president-elect Bill Clinton approved a decision of President Bush to send troops to Somalia to help the United Nations stabilize a bloody civil war. Once in office, the Clinton administration stated a policy of trying to scale back the U.S. military presence worldwide. Then, in June, the clan of Somali warlord Mohammad Aidid killed twenty-four Pakistani peacekeepers. The United Nations responded with an emergency resolution to apprehend those responsible, and the United States flew in a special force of elite troops from the army's Tenth Mountain Division. Their mission was to capture Aidid.

On October 3, 1993, acting on a tip that two of Aidid's lieutenants were in one of Mogadishu's teeming ghettos, Army Rangers mounted an assault on the Olympic Hotel where the men were thought to be. They flew into battle in Black Hawk helicopters in broad daylight. "Mogadishu spread beneath them in its awful reality, a catastrophe.... The few paved avenues were crumbling and littered with mountains of trash, buildings that had not been reduced to heaps of gray rubble were pockmarked with bullet scars."[56] This led to a seventeen-hour battle in which eighteen U.S. soldiers were killed and eighty-four were wounded. More than 500 Somalis died and over a thousand were wounded. Bodies of dead American soldiers were dragged through the streets of the city, and all this was shown on international news reports.

The battle in Mogadishu was the longest and bloodiest one for U.S. troops since Vietnam, and shared characteristics of that flawed conflict. "I was sick about the loss of our troops," said the president, "and I wanted Aidid to pay."[57]

The American populace was outraged, so on October 7, President Clinton withdrew U.S. troops from Somalia. What began as a peacekeeping mission to provide relief to a starving people beset by civil war ended with a failed firefight and a military withdrawal. The lesson seemed to be that America's power could accomplish some things, but not all things, in the post–Cold War world. The retreat showed the world's terrorists and despots that killing a few American soldiers was enough to spook Uncle Sam into leaving.

In his second year in office, Bill Clinton had a mixed record of accomplishment. The Middle East Peace Accord was undoubtedly the high point. Overseas in Russia, Boris Yeltsin crushed a rebellion in Moscow after the army fired on the parliament building to force the surrender of rebels and free hundreds of imprisoned delegates. Clinton gave unconditional support to Yeltsin, and appeared as a supporter of world peace. His most striking performances were always on television, and when he spoke with conviction, the president was compelling. The budget and tax package had barely passed in Congress, but they still passed.

On the negative side, the president was unable to win over many of his critics. They criticized him as a man of good intentions, but without a philosophical core or any keen instinct for the public mood. He had run as a "New Democrat" espousing tax relief and welfare reform, but when in office he enacted a tax increase and announced a "Don't ask, don't tell" policy to allow homosexuals to serve in the military. The ill-fated attempt to reform America's health care system appeared to be a classic, liberal, big government program. Republicans were able to depict it as such, and accused Clinton of trying to socialize American medicine. They were effective in portraying him as a politician who talked one way, and governed another.

Some of Clinton's shortcomings could be attributed to his inexperience. At age forty-seven he was still a man in search of himself. The removal of long-time employees from the White House travel office and the bumbling of the health care initiative were first-term mistakes. To his friends he seemed cautious; to his enemies, reckless. He alienated much of his culturally conservative base in the South with his decisions on abortion and homosexuality, but he did not seem to care. His budget decisions and his defeated job-stimulus package alienated Democratic moderates like Senator David Boren of Oklahoma. The press ran the gamut: "*Time* magazine covers heralded the scope of the Clinton ambition with 'You Say You Want a Revolution,' to calling him 'The Incredible Shrinking President,' to extolling the enormity of his agenda again: 'Overturning the Reagan Era.' "[58]

As the 1994 midterm elections loomed, the president's popularity was in a tailspin. In mid-July, he had lower midterm approval ratings than eight of the previous nine presidents; 42 percent approved the job he was doing, while 49 percent disapproved.[59] Democrats were running for re-election by repudiating Clinton, and Republicans were preparing to attack by identifying any Democratic candidate with the president. The new video technology allowed campaign messages to "morph" the face of any Democrat with an unflattering image of Clinton.

Republicans were quick to realize their opportunity. In the summer, House Minority Whip Newt Gingrich of Georgia gathered more than 300 Republican incumbents and candidates for a rally on the Capitol steps to sign the "Contract with America." The details of the pact had been percolating for some time, and the agreement was seen as an attempt to capitalize on voter discontent nationally. The "Contract" was a set of proposals that Republicans promised to bring to a vote if they won a majority in Congress. The listing of items, such as a balanced budget amendment, Congressional term limits, a line-item veto for the president, and campaign finance reform, were things on which the GOP enjoyed a 55 percent–plus consensus with the voters.

The discontent that year extended beyond Congress. A popular bumper sticker at the time declared: "Re-Elect Nobody." In November of 1994, they did just that. The Republican Party won a majority of the votes cast for Congress for the first time since 1946, and picked up fifty-two seats to become the majority party in the U.S. House for the first time in forty years. They also reclaimed the U.S. Senate, which was lost after the Iran-Contra scandal in the second term of the Reagan administration. In the South, the Republicans gained a majority of House seats in the region for the first time since Reconstruction. The experts decried the low voter turnout, saying the country was undergoing dealignment, defined as a turning away from both political parties, instead of realignment to the GOP.

The Republicans did not care what it was called. They just knew now they were in charge of both houses, and divided government had returned to Washington. Years of Republican presidents cohabiting with Democratic congresses were at an end; now the shoe was on the other foot. Republicans exulted in taking over the major committees and removing Democratic staffers who had been there for years. The criticism was still that divided government left the country with bitter partisanship, policy incoherence, nondecisions, showdowns, standoffs, checkmate, stalemate, deadlock, and gridlock with poor government performance. Republicans were unconcerned with the labels. They looked down Pennsylvania Avenue and saw that only one prize still eluded them: the White House.

It was a strange political year in Washington, as the nation began to reflect on the end of a century named for American omnipotence. The greatest fear, given the weaponry, was still war. Since the first century, historians estimated that 149 million people had died in major war; 111 million of those deaths occurred in the twentieth century.[60] Given the record, one could not help but wonder what the future held. World War I and World War II were epic events, and in the "global village" of worldwide communication and twenty-four-hour news cycles, a vigilant eye was supposed to be on everything that happened. But in 1994 a horrible tragedy went largely unnoticed.

Rwanda is one of the smallest countries in Central Africa, with just 7 million people comprised of two main ethnic groups: Hutu and Tutsi. Although the Hutu were the preponderant majority, the Tutsi minority were considered aristocracy during Belgian colonial rule. Following independence in 1962, the Hutu majority oppressed the Tutsis, who fled to neighboring countries where they formed a guerilla army, the Rwandan Patriotic Front (RPF). In 1990, this rebel army invaded Rwanda, and by 1993, the United Nations placed a peacekeeping force of 2,500 multinational soldiers to preserve a fragile cease-fire. On April 6, 1994, the plane carrying the Rwandan president was shot down, a crime for which responsibility has never been established.

Immediately after this incident, Rwanda plunged into political violence. The genocide of Hutu and Tutsi would be one of history's worst, with 800,000 people killed in the next 100 days. Assailants sought out and murdered targeted individuals, and went systematically from house to house in certain neighborhoods, killing Tutsi and Hutu opposed to the regime. By the middle of the first week, organizers began driving Tutsis to government offices, churches, schools, and other public settings. There, the Hutus engaged in systematic shootings, clubbing, and hacking to death with machetes of defenseless Tutsi families.

A group of Hutu soldiers sit in a Jeep on the road from Kigali, Rwanda to Goma, Zaire. (© Peter Turnly/CORBIS)

Back in Washington, and at the U.N. headquarters in New York, the killings were initially categorized as a breakdown in the cease-fire between Tutsi and Hutu. The two tracks of events in Rwanda—war and genocide—confused policy makers outside that country. From April 8 onward, media coverage featured some eyewitness accounts of massacres, but American officials refused to call what they saw "genocide." Such a designation would obligate the United States to act. An exchange between Christine Shelly, a State Department spokesman, and Reuters correspondent Alan Elsner on June 10, 1994, revealed the hesitancy to respond.[61]

Elsner: How would you describe the events taking place in Rwanda?
Shelly: Based on the evidence we have seen from observations on the ground, we have every reason to believe that acts of genocide have occurred in Rwanda.
Elsner: What's the difference between "acts of genocide" and "genocide"?
Shelly: Well, I think the—as you know, there's a legal definition of this ... clearly not all of the killings that have taken place in Rwanda are killings to which you might apply that label.... But as to the distinctions between the words, we're trying to call what we have seen so far as best as we can, and based, again, on the evidence, we have every reason to believe that acts of genocide have occurred.
Elsner: How many acts of genocide does it take to make genocide?
Shelly: Alan, that's just not a question that I'm in a position to answer.

In the entire three months of the genocide, the Clinton administration never focused top policy advisors on the killings. Rwanda was never seen as an important enough problem to merit top-level discussion. "When the subject came up, it did so along with, and subordinate to, discussions of Somalia, Haiti and Bosnia."[62] The memory of dead American soldiers being dragged through the streets of Mogadishu kept leaders of the world's most powerful nation from doing anything to stop the murders. Rwanda generated no sense of urgency at the White House or on Capitol Hill. The editorial boards of major American newspapers discouraged intervention. The April 17 *Washington Post* editorial lamented the killings, but read, "The United States has no recognizable national interest in taking a role, certainly not a leading role."[63]

The Rwandan massacre was a story of non–decision making and bureaucratic business as usual. Most Americans did not know about it at the time, and felt little guilt about what happened later on. "Never again," said President Bill Clinton when he made a visit to the country in 1998, "must we be shy in the face of evidence." More than shyness explained the darkest shadow on the Clinton Administration foreign policy record; there was a general unwillingness to face the implications of what responsibility came with being the world's only remaining superpower.

9

The Postmodern Nineties

Driven by the force of a peacetime boom, America experienced a high tide of optimism and prosperity in the last decade of the twentieth century. After the sluggishness of the 1970s and the expansion of the 1980s, productivity in the United States rose to levels greater even than those of the time following World War II. The United States was producing one-third of the world's goods. The North American Free Trade Agreement (NAFTA) and the so-called Uruguay Road of international trade negotiations opened emerging markets for the economy.[1] The flow of capital multiplied sixfold in just over six years. Suddenly, America was in a boom cycle.

The structure of the domestic economy changed as agriculture shrank in importance, and the country continued to move from industrial manufacturing to the new information society. The most celebrated tales were of the new entrepreneurs and bold risk-taking venture capitalists who became the richest of the very rich in the information age. Young computer "geeks" and "nerds" enjoyed celebrity status and luxuriant lifestyles beyond their wildest dreams. For example, at age twenty-four Marc Andreessen left the University of Illinois's National Center for Supercomputing Applications to go west to Silicon Valley. He was soon worth $130 million. In the daily press, stories from the California economic wonderland were told over and over: of a six-month waiting list for new Porsches at the car dealership, of a survey showing that sixty-four millionaires were being created each day in Silicon Valley, and of the new executives who paid an additional million dollars beyond the $2.4 million asking price for a house.

The landscape of California's Silicon Valley was transformed almost overnight. Vacant lots were turned into multimillion-dollar homes and office buildings. Shopping centers filled with Bentleys, BMW's, Jaguars, and Rolls-Royces. The new hotshots wore jeans to work, slept under their desks, and paid six-figure signing bonuses to co-workers who designed stock options to catch the upside in the creation of wealth. In 1996, the property tax roll in Santa Clara County increased by $5.2 billion; the next year those figures doubled, and they doubled again in 1998.²

The NASDAQ Composite Index of technology shares was at 500 in April 1991, at 1,000 in July 1995, surpassed 2,000 in July 1998, and soared to over 5,000 in March 2000. A bust would follow, but for a decade the ride took investors to dizzying heights. The stock market followed suit, and consumer confidence exploded. The new economy produced jobs, and no one knew the limit because the technology changed so fast. The so-called dot.com companies like Sun, SGI, Cisco, 3 Com, Netscape, and Yahoo pulled the American economy forward. By 1994, unemployment fell below 6 percent, and by April 2000 it was below 4 percent for the first time in three decades.³ The rich entrepreneurs gathered in the largest gains, of course, but everyone seemed to be better off. Even those at the bottom saw their incomes grow, with the greatest reduction in welfare rolls and poverty since records were kept.

The technology boom and the wealth expansion changed the way Americans lived and worked. Despite advances that were supposed to free people from burdensome tasks and provide more leisure time, most seemed to be working as hard as ever. Just keeping up with the new technology required more time, and once learned, the new knowledge had to be jettisoned because something else was available. There was also the additional burden of commuting to work. Americans lived in cities, worked in office parks, and built new homes in the burgeoning suburbs. Work was not just in the office downtown anymore, since laptops, modems, faxes, beepers, and cell phones made any place a workplace. The young were most familiar with the new technology, and more apt to adjust to it. Soon they were showing their mentors shortcuts and tricks-of-the-trade.

The examples of overnight economic success with employees surpassing their employers were everywhere. In 1995, Pierre Omidyar, a young software engineer working in Silicon Valley, began thinking about how to use the Internet to develop a trading system where buyers and sellers could establish a genuine market price by bidding. Over a long holiday weekend he wrote a computer program to facilitate the exchange. At first, only a trickle of users arrived at his web site, including his girlfriend, who traded PEZ candy dispensers. By the end of the year, however, several thousand auctions had been completed, and interest in eBay grew. From this modest beginning, the company became a global giant, with around 150 million registered users worldwide set to buy and sell goods worth more than $40 billion a year.

Seldom had things changed so quickly for an American generation. In jobs, the young embraced risk, libertarianism, and free agency. Douglas Coupland coined the term *Generation X* in his book of the same name in 1991.⁴ The description was of persons born in the 1960s and 1970s who wanted to hop off the merry-go-round of status, money, and social climbing to find an "authentic" existence. They were the thirteenth American generation since the nation's settlement in 1620. In his book, Coupland wrote about three strangers who chose to distance themselves from society to get a better sense of who they were. The author described the characters as "underemployed, overeducated, intensely private and unpredictable." Another term used to describe them was "slackers," and the description of their life was ridiculed by late night comics and in movies like *Reality Bites.*

The new generation survived a hurried childhood of divorce, latchkeys, space shuttle explosions, open classrooms, political corruption, inflation, the Islamic Revolution, and the shift from G- to R-rated movies. The country watched at the beginning of the decade, as a new movie designation of NC-17 was passed for the adults-only designation to replace the stigma of an "X." As young adults, the cohort had to navigate the AIDS crisis with blighted courtship rituals. In 1991 Earvin "Magic" Johnson, one of the world's best basketball players, retired from the NBA after testing HIV positive. His public confession was a warning, and Generation X'ers dated accordingly. They "worked on their relationships," and talked things out without the luxury of a commitment. As the divorce rate grew, they experimented with alternatives to traditional marriage, from remaining single, to same-sex couples, to living together.

Television made things that were once private now very public. Jerry Springer, the former mayor of Cincinnati, Ohio, introduced a top-rated television show where couples confronted one another with sexual details of their affairs, then engaged in brawls before a live studio audience. Lorena Bobbitt, who claimed to be a battered wife in 1993, was given a suspended sentence for amputating her husband's penis. The wife, who stood trial for felonious assault, claimed to have no memory of the event in question. Six months after the trial, the couple—not surprisingly—divorced. The norm seemed to be that even though money was plentiful, the future was unclear and romance fleeting.

Don Tapscott, in his book *Growing Up Digital,* called the children of the decade the "Net Generation ... the first to grow up surrounded by digital media. ... Computers can be found in the home ... and digital technologies such as cameras, video games and CD-ROMs are commonplace."[5] In the America of the 1990s, higher-income, better-educated "haves" were expanding their use of the new technology. Everyday life was altered in ways few could have imagined, like shopping online, for instance. Within four years of its creation in 1995, the online bookseller Amazon.com was generating $3 million a day in sales of books, music, and videos. Its thirtysomething founder, Jeff Bezos, was another Internet success billionaire.

The new Mecca of moneymaking was outside Seattle, Washington, on a 295-acre campus that was home to the world's wealthiest man, Bill Gates. Microsoft's Redmond corporate headquarters was also the residence of a monopoly that dominated the information age just as much as John D. Rockefeller and Standard Oil dominated the industrial age. The company operated on youth, ambition, and talent; the average age of employees was thirty-four in 1998.[6]

They were called "Microsmurfs," but the label was one of admiration, not derision. Of the 31,000 Microsoft employees at the end of the decade, 21,000 were millionaires. More were on the way. The company culture stressed informal dress, no ties or suits for men, and for women, no heels or jewelry. The Microsoft software was on 90 percent of all computers sold in the world. Behind the "laid-back" West Coast lifestyle image was a twenty-four-hours-a-day, seven-days-a-week regime, with intense competition and pressure to perform. Each six months, every employee at Microsoft had to write down the objectives he or she expected to meet before the next performance evaluation. The accomplishments were tied to stock shares in the company, in what remained as one of the most amazing stories in the history of American capitalism.

In 1975, Bill Gates founded "Micro-Soft" with a boyhood friend. Four years later, the company had twenty-eight employees, and produced $2.5 million in revenue. The big break for the company came in 1983, when the Windows software became the industry standard. By 1999, twenty-four years after its founding, Microsoft had a market value of $507 billion, making it the first company to pass the half-trillion-dollar level.[7] The growth was spectacular, and the future had no ceiling. The company was generating forty cents of profit on each dollar of revenue. Microsoft made Bill Gates the world's wealthiest man, and it was the most highly valued company in the world.

The information society, and the Generation X cohort it inspired, produced a whole new class of working persons. Because so many people were now involved in the manufacture of information, instead of the manufacture of goods, Marx's proletariat was replaced by the "cognitariat."[8] For business, the emergence of the Internet meant a shift from the modern technique of centralized control in an office to the new postmodern model of networking. In the past, information could be spread no faster than human beings could travel, but now information traversed the globe at the speed of light. The result was that people could gain information from almost anywhere on earth in an instant.

As a result, key boundaries and separations that had historically separated people and countries were eroded. Nationalism was out of fashion, especially in Europe, where twelve nations signed the Maastricht Treaty in 1992 to form the European Union. The new culture and global economy created a different order, one that a popular observer called "McWorld."[9] Life in the new world order was a kind of global village, where everyone knew everyone else's business. Americans watched nightly updates on Operation Desert Storm, followed by the election of Nelson Mandela in South Africa, and knew the intimate details behind the divorce of Princess Diana and Prince Charles.

The decade was remembered as having moved slightly away from the more conservative 1980s, but keeping the same mindset. The world experienced a rapid progression of global capitalism following the collapse of the Soviet Union. A reduction in the size and cost of mobile phones led to a surge in their popularity, and the states were left to wonder if they should legislate against taking phone calls while driving. Video games became more advanced. The most popular game systems included the Super Nintendo, the Sony Playstation, and the Sega Dreamcast.

In science, in technology, in medicine, and in military power, Americans had no equal. The explosive growth of the Internet led to a corresponding decrease in the cost of computers. Suddenly people had access to a bewildering store of knowledge, and the question was how to organize it, and search for it, without collapsing under the sheer weight of all the information. In 1994, 3 million people were online; four years later, the figure was 100 million. The new technology affected all fields. DNA identification of individuals had wide applications in the field of criminal law. The Hubble Space Telescope was launched, and it revolutionized astronomy with the detection of extra solar planets orbiting stars other than the sun. On May 11, 1998, J. Craig Venter announced that he would map and publish the entire human genetic code. At the time, the U.S. government's vaunted Genome Project had already been at work for nearly a decade. By decoding the "book of life" that held the key to understanding how every physical characteristic in the human body worked, scientists could embark upon genetic engineering. The new frontier of biology offered something more than an understanding of how genes work; it showed that they could be manipulated to fight disease and change behavior.[10]

Television remained the most popular form of entertainment. The classic television shows of the 1990s included *Beverly Hills 90210*, *Friends*, *Home Improvement*, and *Seinfeld*. "Fanny packs," or purses that buckled on the waist, were popular early in the decade, and along with Adidas Wind pants and baggy jeans, they set a clothing style. The most popular sportswear was by Nike, whose swoosh symbol and motto "Just do it" appeared everywhere. It was fashionable to get a tattoo, which became so common you had to get one just to blend in. Then there was the piercing of body parts. People were getting their tongues, belly buttons, eyebrows, nipples, or anything else pierced. The most popular female hairdo was the "Rachel," a haircut Jennifer Aniston wore on television's *Friends*. It was the 1990s equivalent to what Farrah Fawcett was to the 1970s. Black became a dominant color in fashion. Extreme sports reached new heights in popularity, and by 1995 were given their own annual tournament on ESPN, the "X-Games."

In sum, the 1990s saw the blossoming of a new type of social life that began in the 1960s. That decade introduced a politics critical of the modernist state, with its economy of production and prosperity. The critique by radicals was of a "myth of objective consciousness" as a mask for establishment power. By the 1990s, a new economic order had emerged, euphemistically called postmodern, or postindustrial, or a consumer society of the media, or a spectacle of "globalization," or multinational capitalism. The postmodern ethos was centerless. There were no longer common standards to which people appealed in their efforts to measure, judge, or value ideas, opinions, or lifestyle choices. Gone was allegiance to a common sense of authority, or a commonly regarded and respected wielder of legitimate power. Modernity was itself born out of a secular interpretation of the Christian narrative, which spoke of a rational God who was the creator and sovereign over the universe. Science was the new god, but postmodernism rejected any notion of an overarching truth, and reduced all ideas to social constructions of class, gender, and ethnicity.

The postmodern philosopher Michel Foucault offered a name for the unfocused, postmodern ideal: "hetrotopia."[11] The term was the opposite of utopia, which was the design of a modern society where peace, justice, and love would reign. Now there were no universally agreed-upon values. The postmodern expression of hetrotopia was pluralism, which celebrated diversity and no overarching standard. Postmodern cultural expressions undermined the concept of a powerful, originating ideal, by destroying the ideology of style and replacing it with multiple styles. Jacques Derrida, a leading postmodern philosopher, wrote that the primary form of postmodern discourse was the collage. Contemporary postmodern art works, for example, emphasized disparate images and incompatible meanings, producing "a signification which could be neither univocal nor stable."[12] In short, postmodern art refused to speak with one voice, and its very definition resisted a single meaning.

The collage offered an artist a way to bring incompatible elements together, and allowed many styles to hold sway at the same time. Postmodernism was this

The Wrapped Reichstag by the artist Christo. (Courtesy, Martin Morgenstern)

ethic written on a larger surface. The multiple presentations described a particular view of history, a declaration that society should live in "a perpetual present," without depth, definition, or a secure identity. It had a fixation with appearances, surfaces, and instant impacts, and was ephemeral, existing only for the moment. The artist Christo (which is really two people born on the same day, Christo Yavasheff and Jeanne-Claude Denat de Guillebon) explored the postmodern ideal by wrapping historical buildings in fabric.[13] In 1995, after twenty-three years of negotiating with the German government, the Christos wrapped the Reichstag in Berlin. Over 100,000 square meters of fireproof polypropylene fabric and fifteen kilometers of rope were needed for the project. Veiling was completed within a week, and the "performance" presentation lasted two weeks. The wrapping of the Reichstag had importance for the artists because of the ending of the Cold War and because Berlin had been the scene of significant East-West confrontations. The statement was irrational in the sense that the wrapping had no practical foundation and showed only artistic creativity, making people smile and become more aware of themselves and their surroundings. The work had a deliberate temporary effect to enhance the value and intensity of the viewer. One reviewer mentioned that performance art, like that of Christo, was like the idea of death, and it made people more aware of life's precious brevity.

When Christo staged a well-publicized event, and then took down the fabric and the work of art was gone, so too the significance was not in the work of art itself; instead, the relevance was in the boldness of the artist to confront a modernist conception or stereotypes. The irony of the event was the art. After wrapping the Reichstag, Christo wrapped the Louvre in Paris, making art out of the world's greatest museum of art. The reaction of the audience to the irony in such a statement, including responses of outrage, disgust, and puzzlement, are the work of art itself. The words of Milan Kundera, who quotes Nietzsche in his book *The Unbearable Lightness of Being*, were classically postmodern: "Life is unbearably light when it has no purpose to it."[14]

Technological developments facilitated the penetration of postmodern thinking into the culture, especially the popular culture. Rock music, for example, was a perfect venue because of its "unifying global reach and influence on the one hand, combined with its tolerance and engendering of pluralities of styles, media and ethnic identities on the other."[15] Rock music was multicultural; it easily spanned political borders and was popular around the world. New styles emerged, and yet it remained intrinsically contemporary. Rock depended on technology to prosper, and in the age of Internet mixing, the artists did not have to be together to record or perform.

Music styles multiplied, Latino music grew in popularity, country became mainstream, and Grunge music gained widespread acceptance. The grunge style of music was sometimes referred to as the "Seattle Sound," with lyrics that emphasized feelings of anger, frustration, ennui, sadness, fear, and depression. Factors such as poverty, the environment, discomfort with existing social institutions, and the state of society were evident in the songs. The band Nirvana was generally credited with breaking the genre into the popular consciousness in 1991. Their popularity paved the way for other bands, most notably Pearl Jam. Heroin use among grunge musicians was a serious problem, especially when Kurt Cobain of Nirvana died in 1994 from an alleged overdose.

Another means of postmodern expression was filmmaking, which fit the postmodern ethic by producing something that had the illusion of reality but was not real. "Video can lay claim to being postmodernism's most distinctive new medium, a medium which, at its best, is a whole new form in itself."[16] Movies created events. The release of a major movie became a public relations event that doubled as a birth announcement to the culture that a new campaign with toys, video games, and fast food meals was on the way. A film became a technological artifact, assembled by a variety of specialists, each working with a range of techniques to produce a coherent whole. The unity of the film was largely an illusion. What appeared as a continuous narrative was really an edited compilation of events filmed at various times in wide-ranging locations over months and weeks. The characters were regularly not the same actors, and with the computer, scenes were re-imaged and altered.

Because the unity of a film was so malleable, filmmakers had considerable freedom to manipulate a story in contrived ways. Postmodern film delighted in collapsing events, manipulating space and time situations, and deconstructing a belief in cultural values. In 1991, *The Silence of the Lambs* pushed the moral envelope by making a sympathetic hero of a cannibal. Quentin Tarantino's direction of *Pulp Fiction* in 1994 marked the breaking of postmodern filmmaking into mainstream culture. The story appeared to take place in an undisclosed time period that looked like the 1970s, but the plot was mixed up out of sequence, showing the middle at the beginning and bouncing back and forth in time. The movie ended with a character's earlier life after showing his death.

The postmodern sensibility, since it did not believe in underlying reality, could not be about reality and so it was about itself. The new form presented live action/animation hybrids such as *Who Framed Roger Rabbit* (1988), *Cool World* (1992), and *Monkeybone* (2001), where characters interacted with cartoon fantasy worlds. Other movies like *Hook* (1991) and *Jumanji* (1995) used live-action fantasy to fuse reality with fiction. In advertising, long-dead actors Groucho Marx and John Wayne appeared in cola commercials. Woody Allen's *Purple Rose of Cairo* (1985) had the dashing, romantic movie hero literally walk out of the movie screen into the heroine's pathetic, abused life.

The postmodern take on horror movies was equally ironic; it spoofed the conventions of the genre, while graphically depicting sex and violence. In the dialogue of one scene, a character declares, "But this is life.... This isn't a movie." To which another character responded, "Sure it is.... It's all a movie.... Life is one great big movie... only you can't pick your genre."[17] The underside of life was seen in the dark drama *Blue Velvet* (1986), which juxtaposed incoherent worlds and confused characters asking about the nature of reality in a small North Carolina town.

Among the most important statistics when evaluating postmodernism is the one that television became, and remained, the "most trusted source of news for most Americans." The same postmodern assumptions of filmmaking applied to television, with the addition that it could offer live broadcasting to supplement the static product. Television became the medium through which film invaded the day-to-day life of millions of Americans, so much so that each day the average viewer received some 400 visual solicitations through television, newspapers, and magazines.

After a time, many people came to believe that television presented the actual events themselves—without interpretation, editing, or commentary. As a medium of postmodern culture, television legitimized events. Many viewers did not rate something as important until it showed up on television. Television news shows provided the viewer with a succession of unrelated images: a political speech, a murder investigation, a new medical breakthrough, sporting highlights, advertisements for better batteries, better soap, a laxative commercial, and scenes from a war in a remote country. All the stories and the commercials received roughly the same treatment and time allotments. Add to this collage the provision of dozens, maybe even hundreds, of channels, and you had a visual menu without rank. Television became the ultimate postmodern experience, a plethora of images detached from any reference to reality and floating by in a ceaseless stream. A single television screen might have split, three, or even four images at once and have several running tickers along the bottom of the screen at the same time.

Living in the postmodern era of the 1990s meant inhabiting a world created by images without an agreed-upon metanarrative. If there was one impression the major news stories of the decade left with the viewer, it was that human reason could perceive no logical structure or causes in the external universe. Instead, viewers became collectors of experience, repositories of transitory, fleeting images produced and fostered by diverse media forms. The distinction between truth and fiction seemed to evaporate.

The new power of media to shape events was most evident when a sensational incident was covered by television. If the coverage was intense, then the response by the audience was unpredictable. On the night of March 2, 1991, Rodney Glen King was riding with some friends when he was pulled over for recklessly driving through a residential Los Angeles neighborhood. When police ordered the occupants out of the car and instructed them to lie face down on the ground, two complied, but King remained in the car. When ordered out again, King slowly exited. One officer described him as "smiling" as he stood beside his Hyundai and waved to the police helicopter circling overhead. Rodney King finally complied with the order to lie on the ground, but when a California Highway Patrol officer approached him, a sergeant with the Los Angeles Police Department (LAPD) shouted, "Stand back. We'll handle this."

The LAPD officer subsequently testified that he thought King was on PCP, a drug that made individuals impervious to pain and gave them extraordinary strength. Five Los Angeles police officers swarmed King in an attempt to handcuff and subdue him; he charged them and put some on their backs. Twice, the police attempted to subdue him using 50,000-volt tasers, a power considered to be enough to subdue a normal man but not successful with King.

The lights and commotion awakened George Holliday, a manager of a plumbing company, in his nearby apartment. He walked to his bedroom terrace and pointed his new video camera at the action unfolding some ninety feet away. Holliday recorded a scene of police striking King with metal batons. The nine-minute-and-twenty-second videotape showed over fifty baton blows and several kicks before King was handcuffed in a minute-and-a-half segment of the tape. The video showed one officer stomping on King's shoulder so that his head hit the asphalt. The prisoner was taken in an ambulance to Pacifica Hospital, where he later said he recalled little of what happened after the first blow. "I felt beat up and like a crushed can," recalled the defendant, "that's what I felt like, like a crushed can all over, and my spirits were down real low."[18]

The next day, George Holliday took his video to Los Angeles television station KTLA. News producers found it shocking. One later recalled, "I looked at the pictures and felt a flow of adrenaline surge through my body.... I had never viewed anything like this before."[19] After showing the tape to the police, KTLA played it on the evening news. The response was overwhelming, with national repercussions. CNN picked up the tape, and soon it was a segment on their *Headline News* show. CNN Vice-President Ed Turner said, "Television used the tape like wallpaper." A poll taken in Los Angeles after the broadcasts showed that 92 percent of the respondents believed that excessive force was used against Rodney King. Police Chief Daryl Gates said of the arrest, "It was more than extreme... it was impossible."[20]

Rodney King was subsequently released without charges, but the four LAPD officers involved in the arrest faced a variety of offenses, ranging from assault under the color of authority to failing to file a police report. In the course of the subsequent trial, investigators found that one officer wrote, "I haven't beaten anyone this bad in a long time."[21] Later, the same policeman sent another message describing the scene of a domestic disturbance involving African Americans as one "right out of 'Gorillas in the Mist.' " Los Angeles Mayor Tom Bradley declared that the King arrest proved "a dangerous trend of racially motivated incidents running through at least some segments of the Police Department."[22]

Attorneys for the four officers focused their attention on moving the trial out of Los Angeles County. The change of venue was granted after several appeals, and a year later the officers stood trial in suburban Simi Valley in Ventura County. The jury pool included only a half-dozen African Americans out of 260 people called, and the final jury impaneled ten non-Hispanic whites, one Hispanic, and an Asian. Terry White, chief prosecutor in the case and an African American, claimed that "everyone seemed very pro-police, they all seemed to come from the same background."[23]

At trial, the defense argued that the officers had legitimate reason to believe King was dangerous, and all their actions were justified. The prosecution based their case on the videotape record. The jury debated the officers' fate for seven days. On April 29, 1992, three of the officers were acquitted, and the jury could not agree on the verdict for the other one. At 3:15 P.M. the clerk announced the jury's verdict and all four officers were released. Less than two hours later, Los Angeles was in flames.

The authorities were caught off guard by the reaction. Sixty-two minutes after the verdict was read, five black youths entered a Korean-owned liquor store where they grabbed bottles of malt liquor and headed out the door shouting: "This is for Rodney King." The looting, beating, and hysteria expanded exponentially.[24] Black youths with baseball bats battered a car driven by a white driver. Another white driver was hit in the face by a chunk of concrete thrown through the windshield. Carloads of youths headed out of West Los Angeles brandishing hatchets, beating passersby, and looting shops. Police faced gangs of rock- and bottle-throwing youths.

In one of the most horrific incidents, broadcast live from the scene, Reginald Denny, a mild-mannered truck driver, listening to country music as he drove, was assaulted as a news camera helicopter circled overhead. Denny was at the wheel of his truck, carrying a load of sand, when he was stopped and pulled from his truck into the street. When down, he was kicked, and then beaten in the head with a claw hammer. One attacker smashed a block of concrete on Denny's head at point-blank range, knocking him unconscious and fracturing his head in ninety-one places. The helicopter camera recorded his attacker doing a victory dance as he gleefully pointed at Denny's bloodied figure.[25]

The fighting, burning, and looting lasted five days, and was only quelled when National Guard troops were stationed around the city. When it was over, fifty-four people (mostly Koreans and Latinos) were dead, and hundreds more were injured. The looting and fires resulted in more than $1 billion worth of property damage and an incalculable injury to the city's reputation. Whole neighborhoods looked like a war zone, and over 7,000 people were arrested.

President George Bush and Attorney General William Barr brought federal charges against the four LAPD officers accused in the King case. In 1993, a federal judge sentenced two officers involved in the beating to thirty months in prison. The other officers were not convicted, and this time there was no rioting after the verdict. Although he received $3.8 million in a civil suit against the LAPD, Rodney King was subsequently bankrupt and living in a drug rehab center. Yet it was to the original victim that the most memorable quote was attributed: "People, I just want to say, can we all just get along? Can we stop making it horrible? We're all stuck here for a while.... Let's just try to work it out."[26]

The Rodney King videotape, and consequent trial of four police officers that ignited the riots, was heralded as yet another "Trial of the Century" in America. It joined the Sacco-Vanzetti trial (1921), the John Thomas Scopes "Monkey" trial (1925), the Lindbergh kidnapping (1935), the trial of Alger Hiss (1949–1950), the trial of the "Chicago Seven" (1968), and Lieutenant William Calley's court martial (1971), among others, as contenders for the title. Unbeknownst to the chroniclers at the time, the decade of the 1990s would be host to yet another trial with racial overtones, one that would eclipse even that of the Los Angeles riots. On Friday, June 17, 1994, ABC interrupted its regular programming to declare: "This is a special report from ABC News." Anchorman Peter Jennings described a scene on the Interstate Five freeway in the Los Angeles area, where up to ten police cars with overhead emergency lights flashing were escorting a Ford Bronco while as many as twelve helicopters hovered overhead. "This has been going on for some time now," explained Jennings. "Police believe they have located O. J. Simpson, [who was] wanted on two counts of murder, in this white Bronco going somewhere."[27]

The Bronco was going straight into the living rooms, and cultural consciousness, of all America. NBC interrupted its broadcast of the NBA finals game between the New York Knicks and the Houston Rockets, with live pictures. Word spread in Los Angeles that O. J. was on the freeway with a gun to his mouth, and thousands of people took up positions on freeway overpasses and along the interstate with homemade signs declaring: "We Love You, O. J.," and "Honk for the Juice." At times all traffic on the opposite freeway stopped, and one highway patrolman described the scene as if "a rock concert had let out on the freeway, pedestrians were everywhere.... It was like a parting of the Red Sea to drive." Kim Goldman, the sister of one of the slain victims, asked, "Who would do this?" Another LAPD officer looked at the people and said, "It reminded me of the L.A. riots coming as it did on the heels of Rodney King."[28]

Orenthal James Simpson, known commonly as "O. J.," or "The Juice," was one of the most famous running backs in American football history. After retiring from professional football in 1979, Simpson spent time working as a sports commentator, acting, and leaping over luggage in a Hertz television commercial. Simpson's first marriage ended in divorce, and he later met seventeen-year-old waitress Nicole Brown, whom he married in 1985. Nicole Brown Simpson often complained to friends and family of beatings at the hands of the jealous Simpson, who did not approve of her flirtatious manners. After what was described as a "rocky marriage," Nicole Brown filed for divorce from O. J. Simpson in 1992.[29]

In June of 1994, O. J. Simpson was charged with two counts of murder for the gruesome killings of his ex-wife and Ronald Goldman, a waiter who was her friend. A veteran Los Angeles homicide policeman, one of the first officers to arrive at Nicole Brown Simpson's townhouse at 875 South Bundy Avenue on June 12, called it "the bloodiest crime scene I have ever seen." The bodies of the two victims were found shortly before midnight lying in pools of blood on the Spanish-style walkway leading to the $700,000 townhouse. The thirty-five-year-old ex-wife's throat was slashed through to the spinal cord, leaving a five-and-a-half-inch gash from the left side of her neck to the right ear. She had numerous additional wounds, including four in the left side of her neck and three in the back of her head. Her black cocktail dress was ripped; her bloodied hands were in a defensive position as if she were attempting to ward off an attack. The body of the young man lay ten feet away from Nicole Brown Simpson, partly obscured by bushes. His neck had been slashed on both sides; in all, his body bore twenty-three separate knife wounds. Near his feet a brown leather glove, sticky and soaked with blood, lay near a Navy cap and an envelope containing a pair of glasses. The crime was discovered when Nicole Brown Simpson's dog, with blood on its belly and legs, attracted the attention of a neighbor.[30]

Los Angeles police questioned O. J. Simpson when he returned home from a business trip to Chicago. They asked him a number of questions, especially focusing on a deep cut on his right hand, which he said was a result of a glass he shattered when he heard the news of his wife's death. Eventually the police accumulated enough evidence to obtain a warrant for his arrest. Under an agreement worked out with Simpson's attorney, the defendant agreed he would turn himself in the day after his wife's funeral.[31] He did not show up. His absence led to perhaps the most famous low-speed, fifty-mile chase since Paul Revere. Simpson rode crouched in the back of the SUV, driven by a friend, with a loaded gun pointed at his chin. As the cameras followed the Bronco on the freeway, a Simpson family friend read a rambling letter live on air. In it, Simpson said, "First, everyone understand I had nothing to do with Nicole's murder.... Don't feel sorry for me.... I've had a great life."[32]

The country did not know it yet, but it had just turned a psychological corner. The O. J. Simpson trial would galvanize the interest of Americans. Experts estimated that close to 95 million people watched the Bronco freeway chase. An ABC News poll found that 84 percent of those surveyed expressed disgust with the attention the case was getting in the media—but millions kept tuning in.[33] The constant attention in a pervasive scandal culture led to a mockery of the criminal justice system and reinforced an already pervasive sense of public cynicism. An Op-Ed article by A. M. Rosenthal in the *New York Times* early asked if the press was made up of "journalists or garbage collectors."[34] Given the unverified rumors appearing in print and on air, it seemed like refuse was winning out.

At his second appearance, on July 22, a confident Simpson pled in a defiant tone: "Absolutely, 100 percent Not Guilty." The trial was set for the downtown district of Los Angeles, and the decision was political: a largely white jury in Santa Monica might spark another protest like the one after the Rodney King verdict. The opening day of testimony was set for Tuesday, January 24, 1995, and for the next eight months, with 133 days in court, the proceedings dominated the daily news coverage. Cameras were allowed in the courtroom, and nationwide coverage led to endless second guessing of both the prosecution and defense strategies. Christopher Darden led off by saying: "If he couldn't have her, he didn't want anyone else to have her." What followed was a parade of seventy-two witnesses, who collectively suggested that Simpson was an abusive husband motivated by jealousy.

Simpson hired a team of expensive high-profile lawyers, who argued that their client was the victim of police fraud and sloppy internal procedures that contaminated the DNA evidence. A lead detective was painted as a racist, who planted incriminating evidence at the crime scene. Simpson's daughter took the stand; she was followed by the other members of his family. The most critical witness may have been a soft-spoken Japanese American forensic expert, who provided plausible justification for questioning the prosecution's key physical evidence.

At one point in the trial, the prosecution asked Simpson to put on the leather glove found at the scene of the crime. The glove was too tight for Simpson to wear, which inspired defense counsel Johnnie Cochran to quip in his closing remarks: "If the glove doesn't fit, you must acquit." Polls before the verdict showed the country was divided along racial lines. "Barely a month after O. J.'s arrest, 63 percent of whites answering a *Time*/CNN poll said they thought he would get a fair trial... [but] only 31 percent of blacks felt the same way."[35] The jury of ten women and two men, of whom eight were black, with two Hispanics, one half–Native American, a half-white, and a white female, deliberated only three hours. At 10:00 A.M., on October 3, 1995, after $15 million in expenses, and in front of an estimated 100 million television viewers, a verdict of "not guilty" was announced.

The finding shook white America, but many African Americans around the country reacted with celebration. In the end, race, not domestic violence, or police corruption, or the above-the-law assumptions of professional athletes, or even murder, became the touchstone of the O. J. Simpson murder case.[36] Commentators speculated that the verdict showed the effect money had on the judicial system. After the trial, several jurors said they believed Simpson probably committed the murder, but the prosecution bungled the case. On February 4, 1997, a civil jury in Santa Monica, California, found O. J. Simpson liable for the wrongful death of Ronald Goldman, battery against Ronald Goldman, and battery against Nicole Brown. Unlike the previous trial, cameras were not in evidence, and the jury ordered Simpson to pay $33,500,000 in damages. After the trials, Simpson lost his endorsement and advertising deals. He subsequently won custody of his children, and moved to Florida where his residence could not be seized or collected for debt in the civil case.

The trial raised questions about law enforcement practices and showed the prevalence of domestic violence, even among the wealthy. But it had other effects as well, mainly related to the presence of cameras in the courtroom. The entertainment media trivialized the judicial process, exploited tragedy, and added sensationalism to the proceedings. One KNBC newsman, on stakeout at Nicole Brown Simpson's house, stood by open-mouthed as people drove up to chip blood-stained tiles from the sidewalk as souvenirs. Many figures in the trial unwittingly became celebrities. Presiding Judge Lance Ito, for example, was regularly parodied by comedian Jay Leno on the *Tonight Show* as a troupe of Asian men in black robes called the "Dancing Itos."

In the Los Angeles trials of Rodney King and O. J. Simpson, the "City of Angels" gave the nation something even Hollywood, the American Dream Factory, could not provide: surreal reality as postmodern news coverage. The events created a new type of "immersion" journalism that raised speculation to the level of news and created events to feed an insatiable cycle that lasted twenty-four hours a day. Mobile television minicams and earth-orbiting satellites provided the ability to go live anywhere to add to the collage of newsbreaks. Lurid details, and proliferating cable channels, fed a preoccupation with scandal and rumor. Watching O. J. was the ultimate postmodern event. Guilt or innocence was less important than the performance experience of watching the trial.

At mid-decade, the country had to grapple with a new story: domestic terrorism. The wrinkle was that religion was now an imperative for extremist action. In 1968 none of the identifiable international terrorist groups could be classified as religious, since most were Marxist-Leninist. In the 1990s, the proportion of religiously inspired groups grew appreciably. The repercussions of the 1979 Iranian revolution gave birth to the Islamist terrorists, but there were others who lived in the country with deeply held religious motivations.[37] In February of 1993, Islamic radicals drove a yellow Ford Econoline rental van into the basement of the World Trade Center in New York. Ramzi Yousef and Eyad Ismoil then set a timer to detonate the 1,500-pound, urea-nitrate bomb. The massive blast created a crater 200 feet by 100 feet wide and seven stories deep in the garage of the World Trade Center. The explosion killed six people, injured 1,042, and caused nearly $300 million in property damage.[38]

Although proof was lacking, the suspicion remained that the conspirators considered lacing the bomb with poison. Millions of Americans wondered why the hatred. Several historical forces converged to engender the aversion, the most important being that the political mood in the Middle East after the first Gulf War was strongly anti-American. The six conspirators were motivated by an incoherent mixture of hatred for the United States and personal affirmation with a confusing mixture of geopolitical rationales.

In March of 1995 an apocalyptic Japanese religious cult released sarin nerve gas into the Tokyo subway systems. It was the most serious attack on Japan in modern history, and killed a dozen people while wounding 3,796 others.[39] Three subway lines were targeted, in a bizarre plan to launch gas attacks and other calamities that were ultimately targeted to kill 90 percent of the population in major metropolitan cities. The doomsday cult's teachings were based on tenets borrowed from Hinduism and Buddhism, and taught that the end of the world was near. It seemed to some that any religious faith, if taken seriously, would lead to terrorism.

The religious motivation for terrorism led to more intense acts that in turn produced more fatalities than those perpetuated by secular terrorists. Although religious terrorists committed only 25 percent of the recorded acts in 1995, their acts were responsible for 58 percent of the fatalities. Those attacks that killed eight or more people that year were all perpetrated by religious terrorists.[40] The fanatics' view of society was conspiratorial. They saw it as dominated by leaders who deserved punishment. A profound sense of hostility and isolation permeated the cults, and they often sought to eliminate a broadly defined group of enemies in the belief that such large-scale violence was justified.

Most Americans were horrified by the violence they saw on television and read about in newspapers, and relieved that the deaths in New York and Tokyo were not higher than they were. Overall, a feeling of "it can't happen here" still pervaded the mood of the country. That attitude was about to be shocked out of existence. It happened just minutes after 9:00 A.M. on April 19, 1995. Many of the 550 people who worked in Oklahoma City's Alfred P. Murrah Federal Building were headed to their offices when a truck bomb tore down the north face of the nine-story building. Most Americans, who thought such a thing could only happen elsewhere, were left trying to grasp, and then cope, with the enormity of the act. At the time, it was the worst terrorist attack on U.S. soil.

What happened? A stunned nation watched as the bodies of men, women, and children were pulled from the rubble. Speculation on the cause of the explosion

Consequences of the Oklahoma City bombing. (© Les Stone/Sygma/Corbis)

was lost in a rush to get the wounded out. Alan Prokop was one of the first rescuers to the scene. "I could hear water running in the area and I screamed... that we had to get the water turned off... [and] the rescuer behind the slab hollered that it wasn't water, it's blood, and he held up his hands... covered with blood." Captain Dan Browing, with his dog, Gunny, searched for bodies for forty straight days. "I dream that I'm crawling through the rubble," he recalled years later, "I hear children crying from in front of me and to my right [and] I begin to feel the ground tremble in front of me.... I turn and run, and the kids quit crying and I feel very guilty."[41] When the smoke cleared, and the rescue workers went home, 168 people were dead, including nineteen children and one rescue worker.

The bomb was in a rented Ryder truck, loaded with 5,000 pounds of ammonium nitrate, an agricultural fertilizer, and nitromethane, a highly volatile motor-racing fuel.[42] Just ninety minutes after the explosion, an Oklahoma Highway Patrol officer pulled over twenty-seven-year-old Timothy McVeigh for driving without a license plate. Shortly before McVeigh was to be released on the minor offense, he was identified as the bombing suspect by law enforcement authorities and charged with the crime. With the announcement of the arrest, the country had to face the fact of terrorism within, as well as from abroad; from citizens, and not just from foreigners.

The abiding question remained: Why? McVeigh was a military veteran, and had no prior record of arrest. In dramatic testimony in his subsequent trial, McVeigh's sister, Jennifer, calmly told jurors about her brother's rage against the government for the 1993 siege of the Branch Davidians in Waco, Texas.[43] Timothy McVeigh decided to extract retribution on those he felt responsible—the Murrah Federal Building held numerous federal agency offices, including Alcohol, Tobacco, and Firearms (ATF). In planning his revenge on the second anniversary of the Waco tragedy, McVeigh enlisted the help of his friend, Terry Nichols, to help him pull off his plan. Together they experimented with bombing materials and techniques, and in September 1994 McVeigh purchased the fertilizer and stored it in a rented shed in Herrington, Kansas.[44] All this was baffling. On the day chosen, McVeigh drove the Ryder truck to the building, lit the bomb's fuse, parked in front of the building, left the keys in the ignition, locked the door, then walked across the parking lot to an alley and began to jog.

The effect of the explosion was enormous. Beyond the death toll of 168, the bomb injured 800 people and destroyed or seriously damaged 300 buildings in the area. By some estimates, more than one-third of the nearly one-half million residents of Oklahoma City knew someone who was killed or injured in the bombing. Over 12,000 people participated in the relief and rescue operations. The area was immediately flooded with workers and aid agencies, as well as the news media. Thousands of press agents, along with hundreds of satellite trucks, descended on Oklahoma City, straining the resources of the city just when it was trying to support search and rescue efforts. One CNN reporter recalled calling his office to ask where everyone was. The reply: "They're all at O.J." Within twenty-four hours CNN opened, built, wired, furnished, equipped, and staffed a ninety-two-person bureau in Oklahoma City.

The national focus climaxed when President Bill Clinton spoke on April 23. The president blamed the bombing on anti-government paranoia that led to the rise of militia groups that rejected the legitimacy of federal authority. He specifically criticized radio talk show hosts. "They spread hate. They leave the impression that, by their very words, that violence is acceptable."[45] Clinton did not mention any radio hosts by name in his speech, but later he identified conservative talk radio shows to the press.

The McVeigh trial was moved to Denver, where U.S. District Judge Richard P. Matsch maintained strict control over the courtroom. The judge faced the nearly impossible task of reconciling the emotions of the grieving bombing victim families with the defendant's right to a fair trial. He moved decisively to ban cameras and limit the scope of comments outside the courtroom. The prosecution had to overcome reports of evidence contamination and mistakes in the FBI crime lab. The government pursued a two-pronged strategy of calling survivors to recount the horror of the scene and presenting the least impeachable testimony and evidence.

Prosecutors found McVeigh's fingerprints on a receipt for ammonium nitrate; they had a fake driver's license in the same name used to rent the Ryder truck, and the crime lab found explosive residue on his clothing. But the most dramatic testimony came not from evidence, but from friends and family who portrayed McVeigh as a bomber bent on revenge. The defense was able to impeach some of the credibility of prosecution witnesses, but they could not counter the memories eyewitnesses had of the horror of the bombing and the implication that someone was responsible. After twenty-eight days of overwhelming evidence, the jurors found the government's arguments convincing, and chose to send McVeigh to death by lethal injection. Nichols received a sentence of life without parole some six months later. In his remarks from the bench, Judge Matsch said, "He has been proven to be an enemy of the Constitution." On June 11, 2001, McVeigh was executed, and Nichols was subsequently convicted in an Oklahoma state court to another life sentence in prison.[46]

What little that remained of the Murrah Federal Building was demolished, and a memorial was dedicated. The site was given over to a reflecting pool book ended by two large symbolic "doorways," with a field full of bronze and stone chairs—one for each person lost, including children, and arranged based on what floor they were on when the bomb exploded. On a corner adjacent to the memorial a sculpture was erected by St. Joseph's Catholic Church, one of the first brick-and-mortar churches in the city. It too was almost totally destroyed by the blast.

Timothy McVeigh was a disgruntled American who wanted revenge on those he resented. He was not alone. On April 3, 1996, a family member gave a tip to the FBI that ended the longest and costliest manhunt for a serial killer in U.S. history.[47] After seventeen years of anonymity, the "Unabomber" was exposed by his younger brother. Some thought the family unfaithfulness was rooted in the terror the Oklahoma City bombing brought to light. Within five days of the deadly Oklahoma blast, the Unabomber sent another package in the mail to the president of a California forestry group. For a time in early 1995, it appeared as though the nation was held hostage, in the clutch of dissidents.

Theodore John Kaczynski was an American terrorist who attempted to fight what he saw as the evils of technology by sending mail bombs to various people for a period of over eighteen years. The prospect of receiving a bomb in an unknown package caused thousands of people to refuse perfectly legitimate mailings. The bombs killed three people and wounded twenty-nine. Before his identity was known, the FBI referred to the mail bomber as the "Unabomber," which was an acronym for "university and airline bombers."

The university part was certainly appropriate for Ted Kaczynski. Born in Chicago, he was an intellectually gifted child who was also shy and aloof. He skipped two grades, graduating from high school in 1958 and entering Harvard at the age of sixteen to major in mathematics. Kaczynski graduated in four years to attend the University of Michigan, Ann Arbor, and earn a Ph.D. in mathematics. His specialty was a branch of complex analysis known as geometric function theory. One professor on his dissertation committee at Michigan commented, "I would guess that maybe 10 or 12 people in the country understood or appreciated it."[48]

In the fall of 1967, Kaczynski was hired as an assistant professor of mathematics at the University of California at Berkeley. While there, he was not a popular teacher, and was often described by his students as brilliant, but unsociable. After two years, Kaczynski resigned his position at Berkeley and moved to a remote cabin near Lincoln, Montana, where he lived without running water or electricity for more than twenty years. The former mathematician survived on very little money, occasionally working odd jobs and receiving intermittent financial support from his family.

The first mail bomb exploded in late 1978, and was followed by bombs to airline officials. The FBI became involved after a 1979 incident when a pilot was forced to make an emergency landing when a faulty timing mechanism on the bomb led to a smoking package in the cargo compartment. Original speculation was that the bomber was a disgruntled airline mechanic, but some thought the bombs too sophisticated for such a person and pointed to some academic affiliation. The first serious injury to a bombing victim occurred in 1985, when a Berkeley graduate student lost four fingers and vision in one eye when he opened an unknown package.

The Unabomber targeted computer stores, computer science professors at major universities, and other scientists working in emergent technology fields. A group of agents from the FBI, U.S. postal inspectors, and members of the Bureau of Alcohol, Tobacco, and Firearms conducted thousands of interviews, logged some 20,000 calls, and sifted through a list of some 200 suspects. They found that the bomber used old parts and filed any numbers off incriminating items, and they speculated that he picked components up at junkyards. He was careful, using stamps long past their issue date and scraping the labels off batteries to erase their serial numbers. The Unabomber fashioned macabre signatures for his handiwork.[49]

In 1995, the year of the Oklahoma City bombing, Kaczynski mailed several letters, some to his former victims, demanding that a treatise he had written be published. He threatened to kill more people if the "Unabomber" did not get a hearing. The Justice Department recommended publication of the bizarre tract in the interest of public safety, hopeful that its distribution would result in a lead to break the case. The 35,000-word paper, entitled *Industrial Society and Its Future*, argued that technology was enslaving and should be stopped to free people from its unnatural demands. Eventually, the treatise was published by the *New York Times* and the *Washington Post* in September of 1995 in the hope that someone would recognize the writing style. His brother did.[50]

In the end, the federal government with its advanced technology and large task force was unsuccessful. Kaczynski's younger brother, David, thought he saw his eccentric older sibling's style copied from Joseph Conrad's novel *The Secret Agent*. Kaczynski grew up with a copy of the book by his bedside, and had read it some two dozen times. The Unabomber was arrested at his cabin in April of 1996. On January 21, 1998, he pled guilty in exchange for a sentence of life in prison without the possibility of parole. He was sentenced to the Federal ADX Supermax prison in Florence, Colorado. The Oklahoma City bombing and the Unabomber introduced Americans to the home-grown domestic terrorist, but sadly the nation would get a more dramatic lesson on the subject of terrorism in 2001.

The decade sputtered to exhaustion amid affluence and fear. The resurgence of terrorist violence meant that nothing less than a sea of change in thinking about the threat was needed to counter it. But it was not forthcoming. Instead, the country indulged itself in prosperity and innovation. Americans changed their ways of shopping. Montgomery Ward died; so too did Woolworths, while Wal-Mart, Home Depot, Best Buy, Bed Bath and Beyond, and Staples flourished. Families shopped in minivans and checked the Internet for the lowest prices. The upper middle class went beyond talking about affluence; they moved into half-million-dollar houses and traveled abroad. During the decade, the price of a home in the United States actually dropped, from an average of $128,000 in 1990 to $119,000 in 1999. The decade saw more new models of Mercedes-Benz automobiles introduced than ever before: the "E" Class, the "C" Class, and the "S" Class.

The computer was the dominant machine that changed life for everyone in the new era. At the end of the 1990s people talked about email attachments, "snail mail" (via the U.S. Postal Service) and computer-generated graphics. The home computer pushed the video arcade from the shopping mall and helped accommodate the CD and DVD. A library of information was available at the stroke of a key. "The two most profoundly influential technologies of our times are computing and genetics," said Dr. Robert Cook-Deegean, one of the world's leading experts on cancer research. "The 1990s have been the decade when these two technologies converged in a powerful way."

"Dolly the Sheep" was introduced to the world on February 23, 1997, born seven miles from Edinburgh, in Ruslin, Scotland.[51] She was plump and fat, with a full coat and two soft eyes that seemed to be saying, "Here I am: Deal with it." The sheep was the first mammal to be successfully cloned from an adult cell. The technique that made her birth famous, somatic cell nuclear transfer, involved moving the nucleus from one of the donor's nonreproductive cells into a de-nucleated embryonic cell, which was then coaxed into the development of a fetus. Dolly was created by agricultural research scientists who were working to improve production. The implication of the bleating was clear: what scientists could do for sheep they could also do for humans. Later, it was revealed that Dolly had a debilitating form of arthritis.

That discovery alarmed opponents of cloning who argued that it was inappropriate for mammals, but supporters of the project said the nascent field of applied genetics deserved support. The issue suggested a controversial future; the new knowledge of the information floated in a sea of competing values. Postmodernism took the plausibility and plurality of beliefs seriously. It affirmed that the world was not a given, and any object "out there" had to be known internally first. If all metanarratives were equally valid, then a terrorist cell was a model of postmodernism and its dangers. A group, segmented from the rest of society, insulated by its own beliefs and recognizing no values that transcend its own, strikes out at everyone who gets in the way. Bystanders were not seen as individuals, but as members of a group, and they shared a collective guilt. The challenge at the end of the decade was to try to make sense of the collage growing more complex each day.

— 10 —

Triangulation

Outwardly the capital looked the same as always in January of 1995. The cars on the Beltway were regularly entangled in traffic jams, there were as many parties as ever, and the housing market continued to skyrocket. On Capitol Hill, however, the world's greatest deliberative body stood on the edge of an apocalyptic exchange. For the first time in forty years, Congress convened with the Republican Party in control of both the House of Representatives and the Senate.

Down the corridors of the legislative office buildings, men and women worked furiously to deal with the administrative takeover. "Like the dispirited troops of a defeated army, Democrats and Congressional staff members prepared to relinquish posts and cluttered, file-filled cabinets."[1] Every congressional committee had to be reorganized, and every staff member feared for his or her job. Reporters scrambled to find news sources, and rumors were everywhere. At the heart of the "Republican Revolution," as the 1994 election that brought the minority party to power was known, were the promises in the Contract with America. The ten-point plan to cut federal taxes, balance the budget, reduce social welfare programs, and increase congressional efficiency was at the top of the legislative agenda. The platform was spearheaded by Representative Newt Gingrich of Georgia, the House Minority Whip who replaced Democrat Tom Foley of Washington as House Speaker on January 4, 1995. "We were hired to do a job," said the new Speaker, "and we have to start today to prove we'll do it."[2]

Democratic control of Congress collapsed in the previous session (1993–1994). Dan Rostenkowski, chairman of the powerful House Ways and Means Committee, was indicted on charges of embezzlement, fraud, and coverup. "It's a Congress that will live in infamy for having flunked most of the major tests to which it was put."[3] Support for term limits, the belief that legal restrictions should be placed on the number of years that elected officials could remain in office, soared. The movement was based on the public's dissatisfaction with government and a belief that "professional" politicians were to blame. The GOP capitalized on the mood.

Not surprisingly, the Republicans interpreted their election victory as a mandate for change, almost any change, as long as it was quick. With little apparent irony, Speaker Gingrich promised a flurry of congressional activity not seen since 1933, when the Democratically controlled Seventy-Third Congress passed Franklin D. Roosevelt's New Deal into law. Within the first 100 days of the 104th Congress, the House of Representatives passed every bill incorporated in the Contract with America, with the exception of a term limits constitutional amendment. However, the Senate altered many of the bills and Bill Clinton saw to it that others were vetoed. It did not matter. Republicans had wrested the agenda-setting role from the White House, and they wanted the whole world to know it. The Republican National Committee began running advertisements on television with the tag line, "Making Washington work, for a change."

The president was in a precarious position. He was elected by a plurality, and was held responsible for the midterm defeat. "On the day after the election, I tried to make the best of a bad situation," wrote Clinton years later. "I suggested we work together on welfare reform and the line-item veto, which I supported. For the time being there was nothing more I could do."[4] But there was something he could do, and his support of two items in the Contract with America clearly showed it. It was called *triangulation*. Dick Morris, the president's longtime political advisor, introduced the strategy whereby Bill Clinton would play both parties—including his own—against each other for the sake of his own personal political advantage. On matters like the budget, trade agreements, and social issues, the president would pick things off both programs and pit the parties against each other as a way to rehabilitate himself in the aftermath of the midterm setback. The White House chose a more charitable meaning for triangulation, declaring that it incorporated the best elements of each party for the benefit of all the people.

A low point for Bill Clinton and his new strategy came on April 18, 1995, when he held a primetime press conference. Only one network bothered to broadcast it. In response to a question, the president was forced to talk about his role in the policy process given the new realities of GOP dominance on Capitol Hill. The reporter asked if Clinton, as president, was still relevant to lawmaking. His response was rambling, as if to justify his office. "The president is relevant.... The Constitution gives me relevance... the things we're trying to do gives me relevance."[5]

Central to the Republican resurgence was the public's sense that Bill Clinton was not who he said he would be. He was not a "New Democrat," but an old-fashioned liberal who hung out with Hollywood types and was more concerned with gay rights than with middle-class concerns. Instead of cutting programs, he proposed a complicated, big-government plan for health insurance reform. After 1994, the president changed; and triangulation became synonymous with the words of an old Western adage: "He gave his opponents just enough rope for them to hang themselves."

Clinton's comments after the Oklahoma City bombing were characteristic of his new approach. In a moment of national grief, he sympathized with the victims and at the same time pointed an accusing finger at the conservative radio commentators who supported his opponents. "I say to you, all of you ... there is nothing patriotic about hating your country, or pretending that you can love your country but despise your government."[6] The president complimented popular Republican governor Frank Keating, and offered federal assistance to a state he did not carry in 1992 and would not carry in 1996. In Washington, Republicans found themselves explaining that their criticism of Bill Clinton did not mean they were giving support to domestic terrorism.

More rope for hanging was given in November and December of 1995, when Congressional leaders Bob Dole and Newt Gingrich could not reach a compromise on cuts in Medicare with the White House. The budget impasse resulted in a partial government shutdown on two occasions. Bill Clinton went on the air on November 14, 1995, to say, "My message to Congress is simple ... let's say 'yes' to balancing the budget, but let us say 'no' to these deep and unwise cuts."[7] Clinton's forcefulness in his speech that night won the admiration of the press, and respect in the polls.

The year that began with such shining promise for Republicans ended in deep disappointment for them. The GOP-led House watched its public approval sink from a high of 52 percent in January to less than half that after the shutdown of the federal government.[8] Most of this national animus was directed at Newt Gingrich. The Georgia congressman arrived in Washington in 1979, after two previously unsuccessful attempts at Congress. A contemporary, who was in the same freshman class, recalled that Gingrich was a difficult conversationalist: "He was always talking about taking over, and a new conservative majority."[9] The Georgian's favorite reading material was books on military tactics; he was something of a reverse of the great German General Clausewitz: "*Politics* was the extension of *war* by other means."

In 1987, Gingrich brought ethics charges against Speaker of the House Jim Wright, a Texas Democrat who eventually resigned. Democrats in the Georgia state legislature tried to redistrict him out of a job after the 1990 census; they failed when he moved to another district and won easily. The success of the Contract with America led to his election as speaker from 1995 until 1998. Gingrich thought he was leading a charge against the embattled president; in reality, the noose was tightening around his own neck. In November 1995, the press revealed that one reason for the government shutdown was Clinton's snub of Gingrich and Senator Bob Dole by seating them in the rear of Air Force One when the American delegation was flying to Prime Minister Yitzhak Rabin's funeral in Israel. The *New York Daily News* featured a headline of "Cry Baby" with a caricature of the speaker in a diaper.[10]

Bill Clinton rehabilitated his image, and waited for an opportunity to get revenge and embarrass his opponents. In the summer of 1996, the Republicans gave him that chance. Twice before, the GOP majority had passed welfare reform legislation as one of the major planks in the Contract with America. In the summer, the president surprised his liberal friends and his conservative opponents by signing the Personal Responsibility and Work Opportunity Reconciliation Act. The legislation ended the idea that welfare was an entitlement, and replaced it with the notion that it should be a temporary way of returning people to work. Although the specifics were invented by Republicans in Congress, Bill Clinton successfully took credit for the change.

The results of welfare reform were spectacular. Within three years of its passage, 4.7 million fewer people were dependent on the program. The percentage of the population on the dole fell from 5.2 percent to 3.3 percent. The poverty rate was the lowest since 1979, and credit—to the outrage of the Republicans—went to the president.[11] In the 1996 presidential campaign, Clinton declared that he had "reformed welfare as we know it." The president clung to the ideological middle of the road and marginalized his opponents.

In the summer of the election year, the president turned to his aides and asked them to start thinking about an agenda for his second term. At that time, the request seemed presumptuous. The Republicans were riding high on the gains of the midterm elections, and appeared confident of continued victory. But President Bill Clinton used the symbolic and ceremonial aspects of his office to stretch the powers of incumbency to a new frontier. The boundary was financial. The president's personal goal was to raise $37 million for his re-election in 1995, and then spend a significant amount of it before the Republicans were even at their convention.

As his popularity improved, incumbent Clinton had little difficulty raising money. The early fund-raising plan was designed to reduce any cash that might go to a potential challenger in his own party, and—once that threat was removed—to provide the incumbent with an ability to respond to Republican criticisms. The president personally authorized a variety of perks for top party contributors, including golf games and morning jogs with him, as well as overnight stays in the Lincoln bedroom.[12] In return for these gestures, money was given in party coffers.

The Democrats made a conscious decision not to establish a fully staffed and operational re-election committee. Instead, they focused on the financial component of the operation, and let the president pursue a "Rose Garden" strategy. Bill Clinton did not announce his own candidacy until late in the season, and he did not campaign. As a result, the impression was left to the press, and nation-at-large, that Clinton was working at being president, and not at being re-elected.

Eighteen months before the election, the Clinton campaign launched a preemptive advertising campaign designed to position the president as a moderate and take advantage of Republican unpopularity in the wake of the government shutdown. The 1995 media campaign coincided with accusations that the GOP was out to reduce Medicare benefits. Heavy media buys were made in early caucus and primary states, and then in key electoral states. The early expenditure of so much money was controversial in Democratic Party circles, but Clinton was following a pattern. In 1984, Ronald Reagan used the same strategy to remind voters that it was "Morning in America," and at the same time ride prosperity to a landslide mandate. The strategy repeated itself in 1996. Clinton had no primary opponent, and the Republicans languished in the polls and self-criticism for failing to take advantage of their midterm election victory.

A host of GOP candidates lined up to challenge the seemingly weak incumbent, William Jefferson Clinton. Bob Dole and Pat Buchanan had national name recognition, and were the best known candidates in the field. However, each had problems. Bob Dole did not generate much enthusiasm among party loyalists, and Pat Buchanan came off as an extremist. Pete Wilson, former governor of California, was a throwback to the Reagan years. Lamar Alexander used his two-term experience as governor of Tennessee as a springboard to ride an anti-Washington, anti-big-government bandwagon. Indiana Senator Richard Lugar presented himself as a conservative candidate from the Midwest with foreign policy experience. Arlen Specter was the favorite of GOP moderates upset about the influence of the Christian Right in the Republican Party. Phil Gramm tapped Texas millionaires for his war chest, and appealed to the economic conservatives who were at home in the GOP. Alan Keyes, who had never been elected to political office, appealed to the social conservatives. Steve Forbes was a self-financed multimillionaire whose advocacy of a "flat tax" would become legendary. Robert Dornan, the conservative congressman from California, was a national security conservative. Finally, there was Morry Taylor, an Ohio tire magnate who was self-financed and unknown. He remained that way.

The fragmented field of candidates presented voters with a conflicting cacophony of messages and promises. Lamar Alexander aired the first commercials, in Iowa seven months before the caucuses, and eight months before the New Hampshire primary. In the fall of 1995, multimillionaire publisher Steve Forbes put $1.5 million in an advertising blitz in the two states. The money had its intended effect, pushing the candidate up in the polls. The self-funded ads sponsored by Forbes focused on his plan to scrap the Internal Revenue Service and replace it with an "across the board" flat tax for every American. Although he won only two primaries (Delaware and Arizona), Forbes attracted national attention with his calls for lower taxes and less government.[13]

Bob Dole began his third campaign for his party's presidential nomination as the odds-on favorite. He received the endorsement of twenty-one of the country's thirty-one Republican governors before the primaries got underway, and led all candidates, except those personally wealthy, in fundraising. He endured a less-than-expected win in Iowa and a one-point loss to Pat Buchanan in New Hampshire to rebound in South Carolina, where his strong support overwhelmed Buchanan and ended the campaigns of Lamar Alexander and Phil Gramm.

He followed up this victory with wins in the New England states and New York. By the end of the first week in March, Dole had a commanding delegate lead. Only Buchanan and Forbes remained in the race, and it was clear that they had no chance of winning.

The Democrats had Bob Dole in their sights as soon as he emerged from the fog of primary victory.[14] Underlying the entire Clinton re-nomination strategy was the assumption that the election would be decided before the national nominating conventions, not after them. From the summer of 1995, right up to the Democratic Convention, the president supervised a television blitz that preempted Republicans on key issues like family values, crime, high taxes, and the deficit. The ads presented Bill Clinton as the protector of education, health, and the environment, foreign policy leader, and the voice of reason opposite the radical leadership of the Republican Party in Congress. Robert Squires, the Democratic media consultant, called it "unopposed storytelling," and it had a dramatic effect in major media markets, because the Republicans had no money with which to respond.

In the fall of 1996, Bob Dole ran an aggressive but unfocused campaign, which began and ended with him lagging behind the president. Clinton's objective was to look, sound, and act presidential. "Four years ago, you took me on faith," he said in the first debate. "Now there's a record: 10.5 million more jobs, rising incomes, falling crime rates and welfare rolls, and a strong America at peace.... Let's keep going."[15] He did.

Bill Clinton was the first Democrat since Franklin Roosevelt to win re-election, and he did it with an opposition Congress. The president won 49 percent of the vote to Dole's 41 percent, carrying thirty-three states with 379 electoral votes. The win was almost a carbon copy of his 1992 victory, when he won thirty-two states and received 370 electoral votes. Ross Perot remained a third-party candidate, but got less than half the votes he received in 1992. The media strategy of the Democrats was devastatingly effective, winning twenty-one of the top thirty media markets. The only place Clinton lost ground was in the South, but he more than made up for it by gaining votes in the Ohio River valley and the industrial heartland.

Republicans retained control of Congress in spite of the virulent anti-Congress campaign of the White House. The GOP lost eight seats in the House, but retained a 227 Republican to 207 Democratic edge. The breakdown in the Senate was 55 Republicans to 45 Democrats, a pickup of one for the GOP. The transformation of southern politics from Democratic to Republican allegiance was the foundation of the emergent GOP majority nationally.

American elections have always been about more than who won; they also tell us something about the nation itself. In 1996, Bob Dole looked backward: "To those who say it was never so, that America has never been better, I say, you're wrong, and I know because I was there."[16] Bill Clinton looked the other way, and said, "We do not need to build a bridge to the past; we need to build a bridge to the future ... so let us resolve to build that bridge to the twenty-first century."[17] The GOP did win one consolation from the White House. That election year, in his State of the Union address, Bill Clinton acknowledged that "the era of big government [was] over."[18]

As the new millennium loomed, the problems of the past resurfaced, and the president would be faced with a foreign policy nightmare. Until 1991, Yugoslavia was one nation comprised of six republics, but the ethnic diversity and deterioration of the Soviet Union led to conflict long before Clinton's second term. Serbian nationalism was behind the assassination of Archduke Franz Ferdinand on June 28, 1914, that led to the "Great War." During the Cold War, Marshal Tito followed his own road to socialism, refusing to join the Warsaw Pact or become a puppet of Moscow. In August of 1986, in the dying days of Yugoslavia's communist regime, the province of Kosovo was visited by Slobodan Milosevic. Throughout the 1980s, tensions between the Albanian and Serbian communities in the province escalated. Milosevic came to calm the fears of the local Serbs, and in a speech televised throughout the nation, emotionally declared, "You will not be beaten again." By the end of the year, Milosevic was in control of the Serbian government, and he would fulfill his pledge.

Two years later, strongman Milosevic embarked on a campaign to consolidate Serb power throughout Yugoslavia. Albanians in Kosovo were the first to suffer. Poverty and unemployment reached catastrophic levels. About 80 percent of the population was unemployed, and many Albanians left the country in fear. Those who remained behind found themselves in the clutches of a dictator. Milosevic and other Serb ultranationalists embarked on a campaign to unify all the Serbs into one nation, driving out all minorities through a genealogical process known as "ethnic cleansing." In Croatia, the most infamous incident was the siege of Vukovar, where more than 10,000 civilians were killed and the first major war crime of the era was committed.

Serbian repression radicalized the Albanians and sent others scurrying for shelter. On April 6, 1992, the Bosnian Serbs launched a campaign of aggression with a siege of Sarajevo, and the ethnic cleansing of the Drina River Valley and other areas in the north and northwestern parts of the country.[19] For the next three and one-half years, the Bosnian Serb forces, with the help of Milosevic, laid waste to large parts of Bosnia. Half the population of 2 million had to flee their homes, tens of thousands of women were systematically raped, and concentration camps were established. At the height of their power, the Bosnian Serbs controlled more than 70 percent of the country. The United Nations was already in Bosnia, but when Sarajevo came under attack in 1992, it pulled out to avoid casualties. As the situation deteriorated, the chances of a catastrophe increased.[20]

With the United Nations in retreat, the North Atlantic Treaty Organization (NATO) on the sidelines, and the world generally uninterested, the worst act of the war occurred in the summer of 1995. That was when the Bosnian town of Srebrenica came under attack. The city had been declared a "safe area" by the United Nations, but the international governing body had no troops to back up the pronouncement. Nothing the international community did could deter the Serbs from their avowed goal of purging minorities from the country.[21] In mid-July, the majority forces executed more than 7,000 Bosnian Muslim males, while women and children were evacuated to the nearby sanctuary of Tuzla. President Clinton launched a limited bombing campaign against the Bosnian Serb position. This, along with a supporting Croatian offensive, led to peace negotiations in Dayton, Ohio.

President Clinton appeared on the *Larry King Live* television show to defend his administration's policy in the crisis. The White House had memories of Rwanda in mind. "If you reduce the casualties from 130,000 to 3,000 and you at least have the possibility of cease-fires and ongoing negotiations and you continue humanitarian aid, it seems to me that you are fulfilling your moral obligation."[22] Critics were not so sanguine; they thought the United States should do more.

Both the politics and the warfare seemed hopeless in the complexity of the conflict. The Bosnian Serbs declared U.N. peacekeepers to be their enemy, as well as the Albanians, and they annulled all previous agreements. Both sides took hostages, and then released them on television. International peacekeepers found mass graves, and no one knew for sure who was responsible for them. So-called neutral cities for refugees were shelled with artillery rounds from Serbian guns. America found a new hero in the conflict when Air Force Captain Scott O'Grady survived for six days on bugs, greens, and rainwater after his F-16 fighter was shot down on a bombing mission.[23] He was rescued by U.S. Marines in a drill-perfect, two-minute, radio-orchestrated operation.

The Dayton accords created a tepid peace in Bosnia, but problems remained in nearby Kosovo, which was still under the tight control of Milosevic. The Kosovar Albanians hoped the international community would recognize their plight and come to their aid, just like they did in Bosnia. But it was not to be; even periodic reports of human rights violations, mass murders, and refugee evacuations were ignored. The violence continued to escalate until a group of nations known as the Contact Group (the United States, Britain, France, Germany, Italy, and Russia) brought both Kosovo and Serb negotiators together in Rambouillet, France. The Rambouillet talks began on February 6, 1999. The agreement called for both sides to disarm, but Milosovic refused, and instead increased his placement of heavy weaponry in Kosovo in defiance of the provisions. Finally, NATO threatened to bomb the Serbs if they did not sign and stand down.

Milosoevic remained obdurate. So, on March 24, NATO launched an air campaign against Serb military targets in Serbia, Montenegro, and Kosovo. The Serbian forces responded with an all-out campaign to ethnically cleanse Kosovo of its Albanian population. The United Nations estimated that nearly 640,000 Albanians fled or were expelled from Kosovo during this time. It is impossible to know the full extent of the atrocities, but thousands of people were forced from their homes, and many were summarily executed. Most had their money taken, and there were dozens of massacres in specific villages and prison camps.

NATO's bombing campaign lasted until June 10, 1999. It involved up to 1,000 aircraft along with Tomahawk cruise missiles. The United States was, inevitably, the dominant member of the coalition. The proclaimed goal of the NATO operation was summed up by a spokesman as: "Serbs out, peacekeepers in, refugees back."[24] By June, the NATO countries were thinking about a ground operation, suggesting an invasion of Kosovo. Before that happened, Finnish and Russian diplomats persuaded Milosevic to accept most of the terms of the Rambouillet accords and agree to a military presence within Kosovo headed by the United Nations, incorporating NATO troops. Kosovo lay in ruins, but it was finally at peace.

Shortly after the start of the bombing in 1996, Yugoslav strongman Milosevic and others were charged by the International Criminal Tribunal with crimes against humanity including murder, forcible transfer, deportation, and "persecution on political, racial or religious grounds." Case IT-02-54 alleged that Milosevic "executed a campaign of terror and violence directed at Kosvo Albanian civilians."[25] The charges were upgraded, by addressing accusations of genocide in Bosnia and war crimes in Bosnia. The trial began at the Hague on February 12, 2002, with Milosevic defending himself and refusing to recognize the authority of the court's jurisdiction.

In the early months of Bill Clinton's second term, those closest to him believed that he had finally begun to master the presidency. He had regained his political confidence after a chaotic, even inept, first term. The failed attempt at health insurance reform was replaced by the success of triangulation, favorable budget negotiations, and the use of military force in Bosnia. Just as important as the policy decisions was the personal image the president now projected. In January of 1997, he appeared to have replaced his lifelong desire to have the approval of others with the satisfaction that his re-election proved he had it. A story from the first term that the First Lady had tossed a lamp at the president gained wide, if unsubstantiated, currency. Now it was forgotten.

One rumor refused to go away: infidelity in the marriage of Bill and Hillary Clinton. Gossip about Bill Clinton's sexual behavior went back to his days as governor of Arkansas. He always treated any question about the issue the same way: "If you just go out and divorce your wife, you never have to deal with this.... But, if you work at your problems... then you do."[26] In January of 1998, the labor would begin, again, in earnest.

The president would spend most of his second term swimming in shame. At the center of the controversy was what would become an emerging crisis with the Office of Independent Council (OIC) and Independent Counsel Kenneth Starr. The OIC had been authorized to investigate the president and his wife's dealings in the controversial Whitewater land deal in Arkansas. Whitewater followed the Clintons into the White House and "no day in the eight years was ever free of scandal."[27] In his memoirs, written after he left office, Bill Clinton would write about his appointment of Starr, "It was the worst presidential

President Clinton. (Courtesy, William J. Clinton Presidential Library)

decision I ever made, wrong on the facts, wrong on the law, wrong on the politics, wrong for the presidency and the Constitution."[28] The irony of the whole scandal was that the president himself signed the papers that gave his enemies the means to attack him.

In the investigation of the failed Whitewater land scheme, something that happened before the Clintons came to Washington, Starr and his team were presented with damaging information about the president's sexual life. The evidence was related to another legal matter: the Paula Corbin Jones sexual harassment suit. According to Jones's allegations, in 1991 she was escorted to the hotel room of Clinton, then governor of Arkansas, where he crudely propositioned her. Jones filed a sexual harassment suit against Clinton in May 1994.

As Starr followed the allegations against the president from one woman, he discovered rumors of Clinton's sexual indiscretions with another one. It was not until January 12, 1998, that the world heard about the name and misdeeds of Monica Lewinsky. She was of Russian-Jewish descent, was born in San Francisco, and grew up in Southern California, then moved to Washington, D.C., to take a White House internship. On Saturday, January 17, Clinton addressed the rumors about his personal life. Under oath in a deposition with the independent counsel, the president denied that he had an affair with the by-then former White House intern. He repeated that denial to the nation, in public on January 21 and again on January 28, 1998.[29]

I want to say one thing to the American people [finger waving forcefully]. I want you to listen to me. I'm going to say this *again* [stronger gesture]. I did *not* [vigorous gesture] have sexual relations with that woman, Ms. Lewinsky. I never told anybody to lie, not a single time, *never* [said defiantly with finger pointing]. These allegations are *false* [most emphatic gesture of all] and I need to go back to work for the American people.

Independent Counsel Kenneth Starr used Clinton's denial in the deposition to subpoena scores of White House aides and Clinton associates in an effort to prove that the president lied under oath, obstructed justice, and suborned perjury.

The confrontation of Clinton and Starr was a disjunction of the realms. On one side was President Bill Clinton, a man who suggested that sex did not mean sex, that smoking dope did not mean inhaling, and that sidestepping the draft did not mean avoiding it. He was a man who gained strength in a crisis, and the last time he was confronted with charges of sexual indiscretion he earned the moniker "The Comeback Kid" and won the presidency. In his public denial, the president projected an odd, vacant, almost detached personality. But as time passed he rallied to a defense. "That man is evil," he would tell friends of Starr. "When this thing is over, there's only going to be one of us left standing.... And it's going to be me."[30] In a postmodern era where deconstructionists, feminists, and radical Afrocentrists declared that truth was a relative matter, the president was determined to survive by attending to his job and changing his image in the public eye.

On the other side was Ken Starr, a church-going, suburban-dwelling, Republican, faithful husband and father who believed that knowledge was certain, objective, and good. He thought that the law itself was dispassionate, a necessary means for humans to rationally order their world. He presented the image of a round-faced man, slightly chubby with glasses, who offered homilies about truth and morality and then called the courts as "palaces of justice." Starr always declared he was after the facts, and not the president; he repeatedly disagreed with the press, saying the process was fair and would lead to a conclusion beyond his control. Defenders of the president were never convinced. Early on, when presented with a choice on how to proceed with the Lewinsky matter, Starr could have ignored the overture, presented his already far-too-long-delayed final report on the Whitewater scandal, and gracefully exited. Instead, he continued to "follow the facts" with a thoroughness and persistence that would prove his—and the president's—undoing.

In Washington, political news has always been a parlor game. The 1990s presented the "Old Media" of the three media networks and big daily newspapers, with the realities of the "New Media," like the Internet, conservative talk shows, and "blast" faxes. The suggestion that the president was having an affair in the White House led the "New Media" to "All-Monica, All-the-time" coverage. Reporting was a postmodern parade of personalities, a virtual saturation of the airways with pundits endlessly repeating and analyzing the story. It did not matter that those interviewed had no particular expertise on the matter—what was expertise on sexual harassment or misconduct? After a time, the whole thing wore on the public consciousness.

The endless revelations of salacious tales involving the most powerful and identifiable people in the nation provided titillating entertainment on a scale not known before. Each lurid revelation cheapened public life and encouraged the belief that political leaders had different lives behind their public personas.[31] How many incidents? They met nine times total. Was the sex consensual? Yes, they had oral sex in hallways and offices of the White House. Did they have other encounters? Yes, they had phone sex on numerous occasions. After a time, the pornographic details were numbing, and a society cynical about politics became even more so.

In August of 1998, eight months after her name surfaced publicly, and after a grant of full immunity from the prosecutors, Monica Lewinsky appeared before the grand jury. As part of her immunity agreement, Lewinsky agreed to turn over all relevant evidence bearing on the case. Among the material provided was a blue dress purchased from the Gap that she allegedly wore during a sexual encounter. She also provided telephone message recordings. The physical evidence with identifying DNA coding was the end of speculation in the "he said, she said" drama. The FBI lab report was an indictment: "Semen was identified on specimen Q3243 (the blue dress).... In order to conduct meaningful DNA analysis, known blood samples must be submitted from the victim, suspect or other individual."[32]

The prosecutor made a written request for a blood sample of the president, and lawyers in the White House complied. On Monday, the third of August, at ten minutes past ten in the evening, the president took a chair in the center of the Map Room of the White House to donate four milliliters of blood to the FBI. Two weeks later the FBI reported that the semen stain on the blue dress matched the blood sample with the DNA genetic profile of Bill Clinton, a certainty of 1 in 7.87 trillion. On August 17, President Bill Clinton became the first sitting president to testify before a grand jury investigating his conduct. After the questioning in the same White House Map Room, President Clinton went on national television to admit he had an improper relationship with Monica Lewinsky.[33]

> When I was alone with Ms. Lewinsky on certain occasions in early 1996 and once in early 1997, I engaged in conduct that was wrong. These encounters did not consist of sexual intercourse. They did not constitute sexual relations as I understood that term to be defined at my January 17, 1998 deposition. But they did involve inappropriate intimate contact.... I regret that what began as a friendship came to include this conduct, and I take full responsibility for my actions.... Because of privacy considerations affecting my family, myself and others, and in an effort to preserve the dignity of the office I hold, this is all I will say about the specifics of these particular matters.

On talk radio, what Hillary Clinton would subsequently call the "Vast Right Wing Conspiracy," no separation was made between public and private life. For them, the Lewinsky revelations only confirmed deeply held suspicions about the president, and pushed evaluations the public had of his honesty and morality to new lows. The humiliation in public was expected to be the prelude to the downfall of William Jefferson Clinton.

That summer, middle-class Republicans were feeling their oats. They were proud to be conservative, prosperous, conformist, and vigilant defenders of the American way of life. They were conceited in their conservatism, and they wanted no truck with "Femi-Nazis," "whackos," "Reds," "heretics," "crackpots," "liberals," or "homosexual fascists." College professors and academic "studies" were a special source of scorn. In defiance of academia, talk show host Rush Limbaugh presided over his "EIB Network," an acronym for "Excellence in Broadcasting," that included the mythical "Institute for Advanced Conservative Studies."

Rather than producing a public outcry against the president, the televised confession and continuing press revelations produced one against Washington. The worst elements of American culture were on display in the scandal, and the public blamed their elected representatives. Clinton's demise was widely predicted even though his approval ratings began to rise after his confession. A *New York Times*/CBS poll taken after the president's apology showed high ratings for job performance but a darkening of his moral character in the public consciousness.[34] One of the abiding rules of American politics is that the major advantage presidents have is their guaranteed access to the media. The television medium exalted personality and allowed the man in the White House to promote "himself and his policies by appealing to the American public for support."[35] Bill Clinton was unrivaled in his ability to do this. People did not condone what the president did, but—unlike his critics—they separated it from the job he was doing in office.

Analogies to past scandals in high office were suddenly inadequate. Even Watergate comparisons of twenty-five years earlier were invalid. A great shift in American attitudes had taken place in the interim. Attitudes held so strongly just a generation earlier that no divorced candidate should seek or win the presidency and that sexual monogamy was a requirement in office were now obsolete. Ronald Reagan did away with the former, and John Kennedy was a flagrant philanderer who obviated the latter. Gone were attitudes about national morality, fidelity, and personal behavior. In the 1990s, six of every ten marriages were headed for divorce, more than one-third of the marriages had an experience of infidelity in the first ten years of matrimony, and one-third of births were outside of marriage. School children in major American cities attended sex education classes where condoms were distributed, while their science, mathematics, reading, and writing scores were at an all-time low.[36]

Bill Clinton survived as a postmodern politician catering to a postmodern moment in American political history. He reinvented himself through public gestures, his rhetoric, and appearances. He understood the twenty-four-hour news cycle, and he used it to his advantage. A classic example of his sophistry was his response to the prosecutor's question, "You were alone with Monica Lewinsky, weren't you?" "Well, again, it depends on how you define 'alone.' ... Yes, we were alone from time to time ... but I never really thought we were."[37] The new postmodern culture was quite familiar with two meanings for the word "alone," because only one meaning would imply the existence of a universal truth that could be discovered. The new mood was skeptical of certainties and fixities, and welcomed novelties as long as they provided the audience with satisfaction for the moment. "To posit just one analogy between the two cultures, if we associate *Father Knows Best* with the Eisenhower years, we should associate *Seinfeld* with the Clinton ones."[38] As one of the *Seinfeld* episodes declared, the show was about nothing, yet it was about everything.

As fate would have it, the day after his public apology, the Clinton family left Washington for a twelve-day vacation to Martha's Vineyard. The emotional distance between the president and the First Lady was captured in pictures of the two standing stiffly apart. "At night Hillary would go up to bed, and I slept on the couch."[39] The process of rebuilding the marriage would take months and involved once-a-week counseling for a year and a public confession at the National Prayer Breakfast. Democrats, facing a political verdict at the polls two months in the future, began to distance themselves from the president. Around the country, 140 newspapers called on him to resign.

The atmosphere in Washington was filled with rumors, just like those inside the Beltway twenty-four years earlier before Nixon resigned. Republican congressional candidates, in a campaign orchestrated by Newt Gingrich, began to apply the blowtorch. In crucial media markets, ads appeared hammering the "Clinton scandals," and the speaker privately predicted that the GOP would pick up thirty seats in the midterm elections. Independent Counsel Ken Starr submitted his report and supporting documents to the Congress, and the House

Judiciary Committee began consideration of its recommendations. The prosecutor concluded that the president betrayed his "constitutional duty to faithfully execute the laws" by engaging in a pattern "of abundant and calculating lies" making him liable for impeachment.

In the rock bottom days of the fall, as the clock ticked down to the midterm elections, the Clintons began to rally. Hillary Clinton went to Europe to celebrate her twenty-third wedding anniversary alone, and then returned to accompany her husband to a dinner meeting of the Democratic Business Council, where she introduced him by praising his "unrelenting determination to do what is right for America."[40] The president stepped forward and hugged her, and later that day Hillary Clinton's office released a statement saying "her support, her love, and her forgiveness" were with her husband.

But just because Bill Clinton had moved from the sofa back into the bedroom of the White House did not mean that the prospects for Democrats looked any better in the fall election. Even in an age of excess, with O. J. Simpson, Princess Di, and the Bobbits, America was caught up in the most scandalous of spectacles. The "Starr Report" read like a tawdry novel, with chapters on "sexual encounters," "follow-ups," and "subsequent phone calls." The Congressional Internet site nearly collapsed under the number of hits, and news media outlets reported three times their average number of queries about the story. Grizzled television reporters filed their stories warning viewers to send children out of the room or switch to another channel. In the fallout, Gingrich and the House Republicans continually urged full disclosure of documents associated with the scandal in the belief that the graphic revelations would depress the Democratic vote and motivate the GOP-faithful in the critical midterm elections.

It did not happen. On Election Day, Tuesday, November 3, 1998, the Democrats gained five seats in the House. The partisan division meant that the GOP had the smallest margin of control in forty years. Impeachment politics was a failure. In the wake of the election, Newt Gingrich resigned as speaker and gave up his House seat at the same time. The virulent rhetoric and campaign of personal attack energized the Democrats, and turned off the Republicans.

Before and after the midterm election, the cold war temperatures between the two parties sank to arctic levels. The liberal community regarded the Republicans as vigilantes, and while none of the Clinton-Lewinsky jokes made it into the Congressional Record, the whispering campaign was enough to push Democrats to the edge of rage. Occasionally a voice of reason was heard on the Hill, but such moments were increasingly rare given the atmosphere.

Larry Flynt, the publisher of *Hustler* magazine, offered to pay as much as $1 million to women who would go public and name names about adulterous affairs they had with elected public officials of either party. When Bob Livingston, the Republican speaker-designate from Louisiana, admitted to an affair before his House colleagues, he did so to protect himself from the Flynt blackmail. Other revelations followed, including ones about Newt Gingrich and Henry Hyde, the powerful chairman of the House Judiciary Committee charged with handling impeachment.[41] Society knows few satisfactions greater than the discovery of a puritan caught practicing what he has preached against, and the GOP wore the scarlet letter of "family values" that year.

While Republicans saw themselves as defending the rule of law, Democrats viewed the impeachment process as a threat to the Constitution. Bill Clinton was convinced that nothing he had done, or was alleged to have done, rose to the level of an impeachable offense. Polls showed the nation did not want impeachment, and it was widely believed that the Senate would not convict. No matter. The issue had moved beyond questions of logic or legal findings; it was now in the realm of raw, charged passionate emotions. The virulence of the rhetoric had the desired effect, and the impeachment process was carried along by its own momentum.

Two days after the election, Judiciary Committee Chairman Henry Hyde decided to expand the grounds for impeachment even beyond those suggested by Kenneth Starr. As part of the inquiry, Chairman Hyde sent a list of eighty-one questions to the president, asking him to "admit or deny" the major facts outlined in Kenneth Starr's report. The independent counsel himself appeared in a marathon session before the House Judiciary Committee to outline his case against the president. After receiving Clinton's answers to their query, the Judiciary Committee recommended four articles of impeachment to the full House. Some Republicans on the Committee were outraged at what they saw as President Clinton's evasive and legalistic answers to the Judiciary Committee's questions, but others saw trouble ahead.

The prosecutorial Republicans argued that by committing perjury Bill Clinton violated his oath of office and undermined the rule of law. Democrats responded that the allegations were "only about sex," and did not amount to "high crimes and misdemeanors" as intended in the Constitution. On December 19, the House of Representatives forwarded articles on perjury (passed by a 228-to-206 vote) and obstruction of justice (passed by a 221-to-212 vote) to the Senate. The indictment made Bill Clinton the first elected president in U.S. history to be impeached.[42]

Bill Clinton, and the party he represented, did not take the charges lying down. On the day of the vote in the House, he launched a major military strike against Saddam Hussein in Iraq. The timing of the attacks was suspect, and with good reason. A popular movie at the time, *Wag the Dog* (1997), was about a president who ordered a military action to divert public opinion away from a public sex scandal in which he was involved. A cynical public believed they were being similarly manipulated away from the sex scandal–based accusations. The juxtaposition of these two events, the uncommon impeachment proceedings of a president and the actions of a commander-in-chief exercising his powers in office, strained credibility. The television news had schizophrenic coverage, split screens of two political battles.

The Senate trial began on January 7, 1999, and the mood was summarized by Majority Leader Trent Lott, who said, "We think the best way to keep cool and calm and dignified, is to hear each other and talk to each other."[43] A two-thirds vote, or sixty-seven guilty votes, was required for conviction on either charge. Virtually no one thought a guilty vote likely. The prosecution argued that the president lied, that he committed perjury by lying under oath, and that he concealed the evidence of his actions. The impeachment proceedings, including the lurid details, were read into the Congressional Record. On Friday, February 12, 1999, the Senate rejected both articles of impeachment. The perjury charge was rejected with a 55 not guilty to 45 guilty vote, and the obstruction of justice charge tied at 50 to 50. The vote fell along party lines, with ten Republicans crossing over to vote "not guilty" on the perjury charge, and five GOP senators crossing over to vote with the Democrats on the obstruction of justice charge.[44] The president had avoided conviction, and he suffered no penalty other than censure in the House of Representatives. Later, the Arkansas Supreme Court suspended Clinton's law license. The U.S. Supreme Court did the same thing, and in response to the disciplinary actions, the by-then-former President Clinton surrendered his law license.

Twenty-five days before the impeachment vote, the president appeared in the House chamber to deliver his annual State of the Union address. With the drama of the Senate trial in progress, all eyes were fixed on the Capitol. Invisible questions filled the room: Would Bill Clinton's voice be husky? Would his eyes be glistening, like at the prayer breakfast, and his face lined with fatigue? Would he mention impeachment? From the moment he entered the room, the president captivated the audience. He stood at the podium in the blaze of lights, with the American flag as a backdrop, and delivered a powerful seventy-seven-minute address. Never once did the speaker indicate that he was responsible for the bitter partisan divide in the room, and he never mentioned the word "impeachment." Instead, the president smiled broadly and saluted his wife and baseball slugger Sammy Sosa. He presented an all-encompassing agenda of sentences filled with double meanings. "I reach out my hand to those of you of both parties in both houses," he said, speaking of social security reform. The nation "go[ing] forward as One America" was mentioned in the context of immigration.[45]

The affair, and its sordid details, had fallout not realized at the time. When the gossip broke, the first baby boomer president was traveling the country to urge reform of Social Security. "It would be unconscionable if we failed to act," President Bill Clinton said at a forum in 1998. Seven years later, the next president would have to pick up the mantle of reform and face the abandoned legacy. Another inheritance from the time was the "war on terror." While the nation stood transfixed in the glare of the impeachment disgrace, terrorist enemies planned subversive missions of destruction. The explosion of Pan American Flight 103 in December of 1988 over Lockerbie, Scotland; the World Trade Center bombing of 1993; suicide bombings in Israel; and attacks on U.S. embassies were a prelude to more disastrous things. A patchwork quilt of terrorism was being knit together in these years, and the country neglected its homeland security responsibilities. Safety was in decline.

In Washington, the national capital sank into an exhausted postmortem. After weeks of steady inundation, the sense was that something was terribly wrong, if not in the country's well-being, then its morals, its pride, its self-respect. Since the beginning of the scandal, the populace was too preoccupied with the details, and the president was too vigorous denying what was obvious. Aesop said: "A liar will not be believed, even when he speaks the truth."[46] Although Americans approved of the job Bill Clinton was doing as president, they did not approve of him. If moral behavior was crucial for a man in leadership, then he was no leader. No matter how many headlines he accumulated in public life, the president still used his position to get sexual pleasure in private. For Bill Clinton, the last two years in Washington were hamstrung more than most "lame duck" presidents.

"Every educational system has a moral goal," wrote Allan Bloom in 1987, and the American goal was "openness."[47] But in the 1990s youth itself became a problem, and it was anything but open. High schools in the sprawling suburbs had become behemoth institutions, with thousands of students spread over dozens of campus acres. Within the school itself, students congregated in groups, mutually exclusive groups. The "jocks," the "preps," the "rednecks," the "artists," the "cheerleaders," the "non–college prep," and the "nerds" all existed in a kind of tense adolescent association of nonconformity.

At 11:10 A.M. on Tuesday, April 20, 1999—Hitler's 110th birthday—two students who were notorious outsiders arrived at Columbine High School in Littleton, a suburb of Denver, Colorado. The school had 1,800 students; about half were beginning to go to the "A" lunch. Eric Harris, eighteen, and Dylan Klebold, seventeen, found their identity in what was known as the "trench coat mafia," a group that boasted about owning guns and taking pride in their social alienation. They were pariahs in a high school where athletes, the favored jocks who wore white caps, dominated campus politics and social life. The two boys drove separate cars, but they arrived almost simultaneously. Harris parked in the Junior parking lot, and Klebold in the one for seniors. From their vantage point they could see the first floor cafeteria, just filling with students, and each was covering a main exit from the school.[48]

Columbine was a school, like hundreds of others in the suburban United States, where athletic prowess was granted a license. An investigative report subsequently found that athletes could bully, haze, and harass other students without fear of reprisal. The homecoming king, a star football player, was on parole for burglary, yet still was permitted to play. The school's state wrestling champ was allowed to compete, despite being on court-ordered probation.[49] The fact that Harris and Klebold were social outcasts probably made them conspicuous targets for taunting. One Columbine student said the "trench coat mafia" "didn't look like other people" and "didn't dress or act like other people."

The two boys planned to kill most of the 600-plus students eating in the cafeteria. They planted two twenty-pound bombs near the doorway, and waited for them to explode. Their initial plan was to remain outside the cafeteria until the bombs went off, and then shoot anyone who tried to escape. The delayed-action bombs had enough power to blow up the two floors of the school building. The whole ambush was oddly reminiscent. It was April, the month of the Oklahoma City bombing, which itself recalled the Waco tragedy. Each shooter returned to his car to await the explosion so they could proceed with their plan, but the home-made devices did not work.

When the cafeteria bombs failed to explode, Harris and Klebold armed themselves with shotguns, semi-automatic carbines, and pistols, along with an assortment of other explosive devices they made in their homes. Forty minutes later, twelve students and one teacher lay dead, along with twenty-three students wounded. The nation watched in horror as the television screen replayed the scene. In the end, Harris and Klebold were found dead from self-inflicted gunshot wounds. The murderers were haters, out to punish humanity for its inexcusable insensitivity to them and their beliefs. What was it that they believed? It is impossible to say in retrospect, but it is known that they were both fans of the rock group Rammstein and favored violent video games like *Doom*. Harris was on an antidepressant, and the two maintained a web site where they openly showed hatred for people in Littleton, especially their teachers at Columbine High School.

The crime story, reconstructed from interviews and security tapes after the massacre, read like something from a fictional Stephen King horror script. Dylan Klebold shot one student in the head at close range without a second thought. In the library the gunmen shouted, "All jocks stand up! We'll get the guys in white hats." The shooters carried ammunition in duffle bags from which they calmly reloaded their weapons. Eric Harris slapped the top of a computer desk twice with his hand, knelt down and said, "Peek-a-boo" to Cassie Bernall before shooting her in the head. The recoil from his weapon hit his face and broke his nose. One student, an acquaintance of Klebold's, asked him during the mass execution what he was doing, to which he responded, "Oh, just killing people."

At one point the killers stood before some bathrooms to taunt students held up inside, saying, "We know you're in there" and "let's kill anyone we find in here." For some reason the gunmen left the terrified students in the restrooms alone. The whole horrible event ended in the library, the scene of so much carnage. It was empty except for an unconscious student, another playing dead, and those killed earlier. The two murderers committed suicide a little after noon.

Columbine was the worst school shooting, and the second deadliest attack on a school, in American history. The astonishing thing was that it could have been so much worse if the bombs had exploded as planned. The boys learned how to make the explosives over the Internet and from readily available books like *The Anarchist Cookbook*. The ingredients were easily found in hardware stores and made with carbon dioxide canisters, galvanized pipe, and metal propane bottles. The police SWAT team began a thorough check of every room in the high school—a process that took hours. Aside from the unexploded bombs in the cafeteria, the police found twelve other devices throughout the school.

The massacre at Columbine initiated a spate of copycat imitations at other U.S. high schools. President Clinton sent a letter of condolence, and then flew to Colorado to personally comfort the families. The shooting ignited the gun control battle again across the nation, and the Clinton administration called for new measures to apply the Brady Gun Law prohibitions to juveniles, closing the so-called "gun show loophole" that allowed people to buy guns at events without a background check. Still, after all the investigations and explanations, the media reports and government bulletins, no one had any real answers for why the shooting happened.

At decade's end, some of the more cherished icons of American life lay shattered in the public eye. America might remember its legacy as a "city set on a hill," but the nation's cities themselves were shown to be seething cauldrons of racial animosity. American schools, heretofore sources of suburban pride and real estate inflation, found themselves targets of teenage resentment. Finally, the American presidency, the most visible part of the national government, and the Oval Office, its most treasured symbol, became a rendezvous for sexual trysts. The most enduring legacy of Bill Clinton's presidency was his style and resilience, more than his domestic or foreign policy. From the beginning he was comfortable, some said too comfortable, with people knowing the intimate details of his life. They knew his marriage was not perfect, and in office he showed its shortcomings. He answered a question about his style of underwear on MTV. Clinton seemed to understand the postmodern power of assumed intimacy that accompanied the New Media of television and the Internet. He grasped the notion that the president lived in kitchens and great rooms around the nation, just as much as he lived in Washington. At the conclusion of his term, he was an eolian figure carved by impeachment.

11

9/11

The presidential election of 2000 shaped up as a classic duel between the two political parties. With Bill Clinton leaving office, the race was wide open on both sides, but politics that year had to wait on a more pressing issue: the Y2K bug. The plague was forecast to be worse than the Black Death of the 1330s, only it affected machines, not humans. From the 1960s to the late 1980s, a widespread practice developed in all computer software programs to use two digits for representing a year instead of four digits. As the millennium approached, programs were changed to correct this shortcoming, but the fear was that older software would interpret 00 as 1900 and not 2000, ruining all records and data going back for decades. This was a major problem for the finance industry, but it also threatened businesses like utilities, banking, manufacturing, telecommunications, and the airlines.

The Y2K bug was a ticking time bomb for all major computer applications, which meant it was of concern to all Americans. The rumor in Washington was that the defense industry was especially vulnerable, but of course no one knew for sure. Companies around the world spent huge sums of money to go through their entire applications, looking for the Y2K bug and fixing it. The news media carried endless stories of people racing around trying to make themselves "Y2K compliant." In all, the United States spent some $100 billion preparing for the millennium, including substantial amounts by American multinational corporations overseas. The fear was that other countries would be less vigilant about the social disruption from information malfunction. The State Department withdrew hundreds of government employees and family members from Russia and the Ukraine, Belarus, and Moldova because they feared computer problems there.[1]

The gloom and doom about the year 2000 computer meltdown was exacerbated by apocalyptic paranoia in the society at large. Fear of possible computer glitches drove people to stockpile dehydrated food, generators, lanterns, flashlights, and batteries. In Wisconsin, the maker of a line of solar-powered ovens developed for use in Third World countries where people did not have wood found himself swamped with orders.[2] Some people predicted a complete social breakdown, with the failure of transportation and communication systems. They took cash out of banks and put it away under mattresses, installed solar panels on their roofs, and prepared to purify water to drink. The message from some Christians was that the calendar signaled a culmination of biblical prophesies. In Abilene, Texas, a couple caught up in the hysteria predicting the apocalypse took two neighborhood teenagers into the Mexican wilderness as part of a doomsday cult. They lived in isolation in a cave, ate animals, drank water from streams, and went without food for days on end. When the world did not end and the adults came blinking back into reality, a judge sentenced them to jail time.[3]

The run-up to the 2000 presidential nominations had the surreal quality of the Y2K millennium anxiety. Both nominees were likely to be from the baby boom generation, meaning that their political consciousness was shaped by the Vietnam War, the Watergate scandal, and the Reagan presidency. Democratic gains in the 1998 midterm elections unified them as a party, and the Republican establishment longed for similar accord after Bill Clinton's two victories. Business prosperity removed the economy as a major issue, freeing the primary voters to focus on personality and leadership. Some experts predicted at the outset that the coming race would be close. It was; but that was just about the only prediction about it that proved correct.

The American political system has a remarkable ability to reinvent itself, but each change in the rules has a corresponding change in the results. Beginning in the late 1960s, both parties began using primaries to select delegates to their national conventions. The number of primaries increased from fifteen in 1968 to a constant of about forty in 1992. The key to earning the nomination was to win the early primaries, so more and more states moved their contests up in the election season. The process was called "front loading," and it was designed to allow states to creep toward the front of the calendar and increase their influence in the candidate selection contests. In 1976, half the delegates to the Republican and Democratic conventions were selected by week eleven of the primary season; in 2000, half were selected by week six.[4] The small states of Iowa and New Hampshire, along with South Carolina for the Republicans, exercised an enormous influence in winnowing the candidate field and determining the nominee. The key for any successful candidate was to organize early in the primary states.

It came as no surprise, then, that nineteen months before primary election day, Vice-President Albert Gore made his first excursion to New Hampshire and Iowa. His campaign was founded on the idea that he would be the "steward of change" as the world moved into the new millennium, continuing the success of the Clinton years while adapting to meet the future.[5] Gore was taking nothing for granted. Numerous candidates for the Democratic Party presidential nomination were under discussion. Most of the talk was about House Minority Leader

Dick Gephardt of Missouri, Senator Bob Kerrey of Nebraska, liberal Senator Paul Wellstone of Minnesota, and former Senator Bill Bradley of New Jersey. Speculation in the press was that Academy Award–winning actor, director, and screenwriter Warren Beatty would enter the primaries. After receiving the Eleanor Roosevelt Award of the Southern California Chapter of the Americans for Democratic Action, he held the liberal Hollywood elite in the palm of his hand, asking: "Have we come to the point where the Democratic Party has to have a Republican President before it finds its voice again?"[6] If the Hollywood rumor was true, and politics was just another form of show business, only for "ugly people" instead of glamorous celebrities, then the Democratic Party was about to get a transfusion of glitz.

All the speculation proved feckless when primary season came around, and every mentioned candidate had withdrawn except Bill Bradley. This left the way open for Al Gore, who walked through the door to claim the title of nominee almost without a contest. Bradley positioned himself as the liberal alternative to the establishment Gore, and spent more time campaigning in Iowa than the vice-president. It did not help. On primary day, Gore dashed his rival's hopes by crushing him 63 percent to 35 percent in Iowa, and then beating him 50 percent to 46 percent in New Hampshire. Gore went on to win every primary.[7]

The Republicans came to the process starved for victory. Their effort to unseat Bill Clinton led to defeat in 1996 and to Democratic gains in the 1998 midterm election. The result was a national humiliation. The control of Congress remained in their hands, but control was tenuous, and they were determined to capitalize on their self-declared majority status by taking back the White House. Two candidates were returning after losing in 1996: Lamar Alexander, former Tennessee governor, and Steve Forbes. Secretary of Labor and Transportation Elizabeth Dole, who had national name recognition; former Vice-President Dan Quayle; and U.S. Senators John McCain of Arizona, Orrin Hatch of Utah, and Robert Smith of New Hampshire all joined the fray. Representative John Kasich of Ohio was running after giving up his U.S. House seat; media commentator Pat Buchanan was back for a third time. Gary Bauer, a Republican appointee who headed the Family Research Council, and former ambassador Alan Keyes, both of whom had never held office, rounded out the field. The final candidate was the governor of Texas and son of the former president: George W. Bush.

George Bush, or "W," as he was called in the press, garnered the label of favorite for two reasons. First, he won a landslide re-election as governor of Texas in 1998 with 69 percent of the vote, and the attention of the national press followed accordingly. Second, he was the champion in the more mundane, but critically important, task of fund-raising. In fact, Bush took campaign finance to a new level by taking in a record $67 million in 1999, and that included a record $36.3 million in four months, smashing all records in presidential politics.[8] Bush attracted the most influential GOP fundraisers. The early money lead helped clear the field, and allowed Bush to refuse federal matching campaign funds with their encumbering rules. This meant that the Texas governor could avoid the problem faced by Bob Dole in 1996, when the Democrats pummeled him with ads after he locked up the nomination. In July of 1999, Governor Bush declared, "I'm mindful of what happened in 1996, and I'm not going to let it happen to me. I'm going to win."[9]

The George W. Bush juggernaut was bolstered by endorsements. He enjoyed the backing of twenty-six Republican governors, thirty-nine senators, and 175 House members. In August of 1999, the Iowa Republican Party staged a nonbinding popularity contest for fund-raising purposes. While his rivals flocked to the state to personally campaign, Bush relied on television and his grassroots organization. The strategy led one of his less-well-funded rivals to say, "The rewards this year seem to go to those who avoid meeting with the activists, who drop in the Des Moines airport two or three times, rent a bale of hay and pretend they know Iowa."[10] Bush won the straw poll, even though he was outspent by Steve Forbes two to one.

By the fall of 1999, the original field of twelve Republican contenders had been cut in half. Then in November, the race narrowed to two: George W. Bush and John McCain. The Arizona senator concentrated almost all his early campaigning in three states: by-passing Iowa altogether, he worked hard in South Carolina, California, and especially New Hampshire. In the Granite State, he held a total of 114 town meetings, taking questions for ninety minutes from ordinary voters and granting unusual accessibility to the press.

With McCain not competing in the Iowa caucuses, the election was Bush's to lose. Polls showed that the only question to ask was: How close will it be? The answer was, not very.[11] Bush bested Forbes by 11 points in Iowa, and headed to New Hampshire like General Custer scouting for Sitting Bull, and with the same result. New Hampshire was a state that prided itself on personal campaigns, and the Bush effort was an unsuccessful one of media and mail. On February 2, 2000, Senator John McCain swamped Governor George W. Bush, piling up the widest margin since Ronald Reagan defeated Mr. Bush's father twenty years earlier. The final result showed McCain with 48 percent to Bush's 30 percent. Suddenly, the Republican presidential nomination race was turned upside down.

One week later, Bush won the Delaware primary with ease. Though small in delegate numbers, the placement of the primary was important. Steve Forbes, who devoted substantial time and resources in the state, finished third and dropped out of the race. The single most important showdown took place in the Palmetto State of South Carolina. George Bush used the two weeks prior to the campaign to retool his message; he emerged under the banner "A Reformer with Results." The governor went on the attack, and McCain responded by saying the Texas governor "twists the truth like Clinton." In a fierce response, the Bush campaign pulled out all stops with a "Veterans for Bush" operation in a state with the highest percentage of retired service men and women of any in the country.[12] Even with open primary rules, and a crossover vote of Independents and Democrats participating, Bush won South Carolina handily, 53 percent to 42 percent.

In the two primaries that followed, McCain defeated Bush in Michigan, while the Texan won Virginia. On "Super Tuesday," March 7, Republicans held eleven state primaries and two caucuses, and every one was restricted to registered party members. The Bush campaign spent $3 million a week, and because he had the resources to run everywhere, the Texas governor reaped the rewards and swept to victory in the important contests. McCain suspended his campaign two days later and congratulated Bush, although he stopped short of endorsing him. Bush went out of his way to say he respected Senator McCain, and declared, "I'm sure we can work together."[13]

The presidential race that gave America the closest election in history began early. The traditional starting date of Labor Day was pushed back to March 2000. The contest gave the nation a breathtakingly close race and a dramatic electoral controversy. Both candidates were fifty-something white males with Ivy League bachelor's degrees and politically prominent fathers, Al Gore's a former U.S. senator and George Bush's a former president. Al Gore was seen as intelligent, loyal to Bill Clinton, and as stiff as a railroad tie. The look on his face, whether he was speaking or listening, appeared to be the same. George W. Bush was a more engaging personality, but not seen as serious in his thinking. He had a habit of misspeaking himself, producing what the press called "Bushisms." For example, in New Hampshire he said, "I know how hard it is for you to put food on your family," and in South Carolina he declared, "Rarely is the question asked: Is our children learning?" To his admirers, the words just made him more human, and to his critics, nothing he said could change their minds that he was not worthy of the job. One of Bush's former college friends described him by saying, "Despite his upbringing, he [was], I think, one of the least pretentious people I ever met."[14]

Each candidate followed a strategic plan. Gore appealed to the younger voters, blue collar workers, the liberal constituencies at universities and Hollywood, and residents in the Northeast. These groups had been the core of the Democratic Party since the 1960s. The two great bases of the Democrats were on either coast, with the nation's industrial heartland in the balance. The states of Michigan, Iowa, Pennsylvania, Ohio, and West Virginia had to be won if Gore was to prevail. Gore's built-in advantages were support from organized labor, the friendly press corps, his standing with ethnic minorities, and women's groups. His disadvantages were long memories of Bill Clinton's misbehavior and his consistent inability to excite the core constituencies of the Democratic Party.

George W. Bush promised a determined campaign in any contested state. Like Gore, he planned to zero in on key states and crucial media markets. The object, in his view, was to push through to the election day and bring the campaign to a climax in the crucial markets. Bush's advantages were a substantial campaign war chest and enthusiastic support among the New Right and the South. The GOP had inroads into Hispanic neighborhoods, and good support in the business community. Bush's disadvantages, namely, his military experience and a rebellious past he was trying to live down, were highlighted by his opponents.

The party conventions, which both occurred in August, were of only limited importance. George Bush picked Dick Cheney, who had served as White House chief of staff, congressman, secretary of defense, and president of a Texas-based oil company, as his running mate. Al Gore chose Senator Joe Lieberman of Connecticut, a person of almost unmatched personal integrity and independence. The third-party candidates were Ralph Nader and Pat Buchanan, who together were heirs to the Ross Perot legacy of reforms since 1992. Many political observers believed, in advance of the race, that Gore and Nader were competing for the same voters, and that Buchanan voters would hurt Bush.

The general election campaign officially began after the party conventions, and could be divided into three phases, in retrospect.[15] The first division was from August 18 to September 27, when Al Gore enjoyed a popular lead, capitalizing on the strong economy and a host of favorable domestic issues. For example, Gore was able to win over environmental groups, who flirted for a time with Ralph Nader but gave the Democrats their support in the end. His average support in the polls for this period was 52 percent, but in late September the two candidates were running neck and neck. The second period was from September 28 to October 17, when George Bush capitalized on the national debates to showcase his "compassionate conservative" themes and personal appeal. Gore's numbers plummeted, up to 14 points in some polls. Why? On camera Bush appeared the equal of Gore, and during the debates the vice-president frequently bullied the moderator, interrupted, and was shown shaking his head off-camera as he used a number of facial expressions to show his disregard and even contempt for Bush. The advertising became more confrontational during this phase as well; so-called "contrast ads" highlighted differences in the candidates.[16]

Luck then intervened for Gore, and Bush's advantage slipped away. The core constituencies of the two parties hardened. For the last seventeen days of the campaign, the two were virtually tied. In the final days of October, the pollsters concluded that the race was too close to call. It was not a dead heat all the way, though. On several occasions Al Gore had to return to Tennessee where polls regularly showed him behind. Toward the end, the election was a blur of sights and sounds. Gore spent valuable time trying to undermine the growing support for Nader, and for a time Bush believed he had a chance to carry California. As November 7 loomed, the polls had Bush clinging to a microscopic lead. Privately, aides to the Texas governor were more optimistic, and predicted a big GOP win. Bush stopped in Gore's home turf of Tennessee and Clinton's Arkansas in the last week, while Gore ended with a seven-city, thirty-hour swing through five crucial midwestern states.

Abruptly it was over. Bright weather oversaw a turnout of over 100 million voters. For the first time in more than a century, the winner of the presidential election remained unknown a full day after the polls closed, and then another day, and then another. Gore won the popular vote by a narrow margin of 48.4 percent to 47.9 percent for Bush. Ralph Nader finished in third place, with 2.7 percent, while Pat Buchanan trailed with 0.4 percent. The Democrats won nineteen of the top thirty media markets, while Republicans took ten, and the two shared one market. Both candidates claimed triumph without really declaring victory. The problem was the electoral vote. The fate of the two rivals rode on the verdict in Florida, where an incomplete vote count had Bush leading by 1,784 votes. President Clinton met reporters on the South Lawn of the White House the morning after the election to say, "No American will ever be able to seriously say again, 'My vote doesn't count.' "[17]

In Nashville, Al Gore and his running mate, Joe Lieberman, watched the election returns with a large group of aides on the seventh floor of the Loews Vanderbilt Plaza hotel. At one point, all the major networks called Florida for the Democrats, but in a rare reversal, they withdrew the decision two hours later and said the state was too close to call. The electoral map seemed to be turned on its head. For example, Gore was defeated in Tennessee, becoming the first presidential contender to lose his home state since George McGovern lost South Dakota in 1972.

In Austin, George Bush and his family, including his parents, arrived at a restaurant for dinner. When the race proved tight, they retreated to the governor's mansion. When the networks called Florida for Gore, Campaign Manager Karl Rove told *USA Today*, "The networks refused to call states that in the end gave Bush rather respectable margins, like West Virginia and Ohio, but were eager to award a state that was a lot closer, [like Florida] even in their own exit polls."[18] Shortly after 2:00 A.M., Bush appeared to have won Florida, and Gore prepared his concession speech. When his limousine arrived at War Memorial Plaza in downtown Nashville, Gore was prepared to address a few thousand rain-soaked supporters with a gracious speech. He had earlier called Governor Bush and extended his congratulations. But, as they drove to the plaza, cell phones began ringing in the pockets of aides several vans back in the motorcade. Word reached the top Gore strategists that the Florida vote had dropped from a 50,000 vote Bush advantage to one of 6,000 votes. The news changed everything. About 2:30 A.M. Central Time, Gore placed a second call of the evening to Bush, which became one of the most memorable ones in American political history.[19]

Al Gore: Circumstances have changed dramatically since I first called you. The State of Florida is too close to call.
George W. Bush: Are you saying what I think you're saying? Let me make sure I understand. You're calling back to retract that concession?
Al Gore: Don't get snippy about it! Let me explain, if you prevail in the final count you will have my full support. But I don't think we should be going out making statements with the state of Florida still in the balance.
George W. Bush: My brother, Jeb, has been on the phone to Tallahassee, and on the computer monitoring vote patterns that he understands as well as anybody. His research shows a Bush victory.
Al Gore: Let me explain something. Your *younger brother* is not the ultimate authority on this.
George W. Bush: Do what you have to do.

The controversy would last thirty-six days. State results on election night gave 246 electoral votes to Bush, and 255 to Gore, with New Mexico (5), Oregon (7), and Florida (25) too close to call. Since 270 were needed to win, and both New Mexico and Oregon subsequently went to Gore, Florida would decide who would be president. State law there provided for an automatic recount in any election decided by such a small margin. The Gore campaign lodged a complaint over the state's election results, requesting that disputed ballots in four counties be checked by hand. However, the Bush campaign filed suit against the manual recounts, asking for a statewide settlement or none at all.[20] The 2000 election would be decided in court, where one of Thoreau's maxims held sway: "The lawyer's truth is not Truth, but... expediency."

The battle lines were quickly drawn. Within twenty-four hours, the Gore campaign flew in a planeload of seventy-two people, most of them trial lawyers who volunteered their services, to the controversy. The Bush campaign responded by hiring George H. W. Bush's former Secretary of State, James Baker, to oversee the recounting process from their side. Manual recounts began in Palm Beach and Dade counties, but the process was almost entirely subjective.[21] Voters in south Florida complained about "butterfly ballots" that confused them, nearly 180,000 ballots were not counted because of voter error, and some overseas ballots went uncounted because they arrived late. No guidelines were given, and numerous court rulings went both ways, some ordering recounts because the vote was so close and others declaring that a selective manual recount in a few counties that consistently voted Democratic was unfair.[22] Eventually, the Gore campaign won a decision in the Florida Supreme Court that ordered the recounting to proceed.

Unrelated events escalated the conflict. The controversy moved ahead when Katherine Harris, the Florida secretary of state, certified a Bush victory. The document had to be signed by the governor, and when Jeb Bush pulled out a pen and put his name on the dotted line, he made it clear that he would defy a court order to reverse the decision. The Bush campaign appealed to the U.S. Supreme Court, which subsequently returned the issue to the Florida Supreme Court. The Florida court continued to order a manual recount, which went on. This count was in progress on December 9, when the U.S. Supreme Court stopped the recount to hear the issues in *Bush v. Gore*.

As the nation's nine Supreme Court justices prepared to hear the arguments in the case, thousands gathered outside the staid Corinthian-style building. Some cheered, others chanted before television cameras, and the block in front of the marble building became a walled-off town meeting of protest. Inside, the hearing moved quickly; justices asked pointed questions. Justice Kennedy waited a mere fifty-four seconds into the presentation by Bush attorneys before interrupting to ask, "Where's the federal question here?" Chief Justice Rehnquist asked about how many votes had to be recounted in Florida, and whether any recount could be completed in time for a respectable transition.[23]

Around 10:00 P.M. on December 12, the U.S. Supreme Court handed down its decision, ruling 5–4 in favor of George W. Bush. Seven of the nine justices cited differing vote-counting procedures and standards from county to county, and the lack of oversight of the process was also a reason for their decision. George W. Bush was on the phone in Texas when the Supreme Court came in with its decision. James Baker was on the other end. "Good evening, Mr. President-elect," he said. Bush handed the phone to the vice-president-elect. "Jim," said Dick Cheney, "only under your leadership could we have gone from a lead of 1,800 to a lead of 150 votes."[24] The next evening, in a nationally televised address, Gore conceded. The campaign belonged to history, and Governor Bush became president-elect.

During the Florida recount controversy, former president George H. W. Bush watched television incessantly, but Barbara Bush found other things to do to take her mind off the issue. The temperament of the man about to be in the White House in 2001 was very much a reflection of his mother. The ability to be at ease in the middle of a storm was something that always astonished the people around George W. Bush. The staff cheered when they learned they had won the crucial South Carolina primary, but the candidate lay down to take a nap. As the electoral drama in Florida played itself out, Al Gore followed every twist and turn, but "W" did not watch the news shows or read the newspapers; instead, he spent his time jogging and working on his ranch in Crawford, Texas.

Why the detached decision making? Part of the answer lies in the relationship between mother and son that was forged in the hot Texas sun. While his father was absorbed by business demands, the family suffered a terrible tragedy, the death of baby Robin from leukemia. "Georgie" took upon himself the responsibility to cheer up his parents. From this time in his childhood, he cultivated the qualities of an energetic charmer, a sound judgment of people around him, and a curious sense of humor. Those qualities were strengthened when he married his wife, Laura. In short, the candidate had a common and engaging touch, and people liked him.[25]

The dark side of Bush's character was seen in his drinking and rebellion. He was a charismatic partier until 1986, when his alcoholism caused him to nearly lose his marriage. Laura Bush told him that if he did not stop drinking she would leave him, and take their twin daughters with her. At the crossroads of his fortieth birthday, Bush found God and a future. He began consulting with the Reverend Billy Graham, and joined a Bible-study group. By October, the newly sober and increasingly focused Bush received his share of stock from his oil company sale, which he used as collateral to purchase a share of the Texas Rangers baseball team. The sale from that deal landed him $14.9 million, and provided him with financial stability to seek the presidency.

Even though he was the son of noblesse oblige, George W. Bush never approached politics as gentlemanly work; instead he shunned his upper-class roots for cowboy boot commonality. But he was still criticized for being secretive in his decision making, with a blithe sense of entitlement. He made up his mind quickly, and often dismissed dissenting views with a shrug. As a result, he gave the impression of being either a leader of firm conviction or one carelessly disposed to dismiss his enemies. He barreled ahead with his decisions after listening to his advisors, and ignored his critics.

When Bush took office on January 20, 2001, the Republicans held both chambers and the presidency for the first time since January 1955. But their hold was by the narrowest of wins. Bush won the Electoral College vote, but received a half a million fewer popular votes than Gore. The control of the U.S. House for the Republicans was by the razor-thin margin of six seats, and the U.S. Senate was evenly split, with control only by Dick Cheney as tiebreaker. "George W. Bush received nothing more than a key to his office. Neither party could make a plausible claim to be unambiguously in power."[26] The verification of that verdict came on June 5, 2001, when Senator Jim Jeffords of Vermont left the GOP to become an Independent. Jeffords's decision to vote with the Democrats on administrative and procedural matters gave the Democrats control of the Senate for the first time since 1995.

The mandate may have been invisible, but the new president seized it anyway. In a cold semi-snowstorm, George W. Bush placed his hand on the Bible George Washington used and on the Bush family Bible used by his father, his brother as governor, and himself as governor. His inaugural address was the shortest in recent history, lasting only twelve minutes. "I will live and lead by these principles: to advance my convictions with civility, to pursue the public interest with courage, to speak for greater justice and compassion, to call for responsibility and try to live it as well."[27] The only familiar face missing from the inauguration was Reverend Billy Graham, who was ill, so his son, Franklin Graham, delivered the invocation. That night George W. and Laura Bush went to eight inaugural balls, where they danced for an average of forty-eight seconds at each one. The new president was home, and in bed, well before midnight.

On the campaign trail, George W. Bush promised to "give the Oval Office one hell of a scrubbing," and as the inaugural parade concluded painters finished rolling the hallways and putting up wallpaper in the West Wing. The new president declared that the Clinton practice of allowing people in jeans, t-shirts, and running shoes to enter the Oval Office was over. "Only men wearing a coat and tie, and women in a suit were allowed in."[28] Image mattered, and so too did loyalty. George W. Bush put together a cabinet and senior staff made up of experienced people he trusted, along with family friends.

The centerpiece of the domestic agenda that year was a large tax cut to stimulate the economy. Since the 1980s, Republicans had used the legislation as a prescription for a sluggish economy, and the Democrats always responded that the cuts were only "for the rich." In June of 2001, Congress presented the president with what he asked for, a comprehensive bill which he signed. The economy had fallen into a recession, and the $1.6 billion reduction in taxes included a rebate for every taxpayer. Late night comedians joked about the standard $600 return, but for most Americans the check was a welcome addition to the family budget, and tangible proof that things were different in Washington.

For a change, the immediate foreign policy challenge was not in the Middle East, but with China. Three months after taking office, Bush announced plans to sell eight diesel-powered submarines to Taiwan. The move infuriated Beijing. So, relations were at a low in April when a Navy surveillance plane collided with a Chinese fighter jet over the South China Sea.[29] The plane had to make an emergency landing, and its twenty-four crew members were detained. The crisis challenged the long-standing good relations the Bush family had with leaders of the country, and for a time it appeared that negotiations were at an impasse. Finally, quiet diplomacy won out, and a major crisis was avoided. In the negotiations, Bush took the opportunity to press the Chinese leaders for more religious freedom for their citizens.

Another major domestic issue for Bush was education. In Texas, he overhauled the public schools, and he intended to do the same in Washington. The new administration proposed a program called "No Child Left Behind," which was an attempt to reform education using federal incentives. The consensus among experts was that something had to be done, and soon. Comparative studies regularly showed that the United States was lagging behind virtually every other major industrialized country on math and science achievement, and the press showed ignorance among high school graduates about the basics of history and geography as well. The Bush remedy called for increased accountability, greater choice for parents and students, particularly those attending low-performing schools, and more flexibility in how local districts spend federal money.

The plan also called for a stronger emphasis on reading, especially among younger children. The president was determined to push his plan in person, and that is what he was doing when it happened. He was in Sandra Kay Daniels's second grade class at Booker Elementary School on Longboat Key, Florida. His chief of staff stepped up to interrupt and give him a message that ended with, "America's under attack." "I'm sitting in the midst of a classroom with little kids," recalled the president later, "listening to a children's story and I realize I'm the commander-in-chief of the country that has just come under attack."[30]

The most lethal assault on American soil began on a beautiful fall morning on Tuesday, September 11, 2001. On that day, a series of coordinated events by Islamic terrorists involved the hijacking of four commercial airliners, and resulted in the death of 2,986 Americans. Each generation in American history has had some event that galvanized them, where they remember exactly where they were when they heard the news. For the "Greatest Generation" it was Pearl Harbor, the postwar babies remembered John F. Kennedy's assassination, and Gen Xers would always recall the events of 9/11. The assault was the worst ever, one which exceeded the toll of 2,403 dead after the Japanese attack that began America's entry into World War II. When it was over, America had a new "Day of Infamy."

The attack can never be adequately explained, because it was an irrational response to a series of miscalculated provocations. A highly problematic U.S. intervention in the late 1970s in a civil war in Afghanistan, which proved to be the last great conflict of the Cold War, created the original context for the crisis. The Soviet Union invaded Afghanistan on December 26, 1979, and they stayed as occupiers for a brutal ten years. The United States, along with Britain and Pakistan, spent billions equipping and training Afghan rebels to fight the Soviets. Their resistance efforts were bolstered by Osama bin Laden and the Saudi royal family. Sometime in August of 1988, bin Laden formed a new military group, known as al Qaeda, which roughly meant "the base" or "the foundation."

All of this became clear later. It was not obvious at the time. The 1993 plot to blow up the World Trade Center in 1993 resulted in convictions, and the thrust of terrorism seemed far away most of the time. To the new president, the issue of terrorism concerned Americans in Israel, Mogadishu, or Europe, not so much at home. The administration was aware of vague threats about terrorists' intent on striking specific targets inside the United States, but they lacked substance. The enemy had no strong organization, weapons, or money. At least that is what the president was told.

Hani Hanjour, the pilot of Flight 77 which struck the Pentagon on September 11, 2001, entered the United States in 1990 to take English classes in Tucson, Arizona. Eighteen other suicide terrorists followed. Eleven of them were veterans; they had fought the Russians in the province of Chechnya. The terrorists organized themselves into two groups, with six core leaders, including the four pilots trained to fly advanced Boeing airplanes, and thirteen others who came in pairs in the spring and summer of 2001. They did not match the profile of suicide bombers familiar to television viewers who knew about Middle Eastern terrorists who were young, poor, undereducated, or indoctrinated. Instead, most of them were in their later twenties and thirties, with college educations, and they had lived for prolonged periods of time in western countries. Fifteen of them were from Saudi Arabia, and most of their money was transferred from Saudi banks.

They were a radical paradox. The Middle Eastern men were highly fanatical and religious in their ideology. Thirteen of them recorded farewell videos in Afghanistan; one said, "I am writing this with my full conscience and I am writing this in the expectation of the end, which is near."[31] Yet these fundamentalist Muslims drank alcohol, gambled, and made frequent visits to strip clubs. They had strippers perform lap dances for them, and a couple of the men in Boston tried to hire prostitutes the night before the attack. The interpretation of Islam by al Qaeda went against the mainstream reading of the Koran that prohibited sexual license, suicide, and violence against children and innocents and in no way promised sainthood or eternal happiness for terrorists. None of this mattered to the killer-pilots and their accomplices. They were suicide soldiers, fanatically committed to a cause.

The commercial airlines chosen for the mission had fuel capacities of nearly 24,000 gallons, making the planes flying incendiary bombs. The two flights destined for destruction at the World Trade Center both took off from Boston, and were hijacked shortly after leaving the runway. A flight attendant in one of them called a reservations agent in North Carolina to say, "The cockpit's not answering their phone. And there's somebody stabbed in business class and ... I think there's mace ... that we can't breathe ... I think we're getting hijacked."[32] Doubtlessly the passengers were fascinated, awestruck, terrified, and at odds with one another as to what was happening. At 8:16 A.M. American Airlines Flight 11 crashed into the North Tower of the World Trade Center.

The plane was estimated to be flying at 475 miles per hour, and struck the ninety-third through ninety-eighth floors of the 110-story building. No one above the crash line survived, and approximately 1,360 people died. Below the crash line, approximately seventy-two died, but more than 4,000 were evacuated and survived. If there was any grace in such an unconscionable act, it was that both towers were about half full because many offices did not open until 9:00 A.M., and the observation deck for tourists was not open until 9:30 A.M. Some of the occupants above the crash line made their way upward toward the roof in the hope of a helicopter rescue, but no rescue plan existed for such an eventuality. Faced with a desperate situation of smoke and burning heat from the jet fuel, an estimated 200 people jumped from the burning tower to their death on the streets and roofs below.

Survivors experienced tragedy and a miracle at the same time. A bond trader on the twenty-sixth floor of the North Tower thought the building was in an earthquake, as it swayed back and forth for some time. "When we ran to the windows to see what was going on outside, we saw debris falling everywhere— glass, large pieces of metal, and paper.... As if by instantaneous agreement we all made an unspoken decision to leave the building."[33] In the midst of the crisis, the odd thing was the orderly way people exited the building without panic or instruction. People knew what was happening in a vague way, but the time to speak about the events had not arrived, and they were busy trying to survive.

In Florida, the president was told the incident was an accident, and as a pilot he asked if the weather was bad. Back in Washington, CIA Director George Tenet was eating breakfast with his mentor, former Senator David Boren, when bodyguards converged on the table to hand Tenet a cell phone. Tenet took the call and as he handed the phone back to his aide before leaving he said, "You know this has bin Laden's fingerprints all over it." Vice-President Dick Cheney was whisked away to a secure area, but as he sat in the White House watching the television he was puzzled: "It was a clear day, there was no weather problem—how the hell could a plane hit the World Trade Center?"[34]

Two minutes after impact, CNN was the first major network to show the crash site. Anchor Carol Lin reported, "This just in. You are looking at ... obviously a very disturbing live shot there—that is the World Trade Center, and we have unconfirmed reports this morning that a plane has crashed into one of the towers of the World Trade Center." CNN then switched to Sean Martagh, the network's vice president of finance, who reported, "I just witnessed a plane that appeared to be cruising at a slightly lower than normal altitude over New York City. And it appears to have crashed into...the middle of one of the World Trade Center towers."[35] By now millions of Americans were tuning in and making phone calls to their friends to tell them the news.

One of the people watching was Mike McCormick, head of the New York flight control center, only his thoughts were not on the CNN story. Instead, he was looking at another airplane, United Flight 175, on the radar screen. In Chicago, a systems operations manager had just taken a call from an onboard flight attendant who said, "Oh my God. The crew has been killed; a flight attendant has been stabbed. We've been hijacked."[36] In New York, McCormick guessed what was coming, but he kept watching his screen. "Probably one of the most difficult moments of my life was the eleven minutes from the point I watched that aircraft, when we first lost communications until the point that the aircraft hit the World Trade Center." At 9:03 A.M. the United flight hit the South Tower, as millions of Americans watched on live television. The plane struck between the seventy-eighth through eighty-fourth floors, killing all aboard the plane and 600 people in the tower. The death toll was far lower than in the North Tower because two-thirds of the occupants evacuated in the time since the first tower had been struck.

Now the situation was beginning to become clear. When the second aircraft flew into the second tower, the seemingly unrelated hijackings were revealed as a coordinated terrorist attack on the United States. The country was beginning to come to a collective realization. In Florida, the president ended his photo-op and began to make phone calls. After hanging up with New York Governor George Pataki, he declared to everyone in the room, "We're at war."[37] The country must be warned. But how? The extent of what was happening was unknown.

Around the country, the people in positions of authority began to take command. Government buildings were closed, flights were grounded, and the military sent planes aloft and sealed bases. Messages were relayed to all transcontinental flights warning of the World Trade Center disaster and advising acknowledgment. One caution was sent to American Airlines Flight 77, which left Dulles Airport outside Washington, D.C., for Los Angeles, but it was too late. On board the plane, Barbara Olson called her husband, Theodore "Ted" Olson, who was the solicitor general of the United States, the person who argues the government's position on cases that go before the Supreme Court. Later, Ted Olson recounted her conversation: "She told me that she had been herded to the back of the plane...they used knives and box cutters to hijack the plane."[38]

A little after 9:00 A.M. the hijacked airliner crossed the Capitol Beltway and headed for the Pentagon, but the amateur pilot had made a mistake. The plane was too high, at about 7,000 feet, so to correct its pattern, the huge airliner made a high-speed descending spiral turn. Five minutes later it struck the only side of the Pentagon that had been renovated. Again, the measure of thankfulness was for a small favor, and what happened could have been far worse. The side facing the George Washington Parkway was the only one with a sprinkler system reconstructed with a web of steel columns and bars to withstand bomb blasts. Because of the recent construction, only about 20 percent of the people normally working on that side were at their desks. Still, 189 people died in the fiery crash at the symbol of America's military might. Secretary of Defense Donald Rumsfeld appeared for a time to help with the wounded, but he was soon summoned to a meeting to deal with other aspects of the crisis.

It was not over. A fourth aircraft, United Flight 93, on a regular flight from Newark, New Jersey, to San Francisco, had also been taken when it was out over Ohio. At about the same time the Pentagon was struck, Flight 93 reversed course and headed toward Washington. Marion Britton, a passenger on board at the time, called a friend to say that two people had been killed. Another passenger, Todd Beamer, spoke to a Verizon phone operator with the FBI listening in. He talked for fifteen minutes and told them that the passengers were taking a vote to decide whether or not to take over the plane.[39]

Washington was in the grip of panic. The Capitol and surrounding offices began evacuation as did the White House. Even though the city sat at the nexus of the world's most sophisticated communication network, rumors spread. The Associated Press incorrectly reported that a car bomb had exploded outside the State Department in Foggy Bottom. Reports of a fire on the Capitol Mall were also floated, and quickly found to be false. CNN reported an explosion on Capitol Hill, and then retracted the report twelve minutes later. There were reports that another plane was headed to the Pentagon. On board Air Force One, the president talked to the vice-president, and concluded that the military should shoot down any plane under the control of hijackers.[40]

On television, smoke continued to boil from the World Trade Center. At 10:10 A.M. the South Tower collapsed, plummeting into the streets below. A massive cloud of dust and debris formed and drifted down the building canyons as people ran for cover. About twenty minutes later, the North Tower fell as if it were being peeled apart, with another tremendous cloud of debris and smoke. For the New York City Fire Department, the initial battle in the war on terror took an unimaginable toll. When the alarm came in, units throughout the city were dispatched to the scene. Officials later estimated that as many as 400 firefighters responded to the inferno, and as the people streamed out in evacuation, the firefighters went in. Most were still in the building when the first tower collapsed. Some had stories of fortunate survival, but most did not. Fire Department Chaplain Reverend Mychal Judge was giving the last rites to a firefighter who had been injured by a falling body when both of them were enveloped in cascading rubble. Captain Timothy Stackpole had just returned to full duty after suffering burns. He was off duty, but came in when he saw the need to help and climbed to his death. On September 11 the NYFD lost nearly 350 firefighters, including all the members of thirty companies. The World Trade Center collapse was thirty times worse than any disaster ever suffered by a fire department.[41]

The astonishing thing was that it was all live on television. Later, one of the firefighters explained, "You have two 110-story office buildings. You don't find

A New York City firefighter looks up at what remains of the World Trade Center after its collapse during the September 11 terrorist attack. (U.S. Navy Photo by Photographer's Mate 2nd Class Jim Watson)

a desk...a chair...a computer...the biggest piece of the telephone I found was this big," he shaped a six-inch square. The buildings collapsed into dust, called "debris," "ruins," "wreckage," or "dust."[42] The words failed to capture what it really was. There were no bodies, no remains, nothing to really comb through after the collapse. Governor George Pataki refused to clean his shoes after his first trip to ground zero; they were caked with a gray glue-like substance—the remains of the buildings and the ashes of the dead.

In the skies over Pennsylvania, the last tragedy came to a bitter end. The telephone operator listening to Todd Beamer on board Flight 93 heard people shouting and women screaming, "Oh, my God," and "God, help us." Beamer let go of the phone, and his last words were to nearby passengers: "Are you ready? Let's roll."[43] About the time the South Tower collapsed in Manhattan, Flight 93 crashed into an empty field some eighty miles southeast of Pittsburgh. In the tiny town of Boswell, ten miles away, people reported that the big plane dipped its wings sharply to the left and the right, as it descended low and wobbly. Black box recordings recovered from the crash reportedly confirmed that passengers attempted to seize control of the plane from the hijackers. Captured al Qaeda material subsequently confirmed that Flight 93 was targeted for the U.S. Capitol.

Inside the President's Emergency Operations Center (PEOC), located underneath the East Wing of the White House, Vice-President Dick Cheney was erroneously told that Flight 93 was still in the air and descending on Washington. Cheney ordered the airliner shot down. The fog of war continued to cloud communications. Moments later, the vice-president was mistakenly told that six more commercial aircraft were unaccounted for. Outside the bunker, Washington was evacuating, F-16 fighter aircraft were in the air, and the U.S. military went to Defcon Three, the highest alert for the nuclear arsenal in thirty years. The Secret Service relayed a note to the PEOC that it had intercepted a message declaring, "Air Force One is Next." Cheney called President Bush on the plane to warn him not to return to Washington. Air Force One was routed to Barksdale Air Force Base in Louisiana, then on to the bunker beneath Offutt Air Base in Nebraska. In a video conference call to the PEOC in Washington, President Bush declared, "I'm coming back to the White House as soon as the plane is fueled. No discussion."[44] He did, but it was under a jet escort.

As the huge airplane descended to Andrews Air Force Base, the fires on the face of the Pentagon were still burning, and the emergency vehicles were clustered around. Ninety minutes after landing, at 8:30 P.M., the president addressed the nation, where he affirmed what would become known as the Bush Doctrine. "We will make no distinction between the terrorists who committed these acts and those who harbor them."[45] In a meeting in the PEOC after his address, the president told his advisors, "I want you all to understand that we are at war and we will stay at war until this is done.... Nothing else matters.... This is our only agenda."[46] That night an eerie scene developed in the nation's nearly abandoned capitol city. Armored vehicles lumbered in from military units outside the district, and military policemen took up positions at key intersections. Inside the White House, the president finally went to bed around midnight, but not until he wrote a note in his diary. "The Pearl Harbor of the 21st Century took place today.... We think it's Osama bin Laden."

The next morning, the headlines of the *Washington Post* declared: "Terror Hits Pentagon, World Trade Center." The summary column for the lead story had only one word embedded in the column, "War!"[47] For George W. Bush the weight of the presidency was heavier the next day. The attacks changed America, but they also changed the president. He was serious, emotional, and focused. Franklin Graham, the pastor who knew him well and visited with the president during the following days, emerged to say, "There is a seriousness in him.... He knows what he has to do and he has the inner confidence to do it."[48] The devastating nature of the attacks, and their secret nature, along with the cruelty they represented led him to undertake an enormous challenge.

Four days after the attack, the president called for a National Day of Prayer. In the hallowed halls of the National Cathedral he said, "This nation is peaceful but fierce when stirred to anger.... This conflict was begun on the timing and the terms of others. It will end in a way, and at an hour, of our choosing." The misstatements of the election campaign were forgotten. The president stood in the splendid majesty of the National Cathedral and spoke poignantly of the country's pain. "Our responsibility to history is already clear," he said, "to answer these attacks and rid the world of evil."[49]

After the service, Bush flew to New York City, to tour the devastation left by the terrorists. He waded into a sea of rubble and rain-soaked rescue workers in lower Manhattan. At one point he grabbed a megaphone and draped his arm over the shoulders of retired City Firefighter Bob Beckwith to thank the exhausted workers for their heroic efforts. When one worker screamed from afar, "George, we can't hear you!" Bush shot back, "I can hear you! The rest of the world hears you! And the people who knocked down these buildings will hear from all of us soon!" A thunderous cheer of "U.S.A.! U.S.A.!" welled up from the crowd of hardhats.[50]

The country was united in outrage against the sneak attack. The old distrust of outsiders resurfaced, and it combined to transform the war into a crusade against treacherous infidels. To imply that everyone in the county was a xenophobe would be to compound injustice, but together they wanted to see the cold steel of military revenge.

The president and his advisors had already decided that bin Laden was behind the attacks. CIA Director George Tenet said that al Qaeda and the Taliban in Afghanistan were essentially one and the same thing. Afghanistan is located on the road between central Asia and the Indian subcontinent. Lord N. Curzon described it as "a purely accidental geographic unit," not Persia, not Russia, and not British.[51] Even in the twenty-first century, the country had few roads, poor communication, and laws that were enforced in accordance with local custom and without reference to any central government. Radical Islamists flocked to Afghanistan to fight against the Russians in the 1980s. After the retreat of Soviet troops in 1989, the left-behind warriors collectively became known as the jihad fighters, or mujahedin. Later, the nucleus of these extremists coalesced around Mullah Mohammad Omar and became known as the Taliban leadership.

The country of Afghanistan had frequently been a theatre of fierce battles, and Europeans had not fared well. The British lost, as did the Russians. The mountainous geography, coupled with the nation's multiethnic racial composition, made military operations next to impossible. The main money-making crop in

Standing on top of a crumpled fire truck with retired New York City firefighter Bob Beckwith, President George W. Bush rallies firefighters and rescue workers during an impromptu speech at the site of the collapsed World Trade Center towers on September 14, 2001. "I can hear you," President Bush said. "The rest of the world hears you. And the people who knocked these buildings down will hear us soon." (White House Photo by Eric Draper)

the country was opium poppy, and the United Nations estimated that 39 percent of the world's heroin came from this one country. Since 1996, Osama bin Laden had been a resident of Afghanistan, along with other members of al Qaeda who operated the training camps.

President Bush delivered an ultimatum to the Taliban leaders demanding that they deliver al Qaeda's leaders to the United States, close the terrorist training camps, and "hand over every terrorist and every person and their support structure to appropriate authorities."[52] The Taliban refused to speak directly to the American president, stating that it would be an insult to Islam to comply. Later, as the likelihood of military action became more imminent, they offered to extradite bin Laden to a neutral nation. No deal. President Bush rejected the offers as merely delaying tactics.

On October 7, 2001, U.S. and British forces clandestinely infiltrated Afghanistan to make contact with the Northern Alliance of tribal warlords and organized them to overthrow the Taliban. On the same Sunday, the United States began an aerial bombing campaign, targeting Taliban military and terrorist training facilities. Before the attack, Osama bin Laden released a video in which he praised the nineteen hijackers as martyrs and vowed that the United States would never live in peace as long as the goals of his Islamic group remained unmet. He claimed the United States would fail in Afghanistan and then collapse, just like the Soviet Union did after its incursion in the 1980s. His call, broadcast on television stations throughout the Muslim world, was for a war of jihad against the entire non-Muslim world.

Prewar isolationism was now passing through an extraordinary transformation. America wanted retribution, but it was difficult for the nation to understand what was happening in Afghanistan. The geography was formidable, and it was hard to show the effect of high-altitude bombing, strategic air strikes, and cruise missiles on a dug-in enemy to a television audience. The U.S. forces were methodical, and at the same time flexible. Army Special Forces used motorcycles or rode on horseback, and then used sophisticated global positioning technology to deliver attacks on targets in the cities of Kabul, Jalalabad, and Kandahar. The Taliban lost their ability to coordinate a response, and their morale began to sink. The softening-up phase of the campaign took a month, and critics of the war at home pointed to past failures in the mountainous terrain as a prelude for impending failure.[53] The Americans in the military were perhaps the best-prepared generation ever to go to war willingly, meaning only that it was a job that had to be done and they knew what to do. Afghan fighters, who had been involved in a twenty-three-year-old civil war, had never seen anything like the firepower that accompanied American combat forces. On November 9, U.S. forces captured Mazir-e-Shaif, and as the Northern Alliance swept in, many local commanders chose to switch sides rather than fight.

Nine weeks after the World Trade Center disaster, Laura Bush became the first First Lady to deliver the president's Saturday morning radio address to the nation. "The brutal oppression of women is a central goal of the terrorists," she explained. "Women have been denied access to doctors, education, and other services." "Under the Taliban women "face beatings just for laughing."[54] Allied forces were met by hundreds of women, racing up to thank the troops as liberators. Television cameras documented the collapse of the Taliban regime, with pictures of Afghan women taking off their burkhas as they and their children rejoiced by dancing. U.S. relief acts authorized special funds for Afghan families, and the interim government appointed a minister of women's affairs.

When Americans at home sat down to a Thanksgiving meal, they watched the fall of Kabul, Afghanistan's capital, on television. The Taliban began a systematic retreat to the impenetrable Tora Bora cave complexes on the Pakistani border. The heroes of the Afghan War were the mud-caked Special Forces units who allied with natives to press the attack. Behind them, on air bases and guiding support logistics, were thousands of soldiers who just wanted to get it over. By the time the Americans and their Northern Alliance colleagues arrived in the capital they found only bomb craters, burned foliage, and the remains of

Taliban gun emplacements. Within twenty-four hours, all of the Afghan provinces along the Iranian border fell.

Every war is accompanied by a social revolution at home, and this one was no different. Post-9/11 America began to rethink postmodern ideals, of tolerance with a plethora of metanarratives, which resulted in hostile terrorists flying airplanes into buildings. Many people were in disbelief. How could a free society defend itself against attacks that took advantage of American openness and freedom? The very dimension of what was happening altered the country. The nation had a new executive agency, the Department of Homeland Security. The home front was in reality a battleground of ideas, customs, economic theory, foreign policy, and "what America was really about." The left decried the war, but most Americans supported the foray into Afghanistan. The home country was in a convulsive transformation, though few realized it at the time.

By December, the "Afghan War," as it was called, boiled down to a fight between the U.S.-led Northern Alliance opposite 10,000 Taliban fighters led by foreigners. Kandahar, the movement's birthplace, was the last stronghold of the Taliban. Inside the city, Mullah Omar issued defiant orders, but the result was being decided by the advanced weaponry of the United States. As the Taliban teetered on the brink of losing their last bastion, U.S. forces focused their attention on the Tora Bora cave complex which allegedly hid Osama bin Laden. The war ended on December 17, but it brought no victory.

In the last weeks of the conflict, senior al Qaeda and Taliban leaders escaped to Pakistan, and both Osama bin Laden and Mullah Mohammad Omar successfully evaded capture. Explanations for their departure vary, and all were unsatisfying. The best explanation seemed to be that the local forces, upon whom the United States most relied, allowed bin Laden to get away. By 2002, the Afghan war was widely considered over. It had been labeled a failure because the hard core of the Islamic terrorist leadership escaped, and fears were that the Taliban would later regroup.

Throughout the year, al Qaeda fighters were secure in established sanctuaries among tribal protectors in four southern provinces that formed the original heartland of their movement. The intention of the rebels was to use the region as a base for launching attacks and possibly major offensives in the style of the mujahedin who battled Soviet forces in the 1980s. Not this time. In March, the United States and allied Afghan warlords launched an offensive on the entrenched enemy. The battle was fought in caves and bunkers at altitudes above 10,000 feet. Ground fire from Afghan militia and American forces, along with heavy aerial bombardment, resulted in over 400 al Qaeda and Taliban casualties, according to U.S. estimates. However, fewer than fifty bodies were ever found, and most of the opposition simply melted away.

"War," the Greek historian Thucydides wrote, "is a violent teacher." Both Plato and Aristotle saw the violence and extremism of military conflict as corrosive of human nature and the good society. Perhaps because of the Afghan

War, or the World Trade Center attack, or maybe memories of the impeachment diatribe—for whatever reason, it was characteristic of twenty-first-century politics to be shrill. Republicans and Democrats saw each other as mutual enemies, and the rhetoric was extreme on both sides. As the midterm elections approached, the biggest transport ships the Navy had were setting sail for the Middle East, for yet another confrontation with Saddam Hussein and the Iraqi army. Emotions were at another high. In terms of partisanship, there had been a twenty-year trend of increasing power to the Republicans, but the country was evenly divided. Democrats took consolation in one of the maxims of American politics: the party in power nearly always loses strength in off-year elections. The average since World War II was eighteen seats for the president's party in the House of Representatives in the first term. If that happened again, then the Democrats would return to power in the House.[55]

In view of the even divide between the Democratic and Republican parties at virtually every level, President Bush put his personal popularity on the line to campaign for GOP candidates in tight races. In early November, the president stumped in fifteen states in five days. Voter turnout was predicted to be the lowest since 1942, so the president's message was simple. "You have an obligation as part of the citizenry of America to go to the polls and vote."[56] The president was taking a political risk; if he failed, then his first term would end with divided government.

The results of the election were decisive. The Republicans won twenty-two of the thirty-four Senate contests, for a total of fifty-one seats in the 108th Congress. This was a gain of two seats that shifted control back to the GOP. The outcome in the House was even clearer. The Republicans reversed conventional wisdom, and gained six seats in the midterm elections, leaving the party of Jefferson and Jackson twelve seats short of the majority control they sought. Democrats gnashed their teeth.

Suddenly the talk was of the election outcome signaling a new conservative majority. On the first page of the *New York Times,* veteran reporter R. W. Apple likened Bush to Reagan, arguing that both were often underestimated by their opponents.[57] A Georgia Democratic congressman marveled that Bush could help oust that state's Democratic governor and put in office the first Republican since Reconstruction. Comparisons were being made between George W. Bush and Franklin D. Roosevelt. Few could have imagined two years earlier, when Bush won the presidency without a majority popular vote and as a consequence of a Supreme Court decision, that he would ever be compared to Roosevelt. What changed, of course, was the tragedy of September 11. Americans needed someone to believe in, and lead, and George W. Bush was transformed by the office and the challenge. Dramatic events led to dramatic political change.

More drama lay ahead, embodied in the Navy ships carrying Abrams battle tanks to Iraq.

― 12 ―

Misunderestimated

A characteristic of the television news cycle during the Afghan War was to give the expected daily temperatures in Kabul, Afghanistan, and other Mideast cities. The obvious justification at the time was that thousands of American service men and women were deployed abroad, and their families back home wanted to know every detail of what they were experiencing. When the troops came home in 2002, the weather forecasts stopped, but as conflict intermittently flared in the Middle East, the temperature projections came back.

The media anticipated something. Since the end of the Gulf War in 1991, and especially after September 11 ten years later, Iraq's relations with the United States, the United Nations, and the United Kingdom deteriorated markedly. Saddam pursued a policy of confrontation without regard to postwar sanctions. A U.N. resolution passed in November 2002 stated that Saddam had been in "material breach" of every agreement since the end of the first Persian Gulf War. From time to time, it looked like the troops might be headed back.

After Saddam was evicted from Kuwait in 1991, the United States pursued a policy of aggressive containment. U.S. and British warplanes flew sorties and bombed targets over two no-fly zones established in the north to protect the Kurds and in the south to protect the Shiite Muslims. With the war over, the United Nations became concerned about deteriorating famine and diseases in the country, with catastrophe a real possibility. The thought was that domestic unrest would lead to Iraqis rising up to throw off the yoke of Saddam Hussein. In the meantime, something had to be done to keep the populace from starving. In 1995 the U.N. Security Council adopted an Oil-for-Food program that provided Iraq with the opportunity to sell oil to finance the purchase of goods for the general population. At the time it was implemented, the program was seen as a humanitarian gesture; later it was shown to be a scam, with Saddam Hussein diverting billions to his personal use, and involving U.N. officials in corruption.

A pattern emerged. When more military and economic sanctions were imposed on Iraq they wound up harming the population, while the dictator enjoyed an opulent lifestyle. In fact, none of the international policies of containment or charitable aid had the effect of quieting Saddam's unrelenting hostility to the rest of the world. On August 8, 2000, the twelfth anniversary of the end of the Iran-Iraq War, Saddam appeared on Iraqi television to remind his subjects of their "great victory" over "those who wished our people ill and our nation harm, backed by international Zionism, imperialism and the wicked Jews in the occupied land."[1] In the speech, the Iraqi dictator turned his ire on Saudi Arabia for providing bases for the U.S. and British warplanes in the 1991 war. He continued to manipulate the Oil-for-Food program for his own gain, and used it to create divisions in the French, British, and Russian delegations to the United Nations to get economic sanctions lifted. He was amazingly successful in persuading the international community that his intents were peaceful.

In Washington, George W. Bush was unconvinced. The president was not interested in economic embargos. The antiseptic notion of launching a cruise missile or having fighter pilots bomb in the no-fly zone was an option he categorically rejected. While the president was at Camp David with his senior advisors to discuss the Afghanistan war plans, Iraq was part of the agenda, and no meeting adjourned without discussion of the regime of Saddam Hussein and his role in the support of worldwide terrorism. In the wake of September 11, while making plans to deal with the Taliban in Afghanistan, Deputy Defense Secretary Paul Wolfowitz pushed for a "regime change" in Iraq, arguing that Saddam was indirectly tied to the attacks. The president agreed, and signed a secret National Security Council directive outlining the goals and objectives for going to war with Iraq. Once the United States finished operations in Afghanistan, President Bush was asked what was next. "Our objective is more than bin Laden," he said.[2]

Did the president have an unfulfilled family grudge to settle because his father left Saddam Hussein in power a decade earlier? Was the administration fed up with the endless jabbing Iraq gave the United States in the international press and at the United Nations? We will never know the exact answers to these questions, but it became clear that a case was being made for war. Later, when the president's justification for the invasion was metastasizing through the country, the steps appeared shadowy, imprecise, and disturbing. But from September 11, 2001, until the attack on March 19, 2003, the Bush administration, and the Congress, appeared cautious, and even deliberate, with every move well informed.

In his 2002 State of the Union message, Bush mentioned Iraq as part of an "axis of evil," along with Iran and North Korea, and pointedly did not mention bin Laden.[3] The administration doctrine in the "War on Terrorism" focused on preemptive military action in response to an imminent threat of war by another power. The issue of Iraq's disarmament became significant when the president demanded an end to alleged Iraqi proliferation, and use, of weapons of mass destruction (WMD). Iraq said it had no such weapons. Virtually no one believed that. Saddam had already shown a willingness to use chemical and biological weapons against his internal and external enemies, and in innumerable speeches he had declared he would not hesitate to use WMD against Israel if the opportunity arose. Why, for example, would Iraq not allow inspectors unfettered access to sites around the country? The U.S. administration argued that the country posed a "growing" and "gathering" threat to peace in the region. In October of 2002 the U.S. Congress adopted a joint resolution that granted President Bush the authority to wage war in Iraq. The vote was 296–133 in the House, and 77–23 in the Senate.[4]

The drums of war became louder in November, when the United Nations passed another of its resolutions. This one, which would become infamous, was numbered 1441, and called for the resumption of weapons inspections in Iraq. Force was not authorized by the resolution; instead, the language spoke of "serious consequences" if there was no compliance.[5] The U.N. Security Council deadlocked on what the outcome would be, but U.S. Defense Secretary Donald Rumsfeld left no doubt where he stood when he said the United States would "go it alone" if necessary. The Bush administration began to use a new phrase; the threat Iraq posed was no longer "growing," or "threatening"; it was now "imminent."[6] To meet it, George Bush assembled a "coalition of the willing," made up of some forty-seven countries inclined to act collectively and militarily outside the jurisdiction of the U.N. mandates. The world was not anxious for the United States to go to war, and the home front was just as cautious.

The argument became nationwide. Supporters of the war believed that Saddam Hussein had violated U.N. sanctions, supported terrorists, and harbored weapons of mass destruction. More ambitious "hawks" for the war maintained that the removal of Saddam Hussein could be a catalyst for democracy and bring peace in the Middle East. The "doves" disagreed; opponents contended that the information about weapons was incomplete, and that a preemptive war was likely to have results different from what the administration intended. The lack of hard facts and contradictory information helped explain one of the great mysteries of the Second Gulf War and resolve one of its puzzles, why it became a graveyard for the reputations of eminent American statesmen. For example, on February 3, 2003, Secretary of State Colin Powell addressed the U.N. Security Council. In describing the American case for war, he said, "You will see an accumulation of facts and disturbing patterns of behavior ... [that] demonstrate ... Saddam Hussein and his regime have made no effort, no effort to disarm as required by the international community.... The facts and Iraq's behavior show that Saddam Hussein and his regime are concealing their efforts to produce more weapons of mass destruction."[7]

The Iraq War was presented as a case for removing banned weapons. Most Americans were jaded to the region's periodic convulsions, but the justification seemed valid. The problem was all the evidence was circumstantial, and no one could produce "smoking gun" proof. Before the attack, the head U.N. weapons inspector, Hans Blix, stated that his team had been unable to find any evidence of nuclear, biological, or chemical weapons.[8] No weapons of mass destruction were found by the Iraq Survey Group, headed by inspector David Kay, who subsequently resigned in protest against U.S. policy. The alleged link between al Qaeda and Iraq was often mentioned in the run-up to the war, but evidence for the connection was never conclusively shown. The administration argued that U.N. Security Council resolutions had consistently been ignored by Saddam Hussein, and that the violations warranted action. But the majority of the U.N. Security Council members, both permanent and rotating, did not support an attack for reasons of noncompliance. Although Iraq had pursued an active nuclear weapons development program, and had recently tried to procure materials and equipment for their manufacture, the weapons and materials were never discovered. In the end, none of the objections mattered. The cause for war in Iraq was the cause of America for half a century: to protect the world from its most dangerous dictators. For reasons good or bad, right or wrong, America went to war.

Opposition to the decision was global. Many protestors in Middle Eastern and Islamic countries supported Saddam, while those in the streets of Europe just hated George W. Bush. Part of the outrage stemmed from the fact that the two sides in the conflict were not evenly matched. The Iraqi military was considerably weaker than when Saddam Hussein invaded Kuwait. Main battle tanks for Iraq decreased from 5,100 in 1991 to 2,000 in 2003, armored personnel carriers were down from 6,800 to 1,800, self-propelled artillery from 500 pieces to 150 pieces, and towed artillery from 3,000 to 1,900.[9] What was more, the Iraqi air force could not get even one plane airborne. Like most despots, Saddam's legitimacy rested on his command of the army and the police. While the elite Republican Guard forces did receive more modern equipment, higher pay, and better food, through a lack of maintenance and a shortage of spare parts, they were in no position to take on any developed military, let alone one led by the United States.

The U.S. force was substantially different from the one in 1991, as well. Mainly, it was smaller and more mobile. The Third Mechanized Infantry Division was the heaviest unit on the drive to Baghdad, with 270 Abrams tanks and 200 Bradley fighting vehicles. U.S. and British forces carried Tomahawk cruise missiles that used a sophisticated Global Positioning System (GPS) to hit their targets, making them less likely to miss. In the first Gulf War barely 7 percent of the air strikes used precision munitions; by the second, nearly 65 percent of the weapons were precision guided. One advantage was unchanged. The United States still controlled the air, the sea, and the communications battlefield.[10]

In March of 2003, President Bush sent a letter to Congress giving two justifications for the war: first, he had determined that further diplomacy would not protect the United States, and second, he was taking "necessary action" against international terrorists and terrorist organizations.[11] The president gave Saddam Hussein forty-eight hours to lay down his arms or face an invasion. At 5:30 A.M.

Baghdad time, on March 19, explosions were heard around the city, and "Operation Iraqi Freedom" was underway. An American reporter in the city at the time recalled, "I had just begun to drift off...when I heard a big, muted whoomping noise. My bed moved as if there had been an earthquake rather far away."[12]

The Iraqi strategy centered on delay, to stay in the fight as long as possible in hopes of trading space for time. Iraq was a nation about the size of California, and if Saddam was going to make a stand, it would be in the urban environs of Baghdad, some 350 miles inside the border, with the U.S. troops exhausted and having extended supply lines. The American plan was to sweep up the country from Kuwait in a combined air and group operation, where the mass of forces would be sacrificed for speed, maneuverability, and precision. With a huge advantage in reconnaissance and information, U.S. General Tommy Franks was counting on accuracy and unpredictability to defeat the enemy.

It worked just that way. The accuracy of American technology in weaponry was more important than the size of the battle force. A reporter in Baghdad on the first day of hostilities described watching a cruise missile rip into the roof of the Council of Ministers building, "which was already ablaze, and a great new orange plume of flame rose up.... When it was over I noticed that all the electricity in the city was still on."[13] That was the plan, to win the war on television and on the ground, all the while leaving the lights on.

The immediate target for the U.S.-led coalition was the oil infrastructure of the country, which was secured with limited damage. The U.S. Third Infantry Division moved down a main highway toward Baghdad, in a rapid advance, pausing when they met resistance from Iraqi troops and dust storms. At the same time, the British fought their way into Iraq's second-largest city, Basra, located in the southern part of the country. The biggest tank battle by British forces since World War II took place on March 27 when the Royal Scots Dragoon Guards destroyed fourteen Iraqi tanks in a heated battle. One officer suggested, with typical English understatement, that the contest was like "a bicycle against a motor car."[14] Still, problems remained. No matter how badly equipped the Iraqis were, their ambushes proved worrisome to American troops whose task it was to push on to Baghdad.

The press was "embedded" in this war, which meant that television stories were broadcast back to the nation by satellite. The most gripping story was of a daring American raid behind enemy lines to rescue a nineteen-year-old Army POW, PFC Jessica Lynch, who was held hostage in a hospital after her unit made a wrong turn and she was injured in a firefight. The battles were carried live on television, and the viewers saw the bunkers and the bodies from each encounter. Television was the medium of choice, but not all reporters seemed to agree with the Pentagon rules of coverage. Baghdad correspondent Peter Arnett, who was a familiar figure from the first Gulf War, was fired by NBC for giving an interview to Iraqi television in which he said, "American war planners misjudged the determination of the Iraqi forces."[15]

Print journalists filed their stories electronically. One of them was with four Marines in a humvee, "wired on a combination of caffeine, sleep deprivation, excitement and tedium," who talked about the "hopeless retards" they faced in the country.[16] They were referring to irregulars recruited to supplement the Iraqi military forces. In most cases these fanatics were Baath Party loyalists and believers, but an additional number of religious and other fanatics from Arab lands journeyed to participate in Saddam's defense. Collectively they were known as "Saddam's Men of Sacrifice," or the *fedayeen*. The fearsome balaclava-wearing brigade was commanded by Saddam's eldest son, Uday. When interviewed on foreign television, one fedayeen said: "We are here first to kill Americans, and second to kill any Iraqi that doesn't fight them."[17] Before the war the fedayeen were involved in the beheading of women in families suspected of being hostile to Saddam Hussein. In combat, the fedayeen picked martyrdom over victory. They took advantage of any opportunity to kill Americans, sometimes by playing dead and imploding themselves when soldiers or passers-by approached. They armed pickups and SUVs with pedestal-mounted machine guns and rocket-propelled grenades. One Seventh Cavalry unit reported a fedayeen attack on a motorcycle with a recoilless rifle strapped to the sidecar.[18]

The character of this war, like all of them, was set by the weather. The seasonal "shamal" was a summer, northeasterly wind that blew over Iraq and the Persian Gulf, and was often a strong dry wind during the day, and lighter at night. On March 24, the wind struck for three days, sustained at twenty-five knots with gusts to fifty. The talcum-powder-like dust was everywhere, accompanied by rain squalls, heavy winds, and pelting sand. Saddam and his chief lieutenants calculated that the weather would ground close support aircraft, so they moved their forces forward to engage Coalition troops. In 1991 a decision like this made eminent good sense, but this time around high-flying B-1 bombers and American artillery possessed infrared capabilities that allowed them to penetrate the blowing sands and illuminate moving targets. This time the troop movement proved fatal for the Iraqis.

Three weeks into the invasion, U.S. forces moved into Baghdad. A reporter interviewing civilians in the city found that they struggled for words to describe the devastation from American air strikes. At the same time, there was an everyday nonchalance as Baghdad residents sensed that the bombing would not produce widespread carnage as long as civilians stayed away from government buildings. Initial plans called for armored units to surround the city while Airborne units commenced a street-by-street battle. The most crucial moment of the fighting was in the early morning hours of April 4, when two Bradley fighting vehicles and two Abrams tanks were rushed by a large number of Republican Guard vehicles. In less than five minutes the American armor destroyed twelve enemy tanks. Later in the afternoon, seven tanks and two Bradleys attacked twenty-two Iraqi tanks, six of which were destroyed by overhead aircraft. The fierce fight broke out between the two groups at the relatively short range of 800 to 1,300 meters. Within ten minutes the Abrams tanks destroyed all the Iraqi armor.[19]

Hours after their arrival outside Baghdad, a "Thunder Run" of about thirty tanks left a staging area near the Baghdad Airport to attack the palaces of Saddam Hussein downtown. The column met heavy resistance, including many fedayeen suicide attackers who commandeered taxis, cars, and pickup trucks mounted with machine guns on pedestals. Enemy fire scarred every U.S. vehicle, but with the exception of one Abrams, all were rearmed and refueled without casualties. Within two days the American column established a base downtown. Hours after the seizure of the palaces, television coverage spread the news throughout Iraq, and resistance crumbled in the city. On April 9, 2003, Baghdad was formally secured by U.S. forces and the power of Saddam Hussein was declared over.

Viewers in the United States were able to watch U.S. tanks roll into Baghdad live on television, with a split-screen image of the Iraqi minister of information claiming that U.S. forces were not in the city and were being defeated outside its boundaries. Muhammad Said al-Sahuf, or "Baghdad Bob" or "Comical Ali," as he became known, epitomized the loyal Iraqi whose service was based on fear.[20] He spoke with a quaint British accent and delighted in calling the U.S. and British forces "villains, mercenaries, and war criminals." Days after the collapse of Baghdad, General Tommy Franks confirmed that U.S. officials bribed key members of the Iraqi military elite and the Baathist Party to defect.

The Coalition troops promptly began searching for key members of Saddam Hussein's government. Late Monday evening, on July 21, an Iraqi detainee whispered to American interrogators that he knew where Saddam's two sons, Uday and Qusay, were hiding. The location was in plain sight, at a distant cousin's house right in the middle of the city of Mosul. Soldiers surrounded the building and directed an ascending fusillade of fire, beginning with machine guns and ending with ten antitank missiles. When the noise subsided, Qusay, Uday, a bodyguard, and Qusay's son were all taken from the building, dead.[21]

Saddam Hussein was, of course, the most-wanted man in the country, and the most elusive. While many former leaders were arrested, extensive efforts to find the former dictator proved fruitless. Then, on December 14, 2003, the U.S. civil administrator in Iraq, Paul Bremer, walked into a packed room at 8:30 P.M., Iraqi time, to announce, "Ladies and gentlemen, we got him!" Saddam Hussein was captured twenty-four hours earlier in an underground "spider hole" at a farmhouse near his hometown of Tikrit. The world saw a very different man from the one who appeared on television as the neat, and always in-charge, ruler of Iraq. Now Saddam had a full beard and his hair was longer and curlier than his familiar appearance.[22]

President Bush did not need the capture of Saddam Hussein to verify victory in Iraq. On May 1, 2003, he flew a Lockheed S-3 Viking fighter to the aircraft carrier USS *Abraham Lincoln*, where he announced an end to major combat operations. Estimates at the time were that Iraq had some 24,000 casualties, while the United States had some 1,758 from both combat and noncombat deaths.[23]

But amid the joy of celebrating victory, it soon became clear that the job was not over. Those in Iraq opposed to the occupation were determined to drive the Americans away, and they were willing to die as martyrs in the process. The insurgents were part of at least forty distinct groups. Some were organized by former Baathist Party officials, the fedayeen, relatives of soldiers killed by Coalition forces, followers of radical clerics, foreign fighters, and Sunni Islamists. Together they swore that they would make the Americans pay the highest price possible for their military victory.

A new word entered the American vocabulary: IEDs. The acronym stood for "improvised explosive device," and consisted of former Iraqi military armaments and home-made materials, concealed along main roads to detonate when a convoy or patrol passed. The method of detonation varied from simple wires to cell-phone signals and garage-door openers. In addition, Iraqi guerillas frequently launched ambushes on U.S. convoys and patrols, along with those of the Iraqi security forces. Another form of attack involved hit-and-run mortar and rocket strikes on Coalition bases and convoys. Sabotage was also a part of the insurgency. Using either rocket-propelled grenades or explosives, insurgents regularly destroyed portions of oil pipelines to ruin the economic recovery.

The most terrifying part of the campaign was the unpredictability of suicide bombers. Car bombs were driven by combatants to targets such as Iraqi police stations, recruiting centers for the security services, and U.S. convoys. But the suicides were not limited to these targets. Assassinations also marked U.N. facilities, embassies, mosques, the International Red Cross, Kurdish political parties, hotels, restaurants, and Christian churches. The greater bloodshed led to a change in American tactics. The U.S. military identified hard-core fighters and insurgent neighborhoods, where they conducted dangerous house-to-house searches. Gradually, the U.S. forces turned their responsibility over to the local security personnel of the Iraqi government. The struggle was not over, and Americans worried about the "exit strategy" from the country they saved.

As the war wound down in Iraq, the election heated up at home. One of the ironies of American politics is that any military decision is soon ratified, or rejected, as an issue in a presidential political campaign. The foundation for President George Bush's re-election campaign was ideological conservatism. He cast himself as a "war President" in a worldwide campaign against terrorism. Domestically, Bush stuck to tax cuts for the economy, "faith-based" initiatives for social problems, and opposition to gay marriage and abortion. In the aftermath of the GOP's off-year election successes, George W. Bush's chief political strategist, Karl Rove, developed a grassroots voter contact program to register and identify voters in key states. The new "ground game" for the GOP was designed to avoid the problems of four years earlier, when the get-out-the-vote effort of the Democrats trumped the Republicans, who bought ads on television.

With no major challengers, the president raised over $130 million before March of 2004, and waited to see who would take him on from the Democratic side.

The party of Jefferson and Jackson, of FDR and JFK, and of the "little guy" faced a challenge. In six straight elections their nominee had failed to get 50 percent of the vote. The membership was still incensed about the 2000 outcome, and bumper stickers were printed which read: "Defeat Bush—Again!" When it came to presidential politics, the United States was very much the same country it was four years earlier, so the candidates went out initially to secure their base. The first announced candidate was Vermont Governor Howard B. Dean III, who formed an exploratory committee almost two years before the Iowa caucuses.[24] In December of 2002, John F. Kerry, U.S. senator from Massachusetts, announced his plans to run. His candidacy generated enthusiasm because Kerry was a decorated Vietnam veteran, and Democrats were tired of being on the defensive about their candidate's suitability in the presidential role of "commander-in-chief."

The early announcements were ignored because Democrats were waiting to hear from Al Gore. The sentiment among most party members was that the 2000 nominee had the right of first refusal. Press reports in 2002 and 2003 detailed his efforts to mend fences with various constituencies in anticipation of another run. Then, in a surprise move, Gore announced on the CBS program *60 Minutes* that he would not run again for president. His decision opened the door, and sent a host of Democratic candidates into the pen.[25] Senator Joe Lieberman, Gore's 2000 vice-presidential choice, entered as a candidate with wide name recognition and a reputation for integrity gained from the previous presidential race. The rest of the field included Senator John R. Edwards of North Carolina, Representative Richard A. "Dick" Gephardt of Missouri, and the Reverend Al Sharpton, who had never held elective office, from New York. In February of 2003, former Senator Carol Moseley Braun of Illinois, U.S. Representative from Ohio Dennis Kucinich, and Senator Bob Graham of Florida all entered the fray. John Edwards and John Kerry led in fundraising, but the race remained wide open.

The Democrats were initially overshadowed by the events of the Iraq War, and most of them were on record as being in favor of the effort. The exceptions were Dennis Kucinich and Howard Dean, who were not shy about explaining their antiwar stance. The Vermont governor began his campaign by emphasizing health care and fiscal responsibility, and championed grassroots fundraising as a way to fight special interests. His campaign was remarkable for its extensive use of the Internet, but his forceful criticism of Democrats in Congress for voting to authorize force in Iraq soon eclipsed all other issues with which he was identified. Soon, Howard Dean was the antiwar candidate, and a throwback to the doctrinaire Democrats of the 1968 election, who opposed the Vietnam War when their party was in the majority in Congress. By the autumn of 2003, Dean became the frontrunner for the Democratic nomination.

War politics divided the challengers to Bush, and on January 4, 2004, an incident occurred that changed the tone and rhetoric of the campaign. That was the day on which jubilant crowds in the Iraqi city of Fallujah dragged the burnt and mutilated bodies of four Americans through the streets. The corpses were dismembered and parts were hung from a green iron bridge over the Euphrates River. One observer said the men looked like "slaughtered sheep."[26] The world press captured the images as the bodies were hoisted on the bridge, while nearby the crowd chanted: "We sacrifice our blood and souls for Islam." The outrage at home was muted, but all of a sudden the antiwar rhetoric of Howard Dean began to fall on deaf ears.

Moderate Democrats feared a meltdown much like the McGovern experience of 1972. Several groups began a nationwide campaign to "draft" retired four-star general Wesley Clark for the Democratic Party nomination. The gossip was that former president Bill Clinton and his wife Hillary were giving tacit support to the effort. On September 17, 2003, in Little Rock, Arkansas, Clark announced his intention to enter the primaries.[27] He immediately came under criticism, and sometimes misspoke on the stump, but his advisors and supporters portrayed him as more electable than Howard Dean.

The Dean candidacy—his followers dubbed "Deaniacs" by the press for their youth and enthusiasm—remained in the lead because of formal endorsements by Al Gore, Bill Bradley, and Tom Harkin and an informal endorsement from Jimmy Carter. The late-arriving Wesley Clark, along with Joe Lieberman, did not campaign in Iowa. Carol Moseley Braun dropped out early and endorsed John Kerry. The Dean campaign began to sputter when Saddam Hussein was captured, but most polls still showed him in the lead.

On January 19, 2004, the Iowa caucuses yielded unexpectedly strong results for Democrat John Kerry, who won 38 percent of the state's delegates, followed by John Edwards, who won 32 percent.[28] Howard Dean finished third, with Dick Gephardt in fourth. As the caucus returns trickled in, the story of the night became the disappointment among the wide-eyed and true-believing Dean supporters. To encourage them, their candidate rolled up his sleeves and delivered a stem-winding speech to the more than 3,500 volunteers in his headquarters. Unfortunately for him, the omnipresent television cameras captured every word, and the late night comics dubbed the speech the "I Have a Scream" speech, because it was delivered on Martin Luther King, Jr.'s, birthday.

Soon the Dean campaign came to epitomize political frustration and collapse in the media age of politics. Everyday Democrats believed that Kerry was more electable, and with each passing hour more wind went out of Howard Dean's balloon. The end came in New Hampshire, a next-door state where the Vermont governor failed. As late as one week before the voting, Howard Dean enjoyed a 30-point lead in the polls. On election day, Kerry's triumph in New Hampshire left him in the favorite's role, and it was a position he never relinquished.

With Howard Dean's withdrawal from the contest, John Edwards was the only major challenger to Kerry for the nomination—but he failed to win even one state's presidential primary. After the Super Tuesday primaries in March, Edwards withdrew; later he was rewarded for his generally positive campaign with selection as Kerry's running mate. Both parties went into the race united and determined. The Democrats were a near miss in 2000, and four years later they believed their time had finally come. Unbeknownst to most of the rank and file, there were others who were even more single-minded in their determination to guarantee a Democratic victory.

In the midsummer lull most of the talk was of avoiding the post-election trauma that characterized the race four years earlier. The press picked up on the anger, and began to identify many so-called "Bush haters" in the process that year. One of them was George Soros, a Hungarian-born American businessman who declared on November 11, 2003, that removing George W. Bush from office was "the central focus of my life." Though ignored at the time, it was an important announcement. Soros put his money where his mouth was, and contributed $23,381,000 to independent groups not regulated by campaign laws and dedicated to the defeat of the incumbent. He was not alone in his sentiment. Four other individuals, all known to Soros, donated a total of more than $78 million to independent groups working against the president. The money from just these few individuals was more than the $75 million in federal matching funds received by John Kerry's campaign against George W. Bush.[29] The spending and secrecy of the campaign were worse than anything from the Watergate era, and an embarrassment for the supporters of campaign finance reform.

The McCain-Feingold election reforms enacted after the 2000 election were sold as a way to reduce the influence of big money in politics. The reforms did not work. Both parties found a way to get big checks to nominally nonpartisan groups. They went under the designation of "527" groups, named because of the subsection of the Internal Revenue Code that provided for them. In all, "the grand total spent by Democratic-supporting 527s in the drive to defeat Bush topped $230 million—nearly two and a half times the amount spent by Republican-supporting 527s."[30] In all, the two parties would spend over $700 million in the race for the White House that year, but the "soft money" figures would never be known.

Money raised the stakes in the election, and in 2004 those stakes were at record levels. The country was divided, and both parties were desperate to win. The funds spent on what was called grass roots, which translated the electorate into a detailed profile by household and targeted individuals for attention, were unprecedented. Both campaigns put voters in grids, and organized at the sub-precinct level with block captains and neighborhood meetings. The Republicans, for example, implemented a "72-Hour" push in critical states that included literature drops in the morning and phone calls to supporters throughout the day.[31] With polling information showing that undecided voters made up their minds in the final 72 hours, the heavy reliance on volunteers eclipsed the focus on paid vendors, phone calls, and television ads.

The 2004 presidential election was the first one after the 2000 Census, and the results would dramatically influence the outcome. Four states (Arizona, Florida, Georgia, and Texas) each gained two seats in the redistricting, while four states

(California, Colorado, Nevada, and North Carolina) gained one apiece. The thinking was that the redistricting generally helped the GOP, but since several of the contested states, such as North Carolina, Arizona, Florida, and Colorado, were thought to be competitive, the electoral outcome remained as unpredictable as ever.

The polls showed a dead heat. From the time each candidate received his nomination, neither one ever dropped below 45 percent in the polling.[32] In other words, the election was about less than 10 percent of the electorate in a few "battleground" states. The candidates' strategies offset each other. Kerry gained after he selected Edwards as his running mate, but Bush was the object of his own well-staged convention. John Kerry came back to political life during the presidential debates, where he showed a confidence and command of the facts that were impressive. Then the two men deadlocked to the finish.

Gradually, the Bush campaign was able to shift the focus of the campaign to John Kerry and his record. For example, Senator Kerry made his four-month combat tour in Vietnam a centerpiece of his campaign. When he accepted the Democratic Party nomination in Boston, the first words out of his mouth were, "I'm John Kerry and I'm reporting for duty."[33] In response to Kerry's representation, a 527 Group made up of veterans who served with him formed under the designation "Swiftboat Veterans and POWs for Truth." Their contention was that the Massachusetts senator transferred out of Vietnam early and received at least one of his Purple Hearts as a result of his own negligence, instead of enemy fire. While Kerry explained himself, the president was able to escape scrutiny on his own past and his decision making in Iraq. John Kerry also had a record in Congress, one that showed inconsistencies which the Bush campaign exploited.

The major issue in the campaign remained the Iraq War and the continuing insurgency which was a constant drain on Bush's ability to explain what was happening. In spite of Saddam Hussein's capture, most Americans thought the war was going badly. A generation still flushed with the despair of Vietnam, and dazzled more recently by the success of the first Iraq War and Afghanistan, did not want a stalemate. To many Americans the language of "nation-building," with its advocacy of limited objectives and popular allegiance, sounded sour and heretical. The country was nowhere near the frustration levels of the Vietnam War years, but some prominent Democrats on the Hill were still able to make dissent respectable. Senator Ted Kennedy, for example, said the justification for going to war in Iraq was a "fraud made up in Texas" and had no basis in fact.[34]

The other issue in the election was more nebulous, but just as important. It went under the general rubric of "moral values." On February 4, 2004, the Massachusetts Supreme Court cleared the way for gay couples in the state to marry, by instructing the state legislature to rewrite the state's marriage laws. The expected legalization of same-sex marriage in Massachusetts led to flamboyant public weddings in cities like San Francisco. The controversy created a cultural earthquake and backlash across the country. Some states responded by putting an amendment on the November ballot that stated marriage was between a man and a woman. The effect of the ballot initiative was to galvanize the conservative vote. With eleven states holding referenda to outlaw same-sex marriage, and the issue passing by overwhelming margins in each one, the issue proved important in turning out Republican voters in some closely contested states.

George W. Bush made a deliberate, and successful, attempt to capitalize on the moral controversy swirling around the election. He was one of the most overtly religious presidents in recent times, and the public presentation of his faith played a crucial role in the election. Church attenders gave Bush a consistently high rating, and the president responded with a strong moral message.[35] His vision for the country emphasized stable marriages, sexual abstinence as a way to prevent teen pregnancy, educational accomplishment in schools where "no child was left behind," and the spread of American democracy abroad—especially in the Middle East.

John Kerry was both more subdued in his rhetoric and more hesitant to discuss his faith. Much of the Democratic support came from people who despised Bush, so there was limited benefit in trying to mimic the president. As a result, the Kerry campaign did not develop a broad moral theme, even on the topic of Iraq. Like any challenger, the appeal of the Kerry candidacy was change, but the fact that he was not Bush was not enough to win the election.

On election night George W. Bush won, this time more convincingly. Minor party candidates received only about 1 percent of the total vote in 2004. The election was a clash between the two major political parties with the result again being a virtual draw. The television election drama was in Ohio, where Republican turnout south of Interstate 70, in cities like Columbus, Cincinnati, and Dayton, outstripped the union-backed efforts in cities like Cleveland, Toledo, and Akron. When Bush won the "Buckeye State," he won re-election.

The dominant impression left by the 2004 election was that it mirrored the one four years earlier. Only three states shifted their preference: Iowa and New Mexico went over to Bush, and New Hampshire moved to Kerry. George W. Bush became the first president since his father to receive a majority of the popular vote (50.7 percent) as 3 million more voters chose him over his rival. The voter turnout was the highest since 1968, and was attributed to the clear differences between the party nominees and the grassroots effort. Bush won 286 electoral votes to Kerry's 251.[36] Yet, there were cautions in the numbers; the president's victory was the smallest margin for any sitting president in U.S. history in terms of the percentage of the popular vote. Bush received 2.5 percent more than Kerry; the closest previous margin for an incumbent was 3.2 percent by Woodrow Wilson in 1916. Bush's margin of some 3 million votes was the smallest of any sitting president since Harry Truman in 1948.

After the November 2 election, the talking heads on television and pundits in newspapers had a field day speculating on reasons for "Red" (Republican) and "Blue" (Democratic) allegiance in the various states. The vote was sharply split along geographical lines: the West Coast, Northeast, and most of the Great Lakes region went for Kerry, and the South, Great Plains, and Mountain states went to Bush. Table 12.1 summarizes the voting behavior of the top thirty media

Table 12.1
Top Thirty Media Markets and Political Partisanship, 1980–2004

		1980			1984		1988		1992			1996		2000			2004	
		D	R	I	D	R	D	R	D	R	I	D	R	D	R	I	D	R
1	New York	42	49	9	45	55	50	50	50	36	14	66	34	63	34	3	60	40
2	Los Angeles	35	56	9	39	61	45	55	45	34	21	57	43	55	42	3	54	46
3	Chicago	45	46	9	46	54	50	50	50	34	16	63	37	59	39	2	60	40
4	Philadelphia	43	47	9	47	53	48	52	49	34	17	63	37	61	37	2	46	54
5	Boston	40	44	16	46	54	50	50	46	31	23	67	33	59	35	6	60	40
6	San Francisco	41	44	15	52	48	59	41	57	25	18	68	32	65	30	5	70	30
7	Dallas-Ft. Worth	38	58	4	32	68	39	61	32	40	28	45	55	37	61	2	38	62
8	Washington, DC	44	45	11	51	49	51	49	53	35	12	60	40	58	39	3	48	52
9	Atlanta	52	43	5	38	62	40	60	43	44	13	49	51	45	54	1	45	55
10	Detroit	43	46	11	45	55	50	50	48	35	17	63	37	57	41	2	57	43
11	Houston	38	58	4	38	62	42	58	37	43	20	46	54	40	58	2	41	59
12	Seattle-Tacoma	38	47	15	45	55	52	48	46	30	24	61	39	56	40	4	59	41
13	Tampa-St. Petersburg	41	54	5	36	64	42	58	38	39	23	54	46	49	48	3	48	52
14	Minneapolis-St. Paul	48	40	12	52	48	55	45	46	31	23	61	39	51	44	5	54	46
15	Phoenix	25	65	10	28	72	35	65	33	41	26	49	51	44	54	2	43	57
16	Cleveland	46	45	9	51	49	54	46	47	32	21	62	38	56	41	3	59	41
17	Miami-Ft.Lauderdale	38	53	9	42	58	47	53	49	37	14	64	36	60	39	1	59	41
18	Denver	32	52	16	38	62	49	51	43	33	24	53	47	48	47	5	53	47

#	Market	C1	C2	C3	C4	C5	C6	C7	C8	C9	C10	C11	C12	C13	C14	C15	C16	C17
19	Sacramento	39	49	12	43	57	47	53	42	36	22	52	48	47	49	4	47	53
20	Orlando	32	63	5	27	73	30	70	33	46	21	48	52	47	51	2	46	54
21	St. Louis	41	54	5	38	62	47	53	45	33	22	54	46	50	48	2	51	49
22	Pittsburgh	49	44	7	57	43	60	40	51	30	19	57	43	51	47	2	65	35
23	Baltimore	41	50	9	36	64	39	61	40	42	18	49	51	47	50	3	46	54
24	Portland	41	45	14	46	54	54	46	45	32	23	58	42	52	43	5	56	44
25	Indianapolis	38	62	0	45	55	36	64	32	48	20	41	59	39	60	1	39	61
26	San Diego	27	61	12	34	66	39	61	38	36	26	49	51	46	50	4	47	53
27	Hartford-New Haven	41	44	15	43	57	51	49	44	32	24	62	38	57	38	5	57	43
28	Charlotte	45	51	4	43	57	36	64	38	48	14	45	55	41	59	0	42	58
29	Raleigh-Durham	50	44	6	56	44	48	52	48	39	13	53	47	50	50	0	52	48
30	Nashville	58	39	3	44	56	43	57	49	40	11	53	47	50	49	1	43	57
	Markets Won	6	24	0	6	24	8	18	21	9	0	21	9	19	10	0	16	14
	Markets Split			0			0			4			0			1		0

*Source: Compiled by the author based on election outcomes in media markets.

markets, which collectively had over half the electorate in their broadcast reach. The table is for all elections from 1980 to 2004. The larger media markets in eastern and West Coast cities (New York, Los Angeles, Boston, Philadelphia, and San Francisco) were consistently Democratic, but the Sun Belt cities (Dallas/Ft. Worth, Atlanta, Houston, and Phoenix) were reliably Republican. The cities matched up with the states and were a prelude of what the outcome would be before votes were cast. In the 2004 contest, the GOP won fourteen markets while the Democrats won sixteen. Get-out-the-vote efforts in the suburbs of Philadelphia, in the Virginia and Maryland suburbs of Washington, D.C., and in Florida were significant in the electoral outcome. But the greatest battle, and the one that showed the grassroots campaign value the sharpest, remained Ohio, which determined the outcome.

The country took a deep breath when it was over, but no celebration of process could cover up the partisan polarization. Two presidential elections in a row were breathtakingly close, and rhetoric began to turn apocalyptic. Many conservative Christians spoke of the country being on the verge of collapse if George Bush, a believer who evinced his faith in public, was turned out of office. On the left, filmmaker Michael Moore stopped just short of accusing the president of being an agent of Saudi Arabia in his controversial film *Fahrenheit 9/11*.[37] In the end, the close election showed that an equal number of voters hated one candidate, and the same number loved the other one.

The differences went deeper than the election; the parties represented different geographical and cultural values. "In politics," wrote John Stuart Mill, "it is almost commonplace that a party of order and stability and a party of progress or reform are both necessary elements of a healthy state of political life."[38] The Democrats had been the party of change since 1932, but no more. One of the facts they had to come to grips with after the 2004 election was that the reform ideals of the New Deal and the coalition that supported it had finally played out. In their platform and leadership, the Democrats were remarkably postmodern. The "laid-back pluralism" of California pervaded the Democrats' encouragement of diversity, deconstructionism, and a critique of the existing order. Nancy Pelosi, Barbara Boxer, and Dianne Feinstein all lived within a few miles of each other in the San Francisco area. They were major leaders of the millennial Democratic Party in Congress, and reflected the feminist, pro-choice, and pro-gay values of northern California. Democratic hopes had been broaching and yawing since room for dissent had been virtually eliminated. The values of the Democratic Party in the twenty-first century were increasingly skeptical of religion and transcendent truth, and middle America was not yet comfortable with them. In its domestic policy, Democrats increasingly saw people primarily as members of groups (blacks, Jews, women, Hispanics) and less as individuals. The purpose of government, in their view, was to reconstruct the society along new lines. The old order of rationalism, with its faith in science and unitary view of truth, was obsolete.

The Republicans, by contrast, were reliably and traditionally modern. They were confident about the future, comfortable with science and technology, and reliant on a heavenly foundation. Conservative Christians found a home in the GOP, and recoiled at the ideas of gay marriage and a Pledge of Allegiance without the words "under God" in the commitment. Their new regional base was in the South, the home of Protestantism, NASCAR, football, and "traditional family values." George W. Bush was a product of these values, and comfortable with them. His sincerity allowed him to overcome his oratorical faults, and he connected with his audience because of his values. When he declared he was "misunderestimated," which was a way of saying he was both "misunderstood" and "underestimated," he was right on both counts.[39]

The man and the party he represented were very much alike. Despite Democratic arguments to the contrary, the Republican Party had become by 2000 the majority, the one of the American middle class, and the champion of "common sense" ideas opposite experts with their baffling statistics. The Republicans held to the extravagant expectation that a rational management of life was possible through the use of technology and traditional values. They relished phrases like "good ole American know how," and they stood with their hand over their heart when the flag passed by, and said "under God" in the pledge. Their ideas flew in the face of Democratic skeptics and European secularists. The GOP platform declared that evil had to be confronted after September 11, and that democracy was the best means to do it. From the perspective of 2004, one of the most unusual aspects of politics at the time was the difference both sides had in agreeing on the basic postulates of government.

The remarkable accomplishment of the American political system remained that the people would accept the result without demonstrations or protests, and that virtue was in evidence again at the nation's fifty-fifth presidential inauguration. It was the first inauguration of a president held since the September 11, 2001, terrorist attack, and the first since the war began in Iraq. On January 20, 2005, security defined the day. It was so tight that officers confiscated bananas, water bottles, and bags bigger than a prescribed size. Visitors in town bemoaned the constant searches, the barricades, and the caution.[40]

Emotions remained high well after election day. The president looked out from the Capitol steps to the Mall with a view of snow-covered Washington and the city's magnificent memorials. As Bush neared the end of his speech, several women stood up from their seats in the audience and began shouting antiwar slogans. Security guards moved in, and as they did a man in a suit and tie rolled up a snowball and hit one of the women in the face. The crowd stood and cheered.[41]

The second term of George W. Bush began in a house divided. Nevertheless, the president promised to "spend the political capital he had accumulated in the election" on social security and tax reform, but the main issue remained the war. Despite evidence of pacification, infrastructure repair, and the prospect of governmental stability in Iraq, the television mostly carried stories of more dead Americans. A quick military victory, which surprised everyone, was followed by chaos bordering on anarchy. Gunmen roamed the streets of Iraq at will, young women were kidnapped in broad daylight, and U.S. companies charged with the responsibility of reconstruction refused to begin work until their employees felt safe.

In a country like Iraq, nation-building involved a complex process of getting people to transfer their loyalty from tribes, villages, and ethnic groups led by religious leaders to the larger political system. This job fell to special presidential envoy Paul Bremer in May of 2003. At home, critics in both parties declared that the 150,000 troops in Iraq were not enough to provide protection and serve as nation-builders at the same time. The U.S. envoy thought otherwise. Bremer began decisively, removing all restrictions on freedom of assembly, suspending the use of the death penalty, banning human torture, and establishing a criminal court.

The new man in charge was frequently called an ambassador by the press, but his post was never confirmed by the U.S. Senate, and his credentials were never presented to anyone in Baghdad. Since no true U.S. diplomatic mission was in Iraq at that time, Bremer was the equivalent of an imported dictator. He behaved like one. In a controversial move, Bremer disbanded the Iraqi army, removed Baath Party members from top positions, and fired thousands of school teachers. He went around the country under a heavy guard, and was nearly assassinated in December when his convoy was driving on the dangerous Baghdad airport road.

The criticisms of Paul Bremer, both at home and abroad, fueled the insurgency. After the war, one American combat death was recorded every other day of the occupation. This was compared to three deaths a day during the Iraq War, fifteen a day during Vietnam, thirty a day in Korea, and 112 a day during World War II. The United States was gambling casualties for time.[42] The occupation deaths were deplorable because they were caused in such a cowardly way, as in dropping a grenade from a bridge into an open humvee or launching a grenade at an American on guard duty at a children's hospital. The task remained grim, but the president stayed firm in his resolve to continue and prevail in the end, and so too did his envoy.

On July 13, 2003, Bremer approved the formation of the Iraq Interim Governing Council. The members were appointed by him from prominent ethnic and religious leaders whose only qualification was that they opposed Saddam Hussein. The capture of the former dictator in December sobered the council members to their task. The seizure announcement was made in the presence of the U.S. Army command, members of the British and American intelligence agencies, journalists, and a host of Iraqi council members. The council had responsibility for shepherding the country to a new constitution, which was done on March 8, 2004, with the transfer of sovereignty. In the midst of rising tensions and civil unrest, not to mention a presidential election back in the United States, power was given to the Iraqi interim government at 10:26 A.M. local time on June 28, 2004. To ensure his own personal safety, Paul Bremer left Iraq that same day.

In spite of daunting odds, the country of Iraq stumbled down the road to democracy. In public statements and private discussions, President Bush began to refer to a book he had read. The reference was shocking to his critics, who thought him incapable of such depth, but "misunderestimated" remained the rule of his presidency. The book was by former Russian dissident Natan Sharansky, and was entitled *The Case for Democracy*. Sharansky believed that terrorism was primarily a function of the absence of democracy. His thesis was in defiance of conventional wisdom on the left in Europe and among Democrats in the United States. "I am heartened by the American-led effort," wrote Sharansky, "currently underway in the region to build democratic societies in Afghanistan and Iraq as well as President Bush's determination to see this effort succeed."[43]

The American president repeated on numerous occasions his foremost belief that "freedom is not America's gift to the world, it is God's gift to humanity." In the first months of 2005 the world stood by, dumbfounded, as the words of George W. Bush became a reality. On January 30, 2005, the Iraqi people chose representatives for the newly formed 275-seat Iraqi National Assembly, and in October they approved a new constitution. The initial vote, by over 8 million people representing 58 percent of the population, was the first general election since the U.S.-led invasion. The world press recorded pictures of everyday Iraqis holding up their index fingers marked with purple indelible ink, a security measure to prevent double voting.

Soon the desire for purple ink participation was everywhere. A clash of demonstrators and civil disobedience in Lebanon, mainly in Beirut, led to the withdrawal of Syrian troops in place since the 1980s, in April of 2005. Demands for democratic participation were heard in Egypt, Pakistan, Saudi Arabia, and even Iran. The promise of the Bush administration was to support democracy, and that promise was being proven in countries throughout the Middle East in 2005.

The costliest disaster in American history began as a tropical depression over the southern Bahamas on August 23, 2005. Three days later the head of the National Hurricane Center took the unprecedented step of calling the Mayor of New Orleans and the Governor of Louisiana to personally plead with them to begin a mandatory evacuation of New Orleans. The city is wedged between the Mississippi River on the south and Lake Pontchartrain on the north, and is below sea level, a saucer waiting to be filled. The warning came after a monitoring buoy, located some 240 miles south in the Gulf of Mexico, recorded sixty-eight-foot waves before it was destroyed.

Ray Nagin, the mayor of New Orleans, did not want to evacuate. Since Hurricane Betsy flooded 20 percent of the city in 1965, longtime residents preferred to stay put. A survey taken in 2004 found that if ordered to evacuate, about 30 percent of the residents would stay behind. Invariably the only way to measure the intensity of a storm was to compare it with previous ones in terms of breadth and size. The new storm, named Katrina, rivaled previous ones in power, but since the city has survived them, many reasoned that the latest would be just another close call. That helps explain why so many, roughly 150,000 who were ordered to leave New Orleans and thousands of others along the Mississippi coast, decided not to leave.

It was a decision they would all regret.

Katrina made landfall as a category four storm with winds of 140 mph. The storm ticked to the right as it came ashore just east of New Orleans, and headed over to the swamplands of Mississippi. In Biloxi, 154 miles northeast of the storm's landfall, the twenty-two-foot storm surge lifted the President Casino barge off its moorings in the Gulf of Mexico, floated it across an interstate highway, and placed it atop a Holiday Inn. But the worst tragedy unfolded in New Orleans.[44]

About a fifth of the city residents live below the poverty line, and this disadvantaged population was overwhelmingly African American. Three levees were overtopped or broken, and the city was doomed. Water rose to twenty feet in some places. Efforts to drop sandbags by helicopters failed, and the aircraft were called off to lift food and water supplies elsewhere and assist with the rescue of survivors. Pumps were overwhelmed. Within hours 80 percent of New Orleans was submerged. Stranded residents used chair legs for torches, and helicopters from the Navy, Coast Guard, and Marine Corps used night-vision goggles to look for flickering candles or flashlights to rescue people stranded in their homes.

Incredibly, the seriousness of the situation did not really register with anyone. President Bush had earlier urged people to evacuate, but in the immediate aftermath Washington waited for more information. Things were little different in the Louisiana state emergency command post in Baton Rouge. Everyone was trying to make sense of what had happened. Ray Nagin, the mayor, issued what he called a "desperate S.O.S." to the federal government.

When the news media began to report that the 17th Street Canal levee in the city had been breached, the only conclusion was that New Orleans was in serious trouble of being obliterated.[45] The Superdome and the New Orleans Convention Center were opened as emergency shelters, but no one had any plans to care for the people there or get them out of the danger of rising water. Within hours both shelters were declared unsafe and unsanitary. Reports of rape and beatings were widespread, and several people died within the huge Superdome. Around the city, stores were looted and lawlessness became the norm. Reports were that as many as 20,000 people were around the doomed Dome, and the television regularly carried their pleas for help. The television cameras showed that one federal agency that was supposed to handle disasters, the Federal Emergency Management Agency (FEMA), was dysfunctional.

A panic set in. For two days the evacuees' pleas were ignored. When those able to leave the downtown area walked down the Crescent City Connection Bridge, they found Gretna, Louisiana, sheriff's deputies, who turned them back at gunpoint. Finally, the Texas Department of Homeland Security and Emergency Management and the State of Louisiana agreed to allow the entrapped evacuees to be sheltered in various places in Texas. Overwhelmed local officials tried to handle a crisis without power, water, or medical care. As helicopters landed to disgorge hundreds of filthy, dazed, and weak evacuees, there was no way to care for them. The only solution seemed to be to leave. Within two weeks, more than 230,000 evacuees had escaped to Texas from Mississippi and Louisiana.

The death toll estimates spiraled upward. Estimates were in the thousands, then the tens of thousands. Within three weeks 707 were confirmed dead, but hundreds more were missing. Over a million people were displaced, and as the scope of the disaster became clear, the president federalized the national guard and sent in the active military to maintain order and organize the cleanup. In Houston, San Antonio, Beaumont, and Dallas, evacuees had the same request: "Please help me find my family."

Critics blasted the federal government for its slow response, but under law federal troops could not push aside local officials to rush in.[46] When the breadth and scope of the crisis became clear, the military mobilized some 70,000 troops and hundreds of aircraft in the relief effort. The U.S. Congress immediately approved some $10 billion in emergency aid, and then followed that with another $52 billion package. President Bush enlisted the help of former presidents Bill Clinton and George H. W. Bush to organize additional voluntary contributions, much like they did after the Asian tsunami crisis in 2004. The actual cost of rebuilding New Orleans and the Gulf Coast region of Mississippi was unclear, but estimates were as high as $200 billion.

Epilogue: Epochs

"At each epoch of history," wrote French philosopher and political thinker Jacques Maritain in his book *Reflections on America*, "the world was in a hopeless state, and at each epoch of history the world muddled through; at each epoch the world was lost, and at each epoch it was saved." The America halfway through the first decade of the twenty-first century was more confident, and more watchful, than it had been a quarter of a century earlier. In the twenty-five-year epoch examined here, the country saved itself and much of the rest of the world at the same time. The process of renewal proved once more that "freedom, democracy, human rights and the rule of law [were] not American values... or Western values, but universal values of the human spirit," to quote British Prime Minister Tony Blair.

In 2005 the United States had successfully spread these values by confronting and defeating the Soviet Union and the ethic of communist insurrection. The American military stopped Iraq from bullying its neighbors, and then toppled a dictator who was responsible for the deaths of 250,000 of the people he ruled. In Europe, Yugoslavia disappeared as a political entity, and was replaced by a hodgepodge of ethnic allegiances and crosscutting alliances. The United States helped depose, and then put on trial, Slobodan Milosevic as a war criminal. Saddam Hussein joined Manuel Noreiga in jail, and other dictators waited to see if they would be fingered in the worldwide terror crackdown.

The epoch began with World War II's "Greatest Generation" in charge, and ended with their children running things. George Herbert Walker Bush and his son George W. Bush were a metaphor for leadership change in the whole country. But it was Ronald Reagan who set the tone for politics in the twenty-five years since his election in 1980. At his funeral in June of 2004, President George W. Bush said in the eulogy, "Ronald Reagan belongs to the ages now, but we preferred it when he belonged to us." The Reagan legacy remained. His

President George W. Bush bows at the casket of former President Ronald Reagan after giving a eulogy at the funeral service for President Ronald Reagan at the National Cathedral in Washington, DC, June 11, 2004. (White House photo by Tina Hager)

foreign and domestic policies were the template for all his successors. The words on Reagan's Georgian gray granite headstone could sum up the twenty-five years of American political history discussed here.

I know in my heart that man is good. That what is right will always eventually triumph. And there's purpose and worth to each and every life.

The 1980 election began a rolling political realignment that changed the country from Democratic domination to Republican rule. The important elections were Reagan in 1980, the midterm change in 1994, and united government for the GOP in 2000, finally secured in 2002. The New Deal coalition that brought Franklin Roosevelt to office was made up of blacks, urban workers, union members, ethnic Americans, Jews, academics, and the traditionally Democratic South. For all intents and purposes, it remained intact until 2000—with one notable exception. When the conservative South left the Democratic Party, power shifted from one party to the other, and that change altered national politics in the new millennium. After two close elections, the country was, in the words of political scientist Larry

Sabato in his book the *Divided States of America*, left with a "match-up between Bush and John F. Kerry...a battle of Good versus Evil, or Evil versus Good, depending on one's party and ideological affiliations."

No president in the twenty-five-year period had a commanding legislative majority. The largest legislative majority of any president examined here was for Bill Clinton from 1992 to 1994, but that good will was squandered on the health care debacle. Every president worked with a fragile majority, or no majority, and any resulting legislative agreements were a product of compromise. Narrow legislative majorities did not mean the country was not undergoing change. It was undergoing change, in ways not reflected in votes for politicians.

The deepest changes were cultural, and for that reason they remain the most difficult to explain. On January 1, 2000, the signs of a movement from modern to postmodern thought were everywhere, from the definition of marriage to explanations for what the country was about. Bill Clinton was the first postwar generation president, and his election signaled a move to postmodern values. They could be seen in his "Don't ask, don't tell" policy for homosexuals in the military, in his cabinet "that looks like America" with diversity as the major criteria, and in his attitudes about monogamy in marriage.

Cultural values received a shock with the terrorist attack of September 11, 2001. The polyglot peoples of America had no common heritage and only ideas to bind them together. Now the ideas themselves were up for scrutiny. Until that September moment, the country believed it could play with its convictions the way Hollywood producers re-edited a movie, at will and able to change the ending. No more.

The happy tranquil decade that ran from the fall of communism in 1989 to the Twin Towers disaster of 2001 gave way to a storm of controversy. The contending divide under the surface of the old political culture emerged, showing stark divisions. As Robert Conquest once observed, "our cultures, our histories, grasp us with a thousand invisible fingers." The "red-state" Republicans embraced traditional values and explanations for American exceptionalism with a passion. What would happen to national freedom, they asked, once the "self-evident" truths upon which the nation was founded were not longer self-evident? How could you spread democracy if you did not believe in its virtues? The "blue state" Democratic loyalists, who inhabited either coast, were horrified. They saw the old America of rationalism, order, and faith in a unitary view of truth as oppressive, patriarchal, homophobic, and obsolete. For years they had been defining a new social order of subjective pluralism, diversity, and tolerance, led by a cultural elite that wanted to forget American ideals, and certainly did not want them exported. Now their reform effort was halted by terrorists.

The rhetoric of politics and the culture wars remained shrill because what was really at stake was whether America would be transformed in the name of postmodernity to a place of discretely defined and entitled groups, or whether it would continue to be a nation where individuals competed under the same-roof ideals of the founding visionaries. The revolution of a divide between modern and postmodern tested whether the old values that made America a nation could stretch far enough to keep it one, or if a new culture could nourish the political system as well as the one passing away. To one group the world was lost; to the other it was saved.

Notes

PROLOGUE

1. Bruce Miroff, "Courting the Public," in Steven E. Schier, ed., *The Postmodern Presidency* (Pittsburgh, PA: University of Pittsburgh Press, 2000).
2. Michael Barone, *Our Country* (New York: Free Press, 1990), p. xi.
3. John Kenneth White, *The Values Divide* (New York: Chatham House, 2003), p. 37.
4. Erik Felten, ed., *A Shining City* (New York: Simon and Schuster, 1998).
5. Gabriel A. Almond and G. Bingham Powell, *Comparative Politics: A Developmental Approach* (Boston: Little, Brown, 1966), p. 23.
6. Alexander Pope, *Thoughts on Various Subjects* (1727), in Rhonda Thomas Tripp, ed., *The International Thesaurus of Quotations* (New York: Thomas Y. Crowell, 1970).

CHAPTER 1: MALAISE

1. Peter G. Bourne, *Jimmy Carter* (New York: Scribner, 1997), p. 441.
2. John F. Stacks, *Watershed* (New York: Times Books, 1981), pp. 9–21.
3. *New York Times*, February 12, 1979.
4. *New York Times*, May 5, 1979.
5. *New York Times*, May 11, 1979.
6. *New York Times*, May 27, 1979.
7. *New York Times*, June 21, 1979.
8. *New York Times*, July 30, 1979.
9. *New York Times*, May 19, 1979.
10. *New York Times*, June 22, 1979.
11. *New York Times*, May 13, 1979.
12. *New York Times*, May 23, 1979.
13. *New York Times*, June 12, 1979.
14. John F. Stacks, *Watershed* (New York: Times Books, 1981), p. 10.
15. *New York Times*, July 13, 1979.
16. *New York Times*, July 5, 1979.

17. Haynes Johnson, *In the Absence of Power* (New York: Viking Press, 1980), pp. 277–317.
18. *New York Times*, July 15, 1979.
19. *New York Times*, July 13, 1979.
20. Haynes Johnson, *In the Absence of Power* (New York: Viking Press, 1980), p. 281.
21. *Vital Speeches*, July 15, 1979.
22. *Vital Speeches*, July 15, 1979.
23. *Vital Speeches*, July 15, 1979.
24. Haynes Johnson, *In the Absence of Power* (New York: Viking Press, 1980), p. 284.
25. *Vital Speeches*, July 15, 1979.
26. www.imbd.com/title/plotsummary.
27. *Vital Speeches,* July 15, 1979.
28. *Vital Speeches*, July 15, 1979.
29. Christopher Lasch, *The Culture of Narcissism* (New York: Norton, 1978).
30. *Vital Speeches*, July 15, 1979.
31. *National Review*, July 30, 1979.
32. *Vital Speeches*, July 15, 1979.
33. John F. Stacks, *Watershed* (New York: Times Books, 1981), p. 28.
34. Jeffrey Henderson, ed., *Cicero's Letters to His Friends* (Cambridge, MA: Harvard University Press, 2001).
35. Morris Fiorina and Paul E. Peterson, *The New American Democracy* (New York: Longman, 2001).
36. Jimmy Carter, *Keeping Faith* (New York: Bantam Books, 1982), pp. 457–458.
37. George F. Will, *The Washington Post*, December 30, 1979.
38. *New York Times*, November 12, 1979.
39. *New York Times*, November 12, 1979.
40. Hugh Sidey, *Time*, December 24, 1979.
41. *Time*, December 30, 1979.
42. Erwin Hargrove, *Jimmy Carter* (Baton Rouge: Louisiana State University Press, 1988), pp. 137–142.
43. John F. Stacks, *Watershed* (New York: Times Books, 1981), p. 85.
44. *New York Times*, April 5, 1980.
45. Paul B. Ryan, *The Iranian Rescue Mission* (Annapolis, MD: Naval Institute Press, 1985), p. 141.
46. Jimmy Carter, *Keeping Faith* (New York: Bantam Books, 1982).
47. Paul B. Ryan, *The Iranian Rescue Mission* (Annapolis, MD: Naval Institute Press, 1985), pp. 83–90.
48. Paul B. Ryan, *The Iranian Rescue Mission* (Annapolis, MD: Naval Institute Press, 1985).
49. *Time*, May 5, 1980.
50. *Washington Post*, May 5, 1980.
51. Paul B. Ryan, *The Iranian Rescue Mission* (Annapolis, MD: Naval Institute Press, 1985).
52. Jimmy Carter, *Keeping Faith* (New York: Bantam Books, 1982), p. 467.

CHAPTER 2: 1980 ELECTION

1. Lee Edwards, *The Conservative Revolution* (New York: Free Press, 1999), p. 224.
2. Ann Golenpaul, ed., *Information Please Almanac: 1997* (New York: Simon and Schuster, 1977), p. 31.

3. Lou Cannon, *President Reagan* (New York: Simon and Schuster, 1991), p. 207.
4. Lou Cannon, *President Reagan* (New York: Simon and Schuster, 1991), p. 58.
5. Lou Cannon, *President Reagan* (New York: Simon and Schuster, 1991), pp. 88–92.
6. Dinesh D'Souza, *Ronald Reagan* (New York: Touchstone, 1997), p. 28.
7. John Kenneth White, *The New Politics of Old Values* (London: University Press of New England, 1988), pp. 60–61.
8. Lou Cannon, *Governor Reagan* (New York: Public Affairs, 2003), p. 132.
9. Lou Cannon, *Governor Reagan* (New York: Public Affairs, 2003), p. 79.
10. Interview with the author, March 1985.
11. Frank Van Der Linden, *The Real Reagan* (New York: William Morrow, 1981), p. 87.
12. Reagan's ideas were a continuation of policies begun by Richard Nixon, whose New Federalism of general revenue grants and block grants returned money to the local level. Some deregulation of the trucking and airline industries, for example, began under Jimmy Carter.
13. Andrew E. Busch, *Ronald Reagan* (New York: Rowman and Littlefield, 2001), p. 3.
14. Matthew 9:37.
15. *New York Times*, March 13, 1976.
16. Frank Van Der Linden, *The Real Reagan* (New York: William Morrow, 1981), p. 125.
17. Craig Shirley, *Reagan's Revolution* (New York: Nelson Current, 2005), p. 87.
18. *New York Times*, August 1, 1976.
19. Peggy Noonan, *When Character Was King* (New York: Viking, 2001), p. 105.
20. Kiron K. Skinner et al., *Reagan: In His Own Hand* (New York: Free Press, 2001), p. xiv.
21. Kiron K. Skinner et al., *Reagan: In His Own Hand* (New York: Free Press, 2001), p. 184.
22. Craig Shirley, *Reagan's Revolution* (New York: Nelson Current, 2005), p. 121.
23. Peter Jennings et al., *The Century* (New York: Doubleday, 1998), p. 462.
24. Bill Minutaglio, *First Son* (New York: Times Books, 1999), p. 196.
25. David Maraniss, *First in His Class* (New York: Simon and Schuster, 1995), p. 375.
26. Michael Barone, *Almanac of American Politics* (Washington, DC: National Journal, 2004), pp. 376, 377.
27. William E. Pemberton, *Exit with Honor* (Armonk, NY: M. E. Sharpe, 1998), pp. 89–90.
28. Michael Barone, *Our Country* (New York: Free Press, 1990), pp. 594–595.
29. John F. Stacks, *Watershed* (New York: Times Books, 1981), p. 128.
30. Lou Cannon, *President Reagan* (New York: Simon and Schuster, 1991), p. 123.
31. David Frum, *How We Got Here* (New York: Basic Books, 2000), pp. 291–292.
32. *New York Times*, October 24, 1980.
33. Jimmy Carter, *Why Not the Best?* (Nashville, TN: Broadman Press, 1975), p. 19.
34. William Martin, *With God on Our Side* (New York: Broadway Books, 1996), p. 207.
35. Francis Schaeffer, *A Christian Manifesto* (Westchester, IL: Crossway Books, 1981), p. 133.
36. Paul Kengor, *God and Ronald Reagan* (New York: Reagan Books, 2004), p. 174.
37. Paul Kengor, *God and Ronald Reagan* (New York: Reagan Books, 2004), p. 34.
38. William Martin, *With God on Our Side* (New York: Broadway Books, 1996), p. 214.

39. *New York Times*, October 6, 1980.
40. *New York Times*, October 29, 1980.
41. *New York Times*, November 2, 1980.
42. Michael Barone, *Our Country* (New York: Free Press, 1990), p. 596.

CHAPTER 3: I, RONALD WILSON REAGAN

1. Nancy Reagan, *My Turn* (New York: Random House, 1989), p. 230.
2. Nancy Reagan, *My Turn* (New York: Random House, 1989), p. 233.
3. *New York Times*, January 21, 1981.
4. *New York Times*, January 21, 1981.
5. *New York Times*, January 28, 1981.
6. *New York Times*, January 28, 1981.
7. ABC News, January 22, 1981.
8. *Statistical Abstract of the United States, 1980*.
9. *Wall Street Journal*, August 31, 1982.
10. *Statistical Abstract of the United States, 1980; Time*, January 22, 1981.
11. *New York Times*, January 21, 1981.
12. J. David Woodard, *The New Southern Politics* (Boulder, CO: Lynne Rienner Press, 2006).
13. Lou Cannon, *President Reagan* (New York: Simon and Schuster, 1991), p. 114.
14. John Ehrman, *The Eighties* (New Haven, CT: Yale University Press, 2005), p. 55.
15. *Wall Street Journal*, June 26, 1981.
16. *New York Times*, April 1, 1981.
17. Edmund Morris, *Dutch* (New York: Random House, 1999), p. 428.
18. *New York Times*, April 1 and 3, 1981.
19. Nancy Reagan, *My Turn* (New York: Random House, 1989), p. 5.
20. Michael K. Deaver, *A Different Drummer* (New York: Perennial, 2003), p. 137.
21. *New York Times*, April 2, 1981.
22. *New York Times*, August 9, 1981.
23. *New York Times*, August 24, 1981.
24. *Washington Post*, August 16, 1981.
25. Gallup Poll, 1981.
26. David Brinkley, *Washington Goes to War* (New York: Alfred A. Knopf, 1988), p. 154.
27. David Brinkley, *Washington Goes to War* (New York: Alfred A. Knopf, 1988), p. 139.
28. Graham Allison, *The Essence of Decision* (Boston: Little, Brown, 1971), p. 45.
29. Carl Bernstein and Bob Woodward, *All the President's Men* (New York: Simon and Schuster, 1974), pp. 35–72.
30. Eric Felton, *The Ruling Class* (Washington, DC: Regnery Gateway, 1993), p. 132.
31. Edward Gibbon, *The Decline and Fall of the Roman Empire* (New York: Dell, 1963), p. 49.
32. Dan Golenpaul, ed., *Information Please Almanac: 1971* (New York: Simon and Schuster, 1971), p. 661; U.S. Department of Commerce, *1970 Census of Population* (Washington, DC: Bureau of the Census, 1973), tables 11 and 37.
33. Haynes Johnson, *In the Absence of Power* (New York: Viking, 1980), pp. 90–109.
34. Michael K. Deaver, *A Different Drummer* (New York: Perennial, 2003), p. 113.

35. Peter Schewizer, *Reagan's War* (New York: Doubleday, 2002), p. 1.
36. *New York Daily News*, December 13, 1983.
37. Lou Cannon, *President Reagan* (New York: Simon and Schuster, 1991), pp. 59–60.
38. Hedrick Smith, *The Power Game* (New York: Random House, 1988), p. 109.
39. Haynes Johnson, *Sleepwalking Through History* (New York: W. W. Norton, 1991), p. 94.
40. *Newsweek*, December 21, 1981.
41. Nancy Reagan, *My Turn* (New York: Random House, 1989), pp. 39–43.
42. Hedrick Smith, *The Power Game* (New York: Random House, 1988), p. 396.
43. *Christian Science Monitor*, August 17, 1981.
44. Glenn Gaslin et al., *The Complete Cross-Referenced Guide to the Baby Buster Generation's Collective Unconscious* (New York: Boulevard Books, 1998).
45. John Ehrman, *The Eighties* (New Haven, CT: Yale University Press, 2005), pp. 174–203.
46. Lou Cannon, *President Reagan* (New York: Simon and Schuster, 1991), p. 233.
47. Gallup Poll, 1982.
48. William Grider, *The Education of David Stockman* (New York: E. P. Dutton, 1982).
49. Nancy Reagan, *My Turn* (New York: Random House, 1989), p. 61.
50. Morris Fiorina, *Divided Government* (New York: Allyn and Bacon, 1996), pp. 91–95.
51. Hedrick Smith, *The Power Game* (New York: Random House, 1988), pp. 459–460.
52. Paul Johnson, *A History of the American People* (New York: HarperCollins, 1997), pp. 924–925.
53. *New York Times*, December 21 and 29, 1982.
54. *National Review*, August 31, 1992.
55. David Frum, *How We Got Here* (New York: Basic Books, 2000), p. 238.
56. *New York Times*, September 26, 1982.
57. *New York Times*, August 23, 1982.
58. Vanderbilt Television News Archive, July 20, 1982.
59. *New York Times*, January 21, 1981.
60. *New York Times*, January 21, 1983.
61. Dinesh D'Souza, *Ronald Reagan* (New York: Touchstone Books, 1997), p. 109.
62. Vanderbilt Television News Archive, June 11, 1984.
63. Peter Schweizer, *Reagan's War* (New York: Doubleday, 2002), p. xi.
64. Peter Schweizer, *Reagan's War* (New York: Doubleday, 2002), p. 15.
65. Ronald Reagan Presidential Library, "Speeches," March 8, 1983.
66. Peter Schweizer, *Reagan's War* (New York: Doubleday, 2002), p. 144.
67. *New York Times*, June 21, 1984.
68. *New York Times*, October 26, 1982.
69. Lawrence I. Barrett, *Gambling with History* (New York: Penguin Books, 1983), pp. 73–74.
70. Ronald Reagan Presidential Library, "Speeches," May 9, 1982.
71. Seymour M. Hersch, *The Target Is Destroyed* (New York: Random House, 1986).
72. Jonathan Schell, *The Fate of the Earth* (Palo Alto, CA: Stanford University Press, 2000), p. vi.
73. Edmund Morris, *Dutch* (New York: Random House, 1999), p. 466.
74. Peter Schweizer, *Reagan's War* (New York: Doubleday, 2002), pp. 147–148.

75. Lou Cannon, *President Reagan* (New York: Simon and Schuster, 1991), p. 319.
76. Ronald Reagan Presidential Library, "Speeches," March 23, 1983.
77. Haynes Johnson, *Sleepwalking Through History* (New York: W. W. Norton, 1991), p. 412.
78. Edmund Morris, *Dutch* (New York: Random House, 1999), pp. 500–504.
79. Lou Cannon, *President Reagan* (New York: Simon and Schuster, 1991), p. 424.
80. Edmund Morris, *Dutch* (New York: Random House, 1999), pp. 586–604.
81. *New York Times*, October 24, 1983.
82. Lou Cannon, *President Reagan* (New York: Simon and Schuster, 1991), p. 516.

CHAPTER 4: A RISING TIDE

1. International Financial Statistics: 1957–1998.
2. *National Review*, August 31, 1992.
3. *Barron's,* February 11, 1984.
4. John Ehrman, *The Eighties* (New Haven, CT: Yale University Press, 2005).
5. *Wall Street*, imdb.com.
6. Tom Wolfe, *The Bonfire of the Vanities* (New York: Farrar, Straus and Giroux, 1987).
7. Theodore Dreiser, *An American Tragedy* (New York: Modern Library, 1956).
8. Janet Lowe, *Secret Empire: How 25 Multinationals Rule the World* (Homewood, IL: Business One Irwin, 1992), p. 5.
9. Bryan Burrough and John Helyar, *Barbarians at the Gate* (New York: Harper and Row, 1990).
10. *U.S. News and World Report,* December 12, 1986.
11. John Ehrman, *The Eighties* (New Haven, CT: Yale University Press, 2005), p. 23.
12. Connie Bruck, *The Predators Ball* (New York: Penguin Books, 1986).
13. *Statistical Abstract of the United States, 1990.*
14. *National Review,* August 31, 1992.
15. John Ehrman, *The Eighties* (New Haven, CT: Yale University Press, 2005), p. 109.
16. Charles Jencks, *What Is Postmodernism?* (New York: St. Martin's Press, 1987).
17. Daniel Bell, *The Coming of Postindustrial Society* (New York: Basic Books, 1976).
18. David Harvey, *The Condition of Postmodernity* (Cambridge, MA: Basil Blackwell, 1989), pp. 289–291.
19. Daniel Bell, *The Coming of Postindustrial Society* (New York: Basic Books, 1976), pp. 234–276.
20. Milton Friedman, *Free to Choose* (New York: Avon Books, 1985), p. 7.
21. Marshall Berman, *All That Is Solid Melts into Air* (New York: Simon and Schuster, 1982), p. 54.
22. Ronald Reagan, "Remarks at the Bakersfield Business and Finance Conference," Bakersfield, California, October 24, 1992.
23. David Harvey, *The Condition of Postmodernity* (Cambridge, MA: Basil Blackwell, 1989).
24. Gene Edward Veith, Jr., *Postmodern Times* (Wheaton, IL: Crossway Books, 1994), pp. 179–181.
25. William J. Bennett, *The De-Valuing of America* (New York: Summit Books, 1992), p. 51.
26. Ed Ward et al., *Rock of Ages* (New York: Simon and Schuster, 1986), p. 592.

27. Paul Slansky, *The Clothes Have No Emperor* (New York: Simon and Schuster, 1989), p. 28.
28. www.prince.org.
29. Steven Connor, *Postmodernist Culture* (Oxford, UK: Blackwell, 1997), p. 154.
30. Martha Bayles, *Hole in Our Soul* (Chicago: University of Chicago Press, 1994), p. 334.
31. *New York Times*, August 13, 1989.
32. Naomi Wolf, *The Beauty Myth* (New York: Doubleday, 1991), p. 215.
33. Haynes Johnson, *Sleepwalking Through History* (New York: W. W. Norton, 1991), p. 142.
34. Ed Meese, *With Reagan* (Washington, DC: Regnery Gateway, 1992), pp. 312–314.
35. *New York Times*, December 1987.
36. *New York Times*, October 17, 1987.
37. *Time*, June 26, 1941.
38. *Time*, October 10, 1983.

CHAPTER 5: MORNING IN AMERICA: THE SECOND TERM

1. Richard Reeves, *The Reagan Detour* (New York: Simon and Schuster, 1985).
2. Gerald M. Pomper, *The Election of 1984* (New York: Chatham House Publishers, 1985).
3. William H. Flanigan and Nancy H. Zingle, *Political Behavior of the American Electorate*, 8th ed. (Washington, DC: Congressional Quarterly Press, 1994), p. 64.
4. *New York Times*, January 30, 1984.
5. Gerald M. Pomper, *The Election of 1984* (New York: Chatham House Publishers, 1985), p. 16.
6. *New York Times*, February 12, 1984.
7. *New York Times*, February 29, 1984 and March 2, 1984.
8. *New York Times*, March 13, 1984.
9. *New York Times*, April 12, 1984.
10. *New York Times*, July 17, 1984.
11. *New York Times*, July 18, 1984.
12. *New York Times*, July 20, 1984.
13. *New York Times*, July 24, 1984.
14. *ABC* News, June 6, 1984; *NBC* News, June 6, 1984.
15. Lou Cannon, *President Reagan* (New York: Simon and Schuster, 1991), p. 484.
16. Michael Barone, *Our Country* (New York: Free Press, 1990), p. 640.
17. Kathleen Hall Jamieson, *Packaging the Presidency,* 3rd ed. (New York: Oxford University Press, 1996).
18. Bob Schieffer and Gary Paul Gates, *The Acting President* (New York: E. P. Dutton, 1989), p. 185.
19. *New York Times*, October 22, 1984.
20. Gerald M. Pomper, *The Election of 1984* (New York: Chatham House Publishers, 1985), p. 70.
21. *New York Times*, October 12, 1984.
22. *New York Times*, January 22, 1985.
23. *New York Times*, January 23, 1985.
24. Michael K. Deaver, *A Different Drummer* (New York: Perennial, 2003), pp. 200–202.

25. Jason Manning, "Bitburg," www.eightiesclub.tripod.bitburg.
26. Gallup Poll, June 9, 1985.
27. Edmund Morris, *Dutch* (New York: Random House, 1999), pp. 414–415.
28. Jason Manning, "Bitburg," www.eightiesclub.tripod.bitburg.
29. Lou Cannon, *Presidential Reagan* (New York: Simon and Schuster, 1991), p. 587.
30. Theodore Draper, *A Very Thin Line* (New York: Touchstone, 1991).
31. Theodore Draper, *A Very Thin Line* (New York: Touchstone, 1991), p. 157.
32. Theodore Draper, *A Very Thin Line* (New York: Touchstone, 1991), p. 33.
33. Lou Cannon, *President Reagan* (New York: Simon and Schuster, 1991), p. 611.
34. *New York Times*, April 15, 1985.
35. *New York Times*, October 7, 1986; *ABC* News, October 7, 1986; *CBS* News, October 7, 1986; *NBC* News, October 7, 1986.
36. Edwin Meese, *With Reagan* (Washington, DC: Regnery Gateway, 1992), p. 245.
37. *New York Times*, December 23, 1986.
38. Dinesh D'Souza, *Ronald Reagan* (New York: Touchstone, 1997), p. 247.
39. *New York Times*, February 27, 1987.
40. Edmund Morris, *Dutch* (New York: Random House, 1999), p. 577.
41. Peter Jennings and Todd Brewster, *The Century* (New York: Doubleday, 1998), p. 500.
42. William Harwood, "Voyage Into History: 1986," www.cbsnews.com.
43. www.reaganlegacy.org/speeches/reagan.challenger.
44. *New York Times*, January 29, 1986.
45. *New York Times*, January 29, 1986.
46. *New York Times*, June 10, 1986.
47. Edmund Morris, *Dutch* (New York: Random House, 1999), p. 577.
48. *New York Times*, October 12, 1984.
49. Peter Schweizer, *Reagan's War* (New York: Doubleday, 2002), p. 239.
50. Peter Schweizer, *Reagan's War* (New York: Doubleday, 2002), pp. 256–257.
51. *New York Times*, November 20, 1985.
52. Peter Schweizer, *Reagan's War* (New York: Doubleday, 2002), p. 252.
53. Peter Schweizer, *Reagan's War* (New York: Doubleday, 2002), p. 257.
54. Lou Cannon, *President Reagan* (New York: Simon and Schuster, 1991), p. 769.
55. Lou Cannon, *President Reagan* (New York: Simon and Schuster, 1991), p. 770.
56. www.reaganlegacy.org.
57. William Manchester, *The Glory and the Dream* (New York: Little, Brown, 1973), p. 910.
58. Dinesh D'Souza, *Ronald Reagan* (New York: Touchstone, 1997), p. 192.
59. Peter Schweizer, *Reagan's War* (New York: Doubleday, 2002), p. 276.
60. *Newsweek,* December 18, 1988.

CHAPTER 6: A THOUSAND POINTS OF LIGHT

1. *New York Times*, July 12, 1987.
2. *New York Times*, July 2, 1987.
3. *New York Times*, July 9, 1987.
4. Jason Manning, "The Bork Nomination," www.eightiesclub.com.
5. *New York Times*, September 10–15, 1987.
6. *New York Times*, September 19, 1987.

7. *New York Times*, October 24, 1987.
8. Bob Schieffer and Gary Paul Gates, *The Acting President* (New York: E. P. Dutton, 1989), p. 311.
9. *New York Times*, October 13, 1987.
10. *Esquire*, February 1992.
11. *Newsweek*, October 19, 1987.
12. Peter Goldman, Tom Mathews, et al., *The Quest for the Presidency: The 1988 Campaign* (New York: Touchstone, 1989), p. 215.
13. *New York Times*, January 26, 1988.
14. Peter Goldman, Tom Mathews, et al., *The Quest for the Presidency: The 1988 Campaign* (New York: Touchstone, 1989), p. 221.
15. *New York Times*, February 9, 1988.
16. *New York Times*, February 27, 1988.
17. *New York Times*, April 14, 1987.
18. *New York Times*, May 3, 1987.
19. *Newsweek,* April 13, 1987.
20. *The Miami Herald*, May 10, 1987.
21. Michael Nelson, ed., *The Elections of 1988* (Washington, DC: Congressional Quarterly Press, 1989), p. 48.
22. *New York Times*, April 1, 1988.
23. *New York Times*, August 19, 1988.
24. *New York Times*, August 19, 1988.
25. Kathleen Hall Jamieson, *Packaging the Presidency,* 3rd ed. (New York: Oxford University Press, 1996), pp. 459–484.
26. John Robert Greene, *The Presidency of George Bush* (Lawrence: University of Kansas Press, 2000), p. 39.
27. *New York Times*, September 14, 1988.
28. *New York Times*, September 18, 1988.
29. *New York Times*, September 21, 1988, and September 23, 1988.
30. Michael Nelson, ed., *The Elections of 1988* (Washington, DC: Congressional Quarterly Press, 1989), p. 76.
31. George Bush, *Looking Forward* (New York: Doubleday, 1987).
32. Herbert S. Parmet, *George Bush* (New Brunswick, NJ: Transaction Publishers, 2001), p. 339.
33. *New York Times*, October 19, 1988.
34. *New York Times*, December 14, 1988.
35. *New York Times*, January 21, 1989.
36. *New York Times*, January 21, 1989.
37. *Newsweek,* November 9, 1989.
38. *New York Times*, November 21, 1989.
39. *New York Times*, December 26, 1989.
40. *New York Times*, April 21–May 3, 1989.
41. *New York Times*, April 27, 1989.
42. *New York Times*, January 23, 1989.
43. *New York Times*, December 2, 1989.
44. Herbert S. Parmet, *George Bush* (New Brunswick, NJ: Transaction Publishers, 2001), p. 428.

45. *New York Times*, December 2, 1989.
46. *New York Times*, January 21, 1989.
47. *New York Times*, May 8, 1989.
48. *New York Times*, May 12, 1989.
49. *Washington Times*, May 15, 1989.
50. *New York Times*, January 5, 1990.
51. *New York Times*, September 22, 1989.
52. *New York Times*, October 17, 1989.
53. Herbert S. Parmet, *George Bush* (New Brunswick, NJ: Transaction Publishers, 2001), pp. 428–435.
54. John Robert Greene, *The Presidency of George Bush* (Lawrence: University of Kansas Press, 2000), p. 84.

CHAPTER 7: FROM A DISTANCE

1. Williamson Murray and Robert H. Scales, Jr., *The Iraq War* (Cambridge, MA: Belknap Press, 2003), pp. 15–16.
2. Micah L. Silfrey and Christopher Cerf, eds., *The Gulf War Reader: History, Documents, Opinions* (New York: Times Books, 1991), p. 77.
3. Nasser Ibrahim Rashid and Esber Ibrahim Shaheen, *Saudi Arabia and the Gulf War* (Joplin, MO: International Institute of Technology, 1992), p. 128.
4. Williamson Murray and Robert H. Scales, Jr., *The Iraq War* (Cambridge, MA: Belknap Press, 2003), p. 47.
5. *New York Times*, April 3, 1990.
6. *New York Times*, August 3, 1990.
7. John R. MacArthur, *Second Front* (Berkeley: University of California Press, 2004), pp. 37–77.
8. Herbert S. Parmet, *George Bush* (New Brunswick, NJ: Transaction Publishers, 2001), p. 442.
9. *New York Times*, August 6, 1990.
10. John Robert Greene, *The Presidency of George Bush* (Lawrence: University of Kansas Press, 2000), p. 114.
11. Herbert S. Parmet, *George Bush* (New Brunswick, NJ: Transaction Publishers, 2001), p. 456.
12. Herbert S. Parmet, *George Bush* (New Brunswick, NJ: Transaction Publishers, 2001), p. 451.
13. *New York Times*, August 9, 1990.
14. Williamson Murray and Robert H. Scales, Jr., *The Iraq War* (Cambridge, MA: Belknap Press, 2003), p. 147.
15. *New York Times*, August 9, 1990.
16. *The Nation,* September 10, 1990.
17. Herbert S. Parmet, *George Bush* (New Brunswick, NJ: Transaction Publishers, 2001), p. 471.
18. James Fallows, *National Defense* (New York: Random House, 1981).
19. Herbert S. Parmet, *George Bush* (New Brunswick, NJ: Transaction Publishers, 2001), p. 462.
20. Micah Silfrey and Christopher Cerf, eds., *The Gulf War Reader: History, Documents, Opinions* (New York: Times Books, 1991), p. 263.

21. Herbert S. Parmet, *George Bush* (New Brunswick, NJ: Transaction Publishers, 2001), p. 425.

22. Williamson Murray and Robert H. Scales, Jr., *The Iraq War* (Cambridge, MA: Belknap Press, 2003), p. 175.

23. *New York Times*, January 19, 1991.

24. *New York Times*, January 18, 1991.

25. Micah L. Silfrey and Christopher Cerf, eds., *The Gulf War Reader* (New York: Times Books, 1991), p. 143.

26. *New York Times*, February 22, 1991.

27. Micah L. Silfrey and Christopher Cerf, eds., *The Gulf War Reader* (New York: Times Books, 1991), p. 365.

28. Interview with Rod Andrew, April 5, 2005.

29. Miland Brown, "The First Gulf War," www.libraryreference.org.

30. Interview with Rod Andrew, April 5, 2005.

31. *New York Times*, February 25, 1991.

32. U.S. News and World Report, *Triumph Without Victory* (New York: Times Books, 1993), p. 321.

33. Bette Midler, "From a Distance," www.lyricsorp.com.

34. U.S. News and World Report, *Triumph Without Victory* (New York: Times Books, 1993), p. 369.

35. *New York Times*, February 28, 1991.

36. *New York Times*, February 28, 1991.

37. Herbert S. Parmet, *George Bush* (New Brunswick, NJ: Transaction Publishers, 2001), p. 483.

38. U.S. News and World Report, *Triumph Without Victory* (New York: Times Books, 1993), p. 375.

39. Rick Matlick, "Presidential Approval Ratings: 1953–1996," www.presidentialapproval.com.

40. Herbert S. Parmet, *George Bush* (New Brunswick, NJ: Transaction Publishers, 2001), pp. 490–493.

41. David Brock, *The Real Anita Hill* (New York: Free Press, 1993).

CHAPTER 8: DON'T STOP THINKING ABOUT TOMORROW

1. Landon Y. Jones, *Great Expectations* (New York: Coward, McCann and Geoghegan, 1980).

2. Herbert S. Parmet, *George Bush* (New Brunswick, NJ: Transaction Publishers, 2001), p. 493.

3. *New York Times*, February 9, 1992.

4. Michael Nelson, ed., *The Election of 1992* (Washington, DC: Congressional Quarterly Press, 1993), p. 143.

5. *New York Times*, August 6 and 14, 1991.

6. John Robert Greene, *The Presidency of George Bush* (Lawrence: University of Kansas Press, 2000), p. 144.

7. Michael Nelson, ed., *The Elections of 1992* (Washington, DC: Congressional Quarterly Press, 1993), p. 144.

8. *National Review*, December 1991.

9. Lee Edwards, *The Conservative Revolution* (New York: Free Press, 1999), p. 289.

10. James Ceaser and Andrew Busch, *Upside Down and Inside Out* (Lanham, MD: Rowman and Littlefield, 1993), p. 39.

11. *Boston Globe*, January 30, 1992.

12. *New York Times*, February 27, 1991.

13. *New York Times*, October 22, 1992.

14. Steven E. Schier, ed., *The Postmodern Presidency* (Pittsburgh, PA: University of Pittsburgh Press, 2000), p. 10.

15. Bob Woodward, *The Agenda* (New York: Simon and Schuster, 1994), p. 20.

16. David Maraniss, *First in His Class* (New York: Simon and Schuster, 1995), pp. 358–404.

17. *New York Times*, October 4, 1992.

18. Bob Woodward, *The Agenda* (New York: Simon and Schuster, 1994), p. 30.

19. Bob Woodward, *The Agenda* (New York: Simon and Schuster, 1994), p. 33.

20. *New York Times*, January 23, 1992.

21. *New York Times*, January 27, 1992.

22. *New York Times*, February 19, 1992.

23. W. Lance Bennett, *The Governing Crisis* (New York: St. Martin's Press, 1992), pp. 19–21.

24. www.lyrics.com.

25. James Ceaser and Andrew Busch, *Upside Down and Inside Out* (Lanham, MD: Rowman and Littlefield, 2001), p. 91.

26. *New York Times*, June 18, 1992.

27. James Ceaser and Andrew Busch, *Upside Down and Inside Out* (Lanham, MD: Rowman and Littlefield, 2001), p. 89.

28. Gallup Poll, February 27, 1992.

29. *New York Times*, April 24, June 13, and June 25, 1992.

30. *New York Times*, June 28, 1992.

31. *Boston Globe*, July 12, 1992.

32. Bill Clinton, *My Life* (New York: Alfred A. Knopf, 2004), p. 415.

33. *New York Times*, July 26, 1992.

34. *New York Times*, August 19, 1992.

35. *The Houston Chronicle*, August 19, 1992.

36. *New York Times*, August 21, 1992.

37. *New York Times*, October 7, 1992.

38. *New York Times*, October 20, 1992.

39. *New York Times*, May 23, 1993.

40. David Maraniss, *First in His Class* (New York: Simon and Schuster, 1995), p. 246.

41. Bob Woodward, *The Agenda* (New York: Simon and Schuster, 1994), pp. 120–124.

42. Steven E. Schier, ed., *The Postmodern Presidency* (Pittsburgh, PA: University of Pittsburgh Press, 2000), p. 127.

43. *New York Times*, August 7, 1993.

44. *New York Times*, May 11, 1993.

45. *New York Times*, September 8, 1993.

46. www.clintonhealthcare.com.

47. *New York Times*, September 26, September 30, and October 1, 1993.

48. Gallup Poll, September 29, 1993.

49. *New York Times*, October 30, 1993.

50. *Policy Review*, Fall 1993, p. 15.
51. www.therubins.com.
52. Gallup Poll, February 23, 1994.
53. *Chicago Sun-Times*, January 30, 1994.
54. Bill Clinton, *My Life* (New York: Alfred A. Knopf, 2004), p. 499.
55. Bill Clinton, *My Life* (New York: Alfred A. Knopf, 2004), p. 544.
56. Mark Bowden, *Black Hawk Down* (New York: Penguin Books, 1999), p. 7.
57. Bill Clinton, *My Life* (New York: Alfred A. Knopf, 2004), p. 552.
58. Larry J. Sabato, ed., *Toward the Millennium* (Upper Saddle River, NJ: Prentice Hall, 1997), p. 8.
59. Gallup Poll, July 1994.
60. Haynes Johnson, *The Best of Times* (New York: James H. Silberman, 2001), p. 3.
61. *Atlantic Monthly*, September 2001.
62. *Atlantic Monthly*, September 2001.
63. *Washington Post*, April 17, 1994.

CHAPTER 9: THE POSTMODERN NINETIES

1. Joseph E. Stiglitz, *The Roaring Nineties* (New York: W. W. Norton, 2003), p. 1.
2. Haynes Johnson, *The Best of Times* (New York: James H. Silberman, 2001), p. 23.
3. Joseph E. Stiglitz, *The Roaring Nineties* (New York: W. W. Norton, 2003), p. 6.
4. Douglas Coupland, *Generation X* (New York: St. Martin's Press, 1991).
5. Don Tapscott, *Growing Up Digital* (New York: McGraw-Hill, 1998), p. 1.
6. Haynes Johnson, *The Best of Times* (New York: James H. Silberman, 2001), p. 50.
7. Haynes Johnson, *The Best of Times* (New York: James H. Silberman, 2001), pp. 48–72.
8. Charles Jencks, *What Is Postmodernism?* (New York: St. Martin's Press, 1987), p. 44.
9. *Atlantic Monthly*, March 1992.
10. John R. Vacca, *The World's 20 Greatest Unsolved Problems* (Upper Saddle River, NJ: Prentice Hall, 2004).
11. Michel Foucault, *The Order of Things* (New York: Vintage Books, 1994), p. xviii.
12. Jacques Derrida, *Deconstruction in a Nutshell* (New York: Fordham University Press, 1997).
13. Christo and Jeanne-Claude, *On the Way to the Gates: Central Park, New York City* (New Haven, CT: Yale University Press, 2004).
14. Milan Kundera, *The Unbearable Lightness of Being* (New York: Harper and Row, 1984).
15. Steven Connor, *Postmodernist Culture* (Oxford, UK: Blackwell, 1997), p. 186.
16. Frederick Jameson, *Postmodernism* (Durham, NC: Duke University Press, 1991), p. xv.
17. Brian Godawa, *Hollywood Worldviews* (Downers Grove, IL: Intervarsity Press, 2002), p. 90.
18. Robert Gooding-Williams, ed., *Reading Rodney King: Reading Urban Uprising* (New York: Routledge, 1993), p. 13.
19. Stan Chambers, "Rodney King and the Los Angeles Riots," www.citivu.com.
20. Robert Gooding-Williams, ed., *Reading Rodney King: Reading Urban Uprising* (New York: Routledge, 1993), pp. 21–22.

21. *USA Today*, March 19, 1991.
22. *New York Times*, April 4, 1991.
23. Lou Cannon, *Official Negligence* (Boulder, CO: Westview Press, 1999), p. 141.
24. *New York Times*, May 1, 1991.
25. *New York Times*, May 1 and 2, 1992.
26. *New York Times*, March 14, 1993.
27. Haynes Johnson, *The Best of Times* (New York: James H. Silberman, 2001), pp. 107–108.
28. *New York Times*, June 19, 1994.
29. *New York Times*, June 19, 1994.
30. Donald Freed and Raymond P. Briggs, *Killing Time* (New York: Macmillan, 1996).
31. *New York Times*, September 16, 1994.
32. *New York Times*, June 18, 1994.
33. *New York Times*, February 7, 1995.
34. *New York Times*, June 24, 1994.
35. Haynes Johnson, *The Best of Times* (New York: James H. Silberman, 2001), p. 139.
36. *New York Times*, October 4, 1995.
37. *New York Times*, April 1, 1993.
38. *New York Times*, April 1, 1993.
39. *New York Times*, March 23, 1993.
40. Bruce Hoffman, *Inside Terrorism* (New York: Columbia University Press, 1998), pp. 14–25.
41. Charles Kay, "Painful Memories," www.okc.com.
42. *New York Times*, April 20, 1995.
43. *New York Times*, August 4, 1995.
44. *New York Times*, June 15, 1995.
45. *Washington Post*, April 25, 1995.
46. *New York Times*, June 12, 2001.
47. *New York Times*, April 5, 1996.
48. *New York Times*, April 4, 1996.
49. Robert Graysmith, *Unabomber* (Washington, DC: Regnery, 1997).
50. *New York Times*, June 30, 1995.
51. *USA Today*, February 26, 1997.

CHAPTER 10: TRIANGULATION

1. *New York Times*, January 2, 1995.
2. *New York Times*, January 5, 1995.
3. *St. Petersburg Times*, October 13, 1994.
4. Bill Clinton, *My Life* (New York: Alfred A. Knopf, 2004), p. 357.
5. CNN Early Edition, April 19, 1995.
6. *Houston Chronicle*, April 25, 1995.
7. CNN, November 14, 1995.
8. Gallup Poll, 1995.
9. Personal interview with South Carolina Governor Carroll Campbell, October 1994.
10. *New York Daily News*, November 17, 1995.
11. Anne Marie Cammisa, *From Rhetoric to Reform: Welfare Policy in American Politics* (Boulder, CO: Westview Press, 1998), pp. 101–121.

12. Michael Nelson, ed., *The Elections of 1996* (Washington, DC: Congressional Quarterly Press, 1997).
13. *New York Times*, January 9, 1996.
14. Bob Woodward, *The Choice* (New York: Simon and Schuster, 1996).
15. Haynes Johnson, *The Best of Times* (New York: James H. Silberman, 2001), p. 302.
16. *New York Times*, August 16, 1996.
17. *New York Times*, August 30, 1996.
18. *New York Times*, January 28, 1996.
19. *New York Times*, April 22, 1992.
20. Charles R. Shrader, *The Muslim-Croat Civil War in Central Bosnia: A Military History* (College Station: Texas A&M Press, 1996).
21. *New York Times*, January 12, 1995.
22. *St. Louis Post-Dispatch*, June 6, 1995.
23. *New York Times*, June 9, 1995.
24. *New York Times*, June 6, 1999.
25. International Criminal Tribunal, Case IT-02-54, "Indictment Kosovo," September 2004.
26. David Maraniss, *First in His Class* (New York: Simon and Schuster, 1995), p. 461.
27. Todd G. Shields, Jeannie M. Whayne, and Donald R. Kelley, *The Clinton Riddle* (Fayetteville: University of Arkansas Press, 2004), p. 40.
28. Bill Clinton, *My Life* (New York: Alfred A. Knopf, 2004), p. 574.
29. Haynes Johnson, *The Best of Times* (New York: James H. Silberman, 2001), p. 233.
30. Joe Klein, *The Natural* (New York: Doubleday, 2002), p. 165.
31. William Bennett, *The Death of Outrage* (New York: Touchstone, 1999).
32. Haynes Johnson, *The Best of Times* (New York: James H. Silberman, 2001), p. 354.
33. *New York Times*, August 18, 1998.
34. *New York Times*, August 20, 1998.
35. Samuel Kernell, *Going Public* (Washington, DC: Congressional Quarterly Press, 1997), p. 1.
36. William J. Bennett, *The Index of Leading Cultural Indicators* (New York: Simon and Schuster, 1994).
37. Haynes Johnson, *The Best of Times* (New York: James H. Silberman, 2001), p. 360.
38. Steven E. Schier, ed., *The Postmodern Presidency* (Pittsburgh, PA: University of Pittsburgh Press, 2000).
39. Bill Clinton, *My Life* (New York: Alfred A. Knopf, 2004), p. 803.
40. *New York Times*, October 18, 1998.
41. *Washington Post*, December 22, 1998.
42. The previous impeachment was Andrew Johnson, who was unelected; Richard Nixon resigned under the threat of impeachment.
43. *New York Times*, January 8, 1999.
44. *New York Times*, February 13, 1999.
45. *New York Times*, January 19, 1999.
46. *Aesop's Fables* (New York: St. Martin's Press, 1938), p. 67.
47. Allan Bloom, *The Closing of the American Mind* (New York: Simon and Schuster, 1987), p. 26.
48. Brooks Brown and Rob Merritt, *No Easy Answers* (New York: Lantern Books, 2002).
49. *Washington Post*, June 12, 1999.

CHAPTER 11: 9/11

1. *New York Times*, November 8, 1999.
2. Waukesha, Wisconsin *Journal*, January 12, 1999.
3. *Abilene Reporter News*, October 14, 2000.
4. Gerald M. Pomper, ed., *The Election of 2000* (New York: Chatham House Publishers, 2001), p. 130.
5. *New York Times*, August 26, 1999.
6. *New York Times*, October 1, 1999.
7. Michael Nelson, ed., *The Elections of 2000* (Washington, DC: Congressional Quarterly Press, 2001), p. 37.
8. *New York Times*, August 28, 1999.
9. Michael Nelson, ed., *The Elections of 2000* (Washington, DC: Congressional Quarterly Press, 2001), p. 32.
10. *New York Times*, August 14, 1999.
11. *New York Times*, January 25, 2000.
12. *Greenville News*, February 27, 2000.
13. *New York Times*, March 17, 2000.
14. Bill Minutaglio, *First Son* (New York: Times Books, 1999), p. 106.
15. Richard Johnson, Michael Hagen, and Kathleen Hall Jamieson, *The 2000 Presidential Election and the Foundations of Party Politics* (Cambridge, UK: Cambridge University Press, 2004), pp. 23–26.
16. *New York Times*, October 17, 2000.
17. *New York Times*, November 9, 2000.
18. *USA Today*, November 9, 2000.
19. *New York Times*, November 9, 2000.
20. *New York Times*, November 11, 2000.
21. Julian M. Pleasants, *Hanging Chads* (New York: Palgrave Macmillan, 2004), pp. 43–58.
22. *New York Times*, November 24, 2000.
23. *New York Times*, December 12, 2000.
24. Peter Schweizer and Rochelle Schweizer, *The Bushes* (New York: Doubleday, 2004), p. 495.
25. Bill Minutaglio, *First Son* (New York: Times Books, 1999), pp. 38–65.
26. James W. Ceaser and Andrew E. Busch, *The Perfect Tie* (Lanham, MD: Rowman and Littlefield, 2001), p. 20.
27. *New York Times*, January 21, 2001.
28. Peter Schweizer and Rochelle Schweizer, *The Bushes* (New York: Doubleday, 2004), p. 501.
29. *New York Times*, April 2, 2001.
30. Paul Thompson, *The Terror Timeline* (New York: HarperCollins, 2004), p. 397.
31. Paul Thompson, *The Terror Timeline* (New York: HarperCollins, 2004), p. 196.
32. *Sydney Daily Telegraph*, September 21, 2001.
33. Yassin El-Ayouty, *Perspectives on 9/11* (Westport, CT: Praeger, 2004), p. 18.
34. *New York Times*, September 13, 2001.
35. CNN, September 11, 2001.
36. *New York Times*, September 13, 2001.
37. National Commission on Terrorist Attacks, *The 9/11 Commission Report: Final Report* (New York: W. W. Norton, 2004), p. 48.

38. *Washington Post*, September 12, 2001.
39. *Pittsburgh Post-Gazette*, September 16, 2001.
40. *New York Times*, September 27, 2001.
41. *New York Times*, September 13, 2001.
42. Judith Greenberg, ed., *Trauma at Home After 9/11* (Lincoln: University of Nebraska Press, 2003), pp. 187–188.
43. *Pittsburgh Post-Gazette*, September 16, 2001.
44. National Commission on Terrorist Attacks, *The 9/11 Commission Report* (New York: W. W. Norton, 2004).
45. *New York Times*, September 12, 2001.
46. Peter Schweizer and Rochelle Schweizer, *The Bushes* (New York; Doubleday, 2004), p. 516.
47. *Washington Post*, September 12, 2001.
48. *Omaha Gazette*, September 15, 2001.
49. *New York Times*, September 16, 2001.
50. *New York Times*, September 16, 2001.
51. Joanne Meyerowitz, *History and September 11th* (Philadelphia, PA: Temple University Press, 2003), p. 25.
52. *Boston Globe*, October 12, 2001.
53. *New York Times*, October 4 and October 6, 2001.
54. Joanne Meyerowitz, *History and September 11th* (Philadelphia, PA: Temple University Press, 2003), p. 81.
55. Paul R. Abramson, John H. Aldrich, and David W. Rohde, *Change and Continuity in the 2000 and 2002 Elections* (Washington, DC: CQ Press, 2002), p. 81.
56. *The Ottawa Citizen*, November 2, 2002.
57. *New York Times*, November 8, 2002.

CHAPTER 12: MISUNDERESTIMATED

1. Jon Lee Anderson, *The Fall of Baghdad* (New York: Penguin Press, 2004), p. 21.
2. *New York Times*, January 30, 2002.
3. *New York Times*, January 30, 2002.
4. *New York Times*, October 11, 2002.
5. *Washington Post*, March 8, 2002.
6. *Boston Globe*, October 8, 2002.
7. *New York Times*, February 6, 2003.
8. *New York Times*, February 22, 2003.
9. Williamson Murray and Robert H. Scales, Jr., *The Iraq War* (Cambridge, MA: Belknap Press, 2003), p. 82.
10. Williamson Murray and Robert H. Scales, Jr., *The Iraq War* (Cambridge, MA: Belknap Press, 2003), p. 177.
11. *New York Times*, March 18, 2003.
12. Jon Lee Anderson, *The Fall of Baghdad* (New York: Penguin, 2004), p. 155.
13. Jon Lee Anderson, *The Fall of Baghdad* (New York: Penguin, 2004), p. 167.
14. Williamson Murray and Robert H. Scales, Jr., *The Iraq War* (Cambridge, MA: Belknap Press, 2003), p. 148.
15. *Houston Chronicle*, April 1, 2003.
16. Evan Wright, "The Killer Elite," *Rolling Stone*, June 2003.

17. Jon Lee Anderson, *The Fall of Baghdad* (New York: Penguin, 2004), p. 190.
18. Williamson Murray and Robert H. Scales, Jr., *The Iraq War* (Cambridge, MA: Belknap Press, 2003), p. 102.
19. *Minneapolis Star-Tribune*, April 6, 2003.
20. *New York Times*, April 4, 2003.
21. *Washington Post*, July 23, 2003.
22. *New York Times*, December 15, 2003.
23. *New York Times*, May 2, 2003.
24. *New York Times*, July 14, 2002.
25. *Chicago Sun-Times*, December 13, 2003.
26. NBC News, Janaury 5, 2004.
27. *New York Times*, September 18, 2003.
28. *New York Times*, January 20, 2004.
29. Byron York, *The Vast Left-Wing Conspiracy* (New York: Crown Books, 2005), p. 8.
30. Byron York, *The Vast Left-Wing Conspiracy* (New York: Crown Books, 2005).
31. *New York Times*, July 4, 2004.
32. Michael Nelson, ed., *The Elections of 2004* (Washington, DC: Congressional Quarterly Press, 2005), p. 53.
33. *Boston Globe*, August 1, 2004.
34. *Congressional Record*, September 19, 2003.
35. Gallup Poll, March 2004.
36. *New York Times*, November 9, 2004.
37. Michael Nelson, ed., *The Elections of 2004* (Washington, DC: Congressional Quarterly Press, 2005), p. 187.
38. Mitchell Cohen and Nicole Fermon, eds., *Princeton Readings in Political Thought* (Princeton, NJ: Princeton University Press, 1996), pp. 382–383.
39. Bill Sammon, *Misunderestimated* (New York: Regan Books, 2004).
40. *Houston Chronicle*, Janaury 21, 2005.
41. *Washington Post*, January 21, 2005.
42. Jon Lee Anderson, *The Fall of Baghdad* (New York: Penguin Press, 2004), p. 261.
43. Natan Sharansky, *The Case for Democracy* (New York: Public Affairs, 2004), pp. 14–15.
44. *Atlanta Journal-Constitution*, August 31, 2005.
45. *New York Times*, September 4, 2005.
46. *Newsday*, September 4, 2005.

Select Bibliography

Abramson, Paul R., John H. Aldrich, and David W. Rohde. *Change and Continuity in the 2000 and 2002 Elections.* Washington, DC: Congressional Quarterly Press, 2002.
Adler, Bill, ed. *The Uncommon Wisdom of Ronald Reagan: A Portrait in His Own Words.* Boston: Little, Brown, 1996.
Allison, Graham. *The Essence of Decision.* Boston: Little, Brown, 1971.
Anderson, Annelise, Martin Anderson, and Kirow K. Skinner. *Reagan in His Own Hand: The Writings of Ronald Reagan That Reveal His Revolutionary Vision for America.* New York: Free Press, 2001.
Anderson, Jon Lee. *The Fall of Baghdad.* New York: Penguin Press, 2004.
Anderson, Perry. *The Origins of Postmodernity.* London: Verso Press, 1998.
Arac, Jonathan, ed. *Postmodernism and Politics.* Minneapolis: University of Minnesota Press, 1986.
Barone, Michael. *Our Country: The Shaping of America from Roosevelt to Reagan.* New York: Free Press, 1990.
Barone, Michael. *The Almanac of American Politics: 1976 to 2004.* Washington, DC: National Journal.
Barrett, Lawrence I. *Gambling with History: Ronald Reagan in the White House.* New York: Penguin Books, 1983.
Bayles, Martha. *Hole in Our Soul: The Loss of Beauty and Meaning in American Popular Music.* Chicago: University of Chicago Press, 1994.
Bell, Daniel. *The Coming of Postindustrial Society: A Venture in Social Forecasting.* New York: Basic Books, 1976.
Bennett, W. Lance. *The Governing Crisis: Media, Money, and Marketing in American Elections.* New York: St. Martin's Press, 1992.
Bennett, William J. *The De-Valuing of America.* New York: Summit Books, 1992.
Bennett, William J. *The Index of Leading Cultural Indicators.* New York: Simon and Schuster, 1994.
Bennett, William J. *The Death of Outrage: Bill Clinton and the Assault on American Ideals.* New York: Touchstone, 1999.

Berman, Marshall. *All That Is Solid Melts into Air.* New York: Simon and Schuster, 1982.
Bernstein, Carl, and Bob Woodward. *All the President's Men.* New York: Simon and Schuster, 1974.
Bloom, Allan. *The Closing of the American Mind: How Higher Education Has Failed Democracy and Impoverished the Souls of Today's Students.* New York: Simon and Schuster, 1987.
Bork, Robert H. *Slouching Toward Gomorrah.* New York: Regan Books, 1996.
Bourne, Peter G. *Jimmy Carter: A Comprehensive Biography from Plains to the Post-Presidency.* New York: Scribner, 1997.
Bowden, Mark. *Black Hawk Down: A Story of Modern War.* New York: Penguin Books, 1999.
Brinkley, David. *Washington Goes to War.* New York: Alfred A. Knopf, 1988.
Brock, David. *The Real Anita Hill.* New York: Free Press, 1993.
Brown, Brooks, and Rob Merritt. *No Easy Answers: The Truth Behind Death at Columbine.* New York: Lantern Books, 2002.
Brown, Mary Beth. *Hand of Providence: The Story and Quiet Faith of Ronald Reagan.* Nashville, TN: WND Books, 2004.
Bruck, Connie. *The Predator's Ball: The Inside Story of Drexel Burnham and the Rise of the Junkyard Raiders.* New York: Penguin Books, 1986.
Bugliosi, Vincent. *Outrage: The Five Reasons Why O.J. Simpson Got Away with Murder.* New York: Bantam Books, 1996.
Burrough, Bryan, and John Helyar. *Barbarians at the Gate: The Fall of RJR Nabisco.* New York: Harper and Row, 1990.
Busch, Andrew E. *Ronald Reagan and the Politics of Freedom.* New York: Rowman and Littlefield, 2001.
Bush, George. *Looking Forward.* New York: Doubleday, 1987.
Cammisa, Anne Marie. *From Rhetoric to Reform: Welfare Policy in American Politics.* Boulder, CO: Westview Press, 1998.
Campbell, David. *Politics Without Principle: Sovereignty, Ethics, and the Narratives of the Gulf War.* Boulder, CO: Lynne Rienner Publishers, 1993.
Cannon, Lou. *President Reagan: The Role of a Lifetime.* New York: Simon and Schuster, 1991.
Cannon, Lou. *Official Negligence: How Rodney King and the Riots Changed Los Angeles and the LAPD.* Boulder, CO: Westview Press, 1999.
Cannon, Lou. *Governor Reagan: His Rise to Power.* New York: Public Affairs, 2003.
Carter, Jimmy. *Why Not the Best?* Nashville, TN: Broadman Press, 1975.
Carter, Jimmy. *Keeping Faith: Memoirs of a President.* New York: Bantam Books, 1982.
Ceaser, James, and Andrew Busch. *Upside Down and Inside Out: The 1992 Elections and American Politics.* Lanham, MD: Rowman and Littlefield, 1993.
Ceaser, James, and Andrew Busch. *The Perfect Tie: The True Story of the 2000 Presidential Election.* Lanham, MD: Rowman and Littlefield, 2001.
Christo and Jeanne-Claude. *On the Way to the Gates: Central Park, New York City.* New Haven, CT: Yale University Press, 2004.
Clinton, Bill. *My Life.* New York: Alfred A. Knopf, 2004.
Cohen, Mitchell, and Nicole Ferman, eds. *Princeton Readings in Political Thought: Essential Texts Since Plato.* Princeton, NJ: Princeton University Press, 1996.
Connor, Steven. *Postmodernist Culture: An Introduction to the Theories of the Contemporary.* Oxford, UK: Blackwell, 1997.

Cordesman, Anthony H. *The Iraq War: Strategy, Tactics, and Military Lessons.* Washington, DC: Center for Strategic and International Studies, 2003.
Coupland, Douglas. *Generation X: Tales for an Accelerated Culture.* New York: St. Martin's Press, 1991.
Crothers, Lane, and Nancy S. Lind. *Presidents from Reagan Through Clinton: 1981–2001.* Westport, CT: Greenwood Press, 2002.
Davis, Patti. *Angels Don't Die: My Father's Gift of Faith.* New York: HarperCollins, 1990.
Deaver, Michael K. *A Different Drummer: My Thirty Years with Ronald Reagan.* New York: Perennial, 2003.
Denzin, Norman R., and Yvonna S. Lincoln, eds. *9/11 in American Culture.* New York: Altamira Press, 2003.
Derrida, Jacques. *Deconstruction in a Nutshell.* New York: Fordham University Press, 1997.
Dover, Edwin D. *The Disputed Presidential Election of 2000.* Westport, CT: Greenwood Press, 2003.
Draper, Theodore. *A Very Thin Line: The Iran-Contra Affair.* New York: Touchstone, 1991.
Dreiser, Theodore. *An American Tragedy.* New York: Modern Library, 1956.
Drew, Elizabeth. *Portrait of an Election: The 1980 Presidential Campaign.* New York: Simon and Schuster, 1981.
D'Souza, Dinesh. *Ronald Reagan: How an Ordinary Man Became an Extraordinary Leader.* New York: Touchstone, 1997.
Edwards, Anne. *Early Reagan.* New York: William Morrow, 1987.
Edwards, Lee. *The Conservative Revolution: The Movement That Remade America.* New York: Free Press, 1999.
Ehrman, John. *The Eighties: America in the Age of Reagan.* New Haven, CT: Yale University Press, 2005.
El-Ayouty, Yassin, ed. *Perspectives on 9/11.* Westport, CT: Praeger, 2004.
Evans, Rowland, and Robert Novak. *The Reagan Revolution.* New York: E. P. Dutton, 1981.
Fallows, James. *National Defense.* New York: Random House, 1981.
Felten, Erik, ed. *A Shining City: The Legacy of Ronald Reagan.* New York: Simon and Schuster, 1998.
Felton, Eric. *The Ruling Class: Inside the Imperial Congress.* Washington, DC: Regnery Gateway, 1993.
Ferguson, Thomas, and Joel Rogers. *The Hidden Election: Politics and Economics in the 1980 Presidential Campaign.* New York: Pantheon Books, 1981.
Fiorina, Morris. *Divided Government*, 2nd ed. New York: Allyn and Bacon, 1996.
Fiorina, Morris, and Paul E. Peterson. *The New American Democracy.* New York: Longman, 2001.
Fiorina, Morris, Samuel J. Abrams, and Jeremy C. Pope. *Culture War?* New York: Pearson and Longman, 2005.
Flanigan, William H., and Nancy H. Zingale. *Political Behavior of the American Electorate*, 8th ed. Washington, DC: Congressional Quarterly Press, 1994.
Foucault, Michel. *The Order of Things: An Archeology of the Human Sciences.* New York: Vintage Books, 1994.

Freed, Donald, and Raymond P. Briggs. *Killing Time: The First Full Investigation.* New York: Macmillan, 1996.
Friedman, Milton. *Free to Choose.* New York: Avon Books, 1985.
Friedman, Thomas L. *The World Is Flat.* New York: Farrar, Straus and Giroux, 2005.
Frum, David. *How We Got Here: The 70's.* New York: Basic Books, 2000.
Gallup Poll: 1976–2005. Wilmington, DE: Scholarly Resources, Inc.
Gaslin, Glenn, and Rick Porter. *The Complete Cross-Referenced Guide to the Baby Buster Generation's Collective Unconscious.* New York: Boulevard Books, 1998.
George, Alexander L. *Bridging the Gap: Theory and Practice in Foreign Policy.* Washington, DC: United States Institute of Peace Press, 1993.
Germond, Jack W., and Jules Witcover. *Blue Smoke and Mirrors: How Reagan Won and Why Carter Lost the Election of 1980.* New York: Viking Press, 1981.
Gibbon, Edward. *The Decline and Fall of the Roman Republic.* Vol. 1. New York: Modern Library, 1931.
Giddens, Anthony. *The Consequences of Modernity.* Stanford, CA: Stanford University Press, 1990.
Godawa, Brian. *Hollywood Worldviews.* Downer's Grove, IL: Intervarsity Press, 2002.
Goldman, Peter, and Tom Mathews et al. *Quest for the Presidency: The 1988 Campaign.* New York: Touchstone, 1989.
Golenpaul, Ann, ed. *Information Please Almanac: 1977.* New York: Simon and Schuster, 1977.
Golenpaul, Dan, ed. *Information Please Almanac: 1971.* New York: Simon and Schuster, 1971.
Gooding-Williams, Robert, ed. *Reading Rodney King: Reading Urban Uprising.* New York: Routledge, 1993.
Graysmith, Anne Marie. *From Rhetoric to Reform: Welfare Policy in American Politics.* Washington, DC: Regnery, 1997.
Graysmith, Robert. *Unabomber.* Washington, DC: Regency, 1997.
Greenberg, Judith, ed. *Trauma at Home After 9/11.* Lincoln: University of Nebraska Press, 2003.
Greene, John Robert. *The Presidency of George Bush.* Lawrence: University of Kansas Press, 2000.
Grenz, Stanley J. *A Primer on Postmodernism.* Grand Rapids, MI: William B. Eerdmans, 1996.
Grider, William. *The Education of David Stockman.* New York: E. P. Dutton, 1982.
Hagen, Michael G., Kathleen Hall Jamieson, and Richard Johnston. *The 2000 Presidential Election and the Foundations of Party Politics.* New York: Cambridge University Press, 2004.
Hannaford, Peter. *Ronald Reagan and His Ranch: The Western White House, 1981–1989.* Bennington, VT: Privately printed, 2002.
Hannaford, Peter, ed. *Recollections of Reagan.* New York: William Morrow, 1997.
Hargrove, Erwin. *Jimmy Carter: As President.* Baton Rouge: Louisiana State University Press, 1988.
Harvey, David. *The Condition of Postmodernity.* Cambridge, MA: Basil Blackwell, 1989.
Henderson, Jeffrey, ed. *Cicero's Letters to His Friends.* Loeb Classical Library, Cambridge, MA: Harvard University Press, 2001.
Hersch, Seymour. *The Target Is Destroyed.* New York: Random House, 1986.

Hill, Dilys, Raymond A. Moore, and Phil Williams. *The Reagan Presidency: An Incomplete Revolution.* London: Macmillan, 1990.
Hoffman, Bruce. *Inside Terrorism.* New York: Columbia University Press, 1998.
Hybel, Alex Roberto. *Power over Rationality: The Bush Administration and the Gulf Crisis.* Albany: State University of New York, 1993.
Jameson, Frederick. *Postmodernism: Or the Cultural Logic of Late Capitalism.* Durham, NC: Duke University Press, 1991.
Jamieson, Kathleen Hall. *Packaging the Presidency*, 3rd ed. New York: Oxford University Press, 1996.
Jencks, Charles. *What Is Postmodernism?* New York: St. Martin's Press, 1987.
Jennings, Peter, and Todd Brewster. *The Century.* New York: Doubleday, 1998.
Johnson, Haynes. *In the Absence of Power.* New York: Viking Press, 1980.
Johnson, Haynes. *Sleepwalking Through History: America in the Reagan Years.* New York: W. W. Norton, 1991.
Johnson, Haynes. *The Best of Times: America in the Clinton Years.* New York: James H. Silberman, 2001.
Johnson, Paul. *A History of the American People.* New York: HarperCollins, 1997.
Johnson, Richard, Michael G. Hagen, and Kathleen Hall Jamieson. *The 2000 Presidential Election and the Foundations of Party Politics.* Cambridge, UK: Cambridge University Press, 2004.
Jones, Landon Y. *Great Expectations.* New York: Coward, McCann and Geoghegan, 1980.
Kallen, Stuart A. *A Cultural History of the United States Through the Decades: The 1980's.* San Diego, CA: Lucent Books, 1999.
Kaplan, Leonard V., and Beverly I. Moran. *Aftermath: The Clinton Impeachment and the Presidency in the Age of Political Spectacle.* New York: New York University, 2001.
Kengor, Paul. *God and Ronald Reagan: A Spiritual Life.* New York: Reagan Books, 2004.
Kernell, Samuel. *Going Public: New Strategies of Presidential Leadership*, 3rd ed. Washington, DC: Congressional Quarterly Press, 1997.
Kiewe, Amos, ed. *The Modern Presidency and Crisis Rhetoric.* Westport, CT: Preager, 1994.
Klein, Joe. *The Natural: The Misunderstood Presidency of Bill Clinton.* New York: Doubleday, 2002.
Knights, Michael, ed. *Operation Iraqi Freedom and the New Iraq: Insights and Forecasts.* Washington, DC: Washington Institute for Near East Policy, 2004.
Kundera, Milan. *The Unbearable Lightness of Being.* New York: Harper and Row, 1984.
Lasch, Christopher. *The Culture of Narcissism: American Life in an Age of Diminishing Expectations.* New York: Norton, 1978.
Lawler, Peter Augustine. *Postmodernism Rightly Understood: The Return to Realism in American Thought.* Lanham, MD: Rowman and Littlefield, 1999.
Levy, Peter B. *Encyclopedia of the Reagan-Bush Years.* Westport, CT: Greenwood Press, 1996.
Lowe, Janet. *The Secret Empire: How 25 Multinationals Rule the World.* Homewood, IL: Business One Irwin, 1992.
Lyotard, Jean-Francois. *The Postmodern Condition: A Report on Knowledge.* Minneapolis: University of Minnesota Press, 1979.

MacArthur, John R. *Second Front: Censorship and Propaganda in the 1991 Gulf War.* Berkeley: University of California Press, 2004.
Manchester, William. *The Glory and the Dream: A Narrative History of America, 1932–1972.* New York: Little, Brown, 1973.
Maraniss, David. *First in His Class: A Biography of Bill Clinton.* New York: Simon and Schuster, 1995.
Martin, William. *With God on Our Side: The Rise of the Religious Right in America.* New York: Broadway Books, 1996.
Meese, Edwin. *With Reagan: The Inside Story.* Washington, DC: Regnery Gateway, 1992.
Meyerowitz, Joanne. *History and September 11th.* Philadelphia, PA: Temple University Press, 2003.
Minutaglio, Bill. *First Son: George W. Bush and the Bush Family Dynasty.* New York: Times Books, 1999.
Moore, Robin. *Hunting Down Saddam: The Inside Story of the Search and Capture.* New York: St. Martin's Press, 2004.
Morris, Edmund. *Dutch: A Memoir of Ronald Reagan.* New York: Random House, 1999.
National Commission on Terrorist Attacks. *The 9/11 Commission Report: Final Report.* New York: W. W. Norton, 2004.
Nelson, Michael, ed. *The Elections of 1988.* Washington, DC: Congressional Quarterly Press, 1989.
Nelson, Michael, ed. *The Elections of 1992.* Washington, DC: Congressional Quarterly Press, 1993.
Nelson, Michael, ed. *The Elections of 1996.* Washington, DC: Congressional Quarterly Press, 1997.
Nelson, Michael, ed. *The Elections of 2000.* Washington, DC: Congressional Quarterly Press, 2001.
Nelson, Michael, ed. *The Elections of 2004.* Washington, DC: Congressional Quarterly Press, 2005.
New York Times. *36 Days: The Complete Chronicle of the 2000 Presidential Election Crisis.* New York: Henry Holt, 2001.
Noonan, Peggy. *What I Saw at the Revolution: A Political Life in the Reagan Era.* New York: Random House, 1991.
Noonan, Peggy. *When Character Was King: The Story of Ronald Reagan.* New York: Viking, 2001.
Parmet, Herbert S. *George Bush: The Life of a Lone Star Yankee.* New Brunswick, NJ: Transaction Publishers, 2001.
Pemberton, William E. *Exit with Honor: The Life and Presidency of Ronald Reagan.* Armonk, NY: M. E. Sharpe, 1998.
Pleasants, Julian M. *Hanging Chads: The Inside Story of the 2000 Presidential Recount in Florida.* New York: Palgrave Macmillan, 2004.
Pomper, Gerald M., ed. *The Election of 1984.* New York: Chatham House Publishers, 1985.
Pomper, Gerald M., ed. *The Election of 2000.* New York: Chatham House Publishers, 2001.
Post, Jerrold M., ed. *The Psychological Assessment of Political Leaders: With Profiles of Saddam Hussein and Bill Clinton.* Ann Arbor: University of Michigan Press, 2003.

Preston, Thomas. *The President and His Inner Circle*. New York: Columbia University Press, 2001.
Rashid, Nasser Ibrahim, and Esber Ibrahim Shaheen. *Saudi Arabia and the Gulf War*. Joplin, MO: International Institute of Technology, 1992.
Reagan, Maureen. *First Father, First Daughter*. Boston: Little, Brown, 1989.
Reagan, Nancy. *My Turn: The Memoirs of Nancy Reagan*. New York: Random House, 1989.
Reeves, Richard. *The Reagan Detour*. New York: Simon and Schuster, 1985.
Rozell, Mark J. *The Press and the Carter Presidency*. Boulder, CO: Westview Press, 1989.
Rozell, Mark J., and Clyde Wilcox. *The Clinton Scandal: And the Future of American Government*. Washington, DC: Georgetown University Press, 2000.
Ryan, Paul B. *The Iranian Rescue Mission*. Annapolis, MD: Naval Institute Press, 1985.
Sabato, Larry J., ed. *Toward the Millennium: The Elections of 1996*. Upper Saddle River, NJ: Prentice Hall, 1997.
Sammon, Bill. *Misunderestimated*. New York: Regan Books, 2004.
Schaeffer, Francis. *A Christian Manifesto*. Westchester, IL: Crossway Books, 1981.
Schell, Jonathan. *The Fate of the Earth*. Palo Alto, CA: Stanford University Press, 2000.
Schieffer, Bob, and Gary Paul Gates. *The Acting President*. New York: E. P. Dutton, 1989.
Schier, Steven E., ed. *The Postmodern Presidency: Bill Clinton's Legacy in U.S. Politics*. Pittsburgh, PA: University of Pittsburgh Press, 2000.
Schweizer, Peter. *Reagan's War: The Epic Story of His Forty-Year Struggle and Final Triumph Over Communism*. New York: Doubleday, 2002.
Schweizer, Peter, and Rochelle Schweizer. *The Bushes: Portrait of a Dynasty*. New York: Doubleday, 2004.
Sharansky, Natan. *The Case for Democracy*. New York: Public Affairs, 2004.
Sheperd, David R. *Ronald Reagan: In God I Trust*. Wheaton, IL: Tyndale House, 1984.
Shields, Todd G., Jeannie M. Whayne, and Donald R. Kelley. *The Clinton Riddle*. Fayetteville: University of Arkansas Press, 2004.
Shirley, Craig. *Reagan's Revolution: The Untold Story of the Campaign That Started It All*. New York: Nelson Current, 2005.
Shrader, Charles R. *The Muslim-Croat Civil War in Central Bosnia: A Military History, 1992–1994*. College Station: Texas A&M Press, 1996.
Silfrey, Micah L., and Christopher Cerf, eds. *The Gulf War Reader: History, Documents, Opinions*. New York: Times Books, 1991.
Simons, Jon. *Foucault and the Political*. New York: Routledge, 1995.
Slansky, Paul. *The Clothes Have No Emperor: A Chronicle of the American 80's*. New York: Simon and Schuster, 1989.
Smith, Hedrick. *The Power Game: How Washington Works*. New York: Random House, 1988.
Spencer, Donald S. *The Carter Implosion*. New York: Praeger, 1988.
Stacks, John F. *Watershed: The Campaign for the Presidency, 1980*. New York: Times Books, 1981.
Stiglitz, Joseph E. *The Roaring Nineties: A New History of the World's Most Prosperous Decade*. New York: W. W. Norton, 2003.
Tapscott, Don. *Growing Up Digital: The Rise of the Net Generation*. New York: McGraw-Hill, 1998.

Thompson, Paul. *The Terror Timeline: Year by Year, Day by Day, Minute by Minute.* New York: HarperCollins, 2004.
U.S. Department of Commerce. *1970 Census of Population.* Washington, DC: Bureau of the Census, 1973.
U.S. News. *Triumph Without Victory.* New York: Times Books, 1993.
Vacca, John R. *The World's 20 Greatest Unsolved Problems.* Upper Saddle River, NJ: Prentice Hall, 2004.
Van Der Linden, Frank. *The Real Reagan: What He Believes, What He Has Accomplished, What We Can Expect of Him.* New York: William Morrow, 1981.
Veith, Gene Edward, Jr. *Postmodern Times: A Christian Guide to Contemporary Thought and Culture.* Wheaton, IL: Crossway Books, 1994.
Ward, Ed. *Rock of Ages: The Rolling Stone History of Rock and Roll.* New York: Simon and Schuster, 1986.
Wayne, Steven J. *The Road to the White House, 2004: The Politics of Presidential Elections.* New York: Thomson and Wadsworth, 2004.
Wayne, Steven J., and Clyde Wilcox, eds. *The Election of the Century.* Armonk, NY: M. E. Sharpe, 2002.
White, John Kenneth. *The New Politics of Old Values.* London: University Press of New England, 1988.
White, John Kenneth. *The Values Divide.* New York: Chatham House, 2003.
Williamson, Murray, and Robert H. Scales, Jr. *The Iraq War.* Cambridge, MA: The Belknap Press, 2003.
Wolf, Naomi. *The Beauty Myth: How Images of Beauty Are Used Against Women.* New York: Doubleday, 1991.
Wolfe, Tom. *The Bonfire of the Vanities.* New York: Farrar, Straus and Giroux, 1987.
Woodard, J. David. *The New Southern Politics.* Boulder, CO: Lynne Rienner Press, 2006.
Woodward, Bob. *The Agenda: Inside the Clinton White House.* New York: Simon and Schuster, 1994.
Woodward, Bob. *The Choice.* New York: Simon and Schuster, 1996.
York, Byron. *The Vast Left-Wing Conspiracy.* New York: Crown Books, 2005.

Index

Afghan War, 223, 225
Afghanistan, 10, 100, 214, 220–23, 226, 243
AFL-CIO, 36
age of publicity, 76
Aidid, Mohammad, 156
AIDS, 120, 163
Alexander, Lamar, 187, 205
al Qaeda, 214, 219–23, 228
American Airlines: Flight 11, 215; Flight 77, 214, 216
American Tragedy, An (Dreiser), 66
Anderson, John B., 27, 29, 31
Arafat, Yasir, 155–56
arms-for-hostages deals, 90–91
arms race, 125
Atwater, Lee, 105, 111, 139

"Baby Jessica" McClure, rescue, 76
Baghdad, 124, 131–35, 138, 229–31
Barone, Michael, 27, 83
BATF (Bureau of Alcohol, Tobacco and Firearms), 154, 177, 179
Beckwith, "Chargin" Charlie, Colonel, 11
Beirut. *See* Lebanon
Bergen-Belsen, 88
Berlin Wall, 114, 141
bin Laden, Osama, 214–15, 219–23, 226
Bitburg fiasco, 87–88, 92

Black Monday, 63–64
Boesky, Ivan, 67–68
boll weevils, 36, 47, 79
Bonfire of the Vanities (Wolfe), 66
Bork, Robert, 104–5
Bosnia, 189–91
Brady Gun Law, 202
Branch Davidians, 154–55, 177
Brawley, Tawana, court case, 75
Bremer, Paul, U.S. civil administrator in Iraq, 231, 242
Brown, Edmund G. "Jerry," Jr., 1, 26
Brown, Pat, 21
Buchanan, Patrick J. "Pat," 143, 187, 205, 208
Buckley, William, 89
bully pulpit, 38
Bush, George Herbert Walker, 27, 35, 105, 139, 141, 245; Iraq-Iran War, 127–29, 132; 1988 presidency, 106–7, 110, 112–13, 117, 120–21, 123, 139–40, 171; 1992 campaign, 139–40, 142–44, 148–50; Vice President, 27, 93, 143
Bush, George Walker, 26, 205, 241; "Read my lips...," 110, 129; 2000 campaign, 205–11; 2000 presidency, 212–13, 219–21, 224, 226–28, 231; 2004 campaign, 232, 235–37; 2004 presidency, 240, 243–45

Bush, Laura, 211, 222
Bush Doctrine, 219
"Bush Haters," 235
"Bushisms," 207
Bush v. Gore, 210

Carter, Jimmy, 1–15, 24, 26–27, 29–32, 43
Case for Democracy, The (Sharansky), 243
CBS, 99, 106
Challenger: explosion broadcast, 75, 93–94; mission, 93–95
Chapman, Mark David, 72
Cheney, Dick: Secretary of Defense, 127; Vice President, 208, 211–12, 215, 219
Chernobyl, 98
China, 213; Tiananmen Square, 115–16
Christo (artist), 166
CIA, 39, 52
Clinton, Hillary, 146, 151, 191, 195, 197; First Lady, 150, 152
Clinton, William Jefferson "Bill," 26, 144–45, 245; 1992 campaign, 145–47, 149–50; 1992 presidency, 150–51, 153–55, 160, 178, 184–85; 1996 campaign, 186–88; 1996 presidency, 190–93, 195–200, 202
CNN, 131–32, 170–78, 215–17
"Cola Wars," 74
Cold War, 39, 95, 97, 100
Columbine High School, 200–202
Communism, 24–25, 54; collapse of, 114; U.S. confrontations against, 59, 97
computer, 47, 180–81, 202
Congress, 40, 129–30, 151, 158, 183, 188, 226–27, 240, 245
Contract with America, 158, 183–86

Davis, Nancy, 20. *See also* Reagan, Nancy
Dayton accords, 190
Dean, Howard, 233–34
Deaver, Michael, 37, 87
deconstruction, 70, 71
Delta unit, 11
Democrats, 188, 196–98, 205, 224, 235, 240–41; conservative, 32, 36; political control, 103, 105

Department of Homeland Security, 223
deregulation, 51
Desert Shield, 128
Desert Storm, 129, 131–34; "G-Day" or liberation of Kuwait, 134; ground war, 134–37
détente, 52
divided government, 113, 158, 224
Dole, Robert "Bob," 106–7, 185, 187–88, 206
"Dolly the Sheep," 181
Dow Jones Industrial, 35, 49, 63
Dukakis, Michael, 108–10

economy, 151, 164–65, 212; boom, 51, 96, 152, 161–62; 1987 crash, 64; postmodern, 165; problems, 33, 116, 121; progress, 41, 49, 84, 100; prosperity, 65, 75, 79, 203; "Reaganomics," 47; service economy, 68
Edwards, John, 233–36
energy, 1979 crisis, 1, 3–9, 14–15
EPA (Environmental Protection Agency), 51
Equal Rights Amendment, 29
everyman, 5, 18

Fahd, King, Saudi Arabia, 128
Fallujah, January 4, 2004, 234
Falwell, Jerry, 28
Fate of the Earth, The (Schell), 55
FCC (Federal Communications Commission), 74–75
fedayeen, 230–32
FEMA (Federal Emergency Management Agency), 244
"527" groups, 235–36
flat tax, 187
Forbes, Steve, 187, 205–6
Ford, Gerald "Jerry," 17
foreign policy: Bush, George H. W., 113; Bush, George W., 213; Clinton, William Jefferson "Bill," 155–56, 160, 189; Middle East, 88; Reagan, Ronald, 25, 52, 57, 59
Fox television, 74

Index 279

free market economics, 70, 103
Free to Choose (Friedman), 70

Gates, Bill, 163–64
GDP (gross domestic product), 63
General Motors, 67
Generation X, 162, 164, 213
genocide, 159–60, 191
Germany, 141
Gingrich, Newt, 158, 183–84, 196–97
global communications system, 77
GNP (Gross National Product), 35, 48
Goldman, Ronald, 172–73
GOP, 36, 101, 151, 158, 188, 197, 212, 224, 232, 236, 241
Gorbachev, Mikhail, 95, 97–100, 116, 127
Gore, Albert "Al," 108–9, 144, 149, 204, 207–10, 233
Gramm-Rudman-Hollings Act of 1985, 120
Grenada operation, 58–59, 61
Growing Up Digital (Tapscott), 163
Gulf War, 123–39, 225; Second, 227–28

Hart, Gary, 81–82, 107
health care, 151–54, 191
Health Insurance Association of America, 153
highway of death, 136, 138
hijacking, 54, 88–89, 175, 214–17, 219
Hinkley, John W., Jr., 37
hostage crisis, 8–11, 13, 26, 31, 34; Desert One, 11; "Eagle Claw," 12; Lebanon, 1985, 88–91
HUD (Housing and Urban Development) budget, 50
Hurricane Hugo, 119
Hurricane Katrina, 243–45
Hussein, Saddam, 123–25, 128–30, 132–34, 136–38, 198, 224–31, 234, 236, 242
Hyde, Henry, 197–98

image politics, 77
immigration, 68
impeachment, 197–99
INF Treaty (Intermediate Nuclear Forces Treaty), 97, 100

"Inside the Beltway," 32, 40, 43
interest groups, 8, 80, 117
Iran, 123–24
Iran-Contra scandal, 88–92, 106
Iranian rescue mission, 13–14
Iran-Iraq War, 124, 126, 226
Iraq, 125–26, 128–29, 131, 133–34, 225–26, 228, 242–43; Iraq War, 227–28, 230–33, 236–37, 241; Kurds and Shiites, 138–39; military forces, 126, 129, 134–38, 224, 230, 242
Iraq Interim Governing Council, 242
Iraqi National Assembly, 243
Iraqi Republican Guard, 125, 135–36, 138, 228, 230
Israel, 127, 133, 155

Jackson, Jesse, 80–82, 108–9, 144

Kaczynski, Theodore John "Ted," 178–80
Kennedy, Ted, 26–27
Kerry, John F., 233–37
Keyes, Alan, 187, 205
Khomeini, Ayatollah Ruhollah, 1, 8–10, 14, 124
King, Rodney Glen, 169–71
Kohl, Helmut, West German Chancellor, 86
Kolmeshohe Cemetery, 87. *See also* Bitburg fiasco
Korean Airlines Flight 007, 54
Koresh, David, 154
Kosovo, 189–91
Kuwait, 125–26, 128–29, 131, 134, 137

Lebanon: Iran-Contra scandal, 89–90; 1983 involvement, 59–62; TWA 847 hijacking, 88–89
Lennon, John, 72
leveraged buyout, 67
Lewinsky, Monica, 193–96
Lieberman, Senator Joe, 208–9, 233–34
Live Aid concert, 73
Los Angeles riots, 170–72
Luce, Henry, "The American Century," *Life* magazine, 76

MAD (mutually assured destruction), 52
Madonna, 73
McCain, John, 205–7
McFarlane, Robert "Bud," National Security Advisor, 88–89
McVeigh, Timothy, 176–78
media, 194; campaigns, 81–82, 146, 149, 188; domestic affairs, 172–74, 177, 203; foreign affairs, 131, 134, 160; politics, 140, 194–96
media markets, 31–32, 86, 113, 150, 188, 196, 207, 209, 237–40
Medicare, 121, 185, 187
Microsoft, 163–64
Middle East, 14, 129, 141, 175, 224, 237, 243
Middle East Peace Accord, 155–57
midterm elections, 79, 129, 157, 204, 224
Milken, Michael, 67–68
Milosevic, Slobodan, 189–91
misery index, 27
modernism, 71–72
Mogadishu, 156
Mondale, Walter, 80–82
"Morning in America," 83, 85, 187
MTV, 72

Nader, Ralph, 208
NAFTA (North American Free Trade Agreement), 142, 161
Nagin, Ray, 243–44
NASA, 93, 95
NASDAQ, 162
NATO (North Atlantic Treaty Organization), 189–91
Nelson, Prince Rogers, "Prince," 72
New Democrat, 145, 157, 184
New Orleans, 243–45
New Right, 28, 29
New York City, 220. *See also* terrorism; World Trade Center
New York City Fire Department, 217–18, 220
New York Times, 2, 4, 11, 99, 224
Nicaragua, 91, 118–19
Nichols, Terry, 177–78
1960s, 6, 37, 46
1970s, 3, 6–7, 25–26, 29, 32, 40, 46, 65

1980s, 25, 31–32, 35–36, 46–47, 65–66, 69–70, 72, 77
1990s, 32, 131, 141, 152, 163, 165, 169, 176, 180–81, 196, 199–200
Nixon, Richard, 4, 17
"No Child Left Behind," 213, 237
noblesse oblige, 112
Noriega, Manuel Antonio, 118–19
North, Oliver, 89–92
nuclear: freeze, 55, 56; prospect, 96; war, 55–57

O'Connor v. Donaldson, 50
O'Grady, Scott, Air Force Captain, 190
oil: imports, 1, 9; Middle East, 124–26; shortage, 4
Oil-for-Food program, 225–26
Oklahoma City bombing, 176–77
Olympic Games, 85
Omar, Mullah Mohammad, 223
Omnibus Budget Reconciliation Act of 1993, 151
OPEC (Organization of Petroleum Exporting Countries), 2
Operation Iraqi Freedom, 229

Pahlavi, Mohammad Reza, 8
Panama, 118–19
Papachristou v. City of Jacksonville, 49
PATCO strike, 38, 51
Pentagon, 214, 216–17
Perot, H. Ross, 147–50, 188
Personal Responsibility and Work Opportunity Reconciliation Act, 186
PLO (Palestine Liberation Organization), 155
political coalition, 25
pornography, 75
postindustrial society, 69
postmodern: economy, 165; film, 168; politics, 147, 196, 202, 240
postmodernism, 71–72, 77, 166–67, 169, 181, 193, 223
post–9/11 America, 223
Powell, Colin, 227
press, 128, 131–32, 139, 153, 173, 185, 205, 207, 229

primary campaign, 22, 81, 143–45, 147, 204, 207, 234
prison furloughs, 111

Quaddafi, Muammar el-Quaddafi, 91
Quayle, Dan, 149, 205

Rabin, Yitzhak, 155–56
Rambouillet talks, 190
Rather, Dan, 51, 106–7
Reagan, Nancy, 37, 43, 45, 92
Reagan, Ronald, 15–31, 84, 96, 100–101; anticommunism, 20, 25, 30, 51–54, 59–60, 96, 98, 100; assassination attempt, 37–38; California Governor, 18, 20; conservative, 43; D-Day commemoration speech, 83; Great Communicator, 30; Iran-Contra scandal, 88–92, 99, 103–4; "Morning in America," 83, 85; new philosophy, 34, 49, 51, 54; 1976 campaign, 18, 22–23; 1980 campaign, 22, 26, 29, 31–32; 1980 presidency, 34, 41, 43, 45–46, 57, 79; 1984 campaign, 83–85; 1984 presidency, 86, 88, 96, 99–101; radio and television, 18–19, 24
Reaganism, 33
Reaganomics, 35, 47, 50–51, 116
Reagan Revolution, 35, 63
recession, 35, 46, 63, 121, 142, 212
Reconciliation Act of 1981, 49
Religious Right. *See* New Right
Republican Revolution, 183
Republicans, 142, 185–86, 188, 195, 209, 212, 224, 237, 240–41; liberal, 32; party dominance, 100, 183, 224
reserves, 128
Reston, James "Scotty," 34
rock music, 72–73, 166
"Rose Garden" strategy, 10, 26, 186
Rumsfeld, Donald, 227
Rwanda, 159–60, 190

same-sex marriage, 236–37
San Francisco Bay earthquake, 1989, 119–20
Sandinistas, 90, 93, 119

S&L scandal, 117, 120
Saudi Arabia, 96, 126–27, 131, 133, 214, 226
Schwarzkopf, Norman, U.S. General, 132, 134–35, 137–38
SDI (Strategic Defense Initiative), 57, 97–99
Serbs, 189–91
Shultz, George P., Secretary of State, 59–60, 62
Silicon Valley, 161–62
Simpson, Nicole Brown, 172–73
Simpson, Orenthal James "O. J.," 172–75
Somalia, 156–57
Soviet: advances, 24, 46; communism, 24, 29, 114; Korean Airlines Flight 007, 54; Union, 57, 114, 127, 134, 189
"stagflation," 63
Starr, Kenneth, Independent Counsel, 191–94, 196, 198
START (Strategic Arms Reduction Treaty), 97
Stockman, David Alan, Office Management & Budget (OMB) director, 48
summit meetings, 97–100

Taliban, 220–23
Tate, Sheila, 44
taxes, 35–36, 121, 129, 145, 151, 157, 212, 232, 241
"technocrats," 69
technology, 162, 165
Tehran, 8–9, 11, 124
television, 85, 93, 104, 119, 140, 157, 163, 165, 169, 178, 194, 197–98, 201–2, 216–17, 222; campaigns, 206, 208, 232, 237; commercials, 83–84, 111, 153–54, 187–88; Gulf War, Iraq War, 130–32, 134–35, 137, 225, 229, 231; O. J. Simpson trial, 172–75; talk shows, 74; twenty-four-hour news cycle, 147, 196
terrorism, 90, 175–76, 199, 228, 232, 243; domestic, 176–78, 180, 200; religious, 176; September 11, 2001, 213–20; war on terror, 221–22, 226
Thatcher, Margaret, British Prime Minister, 126

Thomas, Clarence, 140
Thurmond, Strom, 49
Tiananmen Square, 115–16
Time magazine, 10, 13, 76
Trial of the Century, 171, 172
triangulation, 184–85, 191
"trickle-side" approach, 35, 151
TWA Flight 847, 88
2001, September 11, 213–16

Unabomber, 178–80
unemployment, 47, 49
United Airlines: Flight 93, 217, 219; Flight 175, 216
United Nations, 125–26, 129, 156, 159–60, 189–91, 225, 227
university, 69–70
U.S. military, 131, 134–35, 156–57, 191, 221–23, 225, 230–32
USSR, 25, 96; 1989 collapse, 58

Waco, Texas, 154–55, 177
Wall Street, 63
Wall Street (Stone), 65
Wal-Mart, 65, 180
war on terror, 199, 217, 220–21, 223, 226
Washington, 39–41, 120, 150, 158, 196, 200, 215, 217
Washington Post, 13, 219
Watergate, 17
Watt, James, 51
weapons, 132–34, 136, 158, 223, 229; chemical, 124–25; WMDs (weapons of mass destruction), 226–27
Weinberger, Caspar, Secretary of Defense, 59–60, 62
Whitewater scandal, 191–92, 194
Wildavsky, Aaron, President of the Political Science Association, 21
World Trade Center: 1993 terrorist attack, 175, 213; September 11, 2001, 215–19, 224

Yeltsin, Boris, 157
Y2K, 203–4
"yuppies," 67

About the Author

J. DAVID WOODARD is Professor of Political Science at Clemson University and co-author of *American Conservatism from Burke to Bush* (1991) and *The Conservative Tradition in America* (1996). He is also the author of *The New Southern Politics* (2006).